Determinants of
enterprise performance

Manchester University Press

To Molly and Bebe

Determinants of enterprise performance

Derek L. Bosworth

Manchester University Press
Manchester and New York

distributed exclusively in the USA by Palgrave

The right of Derek L. Bosworth to be identified as the author of this work has been asserted by him in accordance with the Copyright, Designs and Patents Act 1988.

Published by Manchester University Press
Oxford Road, Manchester M13 9NR, UK
and Room 400, 175 Fifth Avenue, New York, NY 10010, USA
www.manchesteruniversitypress.co.uk

Distributed exclusively in the USA by
Palgrave, 175 Fifth Avenue, New York, NY 10010, USA

Distributed exclusively in Canada by
UBC Press, University of British Columbia, 2029 West Mall, Vancouver, BC, Canada V6T 1Z2

British Library Cataloguing-in-Publication Data
A catalogue record for this book is available from the British Library

Library of Congress Cataloging-in-Publication Data applied for

ISBN   0 7190 6774 X   *hardback*
EAN   978 0 7190 6774 7

First published 2005

14 13 12 11 10 09 08 07 06 05   10 9 8 7 6 5 4 3 2 1

Typeset by R. J. Footring Ltd, Derby

Printed in Great Britain
by Biddles Limited, King's Lynn

Contents

Figures

Tables

Acknowledgements

I would particularly like to thank Greg Jobome, at Liverpool Business School, for sections 3.2 and 3.4, as well as most of Chapter 7. Greg wrote the original version of this material as part of a report that we prepared for the Council for Excellence in Management and Leadership. In addition, Chapter 11 contains some material that I prepared as part of a joint paper with Mark Smith, at UMIST (now at Manchester Business School, University of Manchester), written as a contribution to a European Commission project on operating times across Europe. The work on unit costs in section 3.3 is drawn from work by Paul Stoneman, which was part of a project we undertook for OFWAT in examining the efficiency of water and sewerage companies. Many other colleagues have helped to form the ideas contained in this book, and I am grateful for all the people I have worked with throughout the world. Needless to say, any remaining errors are my responsibility.

Luke Bosworth produced the original versions of the figures. I am also grateful to Ralph Footring for his excellent subediting work, which revealed a number of important discrepancies, which I now hope are corrected.

Abbreviations

ARDC	American Research and Development Corporation
BIS	business information system
BLC	brand life-cycle (see PLC)
BoD	board of directors
C–B	cost–benefit
CEO	chief executive officer
CIS	Community Innovation Survey
CoPS	complex products and services
DCF	discounted cash flow
DFM	design for manufacturing
DP	data processing (and database management)
DS	Dorfman–Steiner
EBIT	earnings before interest and tax
EM	employee motivation
ESOS	employee skills and organizational structures
EU	European Union
EVA	economic value added
FFE	firm fixed effect
FMCGs	fast-moving consumer goods
GA	growth accounting
GATT	General Agreement on Tariffs and Trade
GDP	gross domestic product
GRATE	gross return on assets
H-form	holding company form
HPWPs	high-performance work practices
HR	human resources
HRM	human resource management
ICT	information and communications technology
IMD	International Institute for Management Development
IP	intellectual property

IPC	international patent class (or classification)
IPRs	intellectual property rights
IRR	internal rate of return
IS	information system (see BIS, MIS and SIS)
IT	information technology
JIT	just in time
LoB	line of business
MDA	multiple discriminant analysis
M-form	multi-divisional (hierarchical) company form
MIS	management information system
MRP	materials requirements planning
MV	market value
MWMTs	metal-working machine tools
MX-form	matrix company form
N-form	network company form
NGT	new growth theory
NIESR	National Institute for Economic and Social Research
NIS	national innovation system
NPCs	non-patent citations (i.e. citations of the scientific literature)
NPD	new product development
NPL	new product launch
NPV	net present value
OECD	Organization for Economic Cooperation and Development
PBOs	project-based organizations
PIMS	Profit Impact of Marketing Strategy (management consultancy)
PLC	product life-cycle (see BLC)
PSEs	professional scientists and engineers
q	Tobin's q – the ratio of MV to the replacement book value of assets
QM	quality management
R&D	research and development
REE	rational expectations equilibrium
ROA	return on assets
ROCE	return on capital employed
ROE	return on equity
ROI	return on investment
RPI	retail price index
RTD	research and technology development
RUC	real unit costs
RUCC	real unit capital costs
RULC	real unit labour costs
RUMC	real unit material costs
RUOC	real unit operating costs

RUTC	real unit total costs
SCP	structure–conduct–performance (models)
SIC	Standard Industrial Classification
SIS	strategic information system
SMEs	small and medium-sized enterprises
SPRU	Science Policy Research Unit (Sussex University)
SSAP	statement of standard accounting practice
TE	top executive
TFP	total factor productivity
TQM	total quality manufacturing
U-form	unitary company form
WACC	weighted average cost of capital
WIP	work in progress
X-efficiency	degree of organizational slack
X-form	residual company form, not elsewhere specified

Imagination is more important than knowledge. Knowledge is limited. Imagination encircles the world.

Albert Einstein

Part I
Introduction

Chapter 1

Introduction: aims and scope

This book focuses on the broad range of factors that determine enterprise performance. Its principal focus is on those private sector enterprises that, to varying degrees, compete in order to survive. In the main, the discussion concerns the factors that improve firm performance and not, for example, the broader social consequences that might result from better performance. In essence, much of the book is concerned with the way in which firms maintain or improve their market position; while this *may* improve welfare in a dynamic sense (e.g. through the introduction of new and higher-quality products and services), it *may* reduce consumer welfare in a static sense (e.g. through the charging of higher prices). The focus is on dynamic competition, which is quite distinct from the perfect competition of microeconomics texts, and the book does not view perfect competition as being some desirable economic state. Consistent with the Austrian school, the arguments put forward indicate that:

> the long-run equilibrium of perfect competition is not an appropriate policy target because it does not represent competition at all but an end-state in which competition has been exhausted. The market is at rest whereas the essence of competition is disequilibrium characterised by continuous change. (Robinson, 1997, p. 6)

The motivation for the book lies in the widely held view that UK companies underperform compared with corresponding enterprises in other countries. There is ample evidence, for example, that the UK lags behind key competitors such as the USA and a number of other industrialized countries – for instance, the level and rate of growth of productivity appear to be lower than for many of the UK's main competitors. The focus of the present book is *not*, however, on UK companies *per se*. The aim is simply to compile and collate the evidence relating to the determinants of firm performance, in other words, to answer the general question 'What factors make some enterprises perform better than others'? In doing so, the analysis draws upon a wide range of international evidence on the determinants of enterprise performance.

While the author is an economist, this book reflects an attempt to bring together a wide range of relevant literature concerned with the determinants of enterprise performance, largely irrespective of the discipline from which it is drawn. It is therefore not a book that most mainstream economists will necessarily recognize. It is eclectic in nature, in bringing together not only evidence from different disciplines, but also lessons from the past as well as the present. Equally, it draws upon the results of large-scale econometric exercises, survey results and case studies. At each stage within the discussion, an attempt is made to tease out the lessons for management strategy suggested by the literature. In addition, however, Chapter 14 is devoted to broader policy issues and the lessons for government. While that chapter focuses on the UK, most of the discussion is relevant to a wide range of other countries.

The book deals with a large number of issues, such as the goals and strategies adopted by enterprises, the quality and nature of management, and the measures that firms adopt to monitor their environment (technologies, markets, etc.). One of its aims, therefore, is to put 'management' and 'management decisions' back at the heart of what are essentially issues of managerial economics. There are two further main themes. The first concerns the discretionary investments of the firm – such as training, advertising, and research and development (R&D) – which play a central role in determining future performance. These are also related to the organization of the enterprise, which is perceived as an organic entity. This is not meant to imply that, at any given moment, the enterprise does not have shape and structure – far from it; these are essential features determining performance, given the environment in which the firm operates. On the other hand, the firm is (potentially) a dynamic entity, changing its shape and structure over time, to deal with both internal and external pressures and opportunities.

The second concerns risk (and uncertainty). While this is not a book about risk *per se*, it is impossible to talk about the determinants of enterprise performance without considering the role that risk plays. For example, it is not possible to deal with issues such as the discretionary investments of the enterprise or the changes in the scale and scope of the company without also talking about the risks attached to these activities. In the case of discretionary investments such as R&D, for example, the analysis deals with the boundary between creating knowledge of various kinds (e.g. invention) and its effect on the behaviour (e.g. innovation) and performance of the enterprise (e.g. growth and profitability). While much of the empirical evidence relates to what happens 'on average' across enterprises (e.g. the effect of an extra $1 million investment in R&D on the market value of the firm), it is essential to recognize at appropriate points during the discussion that, at the level of the individual firm, these investments are inherently risky. It is impossible fully to understand firm behaviour without accounting for the facts not only that the returns to individual firms vary significantly around the industry average but also that the perceived returns are risky or uncertain, with important implications for management decision making.

Thus, the discussion often turns to the issue of managing the risk associated with particular activities. This is a difficult area: 'It is a space in which engineers, managers, economists, policy makers and even venture capitalists all feel uncomfortable' (Branscomb and Auerswald, 2000, p. 1). There is a general view that the more radical the innovation is (whether this is technological, organizational, etc.), in the main, the greater is the degree of risk (Hartmann and Myers, 2000, Figure 3). While the discussion in the present book broadly accepts this position, it also proposes a slightly different angle (a point that the discussion often returns to) – doing nothing can be as risky as innovating and, often, doing nothing is not a realistic option. The analysis should always bear in mind the counterfactual; for example, what would have happened if the enterprise had not innovated?

1.1 An illustration of the focus of the book

The following quotation sets out Ruthven's (1994) 'ten commandments', which outline his perception of the implications of the need for more focus on company structure:

(i) *Leadership* – good managers have (or get) a vision, then lead by example. They direct and control. The best of them are usually competent, benevolent autocrats, who listen better than the democrats, command loyalty (and get it), and lead rather than moderate or 'manage'....

(ii) *Focus* – stay in the business you know best – stick to your knitting. Remember the grass is really brown on both sides of the fence (the green grass is the one you water). Stay in [a] … tightly defined sector of the economy and, if needing to grow, go overseas with that industry, rather than diversify. Know where you are on your own industry's lifecycle and respond accordingly. Know world best practice for your industry and emulate or surpass it.

(iii) *Dominance* – pick your place in the market – develop a safe position in your industry, either ultra niche (1%), niche (5%), or major (25–75%). A niche position within an industry is one which involves dominating (i.e. 50% share) one product group, nationally, or dominating one state (region) or one customer group. In any of these alternatives, do not have more than 5% of the national sales of your industry. A major position is where you have 25–75% share of the national sales of your industry and dominate a select number of product groups or states etc.

(iv) *Be customer oriented* – know your customers and supply their needs. Managers must meet customers regularly. CEOs [chief executive officers] should personally talk at least once a year to the 20% of customers that provide 80% of the revenue.

(v)   *Have the proper organisational structure* – the best structure is the one that helps achieve your strategy and objectives. Structure follows strategy, which follows goals. Put the three facets of function, geography and product in the right sequence for the stage of your industry's lifecycle. Outsource any activity that is not core or which can be franchised/licensed.

(vi) *Manage the business fundamentals relentlessly* – focus on the fundamentals. This starts with the firm's holy-grail: its intellectual property, which must be constantly enhanced. Total quality control is a condition of survival. Employees are the soul of the enterprise; have a hands-on approach – recognize the value and dignity of employees. MIS [management information system] is a critical intelligence component and, with finance and productivity, needs constant vigilance and action.

(vii) *Ensure operations are simple, clear and precise* – the kiss principle (keep it simple, stupid).

(viii) *Keep government out of your business* – one of the three great lies is: 'I'm from the government and I'm here to help you'.

(ix) *Finance the business soundly* – have a lower debt/equity ratio than your competitors most of the time. Know and act on financial performance information.

(x)   *Know the effect on your industry of the economy and business environment at large* – there are ten major environments: world; national resource base; society; economy; market place; labour market; supplies; finance; services; and governments. Monitor them for long and short term implications. Slow economic periods favour good operators in tough industries; fast economic growth periods favour good operators in growth industries.

While the present author does not necessarily agree with these statements, at least in their entirety, they do give a good feel for some of the key issues that the present book deals with in subsequent chapters.

1.2   Contents

Chapter 2 explores what is meant by an 'enterprise'. The word is used with the intention of making it clear from the outset that the focus is on private sector companies that, to a greater or lesser degree, compete in order to survive and flourish. This chapter provides a range of definitions of what is meant by an enterprise (and by the constituent parts of an 'enterprise' or 'enterprise group'). These include economic, administrative, legal and conceptual definitions that attempt to clarify what lies within the confines of a company and what lies outside. In doing so, a transaction cost view of the firm is provided, with some historical discussion of how theory in this area has evolved. Thus, the analysis considers not only the issues of scale and scope but also lays the foundations for the later chapters that explore the 'optimal' design of the company.

Chapter 3 discusses the various financial, accounting and economic measures of enterprise performance. While recognizing that there are broader social and welfare dimensions of performance (some of which are important for understanding the discussion of the public policy aspects of the results), the principal focus is on the *private* performance of enterprises, as perceived by the major stakeholders in the company. As in other parts of the book, the aim here is not only to document the measures but also to produce an 'encompassing' framework within which each measure is nested. In this way, a clearer picture emerges of the role of the 'partial' and 'total' (overall) measures of enterprise performance. In addition, the chapter addresses a number of other important conceptual issues, such as whether the enterprise should be judged against the goals that it sets for itself or against other, potentially different targets, for example ones that the government might view as being, in some sense, in 'the national interest'. These measures are used in subsequent chapters to provide empirical evidence of the differential performance of enterprises, in part to demonstrate how different performance can be across companies and over time. This evidence is linked to the issue of the risky nature of investments and the ability of each enterprise to manage and cope with risk.

While the implication is that the enterprise will monitor its own performance (and that of competitors), it will also need to measure and monitor a much wider range of activities and factors. It is taken as given that these will include the economic climate both generally and within the sector in which the enterprise operates. The discussion in Chapter 4 focuses more closely on the markets within which the enterprise operates (i.e. the role of market research) and the science and technology base on which it might need to call. In subsequent chapters it becomes clear that the areas that the enterprise monitors are generally wider than its current production activities would suggest and for some – so-called 'integrating' or 'systems integrating' firms – significantly wider. This may arise because the firm is always adjusting from its current to some more desired future position and/or because it is effectively taking out options in terms of its knowledge base that enable it efficiently to address possible, currently imperfectly defined future threats and opportunities. An immediate implication is that the range and level of detail of information now available identify the need for efficient and effective MISs.

Chapter 5 explores the goals and aspirations of the enterprise. Again, there is a historical industrial economics literature (e.g. managerial theories and behavioural theories) on the implications of the adoption of different goals on enterprise performance. The analysis demonstrates how these goals are related to one another and, again, can be viewed more clearly in an encompassing framework. The discussion does not dwell on this, however, as much of it is well trodden ground. The chapter uses the empirical evidence to dispel some of the myths associated with the often accepted view that owner managers are essentially profit oriented while professional managers have their own distinct (non-profit) agendas. In addition, it provides some historical context that shows that empirical economics largely failed to grasp the importance of strategy. More importantly, Chapter 5 considers the product and process strategies that companies use to achieve their goals. Finally, the chapter argues that the choice of strategy is dependent upon both internal factors (e.g. the competences of the workforce) and external factors (e.g. the responsiveness of consumers to price and quality changes). In doing so, the analysis demonstrates that it may be possible to achieve the same over-arching goal using different strategies, at least in the short to medium term.

This discussion sets the scene for future chapters focusing upon the various mechanisms used as part of these strategies to achieve the overall goals of the enterprise (see Chapters 8–10). This leads to an important theme of the literature (currently mainly found in the human resource management area), that goals (and strategies) mediate with 'high-performance work practices' (HPWPs) to determine the performance of the enterprise – in other words, that some high-level practices 'work with' and some 'work against' particular goals in the achievement of better performance. Again, this is one dimension of 'synergies', which form an important focus of the book. Finally, the discussion returns to the issue, originally raised in Chapter 3, that, when a government department or agency suggests, for example, the need for greater innovation, this may not be consistent with the goals of the private sector. If the existing goals are the rational outcome of the incentives faced by companies, modification of behaviour and performance will itself require changes to the government policies that affect the incentive structure, in ways consistent with the desired outcome. This provides the foundations for the discussion of government policy in Chapter 14.

Chapter 6 focuses on one of the fundamental issues at the heart of enterprise performance, that of management skills and core competences. Students are often taught that, conceptually, the production function involves not only tangible inputs such as capital and labour, but also enterprise (e.g. entrepreneurship, leadership, management skills). In practice, the role of enterprise has invariably been absent from the empirical estimates of neoclassical theory – at best it lay somewhere in the background assumption of profit maximization (the role of markets) or in the quality of the labour force. The role of enterprise has not even been a clear focus of non-neoclassical approaches, such as evolutionary theory, although it is encountered on the periphery of behavioural and organizational theories, for example, as bounded rationality. Perhaps only in Edith Penrose's work (e.g. Penrose, 1959) was there the embryonic beginning of a clear and central role for management, whereby the future prospects of the firm were shaped by the current management capacity.[1] Chapter 6 therefore focuses on:

(i)   the nature and quality of the management team (the CEO, board of directors, etc.) – a literature that dates back at least to Penrose;
(ii)   the broader issue of the core competences of the enterprise, defined by its intellectual capital base (also considered in Chapter 9).

These factors will have an important bearing on the goals and aspirations of the enterprise, the strategies adopted and the degree of risk the firm faces in the investments that it makes in attempting to achieve these goals. This chapter presents a wide range of empirical evidence indicating the link between management (broadly defined) and enterprise performance.

Chapter 7 focuses on agency and corporate governance and, thus, builds upon Chapter 6 to look at the design of mechanisms that align the actions of the (professional) managers to the goals of the enterprise. In some ways, this chapter may be thought of as dealing with a particular dimension of the 'shape and structure' of the organization. However, it is so bound up with the goals and behaviour of management that it appears more appropriate to deal with it at this stage. The discussion therefore focuses on the governance arrangements, which are driven by both goals/strategies and skills/capacity. Governance issues have always been of concern to stakeholders. However, following the developments in the managerial economics literature, reviewed briefly in Chapter 6, it is clear that they became of more central concern over the last two or three decades of the twentieth century. This new impetus has also been spurred by developments such as the increasing incidence of corporate failure and corporate fraud, against a backdrop of rapid growth in the compensation packages of senior managers, while the average earnings of employees has grown much more modestly. These issues have led to questions about the adequacy of existing governance structures and mechanisms in protecting the owners of the enterprise and, therefore, concerns about the efficiency of resource allocation. Chapter 7 reviews the extensive empirical evidence in this area, including the linkages between management compensation and enterprise performance. Finally, the chapter reviews the response to these concerns, because of which several national and international bodies have established (so-called) 'best practice governance principles' (e.g. Cadbury and the Organization for Economic Cooperation and Development, OECD), as well as the efforts being made at the firm level to comply with the new standards.

Chapter 8 addresses one of the most researched areas of economics and technology management – the role played by R&D and innovation. In particular, it explores the 'knowledge production function' and 'market valuation function' approaches, and relates these to the role of intangible assets in enterprise performance. Again, from a theoretical perspective, it is useful to search for an encompassing framework that allows the reader to make sense of the often partial results found in the literature. The discussion explores the various strands of the literature to examine the implications for a number of areas, including:

(i)   the returns to private R&D;
(ii)   the role of R&D in determining innovation and the success of inno-
       vation;
(iii) spillovers and the social returns to R&D.

Empirical evidence is provided about the results of the international literature in each of these areas. This topic is one where, at first sight, the results
for management decision making appear to be largely consistent (though
not always identical). However, the private and social implications are
generally viewed as being inconsistent (i.e. firms do not generally operate
in an optimal manner from society's point of view).

   In addition, while the results regarding the private returns to R&D
appear broadly consistent, the discussion suggests that it is very difficult for
companies to utilize them in their investment decisions. In particular, the
final part of Chapter 8 questions the focus of the large-scale econometric
models insofar as these report the marginal returns to R&D *averaged
over all companies in the sample*. Such averages convey some information
but clearly fail to address the crucial question of the degree of risk that
companies face in their discretionary investment decisions. The discussion therefore re-examines the econometric evidence to consider where
risk might arise. Most of the discussion, however, draws together a wide
range of conceptual and empirical evidence about the sources and extent
of risk and uncertainty, and the distribution of returns to R&D and other
discretionary investments. The chapter discusses some of the implications
of these results for the nature of the decision-making process, and these
form the basis for the discussion of firm policies in Chapter 13.

   Chapter 9 changes the focus to the role of human resources and HPWPs.
It begins with a discussion of skills and competences and, in particular, the
way in which the enterprise adjusts these in order to improve its performance. Again, the discussion argues that training and recruitment activities,
among others, are important determinants of the intangible assets of the
enterprise, with implications for future performance. While there is a shift
in focus, nevertheless there is a very real link with the previous chapter
in that the inputs and outputs of R&D (and related creative activities)
are knowledge, skills and competences that add to the intellectual capital
of the enterprise. However, the role of higher skills and competences in
driving enterprise performance is not as clear cut as might be expected.
Chapter 9 therefore explores the ways in which skills and competences are
linked to the different dimensions of performance discussed in Chapter 3,
and shows how the demand for skills is likely to be mediated by the goals
and strategies of the company.

The development and use of skills are closely linked with the HPWPs of the enterprise, including human resource management (HRM). Chapter 9 therefore also reviews the results of the literature on HPWPs. This literature, more than any other, has paid most attention to the mediation role played by goals in determining the impact of HPWPs on the performance of the enterprise. In addition, this area has been most active in attempting to synthesize the wide range of 'high-level' practices into smaller, complementary groups of practices, by means of factor analysis. Chapter 9 argues that there are important lessons to be learnt in the approaches adopted by the HRM/HPWPs literature by other areas of research, such as the R&D and innovation literature. In addition to reporting on the conceptual approaches, it is again possible to find a number of consistent results drawn from the international literature. In particular, enterprise performance is improved by the introduction of:

(i)   HPWP/HRM practices;
(ii) a range of complementary HRM/HPWPs;
(iii) practices which are synergistic with the goals of the firm.

Here the discussion reports econometric evidence that is among the first to combine, in a fairly limited way, some of the results of Chapters 5, 6 and 8. The results presented in Chapter 9 also form a key input to the private and public policy debates considered in Chapters 13 and 14.

Chapter 10 turns its attention to the role of advertising (and other marketing expenditures), within the broader context of new product launch (NPL) and brand maintenance and development. This is not a chapter on the management of marketing *per se*, but is a point at which an attempt is made to bring together the parts of the theoretical and empirical marketing literature that appear to be relevant to the main theme of the book, namely, the role of marketing in determining enterprise performance. Potentially, at least, advertising is also a discretionary investment and, of all such investments, perhaps most obviously the one aimed at increasing (future) monopoly power – although it is important to remember that the main welfare aspects of advertising lie outside the scope of the present book. Chapter 10 focuses on the extensive literatures on:

(i)   the concept of advertising and the decision to advertise;
(ii) the determinants of advertising;
(iii) the impact of advertising on enterprise performance.

There is a much smaller econometric literature on the combined effects of advertising and R&D expenditures on enterprise performance (and almost nothing looking at synergies between the two). However, in this instance there is a large and useful survey and case study literature on NPLs, which is located in both the marketing and the technology management areas (see also Chapter 8).

Chapter 11 examines the role of organizational structure and design. The analysis concentrates on the embeddedness of knowledge and the efficiency of information flows within and between organizations. The chapter begins with some of the more static and mechanistic aspects of enterprise structure. It reports the results of a little-quoted article by Radner (1992) that explores the efficiency of information flows within a company, and goes on to produce some interesting results about the 'optimal structure' of the internal organization of the enterprise. Unlike the original work of Nelson and Winter (1982), which focused on the benefits of the embeddedness of repetitive decisions and processes, however, Chapter 11 extends the discussion to examine companies that are continually changing their products and processes. In doing so, it reviews the emerging literature on, for example, the 'optimal' management structure for the production and supply of complex products and services. The chapter again attempts to offer an encompassing framework, based in part on an emerging taxonomy within the literature, that includes U-form, M-form, ..., N-form organizations. The analysis thereby addresses whether there are features of company structure and design that are most suited to particular products (and processes needed to supply such products). For example, it explores the potential advantages of N-form organizations in accessing external information and disseminating this within the company. Finally, it examines the silos where information and knowledge are stored, both formal and informal, as well as the management of information systems.

Viewing the enterprise in this way leads naturally to the concept of the 'learning organization'. The discussion in Chapter 12 makes the distinction between organizational learning in a 'technology transfer' sense and the concept of endogenous 'learning by doing'. The concept of a 'learning organization' developed is much more than just the simple arithmetic sum of the learning undertaken by individuals. There are potential synergies (and conflicts) in learning at the organizational level that the company can exploit (or avoid) (also see the discussion of synergies in Chapter 9). The enterprise can configure itself to be a learning organization. Indeed, the enterprise can 'design itself' in such a way that to some degree it automatically reconfigures itself as necessary, in order to ensure that learning takes place and has the maximum benefit in terms of overall performance. Companies that are capable of doing so are not only likely to be 'information rich' (see Chapter 4) but also to have the necessary systems in place that efficiently and effectively store, retrieve, disseminate and utilize the information and knowledge available.

Chapter 13 draws together many of the key elements of debate from the earlier chapters in terms of the main implications for enterprise policy. It is argued that the results of the empirical literature indicate that, on balance:

(i)   past economic profit is an important determinant of 'discretionary investments' that are aimed at improving the future performance of the enterprise *vis-à-vis* that which would otherwise have been experienced;

(ii)   such investments, on balance, improve the (future) performance of the enterprises that make them (i.e. are investments in future monopoly power).

However, the results are much richer than this would suggest, for a whole variety of reasons, including the following:

(i)   the role of risk at the level of the individual enterprise itself suggests that standard investment appraisal techniques (e.g. discounted cash flow, DCF) are no longer adequate;

(ii)   risk is not entirely exogenous – a variety of interventions can be made by the firm (and government) to produce an environment that 'optimizes', though never removes, *ex ante* risk;

(iii) the extent and nature of these discretionary investments are not independent of the goals of the enterprise (which themselves may be viewed as being more or less beneficial from private and social viewpoints);

(iv)   investments in 'high-level' practices have synergies both internally (i.e. there are, on balance, disproportionately large returns from investing in a number of complementary HPWPs) and between investments (i.e. there are important synergies between R&D, advertising and other HPWPs);

(v)   'nothing is sacred' – even the size and scope of the company, as well as its routines, are the subject of design and redesign in the face of changing technologies, market demands, globalization, and so on;

(vi)   there are spillovers between the high-level activities of one firm and those of others, which result in an underinvestment in such activities if they are left to private decision makers alone.

Chapter 14 focuses on the public policy issues relating to enterprise performance. It is not possible to address every possible issue with regard to the design of the environment within which companies operate – this could easily form a book in its own right. However, it seems important to outline the lessons from the literature discussed in earlier chapters. One example concerns the role of 'goal modification' – the system of rules and incentives can lead a firm to act in a way that is perfectly rationale but that leads to the 'wrong' outcome from society's viewpoint. Also, there are clearly many implications for government policy in terms of setting the right environment to control risk and optimize discretionary investments (e.g. intellectual property laws *re* appropriability, stability of the macro-economic environment, support for basic science), as well as recognizing the implications of spillovers (not just R&D spillovers) in terms of government support for such investments via tax breaks or other mechanisms. The important issue of R&D incentives, for example, has been considered in many countries. Most of the discussion of the role of government in establishing the correct institutional and incentive setting is perhaps best viewed through the context of national innovation systems.

Note

1 Subsequent work on dynamic systems, mainly in other discipline areas, has made it clear that the observed patterns of performance that evolve over time can be extremely sensitive to the starting position (i.e. there is a strong historical dependence). In the present context, this means the initial management team, their skills and competences.

Part II
Understanding enterprise performance

Chapter 2

Enterprise scale, scope and structure

2.1   **Introduction**

Traditional neoclassical theory viewed the 'firm' as a production unit – a 'black box' – and, broadly speaking, while it was possible to observe the inputs and the outputs, little or nothing was said about what went on within the firm. In this theory, control was largely exercised through the market, by the price mechanism. Thus, traditional theory made little con-tribution to various debates, such as those concerning:

(i)   the emergence and evolution of firms;
(ii) the diversity of firm sizes that coexist in a given market;
(iii) governance structures.

    The recent interest in what goes on within the firm has opened up whole new areas for economics – 'The Coasian view, as amended and expanded by the markets, and hierarchies and contracts literatures, has opened up the "black box" of the firm' (Cowen and Parker, 1997, p. 44). This is extremely important in the context of the present book, because it is essential to understand what is going on within firms, the abilities and limitations of the managers and workforce, and how these dynamically affect the size and nature of the firm.

    It is useful to begin this process by outlining the evolution of the litera-ture in the area broadly referred to as 'transaction costs'. The subsequent discussion, however, shows that this area has developed through various stages, including:

(i)   transaction costs (i.e. as the command–market dichotomy) – Coase (1937);
(ii) markets and hierarchies – Williamson (1975, 1985);
(iii) contracts nexus – Grossman and Hart (1986).

    Later, it will become clear that, while transaction cost theory (broadly defined) is a useful starting point for modern managerial economics, it provides a very narrow view of the firm and its behaviour. Our position therefore is much closer to what Hodgson (1998, p. 26) calls the 'plural position', which emphasizes 'human learning and the enhancement of competencies or "dynamic capabilities" while paying some recognition to the role of transaction costs'. Thus, the discussion wends its way from the starting point of transaction costs as a mechanism for deciding why firms exist, to come full circle to the 'optimal design' of the firm (Part V of the present book).

Section 2.2 continues with the definition of a firm. While this appears simple, it becomes clear that the definition varies between different discipline areas. Section 2.3 deals with a question originally posed by Coase (1937) – 'Why do firms exist?' – and reviews the transaction cost approach. In addition, it outlines the range of factors that influence whether a firm will 'make' (i.e. produce in-house) or 'buy' (i.e. let some other firm produce and buy the product on the market). Section 2.4 reviews the subsequent development of the transaction cost approach away from the simple 'command–market' dichotomy through to the 'nexus of contracts' concept and beyond. Section 2.5 then turns to the question of how firms are organized and, in particular, the issues of economies of scale and scope. Section 2.6 considers a more broadly based, competence view of the firm. Section 2.7 then provides a brief review of the empirical evidence on whether diversified or undiversified (focused) firms perform better. Finally, section 2.8 draws the main conclusions of this chapter.

2.2   Definitions of the firm

2.2.1   *Official definitions*

The operational definition of the 'firm' depends crucially upon who is doing the defining and for what purpose. From a legal perspective, for example, the firm is 'A legal entity or corporate body brought into existence by registration under Companies legislation' (i.e. the Companies Acts in the UK) (Rutherford, 1992, p. 83). The UK government has something similar in mind when it refers to an 'enterprise' or 'reporting unit': 'An enterprise is defined as the smallest combination of legal units, which have a certain degree of autonomy within an enterprise group' (Office for National Statistics, 1994). Thus, the 'enterprise' can form part of a broader 'group', where an enterprise group 'is simply a number of enterprises under common ownership' or 'is defined as one or more businesses under common ownership or control' (Office for National Statistics, 1994).

An accounting definition of a firm would encompass the legal definition, but a distinction is made in terms of the 'reporting unit' for the accounts – the question here is at what level (or levels) of the organization are formal accounts published, and which parts of the organization are covered by (or excluded from) these accounts. Note that the 'enterprise' or 'reporting unit' from the government viewpoint is effectively the smallest unit that can provide the type of information being sought (about sales, employment, etc.), but if the unit is part of an 'enterprise group' it would not normally publish official accounts – this type of information about the unit normally would be consolidated in the 'enterprise group' accounts.

A group may comprise:

(i)   the 'ultimate parent company', which may be a foreign-based multi-national with any number of (national) 'parents' worldwide – the accounts of the ultimate parent will normally consolidate those of the national parents;

(ii) a (national) 'parent company' with a number of subsidiaries – the accounts of the national parent, which are published in that national state, generally consolidate all majority-owned subsidiaries, irrespective of their geographical location;

(iii) 'subsidiary' companies, where the parent has majority ownership – the accounts of these subsidiaries would normally be consolidated within the national parent accounts.

A group may have any number of 'establishments' under the control of any particular level of the company hierarchy. Given that an establishment (or some sub-set of establishments) may form an 'enterprise' or 'reporting unit' in the context of official statistics, some care must be taken not to interpret an enterprise as defined by the UK government as if it is necessarily a company.

2.2.2 Conceptual definitions of the firm

'Economic' definitions of the firm attempt to abstract from the practical considerations applied for 'day-to-day' operational purposes. A firm has been described as 'the system of relationships which comes into existence when the direction of resources is dependent on an entrepreneur' (Coase, 1937) and as a 'Conscious, wilful effort to organise economic activity that consists of a collection of contracts when more than one party is involved' (Acs and Gerlowski, 1996, p. 2). Figure 2.1 demonstrates the coordination of economic activity through the market. Here, individuals are the production units, operating through markets; the markets together comprise the economy (Ferguson *et al.*, 1993, p. 9). Figure 2.2 shows the coordination of economic activity through both individuals and firms. Again, individuals and firms interact through markets in capitalist economies (Ferguson *et al.*, 1993, p. 11).

A further way of defining a firm is to note its main features. Firms are characterized by a number of features, including:

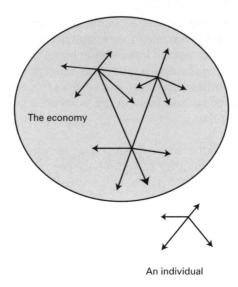

Figure 2.1 Coordination of economic activity through the market. Source: Ferguson *et al.* (1993, p. 9).

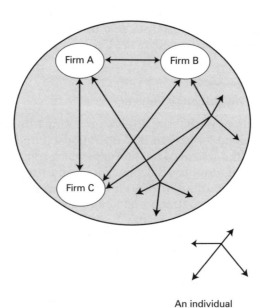

Figure 2.2 Coordination of economic activity by both firms and the market. Source: Ferguson *et al.* (1993, p. 11).

(i)   cooperation of factors;
(ii)   resource owners sign bilateral contracts with management;
(iii) resource owners cooperate in collecting information;
(iv) information is transmitted to the decision makers, who decide and implement the business plan;
(v)   resources within the firm move in line with the conscious wishes of the controller;
(vi) there is both cooperation and authority in the relationships.

Along these lines, Ferguson *et al.* (1993, p. 8) argue that, 'In an economic sense, the identifying characteristic of a firm is the supercession of the price mechanism. Within a firm resources move according to management decision rather than in response to price signals.'

2.2.3 *Firms, products and markets*

In most industrialized economies, the majority of enterprises are small (owner-managed businesses) and associated with one product area – 'For most businesses, the returned data are appropriate to a single "activity heading" (i.e. sector) and fall within a single geographical region' (Office for National Statistics, 1994).[1] However, a few enterprises are much larger (professionally managed businesses) and often operate in a variety of product areas. In most countries, 'Where information covers a mixture of activities, the business is classified according to the main activity' (Office for National Statistics, 1994). Thus, although a business may be allocated (for the purposes of gathering statistics) to one industry, it may be active in another or many other sectors. It will become apparent in later chapters why the range of activities is important. In some countries – the USA in particular – substantial effort has been made to disaggregate information about enterprises by 'line of business' (LoB), but this is not the case in most countries and, as a consequence, the allocation of a diversified company to a single sector can be misleading.

2.3 **Why do firms exist?**

2.3.1 *Transaction costs*

Firms appear to exist because they represent the most efficient method of producing the goods and services that they provide. Coase (1937), for example, argues that:

> Firms arise voluntarily because they represent a more efficient method of organising production … the main reason why it is profitable to establish a firm would seem to be that there is a cost of using the price mechanism and … by organising production under the direction of an entrepreneur these market costs can be reduced.

Coase's explanation for why firms exist is therefore based upon the fact that the costs of using the market (transaction costs) are higher than those of conscious coordination (governance costs). According to Coase, the costs of using the market arise principally from uncertainty; indeed, it is argued that a firm would probably not emerge without the existence of uncertainty (an idea put forward by Knight, 1921).

While risk and uncertainty play a central role (via imperfect information, bounded rationality and opportunistic behaviour), transaction cost theory cites a wider range of determinants for the existence, scale and scope of firms. Transaction costs arise from a wide variety of sources, for example having to devote resources to:

(i)   finding suppliers;
(ii)   establishing market prices and qualities;
(iii) negotiating supply and other contracts, bearing in mind the difficulties in drawing up complete contracts, specifying the transactions to be implemented in the future under different contingencies;
(iv)   monitoring the conditions of the contract;
(v)   enforcing the terms of the contract;
(vi)   terminating contracts where necessary;
(vii) reducing uncertainty and risks.

2.3.2 *Characteristics of markets*

Table 2.1 sets out the assumptions of perfect as opposed to imperfect markets. In a perfect market, individuals have complete information and are able to undertake all relevant calculations with perfect rationality. In addition, all individuals act honestly and the costs of transactions between individuals are zero. Under such assumptions, other things being equal, all activities would be undertaken through the market. A crucial reason why firms exist is that markets are not perfect. To varying degrees, markets are characterized by imperfect and asymmetric knowledge, and individuals are limited in their ability to undertake the whole range of calculations that would result in an unboundedly rational outcome. In addition, individuals act opportunistically in their own interests. As a consequence of these imperfections, the costs of market transactions are positive, and the more imperfect the market, the more likely it is that activities will be routed through firms.

Unbounded rationality arises when agents have full knowledge of all the relevant information and can undertake all relevant calculations – mistakes are never made. Bounded rationality occurs where individuals wish to act rationally, but their ability to be rational is limited because decision makers have a limited ability to collect, absorb and handle information, which is therefore partial and impacted (i.e. known to just a few people).

Table 2.1 Characteristics of markets

	Perfect markets	Imperfect markets
Individual	Unbounded rationality	Bounded rationality
Information	Perfect, total, symmetrical	Imperfect, partial, asymmetrical
Motivation	Honesty	Opportunistic
Transaction costs	Zero	Positive

Clearly, this is generally the case, as most decisions relate to the future and many determining factors are uncertain.

Opportunism is 'a lack of candour or honesty in transactions, to include self-interest seeking with guile' (Williamson, 1975, p. 9). Individuals may behave deceitfully in relation to the quality or price of their product. Such behaviour tends to be less of a problem where large numbers are involved and more of a problem where there is a single supplier. In addition, the problem tends to be larger where there is a lack of information regarding quality or other aspects of trade (i.e. a high level of uncertainty particularly regarding the quality of the goods or services). Under such conditions, dishonesty creates problems and it might be better to 'make' rather than 'buy'.

2.3.3 *Intra-firm efficiency*

The previous section argued that some markets are more efficient and some are less efficient – with consequences for the extent to which they are used in obtaining intermediate goods and services in the production of any given output. In much the same way, firms are differently efficient in organizing production. In the early work, at least, the organization *within* the firm was seen as being analogous with a *command economy* (while transactions between firms took place according to a market economy). Cowen and Parker (1997, p. 10) argue that one view is that 'Modern corporations, with their emphasis on "command and control", are planning systems'. The discussion in section 2.4 demonstrates how this rather restrictive command–market dichotomy perspective has been modified over time.

Much of what is said during the remainder of the book will relate to the efficiency with which firms operate. However, a crucial element in the transaction costs literature relates to the efficiency of the command structure (see Chapter 11). Significant costs are incurred by the firm in policing and directing the use of resources, and ensuring that things are done. These are referred to as 'management costs' and include, for example:

(i)   information costs relating to demand, production processes, rivals' products and so on;
(ii)   the costs of motivating employees and communicating with staff;
(iii) the costs of ensuring both compliance with orders and effective performance of tasks (see Chapter 7).

The higher the costs of 'policing' employee behaviour, for example, the greater is the likelihood of X-(in)efficiencies (Leibenstein, 1966) and of working through the market rather than the firm.

2.3.4   *Transaction versus management costs*

In essence, according to the Coasian theory, the existence of a company in a particular area depends upon the relative efficiency of the market and the firm. This depends upon the relative magnitudes of 'transaction costs' *vis-à-vis* 'management costs'. Thus, in principle, the optimal size (and scope) of a firm is determined by where the marginal costs of internalizing an (additional) external transaction is equal to the marginal costs of organizing that transaction via the market. Some factors therefore limit the size of the firm, including the costs of internal coordination and the costs of entrepreneurial mistakes. Increased efficiency of management and improved organization of the firm increase its potential size, other things being equal (see Chapters 6 and 11).

To be more efficient than its rivals, the firm must identify the appropriate boundary as to which activities should be internal and which external. Factors influencing the relative efficiency of market and firms are shown in Table 2.2.

Table 2.2 Factors affecting the relative efficiency of firms and markets

	Market	Firm
Unexploited economies of scale and scope	+	–
Large numbers of firms	+	–
Governance costs	+	–
Opportunism	–	+
Asset specificity	–	+
Firm-specific knowledge	–	+
Uncertainty about the future	–	+

Source: Adapted from Ferguson *et al.* (1993, p. 11). Note that + indicates a factor favouring use.

Unexploited economies of scale and scope
A small firm cannot achieve economies of scale and scope – which are more readily available to large firms. However, costs may be reduced by

recourse to the market, which may allow access to cheaper components from a specialist supplier if it can aggregate demands from a number of buyers, creating economies of scale and/or scope (Ferguson *et al.*, 1993, p. 12). In other words, in general, a small firm should buy rather than make the components.

Large numbers of firms

Where there are many potential suppliers, the resulting competition will generally ensure low prices, which favours operation through the market (as opposed to making the inputs within the firm). On the other hand, where there are small numbers of potential firms, this tends to give suppliers some degree of monopoly power, reducing the bargaining power of buyers. The existence of monopoly power among the potential suppliers leads firms to avoid the use of the market and make own their own inputs.

Governance costs

These are the costs of the incentives or sanctions required to produce appropriate behaviour. The market will tend to be preferred when the following are greater:

(i)   the incentives required to generate acceptable performance;
(ii)   the costs of sanctions required to discipline inappropriate behaviour;
(iii) the difficulty of controlling opportunism of employees;
(iv)   the complexity of the firm;
(v)   the length of the chains of command.

All these are influenced by organizational structure (see Chapter 11).

Opportunism

Suppliers, in particular, may exploit a lack of information about their products or activities. Such opportunism is more limited where there are repeat orders. Where opportunism exists, internalizing activity helps to guarantee input prices, quality, reliability of supply, and so on.

Asset specificity

This refers to the degree to which resources are specific to their current use – an asset is highly specific if its next best use is scrap. Both human and non-human resources can be specific (e.g. managerial skills or specialist plant and machinery). The concept does not coincide with the distinction between fixed and variable inputs, but involves the concept of sunk costs – the investment costs that cannot be recouped on disposal of the asset. Forms of specificity include:

(i)   site specificity – where the asset cannot be moved;

(ii)   physical specificity – where it can be moved but is of little use else-
        where;
(iii) human asset specificity – where skills are not transferable to other
        firms or tasks;
(iv)   dedicated asset specificity – where the asset meets the needs of a
        single customer.

The greater the specificity, the more likely it is that the activity will be
internalized – owners are aware of the capital losses associated with
redeploying their assets and customers know that they are not able to
find assets as suited to their needs elsewhere.

Firm-specific knowledge
Competitive advantage stems from possession of special knowledge, for
example about the market, product or production technology. Firm-specific
knowledge favours internal activities rather than market transactions.

Uncertainty about the future
In a certain environment, long-term contracts are simple and inexpensive
and the market may be favoured. In an uncertain world, a large number of
contingencies have to be covered, and this makes contracts more complex
and expensive. Greater uncertainty makes coordination within the firm
more attractive.

2.4   Evolution of the literature

While the literature began with Coase's (1937) seminal paper, it was many
years before the importance of this contribution was fully recognized.
The general question that Coase wrestled with was 'given that the market
economy is generally an excellent means of allocating resources, why do
firms exist?' (Cowen and Parker, 1997, p. 35). Coase's initial work suggested that the reason lay in the differential efficiencies of the market
(external) and firm (internal) in delivering different areas of production. The core of the model can be stated in terms of a simple dichotomy
between the relative efficiencies of the 'market' and the 'command'
economy internal to the firm. The heart of this issue was argued to lay in
transaction costs.
   Williamson popularized the transaction costs approach, concentrating
on the distinction between 'markets' and 'hierarchies' (firms). In particular, Williamson began to investigate more fully the sources of transaction
costs, such as bounded rationality, opportunism and asset specificity. The
object then was 'to organise transactions so as to economise on bounded
rationality, while simultaneously safeguarding against the hazards that
one party or another to the contract might take advantage and act

opportunistically' (Cowen and Parker, 1997, pp. 38–39). Williamson (1975, 1985) introduced the idea that transaction costs emphasized the potential benefits of hierarchy (i.e. the M-form company – see section 11.5.2). In time, however, Williamson's work became more critical of the market–command dichotomy and recognized the need to look at intermediate forms of organization, between the market and the hierarchy. Criticism of the dichotomous view was further stimulated by Jensen and Meckling's work, in which they argued:

> The private corporation or firm is simply one form of legal fiction which serves as a nexus for contracting relationships.... Viewed this way, it makes little or no sense to try and distinguish those things that are 'inside' the firm ... from those that are 'outside' of it. There is in a very real sense only a multitude of complex relationships (i.e. contracts) between the legal fiction (the firm) and the owners of labour, materials and capital inputs and the consumers of output. (Jensen and Meckling, 1976, pp. 310–311).

Grossman and Hart (1986) have taken this idea further, refocusing the transaction cost literature on the 'nexus of contracts'. In a fairly recent paper, for example, Williamson argues that firms and markets are 'alternative modes for organising the same transaction ... the different governance structures or contract forms are selected according to their relative efficiencies in terms of transactions costs' (Cowen and Parker, 1997, p. 43). In Chapter 6, the discussion extends this 'nexus of contracts' view of the firm to include informal inter-personal and inter-group relationships. Cowen and Parker (1997, pp. 43–44), however, develop this view in a slightly different direction, arguing that:

> The 'contract view' of the firm, in contrast to the 'command view', emphasises similarities rather than differences between resource allocation in firms and in markets.... By doing so it provides a basis for the application of market principles to resource allocation within the firm ... intra-firm transactions can have market-like relationships.

2.5   Organizational structure

2.5.1   *Central role of organizational structure*

Organizational structure is crucial to firm performance, and this is discussed extensively in Part V from a strategic perspective. Nelson and Winter (1982), for example, argue the importance of 'organizational genetics', in other words, the organizational structure and its evolution over time. However, it is clear that present research in this area is at an early stage – Nelson and Winter note that 'the real work remains to be done'. Nelson (1991) argues that 'differences between individual firms constitute a core problem ... analyses have to consider firm strategies, structure and core capabilities in greater depth'.

2.5.2   *Scale and scope of the organization*

The central shape in Figure 2.3 represents the strategic core of the company. It derives from the employment/ownership of *specific assets* (see section 2.3.4). It is likely to involve the key intellectual capital of the company, including various forms of intellectual property (IP) (i.e. trade secrets, patents, etc.) and other intangibles (i.e. brand names, goodwill, etc.). Team synergies are likely to be high in the core; in other words, the output produced by two (or more) individuals or groups working together in the core exceeds the sum of their individual outputs:

$$Q(A + B) > Q(A) + Q(B)$$

where Q denotes output (Ferguson *et al.*, 1993, p. 223).

   Figure 2.3 also sets out some of the key economic factors that influence the boundary of the firm. In particular, *scope economies* may refer to the improvements in unit costs (C) that derive from an increase in the range of production activities of the firm:

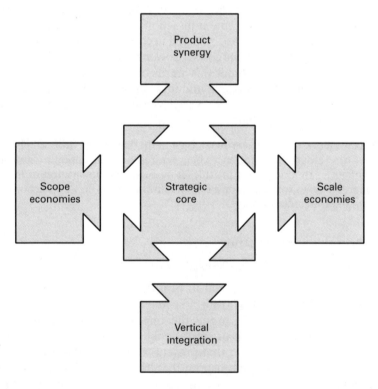

Figure 2.3 Factors influencing the boundaries of the firm. Source: Ferguson *et al.* (1993, p. 225).

$C(I + II) < C(I) + C(II)$

or to improvements from *product synergies* arising from producing a wider range of products – defined, for example, in terms of total revenues (*TR*):

$TR(A + B) > TR(A) + TR(B)$

That is, *TR* is higher from the production of both products than if A and B are produced by different companies.

Scale economies relate to the technical, managerial and/or financial economies that spring from having a larger (smaller) firm. Scope economies arise from operating within a broader range of product markets or with a wider range technologies. The firm may attain scale and/or scope economies via internal growth (or contraction) or external growth via mergers and takeovers (or divestments). Merger activity may also be linked to 'horizontal integration' (i.e. integrating with other firms in the same product area) or 'diversification' (i.e. integrating with firms in other product areas). *Vertical integration* refers to the economies (or diseconomies) that come from integrating some part of the supplier and/or buyer chain. Taking over a sole supplier or a sole buyer, for example, could reduce the degree of monopolistic or monopsonistic exploitation of the company.

2.5.3 *Changing the scale and/or scope*

The discussion above considered the 'optimal' boundaries of the company from a conceptual viewpoint. They are defined as the point where, at any given point in time, the marginal benefits of further expansion (contraction) are exactly equal to the marginal costs of such expansion (contraction) – in any direction. It has been shown that this is to do with various types of economies/synergies (i.e. economies of scale and scope, etc.) and costs (i.e. transaction costs). Figure 2.4 illustrates the practical issues that the firm must resolve in determining its boundaries – these relate to the number and types of relationships and contracts with other organizations.

Changing the organizational structure and, thereby, the routines of the organization is inherently risky. The problem for management is in determining the precise effects of any particular strategy: 'Most important, it is to recognise that the flexibility of routinised behaviour is of limited scope and that a changing environment can force firms to risk their very survival on attempts to modify their routines' (Nelson and Winter, 1982, p. 400). Thus, company structure – in particular, the hierarchy of management, company routines and the nature of formal and informal relationships – becomes a crucial issue for the economist, as, 'At any time, organisations have built into them a set of ways of doing things and ways

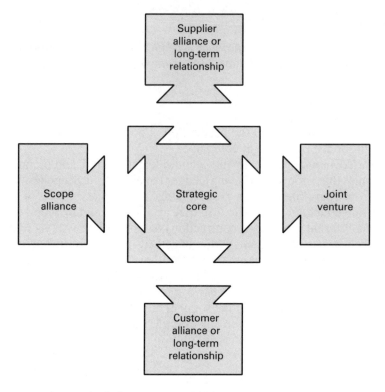

Figure 2.4 Strategic linkages to establish and reinforce the core. Source: Ferguson *et al.* (1993, p. 238).

of determining what to do' (Nelson and Winter, 1982, p. 400). According to Frank Knight (1921, p. 268), 'When uncertainty is present, and the task of deciding what to do and how to do it takes the ascendancy over that of execution, the internal organisation of the productive groups is no longer a matter of indifference or a mechanical detail'.

Ferguson *et al.* (1993, p. 241) set out some of the key strategic relationships surrounding the core (see Figure 2.5). Subsequent chapters explore how the firm handles a number of these relationships and, in particular, how the firm internalizes (moves some of them inside the firm) or externalizes (moves some outside the firm) them in a search for an 'optimal' structure.

2.6   Towards a competence-based theory of the firm

While not denying the importance of transaction costs theory, the main focus of the present book is a competence-based view of the enterprise –

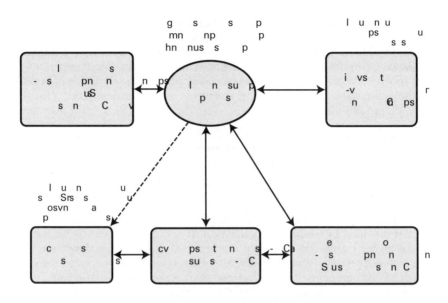

Figure 2.5 Relationships with other organizations in determining the strategic core of an enterprise. Source: Ferguson *et al.* (1993, p. 241).

competences define the strategic core (or the focus) of the company. However, competence is a much more general concept – not only of why this strategic core exists, but also of how it emerges and evolves over time – a dynamic rather than static or comparative static concept. Much of the remainder of the book is about competences, how the firm develops these competences and the implications that this has for enterprise performance. As Hodgson (1998, p. 25) argues, 'The competence-based perspective sees the existence, structure and boundaries of the firm as explained in some way by the associated existence of individual or team competences – such as skills and tacit knowledge – which are in some way fostered and maintained by that organization'.

Hodgson (1998, pp. 36–42) sees the evolution of competence-based theories as occurring through the works of Adam Smith, Frank Knight and Edith Penrose – although there are other contenders, including Joseph Schumpeter. Certainly, Smith's emphasis on the manual 'learning by doing' enabled by the division of labour is an obvious starting point (see the discussion of labour learning in section 12.2.1). While some of the contributions of the other authors are taken up in later chapters, Frank Knight sets the scene. Knight's (1921) work has a number of features of relevance to the present study, not least the role of risk and uncertainty, which he saw as a primary determinant of the existence of the firm (Knight, 1921, p. 244). Extending the earlier quote from Knight:

> When uncertainty is present, and the task of deciding what to do and how to do it takes the ascendancy over that of execution, the internal organisation of the productive groups is no longer a matter of indifference or a mechanical detail. Centralisation of this deciding and controlling function is imperative, a process of 'cephalisation', such as has taken place in the evolution of organic life, is inevitable, and for the same reasons as in biological evolution. (Knight, 1921, pp. 268–269)

Thus, in keeping with a theme of the present book, management plays the key role of coping with uncertainty by 'exercising judgement and developing such capacity for judgement in others' (Hodgson, 1998, p. 38). However, Knight's view is that entrepreneurial and management judgement is idiosyncratic and, thus, according to Hodgson (1998, p. 39):

> Knight's implicit answer to the question 'why do firms exist?' is different from that provided by Coase and Williamson. It is not fundamentally because of the higher transaction costs that the firm cannot be broken down into self-employed producers trading with each other. It is because a complete market for all entrepreneurial and managerial skills is impossible in principle ... in a context of uncertainty, some competences cannot be usefully or readily bought or hired.

Here is the crux that drives the competence view of the firm:

> The very essence of capabilities/competences is that they cannot be readily assembled through markets ... the properties of internal organization cannot be replicated by a portfolio of business units amalgamated through formal contract, as the distinctive elements of internal organization simply cannot be replicated by the market. That is entrepreneurial activity cannot lead to the immediate replication of unique organizational skills through simply entering a market and piecing the parts together overnight. (Teece and Pisano, 1994, p. 540; quoted in Hodgson, 1998, pp. 39–40)

More specifically:

> It is generally believed that the most important resources and capabilities are those which are most difficult for competitors to imitate and difficult to understand, provide potential access to a wide variety of markets, make a significant contribution to the perceived customer benefits of the end product, and are very durable. (Unland and Kleiner, 1996, p. 6)

In essence, the transaction cost theory can be seen as a more static concept that addresses the costs and benefits of leaving out or including particular activities at a given point in time. The competence theory appears more dynamic and encompassing. At any one point in time, the transaction cost theory might suggest that a particular activity would be better done outside the firm, but if undertaking it within the firm nurtures competences, this might be superior in a dynamic sense. Unland and Kliener (1996, p. 6) note that 'Although outsourcing can reduce costs, obtain expertise in non-competitive areas of the business and provide additional flexibility, if not closely monitored, it may also remove core competencies from the company'. Thus, transaction cost theory has a particular focus (i.e. the costs of inclusion versus exclusion), while the competence-based theories help to explain the wide range of activities by which the enterprise can lever improved performance and added value.

2.7 Company focus[2]

2.7.1 *Focus, specialization and diversification*

A distinguishing feature of companies, linked to issues of scale and scope, is the extent to which they are 'focused'. 'Unfocused' is not identical to 'diversified' – in principle, it is possible for a highly diversified company to set up organizational and management structures that enable it to be 'highly focused' in all of the product lines that it produces. However, the range of a firm's different production activities is often taken as an indication of focus, on the general assumption that a 'jack-of-all-trades is master of none'. Industrial economics, therefore, often makes a distinction between:

(i)   *diversification*, which relates to the degree to which a company is involved in different product areas (i.e. the greater the 'diversity' of the products, the greater the degree of diversification);

(ii) *specialization*, which refers to the proportion of the firm's output attributable to its principal product (i.e. the product that is generally used to classify the sector of production of the company).

In a study of large Australian firms, Bosworth *et al.* (1999a, p. 73) attempted to construct an index of *relatedness* (REL) of the outputs of each firm, where REL is the average of the 'distances' of each contributing business (of the company) from the firm's main business.

2.7.2 *Potential advantages of greater diversification*

Bosworth *et al.* (1999a, p. 69) set out some of the strategic advantages that can flow from greater diversification. For example, diversification can help to realize managerial economies of scale, insofar as good managers are good managers anywhere – their skills are not confined by particular products or technologies. If the firm's growth is constrained by the size of the market or anti-trust controls, for example, then the managers' capacity may be more fully utilized if the firm develops new product market activities in other areas (see Chapter 6). This also relates to the earlier discussion, as diversified companies may be able to realize economies of scope (i.e. synergies in production, marketing, etc.).

Diversification may also enable the exploitation of financial synergies. First, if two firms that have volatile but at least partially independent cash flows merge, it is possible that they can reduce the probability of either firm defaulting and, thereby, increase the value of both firms (below, however, it is suggested that this argument is flawed). Second, there are potential tax benefits from merging if the merging firms raise their gearing by increasing borrowing and using the resulting funds to retire equity. The higher post-merger debt can increase the total value of the firm because of the tax deductibility of interest payments (Copeland and Weston, 1992, p. 694). Third, larger, diversified firms may have better access to capital markets, which can help to reduce the risk to those who lend to them (Levy and Sarnat, 1970, p. 801). Fourth, internal (to the firm) capital markets allow a more efficient allocation of funds across competing uses than external (from the financial sector) capital markets (this arises from better access to information and the possibility of better control of the outcomes of investments); therefore diversification will be attractive insofar as it enables greater use of internal funds.

It has also been argued that firms may diversify simply in order to create a portfolio of products that matches that of their competitors (Scott, 1993). The rationale is that such a strategy enables companies to reduce risk and uncertainty in the extent and nature of ongoing competition. Scott (1993) demonstrates empirically that if two conglomerates both operate in one particular LoB, there is a strong likelihood that they will have other LoBs in common. A similar finding is shown for their R&D activities. Scott argues that this is part of a strategy to restrict competition in both a static and a dynamic sense. However, there are many potential strategic reasons why diversification may occur and why the actual reasons may be similar for firms in the same product areas. An example is where managers form a negative view about the expected future profitability of a current LoB, for example because of a general trend in demand for the products of that sector or because of an erosion of the firm's market power through increasing competition. Under such circumstances, the company may choose to diversify into sectors with a more positive outlook, and companies with similar competences and technologies are more likely to choose similar new LoBs.

2.7.3 *Potential disadvantages of diversification*

In recent years there has been a shift in the balance of argument away from the benefits of diversification. It has been pointed out that reducing default risk by merging companies with (at least partially) uncorrelated income flows actually works by changing the relative positions of bond and equity holders – the lenders to the company are more protected but at the expense of the stockholders of each firm, who now have to back the claims of the bondholders of *both* companies. More fundamentally it has been argued that the shareholders did not need companies to merge in order to reduce their risk – shareholders can do so themselves by diversifying their individual portfolios in the stock market. Indeed, diversification may destroy value by interfering with shareholders' ability to diversify their portfolios (Levy, 1991). In holding shares in a conglomerate, the shareholder is effectively forced to hold stock in the constituent businesses in a fixed proportion (i.e. according to the value of the company's equity attributable to each LoB). This ratio is compatible with each shareholder's optimal portfolio decisions only by chance.

Even where diversification aids survival, this may not be efficient from either a private or a social perspective – businesses that would optimally close down or be sold to a company more able to manage them efficiently might continue to operate because of cross-subsidies from other parts of the conglomerate.

Finally, the counterargument to 'managerial economies of scope' is that more focused companies can achieve 'managerial economies of specialization'. These arise because managers develop special expertise in the production and marketing of particular products or services.

2.7.4 Brief review of the literature

An early study by Reid (1968) confirmed a widely held belief that much diversification is management-driven rather than financially justifiable. Reid reported that conglomerate mergers satisfy the desires of managers for larger firms but do not increase earnings or market prices. Later results confirmed that diversification, firm size and management salaries are highly correlated, providing an incentive for managers to diversify even if the result is not in the interests of investors (Hoskisson and Hitt, 1990). Relatedly, an explanation for conglomerate diversification is that it is a mechanism that managers can use to reduce the risk of bankruptcy or takeover. Thus, they are able to reduce the risks to their own jobs through diversification, even though it is associated with a loss in value for the owners – a strategy which is in the interests only of the managers (Zhou, 2004). Pandya and Rao (1998) provide US evidence consistent with these ideas. Their paper concludes that a dominant, undiversified firm may perform better than a highly diversified firm in terms of return, but its riskiness will be much greater. If managers of such firms opt for diversification, their returns will decrease, but their riskiness will reduce proportionately more than the reduction in their returns. Similarly, a number of studies conclude that corporate diversification programmes exemplify the theory that managers of firms with unused borrowing capacity and substantial free cash flows are more likely to undertake low-benefit or even value-destroying investments (Chatterjee and Wernerfelt, 1991; Jensen, 1988). Chatterjee and Wernerfelt (1991) found that excess physical resources, most knowledge-based resources and external financial resources are associated with more related diversification, while internal financial resources are associated with more unrelated diversification. Meyer *et al.* (1992) argued that failing businesses can have too ready access to cross-subsidies when they are part of a diversified firm.

There is some evidence that conglomerate acquirers have an information advantage and are more able to value target companies accurately. Melicher and Rush (1974) report that over the period 1960–1969, conglomerates acquired more profitable firms than non-conglomerate acquirers, and that conglomerate mergers increased the utilization of latent debt capacity. There is, though, evidence counter to this – that conglomerates perform no better than matched portfolios of undiversified companies. For example, Mason and Goudzwaard (1976) compared twenty-two conglomerates against randomly selected portfolios with similar asset structures for the years 1962–1967. They concluded that conglomerates perform statistically worse in terms of their return on assets and return on equity than unmanaged portfolios of similar industry investments. While Smith and Weston (1977) reported that the risk-adjusted performance of conglomerates was significantly better than that of mutual funds, their study was subsequently criticized for its mis-specification of the risk adjustment.

Comment and Jarrell (1995) concluded that in the 1980s there was a trend towards focus and specialization, and that this led to improved stock returns overall. Further, while financial economies of scope were available to diversified firms, diversified firms failed to exploit these economies. Also, Comment and Jarrell reported that diversified firms exhibit lower firm-specific (diversifiable) risk but not lower systematic risk, which supports the argument that diversification at the firm level (rather than diversification by shareholders of their share portfolios) is not value-enhancing.

2.7.5   *Concluding remarks on focus and diversification*

Taken together, these studies suggest that over recent decades there has been a substantial shift in the view taken of diversification. More sophisticated techniques in financial economics (including arbitrage and option-pricing arguments) suggest that previously held ideas about the financial benefits of mergers are misguided. It is perhaps not surprising, therefore, that Ruthven (1994) implies the need to 'stick to your knitting' (see section 1.1) – in other words, the company should keep to its area(s) of *core competence*. He argues that:

> By and large, successful companies believed that the grass was just as green or just as brown on the other side of the fence as it was on their side. They did not succumb to picking up shiny baubles and, in the long run, learned the importance of self control when it comes to delusions of grandeur. They

ran businesses they understood and expanded them locally or internationally before diversifying into other fields. (Ruthven, 1994, p. 21)

Overall, however, the empirical evidence is mixed, which probably partly reflects the problem of using diversification as a proxy for focus, as well as the problems of constructing a counterfactual (i.e. what would have happened to that company in the absence of diversification). Pandya and Rao (1998, p. 68), for example, conclude from reviews of the literature that:

> (a) the empirical evidence is inconclusive; (b) models, perspectives and results differ based on the disciplinary perspective chosen by the researcher; and (c) the relationship between diversification and performance is complex and is affected by intervening and contingent variables such as related *versus* unrelated diversification, type of relatedness, the capability of top managers, industry structure, and the mode of diversification.

On balance, however, it appears that diversifying into related product markets produces higher returns than diversifying into unrelated product markets (Keats, 1990; Kusewitt, 1985; Michel and Shaked, 1984; Rumelt, 1986; Simmonds, 1990), probably because the benefits of integrating operations and core skills outweigh those of reduced variance in sales revenues. In addition, the method of diversification appears important, with some evidence that the R&D and new product development (NPD) route is better than that of mergers and takeovers (Lamont and Anderson, 1985; Simmonds, 1990). The literature also suggests that the strategic reasons for diversifying are important determinants of the subsequent performance of the company.

The result of this relatively recent attention paid to the merits of 'focus' has led to a number of high-profile spin-offs and divestments. At one level, many companies have downsized, often by looking at particular activities and assessing whether these could be best done by the market or by the enterprise itself. At another level, major companies have split into two or more smaller enterprises. Courtauld's decision to spin-off its textiles division from its chemical and industrial activities, as an independent company with its own stock market listing, was announced in 1989. Ferguson *et al.* (1993, p. 24) reported that 'The demerger recognised that the two areas of activity would benefit from management which could focus on their particular requirements.... Forming a separate company allowed existing shareholders to retain a stake in two potentially attractive areas'. Other high-profile examples include the spin-off from ICI in 1994 of Zeneca, with the activities in agrochemicals, genetically modified crops, seeds and pharmaceuticals.

While Ruthven (1994, p. 5) argues that companies should be narrowly focused in terms of what they do, he also suggests that they should:

(i)   be widely focused in terms of the environments in which they operate (and take account of the implications for strategy);

(ii)   think from the outside in (i.e. have a market orientation), not the inside out (i.e. myopic);

(iii) be information-intensive (informed, knowing, astute, wise).

The reader will find that these ideas gel well with a number of the findings that are reported later in the present book.

2.8   Conclusions

This chapter has attempted to provide a definition of firms. In practice, this proved somewhat more problematic than might have been expected, as there are both practical and more conceptual definitions, and some bodies (e.g. the Office for National Statistics) use terms such as 'enterprise' and 'enterprise group' in a somewhat unusual way. In many respects, management decisions are taken at all levels of the firm – the establishment, the company, the group. While it may be true that investments – such as R&D, advertising and, perhaps, training – are more likely to be taken at higher levels within the company or group, even this may not always be so (as in the case of a holding company, where the parent generally leaves such decisions to at least the next level in the hierarchy). In the main, however, financial data are available only from published accounts, which consolidate the activities of majority-owned subsidiaries. Thus, this forms the natural focus for a significant proportion of the research and, for the purposes of the present study, what we would term the 'enterprise'. Even then, there are problems, as the accounts for UK-based enterprises, defined in this way, may be consolidated in the accounts of an ultimate parent, based in another country. It may be that many of the key decisions are taken by this ultimate parent.

The subsequent discussion addressed the issue of why there are firms, rather than just individuals who then trade in the market. Transaction cost theory and its subsequent offshoots, through to the 'nexus of contracts' and 'internal market' approaches, provide considerable insights about the 'make' or 'buy' decision. In addition, the discussion of definitions of the firm and the 'nexus of contracts' approach help to emphasize that the boundaries of the firm are both fuzzy and changing in a dynamic way. A key feature of the transaction cost approach is that, in some sense, activities that are more efficiently done within the firm are internalized and those which are more efficiently done through the market are externalized. At the margin, the net benefits of going within or without are, in principle, equalized around the periphery of the firm. This underlying principle drives both the scale and scope of the firm's activities and, thereby, the organization of the company and its activities.

The present chapter has argued that, while the transaction cost theory offers considerable insights about the existence of firms, it offers much less about the evolution of firms over time, except in the fairly shallow sense of the marginal costs and benefits of internalization. In order to obtain a better understanding of firm dynamics, it is necessary to move to a resource-based or, more accurately, a competence-based view of the enterprise. This theory sees the company as being (relatively) strong in its area or areas of core competence. These areas of competence are linked to key factors, such as skills, management expertise, technology, brand image and so on, which take the discussion much closer to the main foci of the present book. The link with transaction cost theory is that, in the main, areas of core competence are where the firm does things better than the market and, hence, they are internalized, while areas of weakness are externalized.

The implication of this appears to be that more focused firms should outperform less focused firms. The literature on this is far from conclusive, but this is partly the result of the fact that focus is often imperfectly proxied by the extent of diversification. It is probably fair to say, however, that the balance of the literature seems to support a link between greater focus and better performance. It also tends to suggest that related diversification is better than unrelated, and that diversification through R&D and new products is, on balance, better than that through merger and takeover.

Notes

1 'Activity heading' refers to a designation of a sector of economic activity according to the Standard Industrial Classification (SIC) in the UK. The SIC varies according to the level of aggregation (e.g. specified by up to four digits).
2 This section draws upon Bosworth *et al.* (1997) and Bosworth *et al.* (1999a).

Chapter 3

Enterprise performance: indicators and measures

3.1   Alternative measures and approaches to measurement

In studying performance, it is important to be clear about whose performance is to be measured. Performance may be evaluated at the level of individual managers *vis-à-vis* their skills in the task they are appointed to carry out. It may also be studied in the context of the cumulative effect of the skills of all managers on the aggregate performance of the enterprise. The present chapter is concerned with the issue of how performance is to be measured. A number of financial and non-financial measures, as well as combinations of them and relationships between them, are explored. This provides a link to the goals of the enterprise (Chapter 5) and an essential platform for understanding the results of the empirical work on enterprise performance that are reported later in the book.

Section 3.2 discusses the accounting-based measures of performance.[1] It examines the main strengths and weaknesses of such data and outlines the principal financial ratios and financial indices. Section 3.3 outlines the main economic measures, such as productivity, unit costs, profitability and market value (MV). In both sections, an attempt is made to provide an encompassing framework, to indicate how the measures are related to each other. In section 3.3, for example, it is shown how the partial measures of productivity (e.g. labour productivity) are related to total factor productivity (TFP) (and a similar exercise is undertaken for the corresponding unit cost measures). The analysis also demonstrates how productivity and unit costs are related to a firm's profits. The discussion emphasizes the importance of measuring quality change when calculating economic measures of performance. The various measures are then linked to the MV of companies. Section 3.4 introduces the concept of balanced scorecards. Finally, section 3.5 draws the main conclusions of the present chapter.

3.2 Accounting-based performance measures

3.2.1 *Use of financial accounting data*

This section concentrates on the financial measures of performance, in particular those based on the accounting statements of companies (as opposed to market-based financial measures, which are discussed later). It is standard practice to assess the performance of a company by looking at measures derived from its financial statements. A company's financial statements reflect the cumulative effect of numerous individual business decisions. Thus, 'Financial statements are the universal periodic "score-cards" available to track the results of business investment, operations and financing' (Helfert, 1994, p. 99). In a nutshell, the balance sheet, profit and loss account and cash flow statement of a company provide insights into how the business has been run overall and give an indication of its prospects. The skills and capacity of management in taking appropriate investment, financing and operational decisions are expected to be reflected in these financial statements. The role played by management in driving company performance forms the basis for the ongoing debates regarding compensation and 'excessive remuneration', which, along with other corporate governance issues, are discussed in Chapter 7.

The limitations usually associated with analyses of financial statements arise because of the use of alternative and varying accounting policies by companies, which makes consistent comparisons difficult. Particular difficulties relate to inventory valuation, depreciation methods and inflation accounting (Helfert, 1994). More recently, concerns have also been raised about the valuation and treatment of R&D and other intangible assets (it is often debated whether the additional R&D expenditures observed after the introduction of R&D tax concessions are 'real' or just an accounting figment brought about by recategorizing expenditures). In practice, these concerns imply that the analyst would have to restate financial variables on a common and meaningful basis, across time and across firms. Another caveat is that performance analyses based on accounting numbers reflect past data and conditions, and may not form a sound basis for extrapolation into the future (Helfert, 1994).

There are three broad ways in which financial statements are used to measure overall performance:

(i) examining volume trends and growth in financial variables or groups of variables (e.g. total assets, shareholders' funds and debt);

(ii) using ratios that relate various aspects of the investing, financing and operational performance of the company (e.g. return on assets, ROA);

(iii) deriving indices, often from ratios and/or other accounting variables, usually in the context of trying to predict future performance (e.g.

Z-scores derived from discriminant analysis – see section 3.2.3 – and economic value added, EVA – see section 3.2.4).

The first set of measures is basic and most analyses would go beyond examinations of just trends and growth. In what follows, each of the other two broad methods is discussed. These topics are well covered in standard financial management textbooks, such as van Horne (1998). The object is not to replicate these sources, but to highlight the main principles involved and to illustrate their application by discussing a few studies that have used them.

3.2.2 *Financial ratios*

Accounting ratios relate one financial number to another, and facilitate the drawing of inferences about the position or performance of an activity. They enable the analysis to control for size, time and other differences and so foster inter- and intra-firm comparability (Broadbent and Cullen, 1993). In principle, it is possible to compute numerous ratios to relate many items in the financial statements. To be useful, however, the actual ratios computed should be guided by:

(i)   the viewpoint taken (e.g. that of management, owners, lenders, tax authorities);
(ii)   the objectives of the appraisal;
(iii) the standards of comparison.

Helfert (1994) provides a useful summary of the groups of ratios that could be of interest from the viewpoints of three main stakeholders, as shown in Table 3.1. The viewpoints covered are for illustrative purposes only, as there are clearly other stakeholders (e.g. creditors, employees, labour organizations, regulators, government and the public). However, many of the areas (e.g. profitability) are of common interest to all stake-holders – only the degree of emphasis would vary.

The ratios listed in Table 3.1 reflect different aspects of the role of management, and it is possible to assess the skills and capacity of management in terms of operational efficiency, liquidity, resource management, profitability and so on. Furthermore, such (aggregate) assessment must be viewed in the context of the goals of the company, which, here, are presumed to be owner-driven and conditioned by the prevailing arrangements for corporate governance. For purposes of tractability, the assessment of the overall financial performance of management – and so of the skills–performance nexus – is illustrated from the point of view of the owners. There are other grounds for this approach:

Table 3.1 Financial performance measures, by area and viewpoint

Management	Owners	Lenders
Operational analysis	*Profitability*	*Liquidity*
Gross margin	Return on total net worth	Current ratio
Profit margin	Return on equity	Acid test
Operating expenditure analysis	Earnings per share	Quick sale value
Contribution analysis	Cash flow per share	Cash flow patterns
Operating leverage	Share price appreciation	
Comparative analysis	Total shareholder return	
	Shareholder value analysis	
Resource management	*Disposition of earnings*	*Financial leverage*
Asset turnover	Dividends per share	Debts to assets
Working capital management:	Dividend yield	Debt to capitalization
inventory turnover	Payout/retention	Debt to equity
accounts receivable patterns	Dividend coverage	Risk/reward trade-off
accounts payable patterns	Dividends to assets ratio	
Human resources effectiveness		
Profitability	*Market indicators*	*Debt service*
Return on assets	Price/earnings ratio	Interest coverage
Return before interest and tax	Cash flow multiples	Burden coverage
Return on current-value basis	Market to book value	Cash flow analysis
Investment project economics	Relative price movements	
Cash flow return on investment		

(i)   the owners' interest is in the 'bottom line' – the culmination of all management decisions;

(ii) in practice, senior managers are also owners (see Chapter 7).

Profitability and dividend ratios are typical yardsticks in assessing the financial performance of management. The skill and capacity of management to deliver superior resource management and operational efficiency are, in aggregate, reflected in the firm's profitability and the earnings of the owners. This interconnectedness of management and owner viewpoints is clearly illustrated when the ratios are viewed as systems. For example, the profitability ratio, ROA, is derived from 'asset turnover' and the volume of sales, and can be written:

$$\text{ROA} = \frac{\text{net profit}}{\text{assets}} = \frac{\text{net profit}}{\text{sales}} * \frac{\text{sales}}{\text{assets}}$$

3.1

$$= \text{profit margin} * \text{asset turnover}$$

or,

$$\text{ROA} = \frac{(\text{gross profit} - \text{expenses})(1 - \text{tax rate})}{\text{price} * \text{volume}} *$$

3.2

$$\frac{\text{price} * \text{volume}}{\text{fixed} + \text{current} + \text{other assets}}$$

Equivalent statements for return on equity (ROE) would be:

$$\text{ROE} = \frac{\text{net profit}}{\text{equity}} = \frac{\text{net profit}}{\text{assets}} * \frac{\text{assets}}{\text{equity}}$$

3.3

$$= \text{profit margin} * \text{degree of leverage}$$

or,

$$\text{ROE} = \frac{\text{net profit}}{\text{sales}} * \frac{\text{sales}}{\text{assets}} * \frac{\text{assets}}{\text{assets} - \text{liabilities}}$$

3.4

Thus, implicit in the overall measure of profitability is the recognition of the performance expected of management in terms of operational efficiency, resource management and capital structure. To improve ROA, managers have several 'decision levers' (Helfert, 1994, p. 149) at their disposal: improvement of gross margin (e.g. via pricing), control of expenses, utilization of fewer assets and resources, effective management of working capital and tax minimization. A ROE analysis would also yield the same decision levers, plus the role of debt utilization in boosting ROE. Clearly, studies of the relationship between management skills and company performance would do well to gauge management skills in the use of all these key decision levers – which are proxied by the accounting numbers. At the same time, this accounting ratio system provides a framework for evaluating company-wide and, thereby, overall management performance.

3.2.3 *Financial indices*

The ratios discussed above have a univariate nature. Thus, faced with an array of ratios measuring different aspects of management performance, there is a potential for ambiguity. To mitigate this problem, ratios are often combined into a single index of performance, reinforcing the treatment of ratios as a system. This practice has its origins in credit analysis and attempts to predict the likelihood of corporate default or failure. For example, various studies have concluded that the ratios for failing firms differ significantly from those of others (see, for example, Altman, 1983).

Consistently weak performance would lead to default, insolvency, failure, takeover and so on. Since accounting ratios provide an indication of the current or past performance of management, it is likely that any management weaknesses will show up in the data before a takeover or failure. However, the more important question may concern the extent to which past outcomes can be a guide to the future. Equivalently, can ratios be applied in predicting the probability of either takeover or failure? This is the basis for the models pioneered by Beaver (1966) and extended into a multivariate framework by Altman (1968), Deakin (1972) and Altman *et al.* (1981). Generally, the object is to calculate a single value, which is then used as a basis for classifying firms into, for example, 'taken over/not taken over' or 'failed/non-failed' categories.

One common method applied in these studies is multiple discriminant analysis (MDA). Altman (1983) explains the steps involved:

(i)   establish the relevant groups, for example failed or non-failed;
(ii) compute the relevant financial ratios for all the companies in the analysis;
(iii) implement the analysis.

The basic form of MDA aims to derive the linear combination of the characteristics (ratios) that 'best' discriminates between the relevant groups. MDA thus determines a set of discriminant coefficients, which, when applied to the actual ratios, provides a basis for classification into one or the other of the groups. In the process, all the characteristics (ratios) and interactions between them are taken into account, unlike in the univariate case. That is, areas of management performance such as operational efficiency, resource management, liquidity, capital structure and so on can be analysed simultaneously, rather than sequentially. The discriminant function is of the form:

$$Z = V_1 X_1 + V_2 X_2 + \dots V_n X_n \hspace{4cm} 3.5$$

where the Vs are discriminant coefficients and the Xs are the independent variables (accounting ratios). The function transforms the individual ratios into a single discriminant score called the Z-score. Each firm's Z-score is then compared with the predetermined cut-off Z-score in assessing the likelihood of failure. For a further discussion of discriminant analysis, see Hair *et al.* (1995, pp. 178–255).

3.2.4 *Economic value added*

Economic value added (EVA) is a term coined by Stern Stewart & Company, a consultancy based in New York (Dodd and Chen, 1997). EVA is a relatively recent performance measurement tool that also relies on accounting information – it is 'based on operating income after taxes, the investment in assets required to generate that income and the cost of the investment in assets (or weighted average cost of capital, WACC)' (Brewer *et al.*, 1999, p. 5). It is a financial amount calculated as:

$$\text{EVA} = [\text{adjusted operating income after tax}] - \\ [(\text{investment in assets}) * (\text{WACC})] \qquad 3.6$$

A positive EVA means that the firm has earned more post-tax operating income than the cost of assets used in generating that income – that is, it has created wealth; a negative EVA implies that the company is a net consumer of capital (Brewer *et al.*, 1999). It improves on the traditional accounting-based measures by capitalizing intangibles (including goodwill, expensed R&D,[2] etc.), deferred income tax reserves and other items with future earning potential (Dodd and Chen, 1997).

EVA is becoming popular as a tool for aligning corporate and shareholder interests (Ettorre, 1995) and for aligning divisional versus corporate goals (Brewer *et al.*, 1999). Because it focuses on value creation, incentive contracts linked to it would encourage managers to behave in ways that are congruent with maximization of shareholder value and thereby reduce agency costs (see Chapter 7). It forces managers to focus on sales growth, margins, cost of capital, asset value and tax management (Ettorre, 1995). As in the case of the ratio indices discussed above, EVA provides a means of unifying several financial criteria into a single number that can be readily applied in evaluating management performance.

3.2.5 *Application of accounting performance measures in the literature*

As one would expect, numerous studies have employed accounting information and ratios in analysing the performance of firms, either on their own or in combination with non-accounting information. The dependent variable is usually some performance characteristic, which might be linked to the goals of the enterprise – growth, profit, sales, market share, takeover/merger probability, likelihood of failure, credit default probability, and so on. Some relevant examples are summarized in Table 3.2.

All the studies in Table 3.2 used accounting ratios or other accounting data to assess the performance of management. They cover several aspects of the roles expected of managers, such as the management of liquidity, leverage, profitability, asset/resource utilization and operations. A number of these studies modelled poor performance, such as failure, takeover and failure resolution costs (i.e. Altman, 1968; Henebry, 1996). Some examined explicit performance criteria, for example corporate liquidity (John, 1993), default probability (Huffman and Ward, 1996) and acquisitions (Pantalone and Platt, 1993). To reduce the potential for ambiguity arising from computing so many ratios, most combine several measures into a single overall score of management's performance.

From a practical perspective, one may well ask which of the three main approaches is best – univariate accounting ratios, indices based on combinations of accounting ratios (which may be conventional accounting ratios and/or cash flow ratios) or EVA? The problem with univariate ratio analysis was discussed in section 3.2.3 – applied on their own, univariate ratios are potentially misleading.

Regarding the use of indices in the context of estimating the likelihood of failure, no single model is entirely satisfactory. Mossman *et al.* (1998) argue that 'The discriminatory ability of the cash flow model remains relatively consistent over the last two to three fiscal years before bankruptcy, while the [conventional] ratio model offers the best discriminatory ability in the year immediately prior to bankruptcy'. Mossman *et al.* (1998) also suggest that the available results indicate different uses for the models. Thus, stakeholders may be more interested in the cash flow variables as an early warning of financial difficulties, while a large shift in the conventional accounting ratios could be a warning of imminent financial collapse. Cash flows have only recently been applied in the literature for performance analysis – for more discussion of their calculation and use, see Giacomino and Mielke (1993) and Mills and Yamamura (1998).

Overall, the main conclusion regarding the accounting-based measures is that they provide a useful means of assessing management performance in different areas. Used in combination, they are more tractable and could give a reasonable first approximation of overall performance. However, they all suffer from the general weaknesses associated with financial statements identified in section 3.2.1. In addition, the process of combination and the choice of foci further circumscribe their application to varying circumstances. For example, the use of EVA-based compensation would help align shareholders' and managers' interests, but the process of implementation could mean that managers become more short-termist.[3] Furthermore, accounting ratios are the outcome of management actions rather than the dynamic decisions that precede them. One way to improve their use, and to enhance performance measurement as a whole, is to look also at the 'processes' that generate the accounting numbers. This suggests methods that combine accounting and non-financial information in measuring the performance of managers, and these are dealt with in the next section.

3.3   Economic measures of performance

3.3.1   *Principal measures*

This section is concerned with the fact that a variety of performance indicators can be found in the empirical economics literature and, thus, the

Table 3.2 Examples of MDA results

Author(s)	Dependent variable	Accounting information used	Sample characteristics	Estimation method(s)	Main results
Altman (1968)	Failure prediction	WC/TA; RE/TA; EBIT/TA; MVE/BVTD; sales/TA	Sector: manufacturing for the bankrupt firm, mixed for the survivors; 66 matched firms. Hold-out sample from original data; 1945–1965	MDA	Established cut-off: $Z < 1.88$ failed; $Z > 2.99$ healthy; 95% and 72% correct prediction 1 and 2 years before failure, respectively
Coats and Fant (1993)	Distress likelihood	WC/TA; RE/TA; EBIT/TA; MVE/BVTD; Sales/TA	Sector: mostly manufacturing; 188 viable, all manufacturing; 94 non-viable, 54% manufacturing. Hold-out sample 1970–1989	Cascade correlation – Cascor; neural network; MDA	Cascor outperforms MDA on 'type I hits' and over longer horizons
John (1993)	Corporate liquidity and leverage, proxied by: LA/TA; debt/debt+equity; LTD/TA	*Tobin's q (MV/RCA); R&D/sales; advertising/ sales; cash cycle; sales growth; log sales; standard deviation of change in EBIT/TA; EBIT/sales; EBIT/TA; Inventory + plant and equipment/TA; intangible assets/TA*	Sector: mixed, 223 Fortune 500 firms 1980	Ordinary least squares	Corporate liquidity is increasing in proxies of financial distress costs (first 3 explanatory variables) and decreasing in other sources of liquidity
Henebry (1996)	Failure prediction	Numerous 'regular' accounting ratios; cash flow ratios	Sector: banking. Matched by size and location. Hold-out sample; five-year data	Cox proportional hazard model	Adding cash flow variables increases accuracy of bank failure prediction, especially over longer horizon

Study	Objective	Variables	Sample	Method	Findings
Huffman and Ward (1996)	Default likelihood for high-yield bond issues	MVE; MVA; free cash flow/MVA; LTD/TA; net WC/MVA; *change in NWC/MVA; asset growth; collateral assets; EBIT/sales*; EBIT/TA; sales/TA	Sector: non-finance bond issues; 54 defaulted high-yield bonds; 117 random non-default high-yield bonds. Hold-out random sample of 50 issues; 1977–1991	Logit	Asset growth, change in NWC/MVA, collateral assets and EBIT/sales are the key variables in explaining high-yield bond defaults. Highest correct prediction 80%
Foster and Ward (1997)	Failure prediction	Cash flow based: CFfO; CFfI; CFfF	Sector: mixed; 82 failed firms; 264 matched non-failed firms; 1990–1993	Trend analysis of cash flow data	Cash flow trends are good indicators of subsequent failure, especially in the year before
Cudd and Duggal (2000)	Likelihood of takeover	*ROE*; sales growth; LA/TA; LTD/equity; TA (size); MV/BV	Sector: mining or manufacturing. 443 randomly matched firms. Hold-out sample of 473 firms; five-year data	Logit model	76% prediction accuracy, driven mainly by 'type II hits'

Note: Where applicable, italicized variables are those found to be significant or important in the relevant studies.

choice of any one requires justifying – whether it is the rate of growth in TFP or the MV of the company or some other measure. The following discussion reviews the principal alternatives and the relationships between them, and, in doing so, considers their relative strengths and weaknesses.

The static and comparative static measures of performance include:

(i)   partial and total productivity measures (e.g. the rate of growth in labour and TFP);
(ii) partial and total unit cost measures (e.g. the rate of growth of unit labour and total factor costs).

The discussion reinforces the limitations of individual financial ratios, and indicates that, although useful in certain roles, partial measures can be misleading and, in general, total measures give a clearer picture of performance. By providing an encompassing framework, it is also possible to demonstrate the potential importance of taking quality change into account. In addition, all the static and comparative static performance measures are shown to be linked to the economic profit of the firm, although the relationship is closer for the total than for the partial variants. However, traditional accounting measures of profit are highly imperfect in this role, for at least two reasons:

(i)   they do not correspond closely to the economic concept of profit;
(ii) it is not the level or change in actual profit that is important but the difference between the actual profit and the profit that would have been earned without, for example, the productivity improvement or the factor price decline.

Traditional measures, moreover, including those based on profit, can be shown to be 'static' or, at best, 'comparative static', as they do not account for the (discounted) stream of improvements over time. In this sense, data for a number of years can be used to calculate dynamic improvements retrospectively, but it is much more difficult to assess them prospectively. However, the changing MV of companies is a 'dynamic' measure in this sense, as it is related to the discounted sum of future profits. On the other hand, the source of its strength is also a potential weakness, insofar as it is an 'expectational' measure that, in principle, might be biased because of imperfect information and/or short-termism in the capital market.

3.3.2   *TFP, unit costs and profits*

Productivity and unit costs: partial and total measures[4]
Single input, single output. In a single input, single output world, nominal productivity can be defined as X/Y and nominal unit cost can be defined as $(p_X.X)/Y$, where p_X is the price of the input, X the quantity of the input

used and Y a measure of the quantity of output (discussion of quality is postponed until later in this section). The unit cost is a ratio which shows the cost of producing a single unit of output. Given that p_X varies over time with inflation, in order to generate estimates of real unit costs (RUC) it is necessary to correct these nominal costs for inflation. If the deflator is defined as p, then real unit operating costs are given by $p_X X/pY$.

There are a number of alternative deflators that can be used as a measure of p. One candidate is the price of the output of the firm, industry or sector being investigated (i.e. the price of the output Y, p_Y). Use of this measure means that RUC are measured by $p_X X/p_Y Y$, which is simply the share of costs in total sales or total revenues. This can be rejected primarily because this measure does not capture the essence of the concept of RUC. In order to capture this concept, Stoneman *et al.* (1994, p. 3.1) argue that, when working at the sectoral level, an acceptable deflator would be one that reflects the general rise in the price level, such as the retail price index (RPI). This argument leads to a definition of RUC as:

$$\text{RUC} = \frac{p_X}{\text{RPI}} \frac{X}{Y} \qquad 3.7$$

and thus movements in RUC are made up of two parts: changes in the price of inputs relative to the RPI and changes over time in the ratio of the quantity of inputs to the quantity of outputs (i.e. the inverse of factor productivity).[5] In essence, the lower are both of the ratios in equation 3.7, the better the firm is performing, which suggests that the firm should control input prices and improve physical productivity levels. The same picture emerges when the growth in unit costs is considered. Using ° to indicate a growth rate, the growth of RUC is given by:

$$\overset{\circ}{\text{RUC}} = (\overset{\circ}{p_X} - \overset{\circ}{\text{RPI}}) - (\overset{\circ}{Y} - \overset{\circ}{X}) \qquad 3.8$$

where $\overset{\circ}{p_X} - \overset{\circ}{\text{RPI}}$ is the growth of the input price relative to the RPI and $\overset{\circ}{Y} - \overset{\circ}{X}$ is the rate of growth of productivity.

Multiple input, single output. In a world of multiple inputs, using this framework it is possible to define a number of single input, RUC rates of growth. The rate of growth of real unit labour costs (RULC) is calculated as:

$$\overset{\circ}{\text{RULC}} = (\overset{\circ}{w} - \overset{\circ}{\text{RPI}}) - (\overset{\circ}{Y} - \overset{\circ}{L}) \qquad 3.9$$

where w is the nominal wage rate and L is the labour input. The rate of growth of real unit material costs (RUMC) is written:

$$\overset{\circ}{\text{RUMC}} = (\overset{\circ}{p_M} - \overset{\circ}{\text{RPI}}) - (\overset{\circ}{Y} - \overset{\circ}{M}) \qquad 3.10$$

where p_M denotes the price of material (and fuels and other intermediate inputs) and M is the volume of material input. The rate of growth of real unit capital cost (RUCC) is calculated as:

$$\overset{\circ}{\text{RUCC}} = (\overset{\circ}{p_K} - \overset{\circ}{\text{RPI}}) - (\overset{\circ}{Y} - \overset{\circ}{K}) \qquad\qquad 3.11$$

where p_K denotes capital price and K is the volume of capital input.

It is very important to undertake the calculations for all inputs, because the different measures are not independent of one another. For example, a firm may exhibit extremely rapid growth in labour productivity (or a reduction in RULC), but as a result of a heavy investment programme in plant and machinery. Thus, although labour productivity and RULC are improving, capital productivity may be falling and RUCC rising. The same argument applies to the 'materials' input. Indeed, there is another extremely important implication of this – if only capital and labour measures are constructed, then the measure of output should be value added (i.e. 'materials' should be netted out), but if all three measures are constructed gross output should be used in the calculation.

TFP and real unit total costs. The multiple partial measures produce a considerable amount of information about different aspects of company performance and the relationships between them. However, they do not give an overall measure of performance: this requires the construction of TFP and an overall measure of unit costs. This involves combining the measures described above, with appropriate weights. The discussion therefore proceeds by defining measures of the growth of real unit operating costs (RUOC) and real unit total costs (RUTC), where (following from the previous section) RUOC is the sum of RULC and RUMC. Thus,

$$\text{RUOC} = \frac{wL}{\text{RPI}.Y} + \frac{p_M M}{\text{RPI}.Y} \qquad\qquad 3.12$$

from which it is possible to write that,

$$\overset{\circ}{\text{RUOC}} = s\overset{\circ}{\text{RULC}} + (1-s)\overset{\circ}{\text{RUMC}} \qquad\qquad 3.13$$

where s is the share of wages in total operating costs:

$$s = \frac{wL}{wL + p_M M} \qquad\qquad 3.14$$

RUTC is the sum of RUOC and RUCC (RUTC = RUOC + RUCC) such that,

$$\overset{\circ}{\text{RUTC}} = z\overset{\circ}{\text{RUOC}} + (1-z)\overset{\circ}{\text{RUCC}} \qquad\qquad 3.15$$

where z is the share of operating costs in total costs. That is,

$$z = \frac{wL + p_M M}{wL + p_M M + p_K K} \qquad\qquad 3.16$$

RUTC now represents an overall indicator of firm performance, and its component parts reflect the traditional distinction between the short-run focus on operating costs (where capital is effectively fixed) and the long-run focus on total costs (where both capital and labour can be varied). The potential trade-offs between different inputs in driving overall perform-ance (as discussed above) are now made explicit, as is the firm's need to control various input prices (against the backdrop of sectoral or economy-wide inflation) and factor productivities.

Generalized framework
While the previous section demonstrated the links between productivity and unit costs, the present section extends this by introducing the links to profits and also explicitly considering the role played by quality. It is important to include profits in the equation, as the firm should be viewed as undertaking discretionary investments to increase its future monopoly profits (see section 3.3.4). In addition, it is important to include quality, as changes in quality (driven by the discretionary investments) are seen as being a key strategic tool of rival companies. The linkages between profits, productivity and unit costs can be demonstrated from a general accounting tautology (Bosworth and Gharneh, 1996; Bosworth, 1996),

$$RV = pY = \sum_{i=1}^{n} w_i X_i + \Pi \qquad 3.17$$

where: total revenue, RV, is price, p, times output, Y; total costs, C, are formed by factor prices, w, multiplied by the volume of inputs, X, summed across the n different types of inputs, $i = 1, \ldots n$; finally, Π denotes total profit. This expression is initially explored under conditions of imper-fect competition where the prices paid also reflect the quality, Q, of the product, $p = p(Y,Q)$.[6] To do this, it is assumed that price changes reflect both quality change and inflation. Revenue can now be written as:

$$RV = pY = p(\bar{Q})p(Q)Y \qquad 3.18$$

where: $p(\bar{Q})$ denotes the constant-quality price (i.e. the bar indicates that quality is held constant and any remaining price change is a 'pure' infla-tion component) and $p(Q)$ is the price component that can be traced to the attributes or the technical characteristics of the product (see Chapter 4). Using equation 3.18 in the case of output prices and a similar form for input prices, totally differentiating equation 3.17 yields:

$$\overset{o}{\Pi} = \sum_{i=1}^{n} w_i X_i \{ [p(\overset{o}{Q})(1+\varepsilon_p) - w(\overset{o}{Q})_i] + [p(\overset{o}{Q})(1+\varepsilon_Q) - w(\overset{o}{Q})_i] + [\overset{o}{Y} - \overset{o}{X}_i] \}$$
$$+ \ \Pi \left[p(\overset{o}{Q})(1+\varepsilon_p) + p(\overset{o}{Q})(1+\varepsilon_Q) + \overset{o}{Y} \right] \qquad 3.19$$

where ε_p denotes the own-price elasticity of demand, $-\infty \leq \varepsilon_p \leq 0$, and ε_Q is the elasticity of output with respect to quality, where, in general,

$0 \leqslant \varepsilon_Q \leqslant \infty$. In essence, the equation shows that the rate of change in profits is determined by the rate of increase in:

(i)   product price minus the rate of increase in factor prices (appropriately weighted by relative importance) – shown as the first expression in square brackets on the right-hand side;

(ii)   product quality, as reflected in the price consumers are willing to pay for the bundle of technical characteristics and other attributes, minus the rate of change in factor prices that reflect improvements in the quality of inputs that the firm is willing to pay for (appropriately weighted) – shown as the second expression in square brackets;

(iii) TFP, represented by the rate of increase in physical output minus the rate of change in physical factor input, appropriately weighted by relative importance $(w_i X_i)$ – shown by the third expression in square brackets;

(iv)   prices (both quality- and inflationary-driven) and physical output, weighted by profit – shown by the fourth expression in square brackets;

(v)   note also the role that quality and own-price elasticities of demand play in the equation. The effects of quality improvements and own-price changes can be seen to be independent of the distribution of income between profits and factor inputs, but only if the profit's share is constant.

Writing the expression in the form of equation 3.19 brings home the linkages between profitability, productivity and unit costs. Equation 3.19 embodies not only the traditional physical productivity measure, but also a corresponding quality measure and a unit cost (factor price) measure, as well as the effects of imperfect competition. Most of the existing measures found in the literature can be derived from this framework as special cases. The interpretation of the various parts of the equation is discussed in the following sub-sections.

Quality constant/pure price effects. The first term on the right-hand side of equation 3.19 concerns the purely inflationary effects of input and output prices, having held the quality of inputs and outputs constant. Thus, when the expression

$$\sum [p(\overset{\circ}{Q})(1+\varepsilon_p) - w(\overset{\circ}{Q})_i]$$

is positive, the price of output is rising faster than the weighted sum of input prices and profit will be increasing, other things being equal. Thus, again, the result is a clear indication of the firm's need to control input prices *vis-à-vis* the price of its output. The importance of the unit price measures concerns their ability to highlight the role of factor prices, linked to the purchasing function of the firm. Dolan and Simon (1996, p. 6) note that:

> For many companies, purchasing has become a strategic function. The acrimonious situation starting in the mid-1990s and continuing for years involving General Motors in the United States and Volkswagen in Germany was not about the 'defection' of a great car designer or marketer, but rather about Volkswagen's spiriting away of GM's vice president of worldwide purchasing manager, Ignacio Lopez, and GM's allegation that Lopez took supplier information with him.

Note the role that own-price elasticity plays in this part of the equation as $-\infty \le \varepsilon_p \le 0$. The contribution is positive for inelastic products, but negative for elastic products (see the discussion of monopoly power below).

Treatment of quality. The most a firm would pay for an improvement in the quality of its inputs is determined by both the effect this has on its factor productivity and the change in its product quality that consumers are willing to pay for. Ignoring the problems of measurement of the quality-constant deflator (see Chapter 4 and Berndt, 1991), it can be shown that firms perform better if they are able to raise their product quality more quickly than the quality of their inputs. Equation 3.19 contains a relative product–factor quality term, appropriately weighted:

$$[p(\overset{\circ}{Q})(1 + \varepsilon_Q) - w(\overset{\circ}{Q})_i]$$

This suggests that, other things being equal, firm performance increases when product quality rises more quickly than the quality of factor inputs (as represented by the amount the firm is willing to pay for that quality of the input) and falls when the opposite happens. An alternative way of viewing this relationship is that firms seek to lower the quality of inputs (and, thereby, the amount that they pay for such inputs) over the product life-cycle – sometimes moving production to lower-cost countries in order to do so. Note the role that the elasticity of demand with respect to quality plays in this part of the equation as $0 \le \varepsilon_Q \le \infty$. In essence, the more sensitive the market is to changes in quality, the greater is the effect of quality improvements on profits.

From a practical point of view, the key issue is then the extent to which the available (often official) deflators account for quality change (see Berndt, 1991). It can be seen from equation 3.18 that the failure to construct 'pure' quality-constant price indices will result in the underestimation of the growth of real output when product quality is increasing. Deflation by a 'pure' quality-constant price index gives:

$$\frac{p(\bar{Q})p(Q)Y}{p(\bar{Q})} = p(Q)Y \qquad\qquad 3.20$$

which forces quality change into the measure of output (improvements in quality are improvements in output), while the failure to recognize that price changes reflect quality adjustment gives:

$$\frac{p(\bar{Q})p(Q)Y}{p(\bar{Q})\,p(Q)} = Y \qquad\qquad 3.21$$

a 'pure volume' measure (which underestimates the improvements to consumer welfare when quality is rising, other things being equal). On the other hand, the impact on measures of the rate of change in TFP are indeterminate, unless the precise values of the rates of change of both input and output qualities are known (empirical evidence for Japan is provided by Bosworth *et al.*, 2002, 2005b).

Finally, before leaving the important issue of quality, note that the quality elasticity of demand, ε_Q, appears in two parts of equation 3.19. It can be seen that, given it is expected that $0 \leqslant \varepsilon_Q \leqslant \infty$, this produces a positive effect on profits. However, ε_Q has not been the subject of study in the empirical literature and it is difficult to say much about the likely magnitude of this effect. The managerial economics literature suggests an advertising elasticity of demand $0 \leqslant \varepsilon_A \leqslant 1$, but the 'true quality' and the 'advertising' elasticities might be different.

Physical productivity measures. The role of TFP appears in the third expression in square brackets in equation 3.19. This expression can be written as,

$$\frac{1}{A}\frac{dA}{dt} = \sum_{i=1}^{n}\frac{w_i X_i}{pY}\left(\frac{1}{Y}\frac{dY}{dt} - \frac{1}{X_i}\frac{dX_i}{dt}\right) = \sum_{i=1}^{n}\frac{w_i X_i}{pY}(\overset{\circ}{Y} - \overset{\circ}{X}_i) \qquad 3.22$$

where the right-hand side is the traditional measure of TFP. The equation is written in this notation, using the rate of change in A, in order to emphasize the link with the residual factor from growth accounting. Thus, the rate of increase in the profit of the firm is higher when the rate of growth of physical output exceeds the weighted sum of the growth rates of inputs (i.e. the faster TFP rises), other things being equal. Finally, note that the various partial measures, such as output per unit of input, are lodged in equation 3.22 as $(\overset{\circ}{Y} - \overset{\circ}{X}_i)$, appropriately weighted.

As noted above, partial productivity measures may be of interest in their own right; for example, rates of growth in labour productivity in excess of the corresponding growth in product demand are likely to lead to reduced employment. On the other hand, they are difficult to interpret in the absence of information about what is happening to the productivity of other factors. In the UK, for example, a significant proportion of quite rapid rates of growth in labour productivity has been the result of substitution towards capital and, more particularly, intermediate inputs (for a discussion, see Oulton and O'Mahony, 1994). Under such circumstances, improvements in labour productivity may not be reflected in corresponding increases in TFP. A clearer picture of the implications for costs emerges only if total productivity change is known.

There are a whole range of firm strategies devoted to improving productive efficiency, including the introduction of process innovations. Such innovations do not always involve new technologies. For example, in the early 1960s attempts to increase production efficiency resulted in the introduction of materials requirements planning (MRP) (Plossl, 1994, p. 7). This technique improved the productivity of inputs because the firm planned not only what to buy but also when and how much. The costs of carrying excessive inventories included the money used to fund their purchase, which could be tied up in the inventories for some time before being recouped from product sales, as well as the deterioration or even obsolescence of the stocks. However, like all forward planning exercises, these inventory estimates were often imperfect, although there is empirical evidence of a positive effect on performance (Braglia and Petroni, 1999). Some of the problems were overcome by the use of just in time (JIT) systems. The introduction of JIT was reported to be pioneered by the Toyota Motor Corporation and further developed in 1970s – a period when the prices of energy and raw materials were increasing rapidly.

JIT production refers to the organization of production in order to ensure that the right part is in the right place at the right time. 'Part' refers broadly to any item used in the production process, including raw materials, components and work in progress (WIP). In this way, JIT uses capacity as a buffer to variations in throughput rather than inventories and, thus, it minimizes the inventories of the firm in an efficient and cost-effective manner, and contributes to 'lean production'. It is a process by which parts are 'pulled' through the system at a rate to satisfy the operations nearer to completion of the final product (rather than 'pushed' from the previous workstation to the next). Of course, insofar as the use of the capacity buffer is not cost free, there is a trade-off between inventory savings (and the other benefits of JIT) and the costs of the production buffer. Clearly, the introduction of a successful JIT system has implications for the productivity of the raw materials and inputs of intermediate goods to the firm, as well as for capital productivity (and also insofar as firms include WIP as part of their capital assets). However, it will also affect capital productivity (and potentially labour productivity) insofar as JIT reduces underutilized capacity (e.g. by using machines for longer periods). In addition, its use often involves other innovations by the firm, such as the introduction of a Kanban production control system.

JIT is normally taken to apply primarily to repetitive manufacturing processes (i.e. ones where components and end products are produced time and again) and, thus, largely lies outside the area of interest of the present book (the interested reader can find further information in, for example, Agrawal *et al.*, 1996; Anwar and Nagi, 1998). However, it does have implications for the efficient organization of the firm and efficient flows of information within the firm, which are discussed in Chapter 11. It also has important implications for supplier companies and their own organization (it is sometimes reported that JIT for one firm can imply 'just in case' for their suppliers).

Monopoly power. The accounting tautology is perhaps not the best framework for the study of the role of monopoly, at least in a dynamic sense. Nevertheless, the generalized framework set out in equation 3.19 has an implicit role for monopoly through the own-price elasticity of demand, ε_p, which appears in two parts of the equation. Given that $-\infty \leq \varepsilon_p \leq 0$, the equation suggests that a higher absolute value of the elasticity is less beneficial to the growth of profits. As is expected, this effect is infinite for a perfectly elastic demand curve and profits rise proportionately to own prices in the case of a perfectly inelastic demand curve. Note that, while increases in own prices raise profits where demand is inelastic ($-1 \leq \varepsilon_p \leq 0$), they lower profits where own price is elastic ($-\infty \leq \varepsilon_p \leq -1$). Below, however, it is shown that this static view is not very helpful for understanding the dynamic aspects of the creation of future monopoly power (and its destruction by competitors), which operate through, for example, improvements in product quality. As this forms a major theme of the remainder of the book, the present discussion is terminated at this point.

3.3.3 *Profits and MV*

Origins of Tobin q approach
The origins of the MV approach can be traced to Tobin's (1969) original work – the so-called 'Tobin's q', which was defined as the ratio of the market to the replacement book value of a firm's capital assets (Berndt, 1991, p. 258). This is also often referred to as the valuation ratio (Sawyer, 1981, p. 157). Tobin argues that, for any investment project, the following apply:

(i)   there is a demand price for the (marginal) asset – the demand price for an entire firm is the MV of its shares and debt;
(ii) there is a supply price for the (marginal) asset – the cost of producing all new capital goods, and usually measured by the replacement cost of a firm's assets;
(iii) in equilibrium, the demand and supply prices are equal.

Hence, the marginal value of q yields an investment rule:

(i)   when the marginal value of q exceeds unity, the firm should under-take investment;
(ii) when the marginal value of q is less than unity, the firm should dis-invest.

Hence, the long-run equilibrium value of q should be unity, equating supply and demand for investment at the margin. Berndt (1991, p. 257) provides a practical example:

> Suppose, however, that a firm was operating in a relatively profitable environ-ment and that if it added $1 to its capital stock of plant and equipment, its expected profitability would increase sufficiently that its market value would increase by more than $1. In this case the value of the marginal q ratio would be greater than unity, and the firm should invest in the plant and equipment in order to maximize the return to its shareholders.

If the value of the marginal q ratio is less than unity, then the firm should not invest in the plant and equipment – its shareholders could earn a higher return elsewhere. Indeed, the firm might work to improve the posi-tion of its shareholders by selling off some part of its capital stock.

Underpinnings of the MV measure
The MV is a particularly interesting measure of performance, as it is forward looking and reflects the stream of future dividends and profits. By implication, it is not as sensitive to short-term random factors as measures of current profitability (although it is potentially sensitive to the efficiency of stock markets). MV is a natural choice of performance for economies with an efficient stock market because it has both positive and norma-tive connotations. Horne *et al.* (1990, p. 14) note that 'the principle of maximisation of shareholder wealth provides a rational guide for running a business and for the efficient allocation of resources in society'. The value of a firm on the stock market depends directly on the discounted sum of future dividends (Sawyer, 1981, p. 157):

$$\mathrm{MV}_0 = \sum_{t=0}^{\infty} \frac{(1-\eta_t)\,\pi_t^a}{(1+i_t)^t} \qquad\qquad 3.23$$

where: η = profit retention ratio (i.e. $[1-\eta]$ is the proportion of profit paid in dividends); π_t^a is expected accounting profit; and i is the discount rate. Sawyer (1981) shows that, under constant retention ratio and interest rate, as well as steady growth of capital, K, and profits at rate g:

(i)   the rate of profit is constant at ρ, $\pi_t^a = \rho K_t$;
(ii) profits grow according to $\pi_t^a = \pi_0(1+g)^t$;

(iii)   growth is funded from retained profit, $\eta\pi_t^a = gK_t$;
(iv)   hence, $\eta\rho = g$.

Sawyer goes on to show that, under these assumptions,

$$MV_0 = \frac{(\rho - g)(1 + i)K_0}{(i - g)}$$ 3.24

Clearly, the valuation ratio ($v = MV_0/K_0$) follows directly.

Figure 3.1 demonstrates that the variables in the MV equation are not independent of one another. It can be seen that, after a point, increases in the rate of growth increase costs disproportionately and reduce profit rate. In addition, declining profit rates eventually offset the investors' perceived benefits of higher growth, leading to a fall in the valuation ratio. Marris' (1964) managerial theory of the firm was based on these relationships.

Efficiency of the stock market in valuing companies
The use of MV as a measure of performance assumes that the market is the best arbiter of value. If the market is perfectly informed and operates efficiently, then the MV of a company will reflect the discounted sum of its future dividends.[7] Thus, a key issue in the use of this measure concerns whether capital markets operate efficiently – in the case of the UK, for example, it has often been argued that the market is short-termist. This implies a bias against profits further into the future and, by implication, a higher discount rate, i, than would be observed in capital markets that are not short-termist. There is a substantial and largely unresolved literature on short-termism (e.g. Miles, 1993, 1995; Satchell and Damant, 1995; Timmerman, 1994).

While there is a widely held view that stock markets, at least in advanced industrialized countries, are among the more efficient of markets, it should be borne in mind (as shown above) that MV is based on perceptions of the future under limited information. Potential investors may approximate the MV based upon the information to hand and some learning process, although, as Timmerman (1994) points out, the emergence of some rational expectations equilibrium (REE) is far from certain without imposing fairly strict assumptions. Timmerman (1994, p. 779) notes that:

> convergence of learning crucially depends on the prior information agents impose on the learning process. If agents attempt to learn the long-run dynamics of the model without imposing strong prior information, their learning cannot converge to a REE. If, on the other hand, agents have strong priors and impose a unit root on their model, thus confining their learning to the short run dynamics of the model, then their recursive learning may converge to a REE.

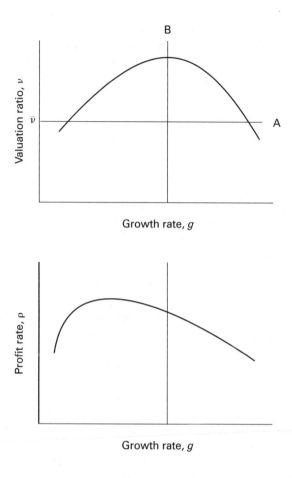

Figure 3.1 Valuation ratio, profitability and growth. Source: Sawyer (1981, p. 158).

However, while potential investors will have at least the minimum information that is available to economists who use MV as a measure of performance in econometric models of MV, they may often have more. Other results suggest agents compile sufficient information for them not to be short-termist (Satchell and Damant, 1995).

There are several related caveats to be made about the use of MVs. First, they are not generally available for companies that are not quoted on the stock market. However, there have been one or two experiments that tend to demonstrate that other measures of firm performance, such as profits, give similar results (Murray, 1996). Second, capital markets are likely to be more imperfect and inefficient in a number of the transitional economies, or the recently established Chinese stock markets. Under such circumstances, the MV either may not be a valid measure or the market may estimate the value of the companies with significant error. Third, the efficiency of valuation may be even more problematic when considering the market's valuation of intangible assets.

3.3.4 *Profits and discretionary investments*

While now quite dated, there are two early studies that form an important foundation on which the present work is based. The first, by Mueller (1967), was far ahead of its time in terms of the way in which the literature subsequently evolved (Bosworth, 1983). Mueller recognized that discretionary investments, particularly the more risky ones such as R&D, were funded largely from profit. Even if additional funds were raised, the extent of the external funding was still strongly influenced by the profitability of the company. Thus, in Mueller's empirical model, all the discretionary investments competed to be funded from the profits of the firm. The result was a recursive set of equations, one for each dimension of discretionary activity, where profit is a right-hand-side variable in each. The system is not closed because, as specified, current profit is not dependent on the past values of discretionary investments. Mueller did not investigate this more dynamic problem, which is an important focus of the present book.

The second contribution, by Grabowski and Mueller (1978), made the crucial distinction between 'economic' and 'accounting' profit. Economic (as opposed to accounting) profit is a measure of the total 'surplus' generated by firms. Economic profit (π^e) is equal to accounting profit (π^a), plus the discretionary expenditures on R&D (R), advertising (A) and training (T) that are expensed in the firm's accounts, but which form investments that yield returns in subsequent periods. Later chapters deal with the question of whether all of the expenditures should be treated as investments or whether some proportion (particularly in the case of advertising) should be expensed. Thus, following the general idea put forward in Mueller (1967) and Grabowski and Mueller (1978), economic profit is defined as:

$$\pi^e = \pi^a + R + A + T = I + D + Tx + R + A + T \qquad\qquad 3.25$$

where, in addition, I, D and Tx represent retained profit for investment in physical assets, for dividend payments and for profits tax, respectively. All of the variables – with perhaps the exception of Tx, can be thought of as investments in future monopoly power, and drive future economic profit (Cowling and Mueller, 1978). The success of these investments should, in principle, be seen against what would have happened to the firm if it had not made them – the counterfactual. In a traditional DCF setting, the optimal level of each investment is where the contribution of the last, say, $1 spent is equal to an addition of $1 to the discounted sum of future net revenues (i.e. revenues minus production costs), thereby increasing future profits. It should be borne in mind, however, that these investments carry some degree of risk, which can affect both the investment decision and the distribution of returns to such activities across companies (see Chapters 8 and 13).

3.3.5 *Links between production function and measures of MV*

The present section further develops the hypothesis that abnormal profits of the firm are the result of past investments in monopoly power and, in addition, provides a link between MV and the production function approaches. Indeed, it is possible to demonstrate that, under fairly heroic assumptions, the production function and MV function give identical results (Bosworth and Gharneh, 1996). The present section simply illustrates the idea, using a Cobb–Douglas production function:

$$Y_t = A K_t^\alpha E_t^\beta RS_t^\gamma \qquad 3.26$$

where Y, K and E are output, capital and employment, while RS is the R&D stock at time t (for further discussion, see Chapter 8). This function has been written in physical terms, but it is easy to see how this can be extended to included product and input qualities – for example, output allowing for quality would be written, $p(Q)Y$. Note also that, while R&D has been used as the driver in this equation, a similar function might be used in which advertising, training and/or any of the other discretionary investments appear on the right-hand side.

   The function can be interpreted as saying that TFP, $Y_t / K_t^\alpha E_t^\beta$, is driven by the R&D stock, RS_t. Section 3.3.2 has already demonstrated that the profits of the firm and, hence, dividends, are linked to TFP – a link which is even closer when the qualities of products and inputs are allowed for (see equation 3.19). Bosworth and Gharneh (1996) show the conditions under which the production function and MV function provide consistent results. It is clear that, in both cases, this is determined by the discretionary investments in R&D, which then determine what happens to the R&D stock, RS, over time. Future TFP (and, hence, future profits and MV) is driven by:

(i) the existing stock of R&D (i.e. by past R&D expenditures appropriately amortized), other things being equal;
(ii) future R&D expenditures that help to maintain or increase the R&D stock (Bosworth and Gharneh, 1996).

3.4   Balanced scorecards[8]

The challenge posed by performance measurement is to identify measures that help managers to understand 'value drivers' and to determine the linkage between strategies and performance targets that are in line with managers' business responsibilities (Capps and Hattery, 2000). While accounting-based measures have a role to play, 'they should be accompanied by a balanced assortment of measures that encompass all the performance attributes critical to long-term success' (Brewer *et al.*, 1999, p. 7).

The 'balanced scorecard' can be viewed as an attempt to provide a unifying framework of the critical performance attributes of a company (Sharif, 2002, p. 63). However, it is more than just a framework for measuring company performance – it can be viewed as:

(i)   an operational control tool (e.g. to highlight areas of underperformance);

(ii)   a strategic planning tool (e.g. to monitor strategic intent at all levels in the firm);

(iii)   a management reporting/MIS tool (e.g. to provide information about all aspects of the organization's activities) (Sharif, 2002, p. 63).

Kaplan and Norton (1992) identify four key performance perspectives in their balanced scorecard:

(i)   customers;
(ii)   internal business processes;
(iii)   innovation and learning;
(iv)   financial.

Similarly, Capps and Hattery (2000) recommend that the process should start with the establishment of the external business value measures that will lead to maximum shareholder value. Thereafter, an internal framework of objectives, strategies and performance measures should be designed. The common performance measurement dimensions they recommend include financial effect, customer activity, process/operational and business activity.

Brewer *et al.* (1999) provide a summary of the steps involved in developing a balanced scorecard of the Kaplan/Norton type:

(i)   *Establish the firm's strategic goals.* The strategic objectives determine the specific measures to be included in the scorecard (e.g. is the firm creating its competitive advantage from cost leadership, product differentiation or a combination of both?).

(ii)   *Select the appropriate measures for each of the four perspectives.*

    (a) One might start from the customer's perspective by identifying measures that define success in the customer's opinion (e.g. customer retention rates, the percentage of on-time delivery or customer satisfaction surveys).

    (b) The internal business process perspective identifies the non-financial measures that indicate of how well the firm is translating inputs into outputs (e.g. cycle time, yield percentage and quality defect rate could be useful here).

(c) The innovation and learning perspective is 'global' in outlook, identifying leading indicators about the firm's competitiveness in the long run (e.g. R&D intensity, NPD over a chosen time scale, the lead time for NPL and the number of new process technology patents – see Chapter 4).

(d) The financial perspective should act as a check, with the financial measures chosen from the range of accounting ratios, indices and EVA methods discussed earlier.

(iii) *Check on the expected financial performance*. Ascertain whether the improvements in operational performance are translated into better financial performance.

(iv) *Back to the drawing board*. If the financial measures indicate otherwise, then the executives should go 'back to their drawing boards to rethink the company's strategy' (Kaplan and Norton, 1992).

With three or four measures representing each perspective, the approach would offer a reasonably complete representation of a management performance that ensures a balance between processes and results and also balances the short and long term.

In support of the use of balanced scorecards, it is useful to highlight the findings of a survey conducted by Ernst and Young's Center for Business Innovation, as reported by Light (1998). The survey sought information on the determinants of investors' buy or sell decisions. From the responses received from 300 brokerage firms and 275 portfolio managers, the report concluded that an average of one-third of the decisions to invest in or sell stock in a company were based on non-financial attributes, such as the quality and execution of corporate strategy, management credibility and innovativeness. These findings lend weight to the need to develop performance measures that reflect a balanced and forward-looking view of the performance of managers.

Sharif (2002, pp. 64–65) sees the balanced scorecard as part of a broader set of performance management approaches. The implementation of such approaches requires considerable architectural and management support (see Part V):

(i) *Development of an information architecture*: data, information, tools, processes, sources, stakeholders, accessibility, security, relevance, timeliness.

(ii) *Design of a technical solution to support the systems architecture*: executive information systems, EIS, management information systems, MIS, decision support systems, DSS, intranet, extranet, knowledge management (KM) system, balanced scorecard, performance management, business intelligence systems, enterprise resource planning (ERP), internet technologies, component based development (CBD) technologies.

(iii) *Alignment of incentives/goals which feed the technical solution*: realising
importance and impact of the architecture and the solution in an operational sense, driven by senior management and the CEO.
(iv) *Application of external resources to develop the tool*: industry standards,
benchmarking (attaining best of breed solutions from different industry
sectors and implementing/adopting them as your own), regulatory pressures (e.g. Securities and Exchange Commission, SEC, Financial Services
Authority, FSA, generally accepted accounting principles, GAAP, tax and
localisation issues), professional services advice.
(v) *Design of a process to control the performance management system*: fluid,
dynamic management and process structure in order to provide visi-
bility, accountability and control of a performance management system.
(Sharif, 2002, pp. 64–65)

Many of these issues are discussed later in the present book. Despite the
potential benefits of such a system, it has to be delivering the correct information and stimuli. Sharif (2002, p. 82) argues that, 'In order to minimize
the risk and maximize the benefit of performance information, there needs
to be an identification of fit with related organizational processes, strategy
and general company-wide initiatives'.

3.5   Conclusions

A wide range of variables used in the empirical literature as measures of
enterprise performance have been identified. The discussion has also outlined how these measures are related to one another. It is fair to say that
the bulk of the measures adopted look at some aspect of profitability – in
line with the view that shareholders are the owners of the enterprise and
performance should be judged by the extent to which the enterprise has
delivered profits or dividends. While it is possible to find other measures
of performance used in the literature, such as the rate of growth of sales,
which are more in line with some of the managerial theories, these form
a small minority of the total. A second feature of taking an overview of
the literature in this area is that partial measures (e.g. a single financial
ratio or, say, labour productivity) may have important applications for
particular managers or parts of the enterprise but, if used individually to
guide enterprise-wide strategy, they can be extremely misleading. Even
TFP measures and, to a lesser extent, RUTC measures are in some sense
partial. The generalized accounting framework demonstrates how all of
the existing economic measures are, in essence, special cases.

The results suggest that profit is perhaps the overarching measure
of the static performance of private sector enterprises and, with some
reservations, MV is the corresponding 'dynamic' measure. However, the
discussion has highlighted the generally different views of profits adopted
by accountants and economists. While it is true that many economists

still use accounting measures of profit, such as earnings before interest and tax (EBIT), for a variety of empirical purposes relating to the evaluation of enterprise performance, the literature on dynamic performance has often worked with a distinct measure of profit that adds in all of the so-called discretionary investments of the enterprise (i.e. those where the returns on expenditures take place in subsequent periods). This is because general accounting practice 'expenses' all discretionary investments at the time they are made, when, often, they should expense only a part of the total. The reason is that accountants view the future streams of income as being inherently risky and, hence, prefer to write investments off against profits or reserves in the same year that they are made. These discretionary investments include R&D, advertising and market promotion and training. Economists, on the other hand, are interested in the total 'surplus' the firm has made, which can be retained for various forms of investment (including those listed above, as well as retained profits for investment in physical capital) or distributed to shareholders. Economists see these expenditures as investments in future monopoly power, which will result in higher *future* economic profit than would otherwise have occurred.

Notes

1 Sections 3.2 and 3.4 are largely based upon material written by Greg Jobome as part of Bosworth and Jobome (2001). My thanks to Greg for letting me use this material here.
2 R&D is generally 'expensed' in firms' accounts. In other words, it is written off as a cost within the period in which it occurs rather than being treated as an investment, which is written off over a number of years.
3 Brewer *et al.* (1999) point out that EVA tends to overemphasize the need to generate immediate results, thus encouraging a short-term orientation. As outlays on innovation tend to be recognized up front, the associated revenue stream can take some years to materialize – this creates a disincentive for managers to invest in innovative products or processes (Brewer *et al.*, 1999, p. 6).
4 This section is based upon Bosworth and Stoneman (1994, ch. 3).
5 As Bosworth and Stoneman (1994) work using sector-wide data, they focus on the overall RPI as the deflator. However, if the unit cost is constructed for an individual firm, *i*, belonging to the jth sector, then RUC can be written as:

$$\mathrm{RUC}_{ij} = \frac{p_{X_{ij}}}{\mathrm{RPI}_j} \frac{X_{ij}}{Y_{ij}}$$

where an estimate of sectoral output prices such as RPI_j is used. The interpretation is broadly the same as before, however, as $[X_{ij}/Y_{ij}]$ is the inverse of the *i*th firm's factor productivity and $[p_{X_{ij}}/\mathrm{RPI}_j]$ is the ratio of input price for the *i*th firm to the output price for that sector.
6 The methods of deriving measures of quality, *Q*, are outlined in Chapter 4, in particular section 4.4.5.

7 It is sometimes argued that capital appreciation is important, but this is itself dependent on the expected stream of future dividends at the time the capital is valued.

8 Thanks again to Greg Jobome for the material that forms section 3.4.

Chapter 4

Measuring and monitoring of key strategic activities

4.1 Introduction

Dynamic and high-performing firms tend to be 'information rich', in that they often access and use a much broader range of information than is strictly necessary for the production of their product or service at a given point in time. A 'fully informed' company would want information at all levels of aggregation (i.e. economy-wide, sector-wide and technology area), in terms of its likely future markets, technologies and possible competitors, takeover targets or collaborators. Thus, the monitoring of information forms a key strategic activity, particularly among knowledge-based and high-technology firms. According to Rappa *et al.* (1992), 'the ability of managers and policy makers to comprehend the pace and direction of technological advancement will largely determine their firm's or nation's competitive performance in world markets'.

The focus of the present chapter is on a range of key indicators available to aid strategic decision making by firms. These measures are distinct from those relating to the overall performance of the firm or its competitors (i.e. productivity, unit costs, profitability, market value, etc. – see Chapter 3). The type of information outlined here relates more to the market and technological environments within which the company operates. Of course, in the real world, companies always operate with incomplete and sometimes inaccurate information, and act with bounded rationality. In addition, the potential volume of such information demands the use of systems to manage its collection, collation, manipulation and interpretation (see Chapter 11).

Table 4.1 gives an overview of the types of indicators currently under consideration by the European Union (EU) in benchmarking research and technology development (RTD) policies (Debackere *et al.*, 2002, p. 228). Such data, when harmonized across countries, reveal whether the rate of technological change is speeding up or slowing down and whether it differs between companies, sectors and countries. Likewise, it can indicate whether the technological focus is shifting, as companies move into new areas of technology and abandon others. Economists have been interested in such measures for many years (see Freeman, 1969; Griliches, 1990; Schmookler, 1966) and viewed such information as essential in informing company strategy and performance (Rosenberg, 1991). The

Table 4.1 Indicators identified in EU RTD benchmarking

Human resources in RTD

Number of researchers in relation to the total workforce

Number of new science and technology PhDs/population in corresponding age group

Public and private investment in RTD

Total R&D expenditures in relation to gross domestic product and breakdown by source of funding

R&D financed by industry in relation to industrial output

Share of the annual government budget allocated to research

Share of small and medium-sized enterprises in publicly funded R&D executed by the business sector

Volume of venture capital investment in early stages in relation to gross domestic product

Scientific and technological productivity

Number of patents at the European Patent Office and United States Patent and Trademark Office per capita

Number of scientific publications and most cited publications per capita

Percentage of innovative firms cooperating with firms/universities/public research institutes

Number of spin-offs generated by universities and research centres

Rate of usage of broadband electronic networks for research by R&D laboratories

Impact of RTD on economic competitiveness and employment

Growth rate of labour productivity

Share of high-technology and medium–high-technology industries in total employment and output

Share of knowledge-intensive services in total employment and output

Technology balance of payments receipts as a proportion of gross domestic product

Growth in a country's world market share of exports of high-technology products

---

Source: Debackere *et al.* (2002).
Note: See also Patel (2000, pp. 132–133), which attempts to identify the level of country, industry, technological field and firm at which a number of these indicators are available.

Table 4.2 Examples of measures of strategic information

Type of activity	Type of data	Source of data	Detailed description
Knowledge gathering		Surveys of information sources	UK Community Innovation Survey and similar surveys for other countries
		Market research surveys	Consumer surveys, purchase diaries, electronic point-of-sales systems, etc.
		Science and technology developments	Scientific papers, conferences, trade journals and trade fairs, etc.
Invention	Input	R&D employment	First destination of university graduates
			Functional activities of employees
		R&D expenditure	Capital, labour, raw materials
			Intramural and extramural
	Output	Scientific output	Numbers of scientific publications
			Peer review
			Extent of citations
		Patent counts	Numbers of patents
			Quality of patents (e.g. renewal data; country coverage; citations)
Innovation	Input	Innovation expenditures	Resources devoted to innovation
			Expenditure on new equipment/capital
	Output	Innovation counts	Numbers of major innovations
			New product counts
		'Hart indices'	Measures of technological performance – speed, luminosity, etc.
		Special large-scale innovation surveys	For example the Community Innovation Survey, based upon the 'Oslo Manual'
		Other intellectual property data	Designs, copyright, etc. – as for patents
		Hedonic indices	Consumer valuation of product characteristics
		Best practice production functions	Productivity growth; changes in unit costs
		Valuation of company's intangible assets	Including intellectual property
Diffusion/ imitation	Input	Expenditure	Resources devoted to technology transfer
	Output		Percentage of firms (or enterprises) adopting the new technology
			Percentage of output produced using the new technology
			Movement towards best practice

Source: Adapted from Bosworth (1986).

present chapter extends the discussion away from the narrow focus of scientific and technological change to broader measures of the evolution of the knowledge base and the growth of intangible assets. This broader view overcomes some of the 'manufacturing' bias of the pure technology indicators (for further discussion, see Bosworth *et al.*, 2003, 2005a).

In providing an overview of the types of measures discussed in the present chapter, for expositional purposes, Table 4.2 adopts a largely 'linear model' view of the technological change process. It begins with 'knowledge gathering' and moves on through the invention (creation), innovation and diffusion processes. The technology indicators are often classified according to whether they focus on 'inputs' (e.g. R&D expenditure) or 'outputs' (e.g. patents granted or NPLs). However, the outputs of one part of the process often form the inputs to other parts (e.g. information disclosed in patent specifications form inputs to R&D). As a consequence, many authors use more than one measure in their studies, and firms track a range of measures to aid their strategic decision making.

Section 4.2 continues with a brief discussion of the survey evidence relating to the main sources of information used by companies. Section 4.3 discusses the important role of market research. While there is not space to consider the types of surveys and survey technologies that companies use to elicit information about consumer preferences and the likely market (i.e. postal surveys, computer-aided telephone interviews, etc.), extensive discussions are available elsewhere (Malhotra, 1999; McMeekin *et al.*, 2003). However, section 4.3 does explore methods of obtaining information about the effects of price and quality on product demand, including conjoint analysis. There are two main reasons for its inclusion: it is an experimental technique used in marketing, which corresponds closely to the hedonic method used by economists; and it is an *ex ante* technique, which can help in research and product design and, therefore, fits well with the discussion in later chapters. Section 4.4 examines some of the science and technology indicators now available to companies. The significant advances in this area are largely the result of the increased availability of electronic databases and computer search techniques. Section 4.5 draws the main conclusions and outlines a number of strategic uses for these types of measure – and suggests that companies can build up a picture not only of competitors, but also of potential collaborators, merger and takeover targets, and so on.

4.2   Sources of information used by companies

While firms do not necessarily use the surveys that are discussed in the present section (although the information is of potential interest), the information gleaned from these surveys point to the ways in which companies garner information and access new technologies, and throws light

Table 4.3 Sources of learning about competitors' product innovations

	Number of industries giving high scores	
	5 or more	6 or more
Licensing	17	4
Patent disclosures	24	5
Publications or open technical meetings	20	8
Consultations with employees of the innovating firm	21	8
Hiring employees from the innovating firm	33	8
Reverse engineering	65	22
Independent R&D	84	19

Source: Nelson (1990), reported in Patel and Pavitt (1995).

on issues of information deficiencies. The results in this section are taken from the first Community Innovation Survey (CIS) in 1994 (European Commission, 1994), although subsequent CISs are now available, as well as parallel surveys for a number of other countries, including the USA and Australia (e.g. Bryant *et al.*, 1996). In an early survey, for example, more than 600 US industrial R&D directors were asked to rank on a scale from 1 (no importance) to 7 (most important) the different means of learning about competitors' product innovations, in 130 lines of business (Nelson, 1990). The results, presented in Table 4.3, are interesting – they show the importance of in-house R&D, reverse engineering and the hiring of staff from other innovating firms.[1]

The 1994 CIS was undertaken across EU member states, although there were some inconsistencies in the questionnaires, and differences in sample sizes and response rates. The unit of observation was the establishment and the questions often used a Likert scale (1 = insignificant to 5 = crucial). Figure 4.1, based on enterprises in all member states, shows a common result – that 'more active' enterprises tend to have greater 'problems'. In this case, innovators report more significant problems than non-innovators, and there is little or no distinction between product and process innovators. Figure 4.2 breaks this down by two areas of information deficiency (market and technology) and by size. Smaller enterprises tend to report less problems than larger ones, and problems of information deficiency are greater with respect to market information than technology information (see also section 4.3).

Figure 4.3 indicates that, consistent with the US survey reported above, internal sources of information ('within the enterprise') are the most important. Note how parts of the buyer–supplier chain are important sources of information – these sources tend to have close links in terms of the technology or market of the enterprise. Further evidence

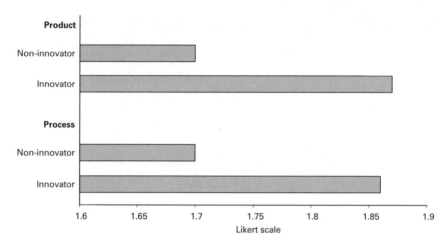

Figure 4.1 Lack of information about technologies: all EU. Ratings on a Likert scale from 1 = insignificant to 5 = crucial problems with lack of information, in the 1994 CIS, for innovator enterprises and non-innovator enterprises, with respect to both process and product innovation. Source: Bosworth *et al.* (1996b).

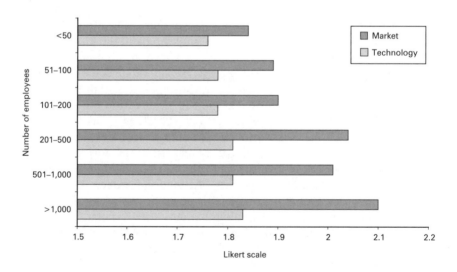

Figure 4.2 Lack of information about technologies and markets: all EU. Ratings on a Likert scale from 1 = insignificant to 5 = crucial problems with lack of information, in the 1994 CIS, by enterprise size (number of employees) and with respect to both market and technology information. Source: Bosworth *et al.* (1996b).

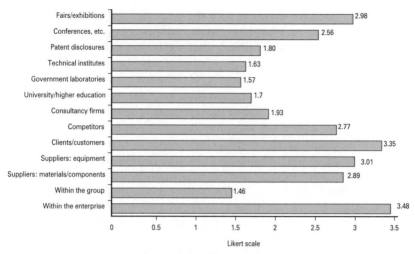

Figure 4.3 Sources of information: all EU. Ratings on a Likert scale from 1 = insignificant to 5 = crucial source of information, in the 1994 CIS. Source: Bosworth *et al.* (1996b).

from the CIS demonstrates that larger enterprises give more weight to all sources of information than smaller ones (consistent with Figure 4.2) and they use a greater range of information sources. Larger enterprises also place somewhat more weight on external than internal sources. The CIS also suggests that, while some sources of information, such as patents, are not very important across the totality of enterprises, they are much more important for certain sectors, and larger enterprises tend to place more weight on patent disclosure than smaller ones (which parallels the extent of use of patent protection). Finally, usage differs across countries, reflecting economic development and industry mix (e.g. Germany makes greater use of patent disclosure than Portugal).

4.3   Market research

4.3.1   *Customer focus*

The literature is unanimous regarding the need for companies to be 'customer focused' – customer retention is essential to business survival, because attracting a new customer is generally much more expensive than retaining an existing one. A starting point for this is to have a system for complaints embedded in the enterprise. As a minimum, this system collects complaints data and provides efficient mechanisms for complaint resolution to feed back to product design or other aspects of supply, in order to ensure such complaints do not arise again. Even this appears to be only a part of a broader picture. For example, while the 1994 version of ISO 9001/2 suggested the need for dialogue with the customer following a complaint (which did not allow auditors to estimate the true customer opinion about the performance of the enterprise), ISO 9001:2000 indicates the need to solicit the opinion of the firm's customer base and react to that opinion via the company's quality management (QM) systems to improve its competitive advantage. Both the reactive and proactive systems have implications for the organizational structure of the company (e.g. the adoption of complaints handling, evaluation and planning procedures, information flows and lines of responsibility), as well as for company practices (e.g. the selection and training of staff, and the provision of technical support).

Given the crucial role of market information, discussion of the key factors that firms measure begins with a brief discussion of market research. The idea of the firm as a technocracy that imposes its new designs and products on the market, levering demand by advertising and market promotion (Galbraith, 1967), is an interesting warning to society, but appears to be far from the real situation.[2] In practice, the evidence overwhelmingly suggests that, to be successful, companies must be consumer oriented and customer aware. Market research lies at the heart of a firm's 'consumer awareness', as it is concerned with the 'collection and analysis of data about consumers and markets' – what is produced is 'information, intelligence and advice' (McMeekin *et al.*, 2003, p. 1). Two key elements stand out – an understanding of the strategic roles of product (and service) price and quality.

4.3.2 *Marketing issues and information*

Figure 4.4 illustrates the relative importance of various marketing issues, based on the responses of 57 US and 129 European (i.e. a total of 186) managers, across a broad range of sectors. It can be seen that pricing issues top the rankings, closely followed by concerns about product differentiation and NPLs.

More generally, the evidence suggests that firms face serious data deficiencies with respect to various aspects of the market. Clancey and Shulman's (1994) survey indicated that only about 12 per cent of US firms carry out what might be regarded as serious marketing research. Similarly, Dolan and Simon (1996, p. 4) argue that the majority of firms abrogate their responsibility for rigorous pricing research on one or more of the following grounds:

(i)   the market sets the price;
(ii)   the firm has to match the price set by competitors;
(iii) the firm uses a standard rule-of-thumb mark-up over cost.

Figure 4.5 indicates the extent to which managers feel well informed about various price-relevant factors. It suggests an important distinction between

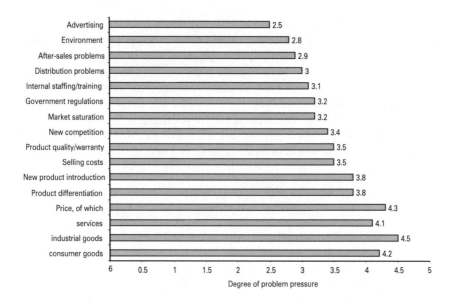

Figure 4.4 Rating of marketing issues by managers (5 = high problem pressure; 1 = low problem pressure). Note that price pressures are also disaggregated by services, industrial and consumer goods. Source: Dolan and Simon (1996, p. 5).

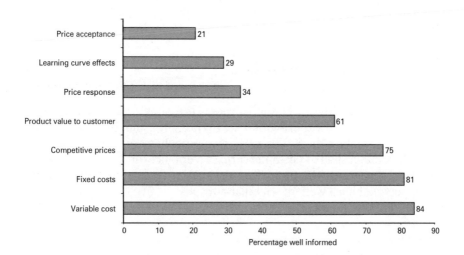

Figure 4.5 Extent to which managers are well informed about price-relevant factors (percentage of managers reporting that they are well informed on each factor). Source: Dolan and Simon (1996, p. 47).

managers' knowledge about price and cost levels (the highest three percentages) and factors such as the value of the product to consumers and the responsiveness of demand to price changes (i.e. price elasticities).

The degree of poverty of information differs between sectors. Mohan and Holstein (1994) argue that, 'Unlike consumer-product firms, industrial-product companies are typically … marketing-data-poor' (consistent with Figure 4.4). Dolan and Simon (1996, p. 8) argue that the relatively small proportion of companies that are most able to price strategically and appropriately (their so-called 'power pricers') are data rich and market knowledgeable:

> A 'power pricer' has data that are more accurate, timely, relevant, and disaggregated than everyday pricers … understands what is happening now – not just what happened two months ago; … knows a product's value to the customer – not just its cost, and … understands what's happening at the individual account or key market segment level.

Thus, the lack of information or its poor interpretation can have severe consequences for a company's performance (e.g. the underpricing of the Mercedes Benz SLC Roadster, which led to a long waiting list and resulted in many customers who received cars selling them on at higher prices).

4.3.3 *Price and attribute data*

From a competitive perspective, the main rivalry appears to take place via price and quality (represented by product or service attributes). Focusing for a moment on prices, Dolan and Simon (1996, pp. 51–77) set out several approaches to the gathering of information, including:

(i) customer surveys;
(ii) planned price experiments;
(iii) unplanned price experiments – analysis of historical market data.

While the discussion covers all of these, it mainly focuses on 'conjoint analysis' (a form of experimental survey), for reasons that will become apparent in section 4.4.5. The various approaches are intended to tease out phenomena such as customer 'price acceptance' and 'demand responsiveness' – some of the areas that the earlier discussion indicated that managers feel least well informed about.

Customer surveys
One approach to customer surveys is simply to ask a series of questions relating to the prices and conditions under which a group of potential customers would purchase the product.[3] Figure 4.6 illustrates the way in which a firm can build up a picture. It shows the responses of potential customers to the question 'What is the maximum price you would be

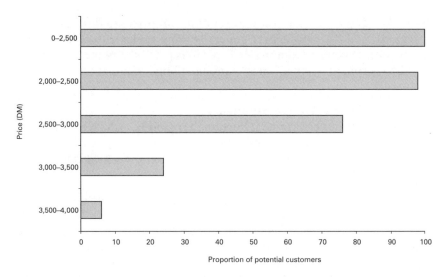

Figure 4.6 Direct survey of potential customers' willingness to pay various prices for a particular computer. Source: Dolan and Simon (1996, p. 52).

willing to pay' on being shown a particular computer (Dolan and Simon, 1996, p. 52). While 6 per cent said that the maximum they would pay was DM3,500–4,000, a further 18 per cent would pay a maximum of DM3,000–3,500 (i.e. 24 per cent would be willing to pay a maximum that exceeded DM3,000, and others would be willing to purchase at lower prices). Dolan and Simon reported that there was a strong threshold at DM3,000 and another, slightly weaker one at DM2,500. Thus, they suggested that the company would consider 'a price just below DM3,000 or DM2,500, depending of course on the cost situation'. The 'optimal price', of course, cannot be decided without data on marginal and average costs, in the way set out in standard microeconomics texts. Note, however, that care needs to be taken in interpreting surveys of 'willingness to buy'. Culkin *et al.* (1999, p. 10), for example, argued that, if manufacturers of leading fast-moving consumer goods (FMCGs) 'have a survey finding suggesting that 30% of customers will definitely buy a particular product, then only a third of this "top box" figure will actually buy the product'. One reason, of course, is that such survey questions do not replicate the situation in which buyers make actual expenditure decisions.

Planned price experiments
Price experiments focus on the effects of price changes (including special offers) on demand and market shares (Dolan and Simon, 1996, pp. 69–70). Such experiments can be conducted in the laboratory, where the market situation is simulated, or in a real-world situation (i.e. 'in-market').

'In-market' tests, for example, may set different prices in different shops or regions, and their results are generally more realistic than laboratory simulations. Dolan and Simon (1996, p. 69) report the findings of a three-month experiment when a German mobile phone manufacturer:

(i)   maintained prices in region A – as expected, the adoption rate was almost identical to pre-experiment;

(ii) made a 25 per cent price reduction in region B – which resulted in a net sales increase of 58 per cent;

(iii) made a 50 per cent price reduction in region C – which caused a 73 per cent rise in net sales.

Such data not only make it possible to calculate crude price elasticities but also to compare marginal revenue with marginal costs under different price scenarios, to give a picture of the profit-maximizing price. These experiments say little or nothing about the relationship between product characteristics and demand *per se*, although it is possible to think of ways to restructure the experiments such that they would have an attribute focus.

Natural price experiments: historical market data
The effects of past price changes, which are not part of a planned experiment (see above), form a natural experiment from which the firm can observe the effects of prices on demand. This generally requires econometric estimation of the relationship between price (or relative prices) and demand (or market shares) (see Chapter 10).

Conjoint analysis: experimental results
Conjoint analysis is an experimental survey method that attempts to value products in terms of consumer preferences with regard to the underlying product attributes (see Hair *et al.*, 1995, pp. 556–601; and the Conjoint Literature Database at www.uni-mainz.de/~bohlp/cld.html). As the approach can be used to evaluate both real and hypothetical products, it is particularly useful in the design and pricing of new products (see Chapters 8 and 10). A consistent approach can be applied to the *ex post* valuation of attributes of existing products using statistical data (see section 4.4.5).

In conjoint analysis, potential customers are presented with a range of alternative brands (or products) with different characteristics or attributes set at different levels; higher-quality mixes of attributes are generally associated with a higher price of the brand in question (see Lancaster's theory of goods – Lancaster, 1966). The conjoint approach is operationalized by presenting potential customers with a range of paired alternative products, comprising a list of attribute levels and price for each alternative, from which they must choose just one from each pair. In effect, the various pairings represent different trade-offs between the levels of attributes available and the overall price of the good. A computer program then compares the choices made to provide a ranking of the attributes implicitly applied by the potential customers, to reveal their willingness to pay for different attribute mixes and levels and, thereby, the implicit value of each attribute. This method yields results for individual customers and for the sample as a whole; given a range of different customers, it can be used to explore potential market segments.

Dolan and Simon (1996, pp. 55–62) set out the seven major analytical steps involved in conjoint analysis. The first three are taken by the firm, in which it has to decide:

(i)   the key characteristics or attributes (e.g. a car manufacturer might choose brand, engine power, fuel consumption, environmental performance and price) – these can be tangible or intangible in nature;
(ii) a range of different but realistic levels of the attributes;
(iii) the nature of the sample that represents the potential customer base for the product or service (e.g. individuals in a certain income category).

In the next four steps, the conjoint software then decides:

(iv) the alternative product profiles to be presented to the sample of individuals in a pair-wise manner, from which they choose one from each pair;
(v)   the individual and average 'importance weights' applied to each attribute – for example, the average weights from (i) might be brand 30 per cent, engine power 28 per cent, fuel consumption 12 per cent, environmental performance 10 per cent, price 20 per cent;
(vi) the value (in price terms) of each attribute level – which yields insights about the marginal value associated with a change in each attribute (e.g. the value consumers attach to an increase in engine power from 100 to 150 bhp);
(vii) overall price sensitivity to the proposed mix of attribute levels (i.e. holding the attributes constant, what would be the effect on consumption and market share of changing price) and the sensitivity of demand to changes in each attribute (or the attribute mix).[4]

Note that the 'optimal' product design (i.e. level and mix of attributes) and price cannot be decided in the absence of information about the (marginal and average) costs of producing each attribute and, thereby, the product as a whole.

4.3.4 *Strategic issues*

Market research clearly plays a crucial role in enabling the firm to take key strategic decisions. In particular, the present analysis highlights the ability of market research to contribute to the firm's understanding of the price sensitivity of the demand for its product and consumer preferences with respect to its quality (attributes). Such activity appears particularly helpful at the NPD stage, and may be of benefit in reducing the risk associated with NPLs (see Chapters 8 and 10). However, such research should also provide information about competitors – a competitive intelligence capability. Not only is it important to monitor and, if possible, predict competitor price, quality and marketing initiatives, but also to know how rivals react to the company's own initiatives. The most obvious of these is the game theoretic issue of pricing strategy (see Chapter 5): 'If management think that a key competitor will [for example] start a price war in response to their new pricing strategy, then … this view should be factored into the analysis process' (Culkin *et al.*, 1999, p. 10).

4.4   Science and technology indicators

This section takes a brief look at the range and strategic use of science and technology indicators (a more detailed treatment can be found in Bosworth *et al.*, 2005a). Science and technology indicators, broadly defined, monitor the progress being made in various fields, with a view to informing the firm's own product and process strategies, as well as throwing light on the activities of competitors and potential collaborators. The range of indicators was illustrated in section 4.1; the present section considers a number of the more important of them and provides examples of their strategic use.

4.4.1   *R&D measures*

Broadly consistent comparisons of R&D activity have been possible at the national level because of definitions provided in the Frascati manual (OECD, 1970).[5] Further consistency at the company level has been introduced by the adoption of accounting standards for reporting of R&D expenditure, which has also encouraged the disclosure of R&D in company accounts. Additional impetus for disclosure has been the introduction of tax breaks for R&D in various countries, such as Singapore, Australia and the UK, although such breaks can also cause distortions, principally the over-reporting of R&D activity. In the main, the definitions of R&D still make clear reference to science and technology (to the exclusion of other areas that firms consider to be R&D), such that qualifying expenditures tend to discriminate against service sector creativity.

The relative extent and strength of R&D activities have been used as key strategic indicators at industry and national levels since the 1950s. For example, the growth in real expenditure on industry-funded R&D per unit of gross domestic product (GDP) from 1967 onwards has been particularly

Table 4.4 Expenditure on R&D as a percentage of sales for selected European countries, 2002

	UK	UK	France	Germany	Switzerland
Number of companies	600[a]	36	31	40	17
All sectors (%)	2.2	2.5	3.1	4.1	4.7
All except pharmaceuticals and oils (%)[b]	2.1	2.9	2.9	3.9	3.0
Pharmaceuticals (%)b	14.6	14.3	15.3	12.8	13.5
Total R&D (£billion)	16.0	10.7	12.7	20.1	5.8

[a]All 600 of the companies in the UK R&D Scoreboard.
[b]Numbers of companies vary by sector.

strong in Japan, with the UK lagging significantly behind, while the USA, France and Germany fall between (Patel and Pavitt, 1995, p. 31; see also Chapter 14). Such results have been central to the debate about the UK's relative technological and economic decline. The first column of Table 4.4 shows data for all 600 of the companies in the UK R&D Scoreboard (Department of Trade and Industry, 2004),[6] while the other columns provide more comparable results for the largest R&D companies (thirty-six of them in the case of the UK). It can be seen that in 2002, overall, the UK lagged some way behind France, Germany and Switzerland in terms of R&D expenditure as a percentage of sales.

The R&D data for individual companies have been published in company reports and accounts in the USA for a long time and these have formed the basis for many studies that have utilized R&D variables (see Hall, 1993a, 2000). Similar information has been available in the UK, particularly since the introduction of the accounting standard statement of accounting practice (SSAP) 13 in 1989, although some companies reported data before that year. UK R&D expenditures are now published in the form of the R&D Scoreboard, which provides an annual ranking of UK companies. Similar rankings can be found in other countries, including Australia, which produces both an R&D and IP scoreboard (Feeny and Rogers, 2000; see below). In the USA, *Business Week* has published R&D expenditures for the 600 largest US companies since the mid-1970s (Patel and Pavitt, 1995, p. 15; *Business Week*, 1992a). These form a major source of information about firm-level R&D activity, which is exploited by companies in tracking competitors and other firms in which they have an interest. Observing the R&D spend of competitors (especially if coupled with information about the direction of that R&D) may help the company decide whether:

(i)   to attempt to be first to invent (i.e. relatively low R&D spend by competitor, with little known focus on the invention in question);

(ii)   to accept coming second (i.e. relatively high R&D spend by the rival, with known focus and competence in that area).

4.4.2   *Scientific publications and citations information*

There is a long history in the sociology of science of using information about the numbers and areas of published articles. Publications and their subsequent citation in the literature are one of the few methods of measuring the output of basic or scientific research. Seminal work by Price (1969), for example, tracked US scientific publications from about 1910 to 1960. The analysis shows a consistent pattern of growth in the total numbers of papers published over the period, with the exception of a dip during World War II. However, the source of sponsorship changed significantly over time, in particular because the US government began funding university research after World War II. In recent times, it has been reported that some 5,000 scientific papers are published each day, in over 3,000 journals (van der Eerden and Saelens, 1991, p. 19).

Creative and high-technology companies in particular (although not exclusively) scan the literature for advances relevant to their current and future performance. Given that companies near the science base tend to share some of their findings in the scientific literature, publication and citation enable the tracking of their activities and their scientific and technological trajectories. For example, biotechnology firms, which tend to be heavily dependent on the science base, might search for authors from firms or universities with which they want to cooperate or trace the growing knowledge base of their competitors. Art and design, textiles or pottery manufacturers might track changes in fashion, materials and so on, while music companies might follow developments in anti-counterfeiting software and devices.

Citation analysis began its life in areas of more basic science, tracing the linkage between articles via the references to other publications.[7] The underlying principle is that the antecedents to published papers can be traced through their citations. The number of subsequent citations is often used as a measure of a paper's scientific importance, and these citations are collated and published in standard reference texts.[8] The main sources of citations information include the *Science Citations Index* and the *Social Science Citations Index*; other more specialist indexes are also available. Despite the continuing debate about the problems of citation-based indices (e.g. the lags in publication, the differing quality of the journals and publishing houses, the bias towards the citation of outputs published in English and so on), the use of such measures is now widespread. The general view is that, if treated with caution, the measures can reveal interesting results. For example, a paper by Hicks *et al.* (1994) suggested that large Japanese firms cooperate extensively and closely with Japanese universities in the production of basic research and scientific outputs.

The citation information also provides insights about the performance of science-based institutions – if a given firm or university is the source of a highly cited cohort of papers, this may be taken as an indication of its scientific contribution and even an indication of its long-term commercial value. Brusoni *et al.* (2003) used scientific papers cited by company patents to calculate the breadth and depth of the science and technology base across the world's largest pharmaceutical companies. They used these data to investigate the suggestion that large firms can be more diversified in terms of the technologies 'they master' than the products that they make (Brusoni *et al.*, 2003, p. 5) – in other words, they are 'information rich' (Chapter 2). They used the range of disciplines cited to identify the 'breadth' of research, with a view to identifying firms that 'maintain capabilities on most (if not all) the bodies of scientific and technological knowledge that impinge upon the development of the specific product market in which they compete' (Brusoni *et al.*, 2003, p. 5). In addition, the whole range of 'levels' of research the citations referred to, from basic to applied (across the range of relevant disciplines), was used as a measure of the 'depth' of research. High capability across both 'breadth' and 'depth' is indicative of 'integrating firms', which have the flexibility to contribute to problems anywhere in the value chain (Prencipe, 2000, 2004).[9] To put this into a more strategic context, firms wishing to be 'systems integrators' need to maintain knowledge about most or all of the technologies of relevance to the product market in which they compete (Brusoni *et al.*, 2003, p. 5).

4.4.3 *Patent-based measures of technological change*

Background
While R&D expenditure has traditionally been viewed as a measure of inventive input, the patents granted to protect the associated intellectual property rights (IPRs) were, at least initially, viewed as a measure of inventive output. Subsequent work, which suggested that significant R&D often occurred after the patent was granted (e.g. to commercialize the product or process), led researchers to look on patents more as an input than an output measure. Nevertheless, the timing of the patent application provides a spot date at which a sufficient germ of the invention is complete to warrant the application. Before granting patent protection, the Patent Office searches the literature and determines whether, with certain caveats, the product or process can be viewed as being novel, involving an inventive step, and having utility.

The early work on technological indicators generally used simple patent counts – the number of patents granted to a particular firm, sector, economy, and so on. The seminal work, culminating in a book by

Schmookler (1966), provided industry-level series of patent counts for the USA. Despite some dissenters, a number of early authors found patent statistics to be a good proxy for the rate of inventive activity (Comanor and Scherer, 1969; Mueller, 1967; Scherer, 1965; Schmookler, 1954, 1966). Early evidence also provided empirical links between R&D and patent series (Freeman, 1962; Gilfillan, 1964, ch. 3; Schmookler, 1966). Freeman (1962), for example, reported that, excluding the aircraft industry,[10] the Spearman rank correlation coefficient between patents and R&D activity across sectors was 0.933. Scherer (1971) and Mueller (1967), drawing upon broadly consistent evidence, suggested that patent data formed a useful index of inventive activity but that they were perhaps a better proxy for research inputs than outputs.

Disaggregated patent count information

The most obvious technological indicator is the aggregate level (see below) of patenting activity for each company.[11] However, patent data are potentially much richer than this. According to Campbell and Levine (1983, p. 3), the various dimensions of the patent data can be used:

(i)   to detect shifts away from past technological directions into new areas:
(ii)   to measure the rate of change in a technology;
(iii) to determine whether a technology is growing, maturing or stagnating;
(iv)   to determine the relative patent position (i.e. technological strengths) of competing firms in a given area of technology.

Thus, while this work is often reported at the company (group) level, it can also be disaggregated by area of technology, as the international patent class (or classification) (IPC). Take the case of patents held by pharmaceutical companies in the area of cephalosporins (Dixon, undated, p. 27).[12] The numbers are highly skewed, with a small number of companies taking out a large number of patents (in Dixon's sample, thirteen companies had taken out twenty-one or more patents) and more firms taking out relatively few (eighty-nine companies had taken out just one patent). It is also possible to trace the date of entry of a given company into a given field (Hyams and Oppenheim, 1983, Figure 7). Eli Lilly and Fujisawa were both relatively early entrants into the area of cephalosporins, compared with, say, Asahi Kasei, which entered over ten years later. Figure 4.7 gives the cumulative numbers of patents, by priority year (i.e. year of application), for the five most active firms in this area.

It is possible to illustrate strategic information about the position a company has reached in any particular area of technology at any given point in time. Table 4.5 sets out the relative importance of patenting activity (under the Patent Convention Treaty) for four companies under six

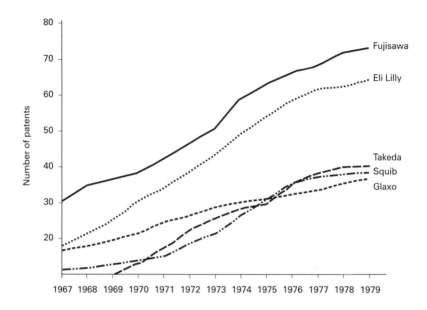

Figure 4.7 Cumulative numbers of basic cephalosporin patents by priority year taken out by the top five companies in the area. Source: Hyams and Oppenheim (1983, Figure 7).

different IPC patent headings relating to cephalosporins, using Derwent data (Hyams and Oppenheim, 1983, p. 11).[13] The first number in each cell is the number of patents, the second gives the relative importance of this area of technology for each company (i.e. number patents as a percentage of the row total) and the third provides the relative importance of each company in that area of activity (i.e. patents as a percentage of the column total). Thus, for example, 50 per cent of Eli Lilly's patents under the six headings fall in the area of 'fused ring heterocycles' (IPC B02). Although this was an important area for Eli Lilly, in relative terms it was even more important for Fujisawa (forming 56 per cent of its patents under these six headings). From the column information, it can be seen that, of the four companies, Eli Lilly was the most important, although other competitors had similar levels of patents (i.e. Hoffman La Roche).

More broadly based comparisons of the importance of companies within cephalosporins, as well as the importance of cephalosporins within the companies' patent portfolios, are also possible (Bosworth *et al.*, 2003, 2005a). This type of information can also be used to track the changing science and technology trajectories of companies over time – subject to the normal limitations of patent data. As noted above, the data reveal entry into and exit from particular areas of technology, related to the dynamic strategies of the firm – while certain areas offer high-technology

Table 4.5 Technological specialties of four companies within the field of cephalosporins, 1976–1981

	B01 Steroids	B02 Fused ring heterocycles	B03 Other heterocycles	B04 Natural products	B05 Other organics	B07 General	B01–B07 Total
Eli Lilly							
Number of patents	4	241	83	57	84	13	482
Importance of activity (%)	0.83	50.00	17.22	11.83	17.43	2.70	100.00
Importance of company (%)	7.41	36.63	19.90	26.89	19.91	21.31	26.37
I G Farben							
Number of patents	0	74	182	36	133	13	439
Importance of activity (%)	0.00	16.86	41.46	8.20	30.30	2.96	100.00
Importance of company (%)	0.00	11.25	43.65	16.98	31.52	21.31	24.02
Fujisawa							
Number of patents	1	139	35	23	40	9	248
Importance of activity (%)	0.40	56.05	14.11	9.27	16.13	3.63	100.00
Importance of company (%)	1.85	21.12	8.39	10.85	9.48	14.75	13.57
Hoffman La Roche							
Number of patents	49	204	117	96	165	26	659
Importance of activity (%)	7.44	30.96	17.75	14.57	25.04	3.95	100.00
Importance of company (%)	90.74	31.00	28.06	45.28	39.10	42.62	36.05
Totals							
Number of patents	54	658	417	212	422	61	1828
Importance of activity (%)	2.95	36.00	22.81	11.60	23.09	3.34	100.00

The importance of the activity is the percentage of the row total and the importance of the company is the percentage of the column total.

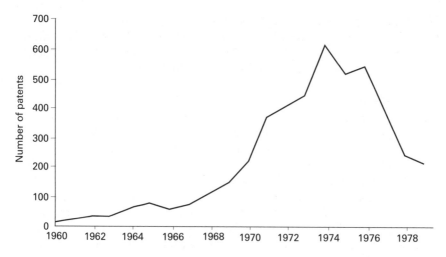

Figure 4.8 The 'technology life-cycle' – total annual numbers of cephalosporin patents, 1960–1979. Source: Hyams and Oppenheim (1983).

opportunity at a given time, they eventually become saturated by potential inventors and effectively 'mined out' – and subject to net exit. Figure 4.8 shows total annual patent activity in the area of cephalosporins and illustrates the 'technology life-cycle' in this area.

Quality weightings
Simple patent counts assign a value of one to all patents, despite evidence that the distribution of patent values is highly skewed. Several methods have been used to attempt to weight patents according to their 'importance'. An early attempt to account for quality differences weighted patents by their longevity,[14] based on the argument that longer-lived patents were likely to be commercially more important (Bosworth, 1973; Federico, 1958; Schankerman and Pakes, 1986; for further information, see Bosworth *et al.*, 2003, 2005a). A second approach using patent citations can be traced back at least to Seidel (1949) and Hart (1949).[15] In essence, the importance of a given invention is determined by the number of times the associated patent is cited in subsequent patent applications. Thus, if a company holds a portfolio of highly cited patents, this indicates it has control of 'important technology'.

The resemblance of the distribution of citations to the one for patent values provides some support for the use of citation information as an indicator of patent value (Hall *et al.*, 1998; see also Hall, 2000). As with other measures of importance and value, citations tend to be highly skewed, with a small number of highly cited patents and a large number rarely (if ever) cited. The literature has revealed what appears to be a strong link between citation-based measures of 'technological significance' and the 'commercial value' of patented inventions (Albert *et al.*, 1991; Carpenter *et al.*, 1981; Harhoff *et al.*, 1997a, 1997b; Narin and Noma, 1987; Trajtenberg, 1990; for brief reviews see Bosworth *et al.*, 2003, 2005a).

Other uses of patent and citation information[16]
In comparing the degree of correspondence between companies' techno-logical activities, and their changes over time, it is possible to construct citation measures of closeness or distance (for a review see Griliches, 1992). Given that such technology mappings (see above) can establish the degree of specialization or diversity of technology areas (and changes over time), such measures can also indicate how similar or different two companies are in terms of their science and technology bases. This can be of great value where a company is searching for a collaborative partner or a takeover or merger target. Other related strategic data can be obtained. The Battelle Institute in the USA, for example, distilled ten patent indi-cators from more than forty objective variables (Campbell and Levine, 1983). Of these ten patent indicators, three concern:

(i)   *immediacy* – the age of earlier patents that are cited by more recently issued patents;
(ii)   *dominance* – a matrix of cross-citation that highlights particular firms that dominate patent activity in a given technology area;
(iii) *scope* – a mapping of citations to define the boundaries of a techno-logical area.

The resulting patent maps can:

(i)   show which patents are strategically important;
(ii)   differentiate basic, defensive and offensive patents;[17]
(iii) identify technology clusters;
(iv)   map the relationships between patents (see also Debackere *et al.*, 2002, pp. 226–227).

In addition to their role outlined in section 4.4.2, non-patent citations (NPCs) offer a means of examining the relationship between the science and the technology base (Meyer, 2000). The main attribute of NPCs – their ability to reflect the influence of science on technology (or vice versa) – opened the way for a stream of research quantifying science–technology linkages. However, a number of the studies argue that science and tech-nology interact in multiple ways and while NPCs can capture the intensity of this interaction, it is more difficult to be certain of the direction of the relationship (e.g. Meyer, 2000; Tijssen, 2002). The close association between highly scientific/technological areas (such as gas lasers or prosta-glandin) and NPCs dates back as far as the mid-1970s (Carpenter *et al.*,

1981). A later study validated the use of NPCs as indicators of science dependence via the degree of agreement between the number of NPCs and the science dependence of innovations as estimated by field experts (Carpenter and Narin, 1983). Subsequent results show an increasing linkage between science and technology over the past two decades (Narin *et al.*, 1997). Citations can also be used to determine the spatial dimension of knowledge flows. Although not all citations represent knowledge spillovers, they are often used as 'signals of spillovers' (Jaffe *et al.*, 2000). The findings suggest a geographical localization of citations, which implies a higher propensity to diffuse when the spatial distance between recipient and originator is smaller (Jaffe and Trajtenberg, 1996). However, this effect tends to fade over time (i.e. with time, the knowledge spreads more widely). In addition, citations can capture cross-border knowledge flows and demonstrate the effects that investments in knowledge transfer mechanisms have on knowledge diffusion (Hu and Jaffe, 2001).

4.4.4 *Measures of innovation activity*

Innovation counts
The seminal work on innovation counts in the UK was carried out at Sussex University's Science Policy Research Unit (SPRU) (e.g. Townsend *et al.*, 1981). Townsend *et al.* define technical innovation along the same lines as the Department of Trade and Industry (although predating the latter by many years), as 'the successful commercial introduction of new or improved products, processes or materials'. It is an interesting question as to whether the adjective 'successful' should be present – certainly it is important to know whether the innovations are successful or not – but the unsuccessful also contain useful information. Nonetheless, innovation counts have similar problems to patent counts, in that different innovations have different technical or commercial significance; many authors therefore attempt to distinguish between minor and major innovations. The SPRU study, for example, indicated that 'significant innovations in each sector were identified by groups of experts knowledgeable of the sector' (Townsend *et al.*, 1981, p. 1). The resulting series of 'significant innovations' increased fairly steadily from 1945 to just before 1970, before falling back and continuing at a roughly constant but slightly lower level.

This form of measurement, when undertaken over a long period, reveals considerable insights into the nature of the innovation process. Gomulka (1990, p. 29) argues that 'the rise of substantially new branches of economic activity and radical changes in the existing branches can almost always be traced to the discovery, respectively, of substantially new products and radically new processes' – in other words, radical innovations. The work of Mensch (1978) provided evidence that the rate at which radical innovations appear varies significantly over time and that innovations are often 'bunched' in particular periods. These findings have linked the economic long cycle (the Kondratieff cycle) to prior radical innovations (see Freeman and Soete, 1997, p. 19).

Survey data

The CIS collects information about innovation expenditures based on the Oslo manual's definition of innovation:

> A technological product innovation is the implementation/commercialisation of a product with improved performance characteristics such as to deliver objectively new or improved services to the consumer. A technological process innovation is the implementation/adoption of new or significantly improved production or delivery methods. It may involve changes in equipment, human resources, working methods or a combination of these. (OECD, undated, p. 10)

The extent of innovation activity is presented in the first CIS report (European Commission, 1994, p. 58). It distinguishes expenditures on:

(i)   R&D;
(ii)   acquisition of patents and licences – product design;
(iii)   trial production, training and tooling up;
(iv)   market analysis (excluding launch costs);
(v)   'other'; as well as
(vi)   related expenditures on specialist services outside the enterprise (e.g. for R&D, patenting, training and design);
(vii)   investment in plant, machinery and equipment linked to NPD.

Despite debates about the definition and phrasing of the survey questions, the resulting data have provided an important advance in our knowledge of the magnitude and nature of the innovation process.[18]

New product launches

A further extension of innovation counts is the work on NPLs, which is based upon innovations reported in the trade literature (Acs and Audretsch, 1990, 1993; Kleinknecht, 1991, 1993; Kleinknecht and Reijnen, 1993). Acs and Audretsch (1990, 1993), for example, use the US Small Business Administration's Innovation Data Base, which gave details of 8,074 innovations registered in a single year. The database examines the product announcements in 100 technology, engineering and trade journals for announcements of innovations. The source of the innovation is allocated to a particular industry (within a four-digit category) and classified by firm size, based on the number of employees. In addition, an attempt is made to distinguish the importance of the innovations. Acs and Audretsch reported a positive and fairly strong relationship between patents per innovation and R&D expenditures, and a sectoral link between innovative activity and high patent and R&D activity. With regard to the issue of firm size, they concluded that small and new enterprises, as well as large incumbents, make important contributions to innovation activity.

The motivation for Kleinknecht's work can be traced to the earlier study by Edwards and Gordon (1984), which also made use of the US Small Business Administration's Innovation Data Base. Kleinknecht's main contribution was the introduction of a refined classification, which separated product differentiation from incremental differentiation, where the former offered a 'pure' innovation measure. The data comprised innovations announced in 1989, which were compared with the 'input' innovation database for 1988, to try to establish whether the inputs were used efficiently. Kleinknecht suggested there were at least nine possible uses of the innovation indicator:

(i)   production of a direct measure of product differentiation;
(ii)   production of a direct measure of the flow of imports of foreign innovations;
(iii)   the collection of discrete cases for later in-depth studies;
(iv)   examination of classical industrial organization issues (e.g. the role of firm size in innovation);
(v)   firm-level data that can be aggregated to higher levels (e.g. sector and, in principle, economy);
(vi)   comparisons of trends with other countries;
(vii)   linkages to other innovation databases;
(viii) linkages to other types of database;
(ix)   examination of innovations developed in one sector but used in another.

While NPL data may be of interest to firms, in monitoring the activities of competitors, the information may be too dated. This form of innovation reporting is done some way downstream from the invention activity reflected by R&D or patents (Campbell and Levine, 1983, p. 5). The selection of journals for such studies is crucial and, even then, it seems likely that process innovations will be under-reported, because firms are more likely to announce new products than processes. In addition, it is important that the person who evaluates the innovation announcement is skilled in classifying the sector (bearing in mind the distinction between sector of origin and sector of use) and the degree to which the innovation is radical. Finally, from a broader policy perspective, it is important to have a database that offers information about changes over time.

Innovation scoreboards
A number of authors have suggested the need for 'innovation scoreboards' (e.g. Tidd *et al.*, 1995), as an extension to the IP scoreboards outlined above. Tidd *et al.* (1995, p. 155) argue that the main interest among businesses is not for improved measures of R&D, patenting activity and so on,

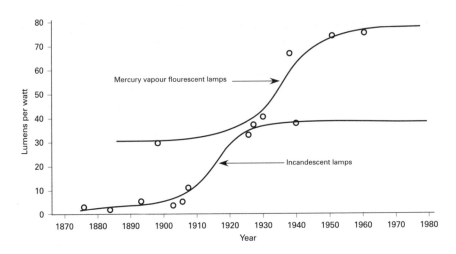

Figure 4.9 Example of a technological index: lumens per watt achieved by evolving bulb technologies, 1875–1960. Source: Wills (1972, p. 108).

but for measures of the effectiveness of innovation and its success. In the final analysis, as with most scoreboard approaches, the authors suggest a synthesis of measures (p. 164). In the absence of any real alternative, the approach is based on an underlying linear model of the innovation process, although the authors clearly recognize the limitations of this (for further discussion see Bosworth *et al.*, 2003, 2005a). Tidd *et al.* (1995) produced a trial scoreboard for forty companies. The trial innovation scoreboard they described (Table 3, pp. 168–169) appears to set out the various measures as a series of indicators for each company, without attempting to produce a composite measure by principal component or regression analysis. However, the authors began the synthesis process by reporting a number of tentative regressions between financial performance, R&D and innovation variables.

4.4.5 *Attributes, technical characteristics and hedonic indices*

Technological indices
There is a wide range of measures of technological performance, such as the maximum speed or height at which an aircraft can travel, or the number of passengers it can carry and so on. Such indices can be traced back at least to the work of Hart (1957), who attempted to measure inventiveness by direct measures of the rate of technological advance. Hart indices measure the 'results of innovation' rather than invention *per se*. Figure 4.9 provides an illustration of the development of lamps, and shows how the brightness achieved changed over time (measured in lumens per

watt). It also illustrates how each particular technology (e.g. incandescent filaments) has a physical limit that results in an 'S-shaped' (or sigmoidal) curve and how one technology supersedes another (e.g. mercury vapour fluorescence technology superseded incandescent filaments). Thus, if lumens per watt is plotted across all technologies, its increase can be exponential for a much longer period (as one technology replaces another); even so, there is an upper limit to development (i.e. the conversion of all electrical energy into light), which produces a sigmoidal curve for the whole batch of technologies.

Hedonic indices

Given that each product has a potentially large number of (Hart) indices, with different rates of change, the question arises of whether to weight them together or pick a key indicator that is either representative or more important than the rest. Hedonic price methods, which use actual, historical data, provide one method of weighting the different characteristics or attributes to form an overall index of 'quality'. Hedonics also provide a direct link with the largely experimental conjoint analysis outlined in section 4.3.3. Hedonic theory brings together the characteristics of a product or service (Lancaster, 1966) and then uses their relationship with observed prices to provide a method of aggregating them. Even the simplest of products can be thought of as bundles of attributes, as in the case of bread (see Table 4.6). More complex products, such as tractors or cars, may have a longer list of key technical characteristics and other attributes.

It is therefore possible to relate differences in the prices of various brands to the differences in the technical characteristics or attributes that each offers (e.g. a Mini and a Rolls-Royce – Cowling and Cubbin, 1972). This allows the isolation of a 'shadow price' of each of the technical characteristics, in other words, the amount consumers are willing to pay for more speed, greater comfort or increased reliability in a car. These 'shadow prices' are used to weight together the bundle of technical

Table 4.6 Examples of characteristics of simple and more complicated products

Bread	Automobiles
Flavour	Seating capacity
Texture	Leg room
Colour	Engine capacity
Nutritional content	Fuel economy
	Acceleration
	Delivery date
	Reliability

characteristics to form a measure of quality change over time. Equation 4.1 illustrates the nature of a relationship that can be estimated across a group of brands (i) over time (t):

$$p_{it} = f[T(1)_{it},..., T(n)_{it}, D_t, B_i] = \alpha(1)T(1)_{it} + ... + \alpha(n)T(n)_{it}$$
$$+ \beta_i B_i + \gamma_t D_t + u_{it}$$

4.1

where p denotes the brand price, $T(j)$ denotes the jth ($j = i, ..., n$) attribute or technical characteristic, D is a time dummy (which picks up pure-inflation effects), B is a brand (or company) dummy (which picks up brand-specific or company-specific effects) and u is the error term. The second expression on the right-hand side shows a simple linear representation of the model. Thus, the path of D_t over time is an indication of the inflation over this group of brands or products and $[\alpha(1)T(1)_{it} + ... + \alpha(n)T(n)_{it}]$ is an index of brand quality, which, for the segment of the market in question, can be calculated using mean values of the technology or attribute variables $[\alpha(1)\overline{T(1)}_{it} + ... + \alpha(n)\overline{T(n)}_{it}]$.

As an example, Figure 4.10 provides a long index of the level of quality, specifically that of tractor production, by linking the results from two studies (Cowling *et al.*, 1970; Gibbons *et al.*, 1981). While there are some differences between the two indices during the period that they have in common, they follow each other reasonably closely. It can be seen that, using consumer (farmer) valuations of the changing technical characteristics of tractors as weights, the quality index rises by a factor of more than 5 from 1948 to 1978. This is an enormous increase in quality, which, in turn,

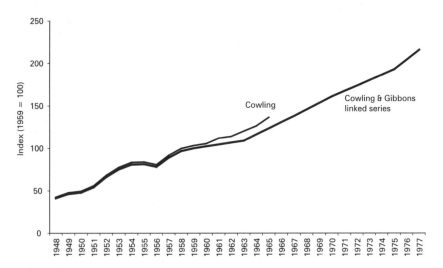

Figure 4.10 Hedonic index of tractor quality. Source: Constructed from data reported by Cowling *et al.* (1970) and Gibbons *et al.* (1981).

was reflected in agricultural productivity over this period. The development of tractors displaced the use of horse power on farms (Cowling *et al.*, 1970, p. 97) – consistent with the Schumpeterian concept of 'creative destruction'.

Linkage between hedonic and patent measures
Bosworth (1976) provides a link between patent measures and hedonic prices, by using patent data as a proxy for changes in the technical attributes of various types of metal-working machine tools (MWMTs). The following regression was used:

$$\log p_t = a + bt + c\log W_t + d\log P_t + u_t \qquad\qquad 4.2$$

where P is a cumulative patent term, W is a measure of weight, a to d are constants and u is an error term. The results suggested significant links between the patent proxy for changes in MWMT quality and the nominal price observed on the market. Bosworth *et al.* (2002, 2005b) undertook a similar analysis at the highly aggregate level of the Japanese economy, and showed that patent (and other IP) data can capture quality changes for which the Japanese population were willing to pay higher prices.

Strategic issues in quality
Hedonic prices are extremely important because they reflect, through the $\alpha(j)$, the values that consumers are willing to pay for a level (and mix) of attributes of a given product or service. The value of the brand coefficient, β_i, shows the price consumers are willing to pay for the ith brand (or product), controlling for all measurable characteristics. Thus, relative values of β_i reflect various unmeasured intangibles, such as brand image, which create differential premiums across firms over the sample period as a whole. It is possible to think of variants of equation 4.1 that would also allow the firm to measure both the level of and changes in brand-specific premiums. Thus, conjoint analysis, coupled with the hedonic methodology, offers a powerful set of tools that the firm can use to explore its product design and other characteristics, both before launch (conjoint) and after launch (hedonic).

4.5   Conclusions

There are benefits to be gained by companies from being 'information rich'. In having a broader range of information than is necessary for current production activities, the firm has effectively taken out options that allow it to respond in a meaningful way to opportunities and threats. Indeed, 'information richness' appears to offer a greater ability to be proactive rather than reactive. All of the indices reported above are of potential interest to firms in assessing their own activities, those of competitors and those of potential collaborators. The indicators can provide a picture of the level, distribution and the quality of each firm's technological efforts (van der Eerden and Saelens, 1991, p. 18). In particular, the firm may need to explore measures that allow it to know well in advance of a competitor's NPL in order to introduce NPDs of its own. The potential strategic importance of information about competitors' technology is illustrated by the following quotation of Thomas J. Watson, a retired chairman of IBM:

> I believe that when we make a new machine announcement, we should set up a future date at which point we can reasonably assume that a competitor's article of greater capability will be announced. We should then target our own development program to produce a better machine on or before that date. (Quoted in Ordover and Willig, 1985, p. 311)[19]

In addition, the firm needs to monitor innovations relating to its inputs; for example, there have been major developments in materials science. Equally, there have been important changes in the ways in which goods and services have been delivered; for instance, call centres have often replaced retail outlets for the sale of insurance or to answer technical enquiries. The growth in the supply of products through the internet has important implications for both the purchase of inputs and the sale of the firm's products and services. Note that the firm should also be monitoring innovation in HPWPs, such as training, HRM practices, flexible working, JIT techniques, total quality manufacturing (TQM) techniques, optimal organizational structures and so on. In addition, firms should not only track patenting activity (where appropriate) but also other forms of IP of relevance. Trademark activity is often a sign of a NPL or product modification by other companies (or an indication of strategic changes in the level or nature of their marketing activity and, thereby, their brand image). In addition, it is important to ensure the company does not infringe other companies' patent, trademark, domain names and so on.

However, it is important to temper these conclusions. While it is possible to put forward a strong case (partly based on evidence from the CIS) for firms to review the extent and nature of their market research activities, it has been acknowledged by some researchers that many firms are simply too small to afford the market research budgets necessary to inform advertising decisions (Lilien *et al.*, 1976). Similarly, there are issues associated with high-technology markets: 'The suggestion that the design of a marketing strategy can be based on careful research of a marketplace can seem unrealistic in high-tech markets. The reason for this is the very high levels of uncertainty (customer as well as supplier) which are characteristic of such markets' (Beard and Easingwood, 1992, p. 5). In addition, it is clear that maintaining an information base wider than is strictly necessary for current production has a cost that must be justified by improvements to the dynamic performance of the firm. While it is quite clear that the sudden emergence of an unexpected product or process technology could be catastrophic for a company, this is an extreme example. Firms have to balance the additional costs of being more information rich with the expected benefits, at the margin.

It is clear from the diversity and wealth of indices reported above that, in some cases, the problem is not the absence of relevant information but its sheer volume (Culkin *et al.*, 1999). Thus, the task is to abstract and synthesize the elements that are crucial to the knowledge base of the firm and to strategic decision making. A number of authors have attempted to reduce the diversity of the indices available by looking at correlations between them – and asking whether the indicators tell the same story or provide different aspects of the story. Jacobsson and Philipson (1993), for example, provide a number of correlations between R&D, patent and educational statistics. A number of these are quite high. However, such correlations require a more thorough understanding of what the statistics are measuring and the 'behavioural relationships' between them (e.g. whether R&D is a determinant of patenting or vice versa, and the factors that make this relationship far from perfect). As attempts to provide a synthesis become more sophisticated (Tidd *et al.*, 1995), these relationships begin to form the basis of specifications that, when estimated, yield weights that allow the different indicators to be aggregated (see Chapters 8 and 9). However, the wealth of information also gives rise to a fundamental need to design the organization in a way that assists with this process, including MIS (see, for example, Kourteli, 2000; and Chapters 11 and 12). In particular, Kourteli's view that the communication structure and the organizational design are intimately related to the internal and external scanning activities of the firm seems particularly important. Finally, note that, despite the wealth of data available, not all the market- and technology-related efforts of firms are manifested in measurable outputs, such as scientific papers or patents. It is important not to lose sight of the fact that these remain only a part of the total – that part associated primarily with formal or codified knowledge. There is also the unobserved part of the iceberg, associated with informal or tacit knowledge (again, see Part V).

Notes

1 Given that the respondents were R&D managers, patent disclosures are more likely to have been reported as being important than if the respondents were non-R&D managers or managers from non-R&D enterprises.

2 Ford's design of the Edsel and its subsequent market failure, as well as the high failure rate of NPLs, provide salutary lessons (Brooks, 1971; and Chapter 8).

3 Dolan and Simon (1996, pp. 48–51) also report on surveys of experts in the field (e.g. managers of retail outlets in potential regional markets). Managers were asked similar questions to those in the consumer surveys, that is, the lowest and highest realistic prices (and some 'medium price'), along with the associated sales

volumes at each. This method is relatively inexpensive, and flexible in terms of product and service situations, including product proposals at the design stage.

4 Allowing competitor prices and attribute mixes to change requires exploration of alternative scenarios.

5 'Research and experimental development may be defined as creative work undertaken on a systematic basis to increase the stock of scientific and technical knowledge and to use this stock of knowledge to devise new applications' (OECD, 1970, p. 8).

6 The latest Scoreboard reports information for 700 companies.

7 One of the earliest examples is the *Science Citation Index*, published by the Institute for Scientific Information from 1963 (Cawkell, 1977).

8 There are numerous problems associated with such indices. For example, they are based only on a part of the total set of journals (in particular, non-English-language journals are under-represented) and references to a particular paper may be made merely because it contains errors.

9 Porter's (1985) value chain covers inbound logistics, operations, outbound logistics, marketing and sales, and service activities (e.g. customer support).

10 Exclusion is justified given that the high defence/government orientation of this sector results in a low propensity to patent.

11 A 'patent scoreboard' appeared in the USA during the 1990s (*Business Week*, 1992b), in Australia since the late 1990s (Feeny and Rogers, 2000) and more recently for the UK (Greenhalgh and Longland, 2004).

12 'Cephalosporins are anti-infective agents (as antibiotics are also known) ... they are used either after other often less expensive anti-infective agents have been tried or when a certain uncommon type of infection is believed present' (www.fda.gov/bbs/topics/CONSUMER/CON00017.html).

13 Derwent is an international company that collates and reports patent data. It is now part of the Thomson Derwent Group.

14 Although patents have a maximum life (normally twenty years), they have to be renewed annually (normally after the fourth year). As renewal involves the payment of a fee, not all patents survive the full twenty years.

15 Evolution of this work is documented by Narin and Olivastro (1988a, 1988b), and further innovative uses of citations continue to appear in the literature (e.g. Engelsman and Raan, 1994; Hall, 2000).

16 Thanks to Despoina Filiou for her work on a literature review that the present section draws upon.

17 Basic patents may be interpreted as likely to lead to the development of an important new area of technology. Offensive patents are blocking ones intended to shut out competitors. Defensive patents are intended to help ward off legal suits and reach deals with competitors.

18 Given that many companies are becoming used to answering these questions, some will construct accounting mechanisms to make the provision of such data more straightforward.

19 Note that competition may not come from the most obvious source – with radical inventions and innovations, competition may come from technologies some distance away, possibly far away (e.g. railways replaced canals, roads replaced railways, glass and carbon fibres replaced metal).

Part III
Management and enterprise strategies and goals

Chapter 5

Goals and strategies

5.1 Goals in context

The earlier chapters provide some strong hints about the potential goals of the firm. The transaction cost approach outlined in Chapter 2, for example, had an 'efficiency' aspect – allocating activities between the firm and the market according to the relative efficiency with which they are carried out. Chapter 3 outlined a range of financial, economic and other measures of enterprise performance. Most of these can be considered to be 'higher-level' measures in the sense that they are relevant to or can be applied at the level of the overall performance of the company. The discussion demonstrated that the majority were closely related to profitability. They highlighted key areas of management focus and concern, such as the control of input prices, the improvement of physical productivity and the increase in product quality. However, the goals reportedly adopted by companies often do not appear to relate so closely to issues of profitability. What is immediately clear from the literature is that different types of companies (e.g. private versus public sector, quoted companies versus worker cooperatives), insofar as they adopt goals, are likely to adopt quite different higher-level goals. Even companies in the same sector can have quite distinct goals.

Importantly, the goals (and, as demonstrated below, the strategies) adopted often do not correspond with those imagined (or hoped for) by government. Thus, when the government is critical of enterprise performance (firms are not innovative enough, not growing fast enough, etc.), this may not be the view of companies themselves. In other words, the companies may be achieving the goals that they set for themselves, but not the goals that the government perceives to be important. It is therefore important to investigate why there is such a diversity of goals as well as the implications not only for company and national performance, but also for government policy (see Chapter 14).

The literature suggests several reasons for the lack of focus on profits among some private sector firms. First, some of the owners of the company may not see profits as the only driving force; this is easy to demonstrate for some owner-managed companies, but it may also apply to some professionally managed companies (e.g. where shareholders are concerned about employee welfare or 'green issues'). Second, the managers of the company may have their own interests and agendas. Thus, an important theme of the present chapter concerns the managerial goals of the firm, while Chapter 7 looks at the mechanisms that attempt to align the goals of professional managers with those of the owners. Third, managers may not be able to maximize profits or closely related variables, even though they seek to do so. Here firms are considered as complex organizations (an issue that is dealt with in Part V) and, thus, a further important theme concerns the behavioural theories of the firm, in which companies can have multiple goals and may not optimally implement any one of them (let alone optimize overall firm performance). The discussion below of the last reason also touches upon the insights from institutional theories of the firm. Finally, it addresses the dynamics of companies, drawing upon evolutionary theory and, in the context of whether markets operate in favour of selecting firms that have a greater profit focus, upon the ecological school of firm dynamics (again, see Part V).

Section 5.2 distinguishes between goals and strategies and then develops a taxonomy of them. Section 5.3 considers the early evolutionary view that it may make little sense to try to pin down explicitly the goals and strategies of particular companies, as business actions are often instinctive. However, the present discussion makes the case for an increased focus on goals and strategies, as this affords a greater understanding of the way in which enterprises behave and perform. Section 5.4 considers the goals of owners from two special perspectives: first, the 'greening' of companies (i.e. the reaction of shareholders to green and ethical issues); second, the goals set by owner managers, often of smaller companies. The aim is to show that groups that are often assumed to be profit maximizers may have quite different goals. Section 5.5 focuses on the assumptions of the empirical structure–conduct–performance (SCP) models and the distinctions between the managerial and behavioural theories. Section 5.6 then turns to the strategies that firms adopt in attempting to achieve their goals. This section explores the origins in the literature, in particular the role of game theory, and the development of the strategic management literature. Section 5.7 examines the issue of whether, if firms adopt different strategies, the market will weed out suboptimal strategies via a process of natural selection. Finally, Section 5.8 draws together the main conclusions of the study.

5.2   Towards a taxonomy of goals and strategies

It seems important to make a distinction between goals and strategies and, as far as possible, not to use the terms interchangeably. Some studies adopt the useful distinction between higher- and lower-level goals – higher-level goals relate to the enterprise as a whole, while lower-level goals are set at an operational level in different functional areas, divisions of the enterprise and so on. The higher-level goals are often set in financial terms (e.g. sales targets, share prices, MV, profits), while the lower-level goals may be financial or physical (e.g. units produced, rejection rates). Bosworth (2001) provides UK empirical evidence about the dominant, higher-level, enterprise-wide goal and other, lower-level goals.

While the higher-level, enterprise-wide goal indicates what the enterprise is attempting to achieve, it does not give any information about the mechanisms used. Some understanding of the mechanisms can be obtained from a picture of the lower-level goals, but a clear picture emerges only from information about enterprise strategy. The area of strategy and strategic decision making is vast (for an excellent review see Mintzberg *et al.*, 1998). Strategic issues include, for example: what products to make and to what quality, which markets to sell in (e.g. Europe, USA), where to base production (domestically or abroad) and what price to set.

Enterprise strategy effectively describes the approach adopted in order to achieve the higher-level goal. To illustrate the idea, while the enterprise may define the goal as profit maximization, it may achieve this by product improvements that command higher prices (given control over costs) or by cost reductions (given control over quality), or some combination of the two. The distinction between 'quality' and 'cost–price' strategies permeates the literature, especially the HRM/HPWP literature (e.g. Youndt *et al.*, 1996; see also Chapter 9). It also underpins the traditional economic notion of price versus non-price competition (Tirole, 1990, pp. 205–206). In addition, it appears in Porter's (1985) generic strategies of:

(i)   cost leadership (where the strategy is to be the low-cost producer in the sector);
(ii)   differentiation (where the strategy is make distinct products of high quality that can generate customer loyalty);
(iii) focus (where the strategy is to concentrate on a particular niche or market segment through either cost leadership or differentiation);
(iv)   'stuck in the middle' (where firms that fail to do any of these achieve mediocrity and below-average performance).

Bosworth (2001) focuses on what might be termed 'moving up-market', which implies a 'quality-improving' strategy, rather than an 'efficiency-increasing' strategy with existing products. However, subsequent research by the author suggests that it is important also to distinguish between an efficiency-increasing strategy and a cost-reducing strategy – the former operates through factor productivity improvements and the latter by moving to cheaper inputs (Skills in England, 2003). One interesting suggestion is that the different strategies adopted have different implications for risk. Mintzberg *et al.* (1998, p. 9) note that 'A company that perpetually markets the most expensive products in its industry pursues what is commonly called a "high-end" strategy, just as a person who accepts the most challenging of jobs may be described as pursuing a "high-risk" strategy'. This link between high-end strategies and risk is developed throughout the remainder of the present book.

Companies need to ask a series of questions in order to identify their key strategic issues.[1] These questions may relate to the following, for example:

(i)   the principal changes likely to affect the company's operations –
      (a) demographics of stakeholders (number, values, resources, power, etc.);
      (b) rules and regulations (accounting codes, health and safety regulations, trading standards, etc.);
      (c) tastes and needs for products and services (fashions, designs, quality trends, etc.);
      (d) emergence of potential new competitors (new entrants, large firms diversifying, growth of foreign competition, etc.);
      (e) leadership and staffing (changing skill and competence needs among managers, other employees, etc.);
(ii) the likely effects of these changes in terms of threats or opportunities;
(iii) the changes that must be introduced in order to address the threats;
(iv) the strengths that should be built in order to take advantage of the opportunities.

To complicate matters further, companies in the same sector with the same goal may adopt different strategies and operationalize these strategies in different ways. Elsewhere an attempt has been made to provide a taxonomy of higher- and lower-level goals, strategies and the way that they are operationalized (Bosworth, 2001). In some firms, for example, a product innovation or quality-increasing strategy may be the best way of improving profitability, while in other firms an efficiency-increasing strategy may be more effective. Subsequent chapters demonstrate that the choice of strategy depends crucially on the internal (e.g. competences, skills, etc.) and external (e.g. degree and nature of the competitive process) environments of the firm.

The literature tends to imply that strategies demand 'either/or' choices (e.g. differentiation or cost–leadership). This view appears to arise from a misconception linked to the idea that an enterprise that is oriented towards high product quality is likely to accept that it will operate at a higher unit cost level and, which is where the problem lies, to be less concerned about the costs of production (section 5.3 discusses the more conceptual issues). Indeed, simple game theoretic models tend to reinforce this misperception – as the enterprise may be modelled as choosing between a 'high-cost, high-quality strategy' and a 'low-cost, low-price' strategy. This need not be the case – firms can attempt to lower cost (below the level it would otherwise have been) and increase quality at one and the same time. This may be because a given enterprise adopts different strategies for different market segments, as described by Porter (1990), but it may also occur in response, for example, to a need to save on production costs to find the resources to develop and launch a new product. More fundamentally, the two may exist side by side because the enterprise wants to offer the best 'value for money'.

The way in which the overall strategy of the enterprise is operationalized is reflected in the lower-level goals, that is, those set for individuals or teams of workers. This requires a much more detailed knowledge of the nature of the product, the technology of production, the structure of the enterprise, management styles and so on. The actions taken to operationalize the strategies may include activities such as technological innovation (e.g. new and different equipment) or new working practices. However, a number of these lower-level actions may be partly or even wholly subsumed in the organizational structure and/or the routines of the enterprise. The higher the degree to which the strategies and the actions taken to achieve them are 'tacit', the more difficult they may be to rationalize – a point emphasized by the evolutionary economics literature – and the more difficult they may be for other firms to copy.

5.3 Conceptual problems in measuring goals and strategies

5.3.1 *Early evolutionary view*

While the evolutionary literature has made a substantial contribution to understanding many economic issues, it has sometimes adopted a negative stance about the ability to investigate (and measure) goals, strategies and management skills, because of the degree to which they become 'tacit'. Nelson and Winter (1982) present a critique of orthodox economic theory as portrayed in the literature of the 1960s and 1970s. By 'orthodox', they appear to mean the managerial theories of the firm (see section 5.5). They argue that:

> The economic theorist's abstract account of business decision making is not to be confused with the businessman's skills; it serves different purposes and those purposes place a high premium on articulation. Clear articulation of his methods may be valueless, or even counterproductive, for the businessman. It is therefore quite illegitimate to seek to appraise the validity of the theoretical

account of business decisions by asking businessmen whether their procedures match the theoretical constructs. Such a method founders first on the general observation that the possibilities for articulating the basis of high skill are limited; second, even if this fact were somehow of minimal importance in the specific context of business decision[s], there would be no reason to expect that the language chosen by the businessman to articulate his skill would be the language of economic theory. There is, after all, no reason to expect a bicyclist to be able to explain in the language of physics how he remains upright, but this does not imply that he usually falls over. (Nelson and Winter, 1982, p. 92)

Nelson and Winter (1982, p. 93) raise the issue of whether it makes any sense to try to codify what is essentially a set of tacit skills:

> However, merely noting that the central problem is how to model skilled behavior opens the way for a substantial clarification of the issues. Orthodoxy treats the skillful behavior of the businessman as maximizing *choice*, and 'choice' carries connotations of 'deliberation'. We, on the other hand, emphasize the *automaticity* of skillful behavior and the suppression of choice that this involves. In skillful behavior, behavioral options are selected, but they are not deliberately chosen. This observation directs attention to the processes by which skills are learned, the preconditions for the effective exercise of skill, and the possibilities for gross error through automatic selection of the wrong option.

Their theory is in many respects an extension of the behavioural theories of the firm. While behavioural models accepted satisficing (rather than optimizing) behaviour,[2] they nevertheless adopted goals of the firm (see section 5.5.2).

5.3.2   *Necessity of pinning down goals*

It is difficult fully to understand the performance of companies unless one knows what their goals are. While it is possible to adopt some common standard – such as profit maximization, as this is consistent with Pareto optimization – this may judge the company by some metric that it was not focusing on. Equally, the company may be judged by its dynamism, in the sense of its degree of involvement in invention and innovation. On the other hand, a particular company may have no interest in such activities. Thus, the key rationale is that company performance is, in part, driven by the goals it sets itself. Historically, for example, this has shown up in a wide variety of contexts, such as the 'worker orientation' of the Swedish companies versus the 'financial orientation' of UK companies, found in comparative international case studies of firm performance (Bosworth *et al.*, 1992). This raises a second, even more thorny issue: is the goal of the company the 'correct' one? There are many issues bound up here. Not least is the question of who owns the company and who benefits from the operations of the company. In some instances, ownership and management are one and the same, while in other instances they are separate.

The focus of the original managerial theories was on this separation, and specifically with whether professional managers might act in their own 'self-interest' to the detriment of shareholders (see Chapter 7).

The rather simplistic SCP models (see section 5.5) tend to assume a mechanistic link between size or market structure and conduct. The rationale again lies in the separation of ownership from management, which results in increasing degrees of managerial discretion in larger, more monopolistic firms. Even if this were true, different managerial theories point to different goals, with different performance outcomes. However, the link need not be mechanistic in the way this suggests. Firms in the same market of the same size may be differently equipped for product innovation (e.g. because of a difference in the quality of their managers or workforce), which produces a difference in the rate of return on investment in quality improvements as opposed to cost savings (see Chapter 13). Hence, otherwise comparable firms can have quite different behaviour and outcomes.

There is a separate issue, however – whether the managers of the firm in some sense adopt the 'correct' or 'optimal' goal. If the goal of the firm were changed, would the company perform 'better' from the manager's, owner's or society's perspective? This problem is associated with one aspect of *latent skills deficiencies*, namely that with greater levels of skills/competences, the manager would have adopted a different and 'more appropriate' goal. So one aspect of *latency* concerns the extent to which firms would perform better if the level of skills or competence (in this case of the managers) were higher. The broader range of latency issues is considered in Chapters 13 and 14 (see also Bosworth *et al.*, 2001).

5.4 Goals of owners

5.4.1 *Ethical and green issues*

The globalization debate has raised considerable public concerns over the goals and actions of companies. While this has resulted in protests at events such as meetings of heads of state, there is also a small but important group of shareholders who voice their opinions regarding the conduct of particular companies, notably in relation to ethical and green issues. The concerns of such individuals include:

(i) the nature of the products (e.g. genetically modified crops);
(ii) the sourcing of raw materials;
(iii) the safety and sustainability of manufacturing processes used;
(iv) the nature of wastes produced, and methods and extent of reuse, recycling and disposal;
(v) the ethics of relationships with other stakeholders, including employees, communities and the environment;
(vi) the quality of information provided to the media by companies;

(vii) donations to political parties, lobby groups and ideological 'think tanks' by companies.[3]

The most obvious way in which such individuals can voice their concerns is by attending and raising questions at the company's annual general meeting, but they can also put pressure on companies in a wide range of other ways, such as writing to the chairperson or CEO.

The extent and importance of this movement can quickly be ascertained in a web search. A number of companies have taken action to change their image, such as BP, which revealed its new 'green' brand image in 2000, in 'an attempt to win over environmentally aware consumers'. It replaced BP's shield logo with a green, white and yellow logo, which was intended to indicate its commitment to the environment and the development of solar power. The company also changed back to BP (from BP Amoco) and undertook an extensive rebranding exercise. In doing so it was reported that it spent $7 million researching the new brand and around $100 million a year in supporting the brand change.[4]

The adoption of green goals also has implications for a firm's strategy – cost-reduction and quality-improvement strategies become affected by the need to produce and distribute in environmentally friendly ways. The enterprise that formerly had a cost leadership strategy may now moderate this to allow for higher costs, to produce less pollution (e.g. fitting scrubbers to reduce air pollution). The company that formerly had a differentiation strategy may now have to modify product design in line with industry standards such that the product itself produces less pollution (e.g. producing cars with lower acceleration but reduced exhaust emissions). Various actions can be taken by the company to minimize the effects of such strategy changes on profits:

(i) lobbying for government legislation for a 'level playing field' for all companies in the sector;
(ii) encouraging consumers to value the improvements and be willing to pay a price premium (e.g. paying more for organic foods);
(iii) convincing shareholders to accept a lower rate of return on their investments.

The balance is difficult – the company may be harried by lobby groups, regulation does not always produce a level playing field, and consumers and/or shareholders may place no value on the environmental benefits.

5.4.2 *Goals (and strategies) among small firms with owner managers*[5]

Given that the divergence between owners and professional managers tends to occur in larger companies, one interesting place to look at the goals of owners is in the literature on small firms with owner managers.

The general presumption in the early economics literature was that, in the main, small firms are owner managed and could be expected to be 'profit seeking' (where profit can be viewed as the surplus the business earns over total costs – where total costs exclude the owner manager's income). The findings of the subsequent literature on this topic, however, suggested that, on balance, material reward is rarely the primary motivation for business ownership (Gill, 1985): owner managers place more weight on job satisfaction and personal fulfilment (Clutterbuck and Devine, 1985; Ritchie *et al.*, 1982), which can be traced to close contact with the business client group (see also the discussion of social capital in section 6.5.6 and Part V). These types of finding continue to appear in more recent studies; for example, a survey of owner managers in the rural tourism and hospitality sector in Western Australia suggested that lifestyle and family-related goals are predominant, although there was also recognition that the business must be profitable (Getz and Carlsen, 2000).

The literature in the early 1980s suggested that the owner managers of small firms were often characterized by an artisan philosophy, centring on client satisfaction and the perceived quality of the service or product (Gill, 1985). When this artisan philosophy is associated with an aversion to bureaucracy, it inhibits the motivation for growth (Scase and Goffee, 1980; Stanworth and Curran, 1986). Minguzzi and Passaro (2001) argue that owner managers of small and medium-sized enterprises (SMEs) often demonstrate a 'resistance to change' that limits competitiveness. They attribute this, often, to a 'cultural entrepreneurial homogeneity' that is a consequence of the similarity of the social, educational, and entrepreneurial experiences of the owner managers, which results in distrust of innovation and discontinuity.

While the term 'entrepreneur' is sometimes used to cover all owner managers of small businesses (as in the case of Minguzzi and Passaro, 2001), the present discussion prefers the modification in the literature that recognizes at least two types of owner managers: the 'craftsperson' and 'opportunistic' owners (Smith, 1967), or the 'artisan' and the 'entrepreneur' (Stanworth and Curran, 1986), who can exhibit quite different attitudes towards growth. The adoption of the two different groups often implies something about the area of technology – with the former more traditional and the latter more innovative. Miller and Friesen (1982), for example, use the alternative terms 'conservative' and 'entrepreneurial' firms, where the latter seek competitive strategies, often linked with more radical innovations. Covin (1991) also makes this distinction, adding alongside the innovativeness of entrepreneurial firms their proactivity, risk taking, openness and adaptability. The use of the terms 'opportunistic' and 'entrepreneurial' imply something about market orientation and drive – people who, according to Adam Smith, were 'self-seeking' and, according to Joan Robinson, possess 'animal spirits' (see Chapter 6).

Of course, the dichotomous approach is simplistic and many other writers have suggested somewhat more complex taxonomies (e.g. Chell *et al.*, 1991). Quince and Whittaker (2002, p. 34) pointed to a significant diversity of high-technology firms and the markets within which they operate. While they found that, effectively, all small high-technology firms operate in niche or segmented markets, there are important differences across niche markets in terms of the technology and the manner in which the technology is embodied – ranging from where it is embodied in an individual (or group) to where it is in the product or service. They argue that all these types of firm have a role to play (in part in supporting each other), but also note that they require quite distinct government policies (e.g. R&D tax breaks are essential for some, but irrelevant for others).

While ownership (and the status that this confers) may be perceived to be more important than salary (Clutterbuck and Devine, 1985; Ritchie *et al.*, 1982), the distinction between material reward and ownership is not clear – as there is an economic value of ownership (i.e. the discounted sum of future earnings, including the end-of-period capital value). Nevertheless, the literature clearly indicates that ownership confers much more than just a stream of future income on the owner manager. It may be questioned whether this is true of different types of small firm (e.g. artisan and entrepreneurial, low and high technology) but, in practice, it seems to be, at least to some degree. Quince and Whittaker (2002, p. 3) reported that:

> The 1998 survey showed that high-tech entrepreneurs in the UK espouse a number of objectives of which financial gain is not paramount, that high technology entrepreneurship is very much a collaborative activity, and that most adopt a cautious approach to expansion and the development of their business.

The literature also suggests important differences between male and female owner managers. Males exhibit a drive for independence and a desire to control their working environments and their lives (Clutterbuck and Devine, 1985; Gill, 1985; Ritchie *et al.*, 1982). The 'desire for control', which includes the control of others, can be an important influence on the direction and rate of growth of the small business. The males' dislike of bureaucracy is an important motive for starting up a small business, but also a barrier to growth (Gill, 1985; Stanworth and Curran, 1986). 'Control loss' occurs as successive layers of administration transmit information less and less accurately and reliably (Williamson, 1967b), which is linked to the failure of management and the organizational structure to cope with company growth.

While females may share the male desire for control and need for independence, historically at least they experienced the added frustration arising from the ethos of the male-dominated business world (Clutterbuck

and Devine, 1985). Early work in this area suggested that a larger percentage of UK female owner managers adopt a more parental (maternal)
role model, focusing on creativity and team work, rather than a model
based upon authoritarian control (Watkins and Watkins, 1986).

Historically in the UK, owner managers of small businesses were
thought to lie on the right of the political spectrum, which, when linked
with their desire to maintain control of their businesses, can negatively
influence growth. There are several reasons for this. First, owner managers are reported to fear the difficulty of ensuring compliance with their
decisions as the degree of hierarchy rises (Sawyer, 1981, p. 55). Second,
owner managers perceive union power and activity to increase with firm
size (Bain and Elias, 1985; Sawyer, 1981, p. 55). In addition, the empirical
evidence supports a trade union 'wage mark-up' (Stewart, 1983), even if
this is smaller than originally supposed (Minford, 1983).

Growth is linked with the potential loss of control in other ways. The
managerial growth model, for example, suggests that the valuation ratio
of a company initially rises with growth and then declines (Marris, 1964;
Wildsmith, 1973, pp. 929, 113–122). Thus, continued ownership and control
depend on avoiding under- and overperformance of the firm, which can
result in liquidation or takeover. While this is true of both professional
managers and owner managers, growth appears to figure more heavily in
the utility function of the former than the latter and, hence, may result in
a higher rate of profit and lower growth for the owner-managed firm.

5.5 Structure–conduct–performance (SCP), managerial and behavioural models

5.5.1 *SCP models and contestability*

While there is a wide-ranging economics literature on the goals of the
enterprise, it is largely conceptual in nature. The starting point is probably
the early empirical work on the SCP models of the industrial economics
literature. This group of models suggests that market structure (i.e. the
number of suppliers of a given product or service, representing the degree
of market power) determines the conduct of the enterprise and, thereby,
company performance. In the majority of the empirical SCP models, performance was measured either by profit (the 'static' SCP models) or by
the extent of inventive or innovative activity (the 'dynamic' SCP models).[6]
In particular, the dynamic models purported to test the Schumpeterian
hypothesis that larger and more monopolistic companies were the principal drivers of technological change. 'Conduct' referred to various actions
and, thereby, the behaviour of firms, rather than the goals *per se*, but the
literature was never at all clear about what was meant by 'conduct'. Many
of the writers on this topic did not even provide a definition of conduct,

although some provided examples, such as 'Aggressive marketing via price discrimination, aggregated rebates, insistence on exclusive purchasing' (Pickering, 1974, p. 29). Other authors have viewed conduct (and behaviour) as being linked to the goals of the firm. Thus, firms with the goal of maximizing profit may attempt to restrict entry to a market, for example via limit pricing[7] (the conduct) on the grounds that this improves future profit flows (Sawyer, 1981, p. 73).

Contestability adds the issue of the role played by entry and exit on the behaviour of firms within the market (Baumol, 1982). This has given rise to interesting concepts, such as the role of sunk costs – those that cannot be retrieved by a firm on exit. It has also provided a further link with strategic behaviour, both in terms of the new entrant (i.e. entry strategy) and in terms of the incumbent (i.e. in terms of price and non-price behaviour to limit entry or to accommodate the new entrant). This has also been dealt with in the context of game theoretic approaches (e.g. the credible threat of entry) (see section 5.6.1).[8]

The SCP framework was used by Porter as the basis for understanding the strategic challenges faced by the enterprise as managers attempt to maximize profits (for a discussion, see Keat and Young, 2000, p. 408). Porter's 'five forces' model effectively establishes the competitive framework and the likely profitability of the sector (i.e. role of potential new entrants, power of suppliers, power of buyers, threat from substitute products, intra-market rivalry). Within this framework, Porter discusses the firm-level strategies that can lead to higher than average profit. The two 'generic' strategies are very similar to those that were discussed in section 5.2 (i.e. narrow or broad 'differentiation' and 'cost leadership').

5.5.2 *Managerial and behavioural models*

The managerial literature, in particular, said little, if anything, about strategy. Strategy implies something more fundamental and forward looking than conduct or behaviour. For example, a strategy to compete increasingly through the development of new products with higher value added may imply a range of actions (e.g. increase and refocus R&D spending, undertake a new advertising campaign, improve the skills of the workforce). In addition, while conduct may be proactive, the managerial literature suggests the predominance of actions of a more reactive nature – such as actions contingent on or proscribed by market circumstances. For example, managers in larger, more monopolistic firms are able not only to adopt different goals but also to behave differently to the managers of smaller, highly competitive firms. This is not to say that conduct is uniquely determined by the particular market structure, but that the range of conduct is defined for each market, as certain actions are more likely to be chosen in the light of the environment. Strategy, on the other hand, appears to be essentially forward thinking and proactive in nature, and contingent on competitor and other responses.

While strategies were largely absent from this generation of literature, goals played a central role in two major streams of mainly theoretical contributions:

(i) managerial theories of the firm, which involved some form of optimizing behaviour (e.g. maximization of profit, revenue, growth or managerial utility) – see, for example, Marris (1964) and Williamson (1963, 1967a);[9]

(ii) behavioural theories, which assumed satisficing behaviour, on the grounds that optimization was impossible – see, for example, Cyert and March (1963), Cohen and Cyert (1965) and Simon (1959).[10]

In the case of the managerial theories, normally only a single, higher-level, enterprise-wide goal is chosen (e.g. Marris's growth maximization). While this is also true of Williamson's model, based upon managerial utility maximization, utility was argued to be a function of a number of different elements (profits, number of staff controlled, emoluments, etc.). These models have no strategic content; for example, they do not say that growth should be achieved using a low-cost, low-price strategy, or a quality-increasing strategy. One interesting feature, however, is that while the various managerial goals do not result in maximum profits, profits figure somewhere in the model, either as an argument of the utility function or as a constraint (e.g. at least a minimum profit must be achieved), which limits managerial freedom. Thus, profit maximization is invariably a special case in such models. For example, it arises in the model in which sales revenue is maximized, when shareholders are able to set the minimum-profit constraint equal to the maximum-profit outcome.

Evolutionary theories draw quite heavily on behavioural theories. This is because behavioural theory was the first to assume non-optimizing behaviour, limited information, bounded rationality and so on. While the managerial literature had two main mechanisms by which a single goal would emerge for the enterprise,[11] according to Cyert and March (1963) 'neither solution is entirely happy'. They argue that, in practice, organizations are coalitions of individuals and groups, with potentially different and conflicting goals. Thus, the enterprise sets (many) aspiration levels but it does not optimize. These aspirations form the 'goals of the firm'. Cyert and March (1963) argue that goals are formed as a result of three processes:

(i) 'bargaining', which determines the form of the coalition between participants in the firm, who have disparate views and demands;

(ii) an 'internal organizational process of control', by which objectives are stabilized and elaborated;

(iii) 'learning and adjustment' from experience.

The goals themselves may conflict with one another. The authors argue that they can coexist not only because the enterprise does not optimize but also because it deals with each in a 'fire-fighting' manner – if a goal is being satisfied it drops down the list of priorities, while the one that is least satisfactory rises to the top. Each goal has a level and a smoothing aspect (i.e. the level of sales or inventories and the rate of change in sales or inventories), as well as an aspirational level, which *may* be raised (if the goal is easily satisfied) or lowered (if it is often unsatisfied).

Both managerial and behavioural approaches have made a contribution to our understanding, but both have weaknesses. The managerial theories are economic in nature, but weak in institutional and sociological content, while the opposite is true of behavioural theories. As a consequence, a particular managerial theory gives a single (but possibly wrong) outcome, while a particular behavioural theory gives multiple outcomes (only one of which is potentially 'right').

5.6   Strategy: origins in the literature[12]

The principal areas of focus for strategic behaviour concern which products or services to produce (and, thereby, product mix), product price and product quality. The strategy may, for instance, be to introduce a higher-quality product before a competitor launches its new product. However, the literature often also focuses on lower-level strategies (as described in section 5.2), which are more concerned with the mechanisms used to deliver these higher-level strategies (e.g. the extent and nature of the R&D, advertising or training programmes – see Part IV). This section briefly reviews the contribution of game theory and then the contribution of the strategic management literature, before a strategic theory of the firm is sketched.

5.6.1   *Game theoretic origins*

A strategy can be thought of as a 'blueprint for action', aimed at a particular goal (Dutta, 1999, p. 20).[13] For example, the strategy may be to develop a higher-quality product in order to increase future profits. The very idea of adopting a strategy implies that there is a choice – that the enterprise has reached some point (a 'node') at which it has two or more options that it must decide between. In addition, it implies that this is not done in isolation – that the actions of one enterprise will affect those of others (and are therefore contingent upon them). Thus, strategic behaviour lies at the heart of game theory. Montet (1991, p. 343) argues that:

> Game theory is concerned with the analysis of conscious interactions between agents. Each player behaves strategically in the sense that, in deciding which course of action to take, [s]he takes into account the possible effects on the other players and the fact that the latter behave in the same way.

In work by Schelling (1960, 1966), more complex forms of strategic behaviour have been outlined. In this, a strategic move is an action that 'influences the other person's choice, in a manner favourable to oneself, by affecting the other person's expectations of how oneself will behave' (Shelling, 1960, p. 160). This leads on to the discussion of issues such as 'credible threats'.[14]

Game theoretic approaches have formed a major additional tool that has thrown light on numerous economic and social issues, not least of which is decision making on the part of firms. However, it seems important to recognize their limitation in the context of an empirical study of decision making and the consequences for company performance. This can be illustrated using the simplest payoff matrix for a one-shot game between two competing firms (A and B), with two alternative strategies ('move up-market' and 'move down-market'), as set out in Table 5.1, where the payoffs are 5,5 (for A and B, respectively) if they both play 'up-market' – the other payoffs follow the same pattern, dependent on the combination of strategies played.

It can be seen that, if A chooses to move up-market, it pays B to move down-market (a payoff of 10 rather than 5); if A chooses to move down-market it still pays B to move down-market (a payoff of 2 rather than 1). Precisely the same outcome occurs for A's response to B's choices (i.e. if B chooses up, A chooses down, and if B chooses down, A still chooses down). Thus, the two firms both move down-market. There is a better outcome for both players in the market (i.e. both move up-market and receive payoffs of 5 each) if the two firms can cooperate.

One of the problems of standard approaches to game theory is that they assume a certain level of knowledge by and about the players, including:

(i) the goals of the firm – the goal is reflected in the units in which the payoff is measured (for example, 1,1 may be the expected profits of A and B respectively, and the aim of each firm is to maximize its profit in the light of the competitor's possible choices);
(ii) alternative strategies – to raise or lower product quality (only one of which will be chosen);

Table 5.1 Payoff matrix for firms A and B

Firm A	Firm B	
	Move up-market	Move down-market
Move up-market	5,5	1,10
Move down-market	10,1	2,2

(iii) the outcomes (i.e. the precise payoff that accompanies any com-
       bination of strategies adopted by A and B), which may be in Nash
       equilibrium (i.e. where each firm cannot do better *given the strategy
       that its competitor has adopted*).

Thus, although, in some sense, game theory deals with risk (i.e. adopting
the 'right' or 'wrong' strategy), the treatment of imperfect information
and risk are generally very limited. This can be illustrated with a quote
from Dutta (1999, p. 20): 'A strategy is a blueprint for action; for every
decision node it tells the player how to choose'. Games with incomplete
information are significantly more difficult to specify, and it is not certain
that an equilibrium outcome will emerge (Weber, 1989). More complex
games have been studied, including 'multi-criteria strategic form games'
(as opposed to ordinary strategic form games), which appear to date back
at least to Blackwell (1956), in which there can be an arbitrary number of
criteria (types of payoff) for any given choice of strategies made by the
players involved – indeed, the set of outcomes for any given player comprises a range of payoffs that can be intrinsically non-comparable.

Repeated games (i.e. where the same game is replayed over a number
of periods) introduce the possibility of learning, policing and punishment,
which will influence the process of decision making and the decisions
taken. Thus, the game theoretic literature talks of the 'credible threats'
that one firm can make to another in order to influence the other firm's
behaviour. As a consequence, the decisions in repeated games may develop
forms of implicit cooperation between players, in which their choices
depend upon the degree of trust that has been established. Game theory
is particularly good at illustrating the costs and benefits of opportunistic
behaviour and, hence, in principle, may be able to identify situations
where transaction costs are likely to be sufficiently high to make production within the firm the optimal outcome.

The need to set the parameters of such games in order to investigate the
process of decision making has given rise to the area of experimental economics, an area on the boundary of economics and psychology (Loomes,
1991). Thus, work on bargaining outcomes, for example, shows that considerations other than profit – such as justice and fairness – are often
taken into account by decision makers (Roth, 1988; Thaler, 1988). As
a consequence, even if the higher-level goal is known, the strategy and
outcomes are not always those suggested by standard theory (Loomes,
1991, p. 610).

5.6.2 *Strategic management literature*

There is not space here to review the entirety of the vast, still growing and
fascinating literature on strategic management. Luckily Mintzberg *et al.*

Table 5.2 Strategic management: schools of thought

Name of school	Process of strategy formation
Design school	Strategy formation as a process of conception
Planning school	Strategy formation as a formal process
Positioning school	Strategy formation as an analytical process
Entrepreneurial school	Strategy formation as a visionary process
Cognitive school	Strategy formation as a mental process
Learning school	Strategy formation as an emergent process
Power school	Strategy formation as a process of negotiation
Cultural school	Strategy formation as a collective process
Environmental school	Strategy formation as a reactive process
Configuration school	Strategy formation as a process of transformation

Source: Mintzberg *et al*. (1998, p. 5).

(1998) have provided such a review and the present discussion draws a few concepts and ideas from their work. First, however, it is important to note the potential linkage of strategies with the game theoretic approach discussed above. The writings on military strategy go back at least as far as Sun Tzu's thesis *Art of War*, around the fourth century BC (Mintzberg *et al.*, 1998, p. 18). Military strategy gives a good feel for what is meant in an economic or management context – the *Concise Oxford Dictionary*, for example, defines strategy as the 'art of so moving or disposing troops or ships or aircraft as to impose upon the enemy the place and times and conditions for fighting preferred by oneself'. Its application to management appears to be traced back at least to the early 1960s; however, the strategic management literature is wider-ranging and more diverse than an application of game theory.

Mintzberg *et al.* (1998, p. 6) identify ten schools of thought, shown in Table 5.2. The first three are mainly prescriptive in nature – they indicate how strategies should be formulated. The next six consider the process of strategy formulation and describe strategies or how they are actually formulated (rather than how they should be formulated). The last school attempts to combine a number of the features of the other nine.

In addition to the conceptual game theoretic definition of strategy, many authors contributing to the broader strategic management literature also attempt to define what the term 'strategy' means. Mintzberg *et al.* (1998, p. 9) note that 'Most of the standard textbooks on strategy offer the definition … more or less as follows: top managements' plans to attain outcomes consistent with the organization's missions and goals'. Mintzberg *et al.* (1998, pp. 9–15) argue that, given the variety of approaches and schools of thought, there is no single definition. They propose five 'definitions', whereby strategy is a:

(i)   plan – when it is forward looking and sets out a series of actions to achieve the enterprise goals;
(ii)   pattern – when it is realized as consistency in behaviour that has emerged over time;
(iii) position – particularly when it is in relation to the location of products in particular markets;
(iv)   perspective – when it is inward and upward looking, and incorporates the ethos and thoughts of key managers in the light of the 'grand vision' of the enterprise;
(v)   ploy – when it involves the enterprise making credible threats in order to modify the behaviour of competitors (or suppliers or customers).

The authors then argue that strategies have the following effects. They:

(i)   set direction – 'charting the course of an organization';
(ii)   focus effort – providing the chosen route by which the enterprise's goals are to be achieved;
(iii) define the organization – providing a 'shorthand way to understand the organization and to distinguish it from others';
(iv)   provide consistency of thought and action – to reduce ambiguity and to increase consistency and order (Mintzberg *et al.*, 1998, pp. 15–18).

Each of these should be viewed as the 'net effects' of positive and negative influences on enterprise performance, often associated with the balance of the benefits and costs of continuity (and rigidity) with those of change (and flexibility). Insofar as strategies are ongoing and largely invariant (or only slowly evolving), they tend to become built into the organizational routines and structure (see Part V). This has some advantages because 'Even chief executives, most of the time, must get on with managing their organizations in a given context; they cannot constantly put the context into question' (Mintzberg *et al.*, 1998, p. 17). Changes, however, have a cost, as 'The very encouragement of strategy to get on with it – its very role in protecting people in the organization from distraction – impedes their capacity to respond to changes in the environment' (p. 18). It is clear that strategic management runs on a knife-edge of reinforcing existing strategies – to exploit an existing market position to the full – and developing new strategies reactively or proactively in the light of the changing market environment.

5.6.3 *Towards a strategic theory of the firm*

Phelan and Lewin (2000) argue that there is a need for a 'strategic theory of the firm'. They point to the criticisms by strategists of the 'economic theories' of the firm (i.e. those theories that have grown out of the transaction cost theories – see Chapter 2). In essence, the strategists argue that the existing 'economic theory' of the firm is largely static, in the sense that it views the firm as being in equilibrium (or in the process of equilibrating). In effect, the firm is seen as the most efficient structure in terms of current scale and scope for the delivery of the products and services that it produces. Chapter 2 has already argued that a more dynamic view of the optimal scale and scope of the enterprise is required, and there is now an emerging literature on 'strategic theories of the firm' (Foss, 1998), which dates back at least to Rumelt (1986) and is arguably traceable to Penrose (1959) (Phelan and Lewin, 2000, p. 312). The common elements to be found in the emerging strategic theory school are:

(i)   the resource-based nature of the firm;
(ii)   the focus on the determination of the boundaries of the firm;
(iii) the existence of bounded rationality.

Some flavour of the difference in focus of the emerging strategy theories is given by Demsetz (1997, p. 428):

> This creates a productive role for management where none exists in neo-classical theory. Imperfect information … makes the judgement of managers and owners a source of productivity enhancement. The main source of management's productivity in contemporary theory has been in its response to agency problems. Shirking, opportunism, and reputation are brought to the fore. This effort has led to the neglect of information problems that do not involve agency relationships. These are associated with planning in a world in which the future is highly uncertain, and they include problems of product choice, investment and marketing policies, and scope of operations. Neglect of this class of problems is unfortunate. (Quoted by Phelan and Lewin, 2000, p. 314)

Thus, a key area of dispute with the traditional 'economic theory of the firm' relates to the assumption that resources are put to their most efficient use when, in a world of imperfect information and uncertainty, this clearly is not the case. In addition, the focus on the firm as 'a tool for guarding shareholders from hold-up and opportunism' (Phelan and Lewin, 2000, p. 316) is myopic and misses a number of the key strategic issues faced by managers. On the other hand, most of the strategy literature has ignored the need to protect the firm from opportunism (Phelan and Lewin, 2000, p. 319).

Foss (1998) argues that the strategic theory of the firm has two essential propositions. First, firms exist because they are able to create specialist assets that cannot be created by the market (shareholder understanding, culture, reputation, identity, learning ability, tacit knowledge, etc.). Second, managers of firms have flexibility in the deployment of resources, without the need to negotiate with the market. However, the main focus of the strategic theory of the firm is on the methods of creating value. What is needed is some accommodation by both the economic and strategy schools, given that 'the most efficient economic organisation will be the one that best creates and protects value' (Phelan and Lewin, 2000, p. 319). Later in the book (Part IV in particular) it will be shown that other streams of economic research particularly stress the creation (and protection) process, and focus on such key strategic variables as product innovation and market promotion.

5.7   Goals, strategies and natural selection

The present section explores whether the market mechanism selects firms which maximize profit in preference to those with alternative goals. While, as we expect, the more profitable enterprises survive and the less profitable are taken over or go bankrupt, are the more profitable firms the ones that maximize profit?

5.7.1   *Goals and survival*

Evolutionary theory and its behavioural counterparts are unwilling to assume optimization of profit (or anything else). Nelson and Winter (1982, p. 8), for example, explicitly reject 'the assumption that economic actors are rational in the sense that they optimize'. The traditional response of economists is that this may not matter too greatly, as the market buys from the firms that offer the lowest quality-adjusted price – in other words, firms that charge a higher price for a given level of quality and firms that offer a lower level of quality at a given price lose customers to those that offer lower prices or higher-quality, respectively. Of course, the extent to which the market achieves this result depends crucially on how efficiently it operates. The costs of information search, the resulting degree of imperfect information, the bounded rationality of potential consumers and so on will all affect this result. Nevertheless, on balance, it would be anticipated that most markets will operate in this way, and the companies producing the highest-value products in this sense will generally have the highest discounted sum of future *economic* profit (which need not be the same as the discounted sum of future accounting profit). In addition, firms that fail to offer products of sufficiently high value will fail. Hodgson (1998, p. 42) argues that limited elements of modern evolutionary theory can be traced back to the argument by Alchian (1950) about the role of market forces in the selection process that determines which firms survive:

> Alchian saw the idea of evolutionary selection … more as an alternative to the assumption that individual firms are actually attempting to maximise their profits. Although individual behaviour cannot be predicted, evolutionary processes ensure that patterns of development can be observed in the aggregate.

Similar arguments were presented by Johansen (1972) in terms of the effect of markets on the range of observed production units that are economically viable. The whole range of evidence from product and factor demand functions supports the operation of prices in this selection process, although less work has been done on the role of quality.

However, this is quite different to saying, as Friedman (1953) hypothesized, that this market selection process will result in the survival of profit-maximizing firms and the demise of others. This was rejected by Winter (1964), who demonstrated that 'under plausible conditions the "natural selection" of profit maximisers would not work' (Hodgson, 1998, p. 43). The fact that product demand will tend to flow to the enterprise offering lower quality-adjusted prices (value for money at given income levels) has nothing at all to do with whether profit-maximizing firms (or in our case firms with a MV focus) will offer the best-value product. While it seems natural to suppose that firms that have a greater (dynamic) profit focus are more likely to generate higher profits than firms that adopt some other, quite different focus, there is no certainty that this will be the case. Thus, firms may have some arbitrary set of routines and rules that enable them to survive in the long run, even though there is no attempt to maximize profit. These established patterns and routines form the genotype (the genetic constitution of the firm), which is passed on from day to day and, potentially, from generation to generation.

5.7.2 Strategy and survival

This present section now demonstrates that firms can also adopt quite different strategies and survive, at least for long periods. Here a hedonic approach is adopted to compare the outcomes for:

(i)   a firm with an attribute-improvement strategy, which is moving to products and services of higher value added – competing through quality;

(ii) a firm with an efficiency-increasing (cost-reducing) strategy – competing via price.

This is simple to represent, where the market operates well, as the two firms need to offer a constant quality-adjusted price (see equation 5.1):

$$\frac{p_1}{p_1(Q)} = p_1(\bar{Q}) = \frac{p_2}{p_2(Q)} = p_2(\bar{Q}) \tag{5.1}$$

where the subscripts refer to firms 1 and 2, p_i denotes the nominal prices, $p_i(Q)$ denotes the element of price that reflects the level of quality, Q, and $p_i(\bar{Q})$ denotes the pure price element. It is immediately apparent that, if firm 1 raises its quality over time, it is possible for firm 2 to maintain this equality by reducing its costs and lowering p_2 (while keeping $p_2(Q)$ constant). Indeed, maintaining the equality simply requires firm 2 to reduce its nominal price at the same rate that firm 1 is able to increase the price that consumers are willing to pay for the higher quality. Thus, the two diametrically opposed strategies (quality and cost) can, in principle, result in the continued coexistence of the firms in the market.[15]

Subsequent chapters demonstrate that the choice for firms depends upon a wide variety of factors, including the degree of technological opportunity in the sector, and the internal capabilities of the firm with regard to R&D and innovation. The implications of the choice are not only extremely important for the firms involved, but also for the employees and for society as a whole (see Chapters 13 and 14). A 'down-market strategy' will generally involve pressure to maintain or lower factor prices (e.g. wages), shifting to lower-quality inputs (e.g. less skilled workers), and so on, while an 'up-market strategy' is likely to increase the skills and competences of the workforce.

5.8   Conclusions

The literature makes a useful distinction between the higher- and lower-level goals of the enterprise. It has been shown that these goals are largely distinct from the strategies adopted to achieve them. For example, a profit goal may be achieved by raising the quality of the product or reducing costs of production. The choice of strategy for any given goal will be premised on the characteristics of the manager or management team, and the nature and quality of the workforce. 'High-quality' strategies, for example, appear much more likely to arise in the case of high-quality employees, who are paid higher wages, than in enterprises with low-quality employees who are paid low wages.

The early discussion of the goals of the firm that developed in the economics and management literatures was rarely empirically based or empirically tested. For example, the managerial theories of the firm are largely theoretically rather than empirically driven. There have, however, been some attempts to test the behavioural models (and, more recently, the evolutionary models) using simulation techniques, with some comparisons of the outcomes with those found in the real world. The evolution of game theoretic approaches, even though they often tend to simplify the 'real world' nature of the choice of goals and of the strategic choices, help to highlight the absence of these issues in traditional economic approaches and have led to some interesting developments in experimental economics.

Even the SCP models of industrial economics, which are highly empirical in nature, never address the 'conduct' link explicitly, but concentrate on the link between structure and performance. What economists mean by conduct is a form of action or behaviour rather than a strategy. In the present chapter it is clear that the choice of these actions (i.e. the set of actions and behaviour chosen) is dependent not only on the goals of the firm, but also on the strategies adopted to achieve those goals. Even within the confines of what SCP models attempt to examine, the results are often weak and conflicting. In retrospect, the SCP models appear inherently flawed, as they focus on the industry rather than the firm, and in doing so omit the empirical modelling of strategic behaviour and the mechanisms for operationalizing the firm's strategy (R&D, NPL, advertising, training, process innovation, etc.). While each of these mechanisms is now the focus of empirical attention, as yet they have not been moulded into a coherent strategic theory of the firm, let alone tested in the context of such an over-arching strategic theory.

Despite the inherent weaknesses of managerial and industrial economics, the associated models highlight the agency and governance problems in professionally managed enterprises. Despite their often simplistic character, and their myopic adoption of optimizing behaviour based upon a single goal, the managerial models that are based on the maximization of sales revenue, growth or utility are able to demonstrate that profit maximization is a special case and not the general outcome. By implication, professional managers, left to their own devices, appear likely to behave in a manner that benefits themselves rather than the owners (often shareholders) of the enterprise. As a consequence, it is clear that incentives and penalties are required to align management interests more closely with those of shareholders. These issues are dealt with in Chapter 7.

The personal characteristics of managers may be important in driving goals and strategies. Relatedly, the qualifications of the managers and the workforce may be important determinants of the strategies adopted (see Chapter 6). Indeed, the remainder of the book develops the hypothesis that the strategies adopted are likely to be related to the competences of the enterprise – leading to the issue of low-skills trajectories for companies and low-skills equilibrium within the economy as a whole (see, in particular, Chapters 13 and 14). The underlying hypothesis regarding competences is that a low-skill base raises the stakes in the high-risk strategy of moving up-market (i.e. to products and services of improved quality, with higher value added) and makes it more likely such companies will choose a strategy of increasing efficiency and competing on grounds of price rather than quality. Some hint of the importance of skills and competences is given in the following quote:

> The challenge to ... firms is to develop the skills, products, services and technologies that customers are willing to pay for. A greater focus on high-quality segments and differentiation strategies will require ... firms to upgrade, and add to, their existing capabilities. (Crocombe, 1991)

The present chapter also highlights some of the practical issues of measuring goals and strategies:

(i)   while accepting that goals and strategies may be difficult to articulate in a wholly meaningful manner, it is clear that it is essential to do so (at least as a first approximation) in order to measure and understand enterprise performance;

(ii)   the goals and strategies of enterprises can be diverse and not always what standard economics textbooks suggest (the small-firms literature, in particular, throws light on this issue);

(iii)   the performance of the enterprise can be judged against the goals that it sets and against those perceived by society and articulated by the government;

(iv)   most of the empirical literature imposes some external benchmark of performance (e.g. productivity, profits or MV) rather than the goal that the enterprise sets for itself (Part IV investigates various strands of the literature, such as that on HPWPs and returns to R&D, that impose benchmarks and, by implication, set goals);

(v)   the diversity of enterprises themselves, with their different niches in the market, different resource bases and so on, makes it extremely difficult to say, for any particular enterprise, whether its strategy and the actions that it takes to operationalize that strategy are the most appropriate;

(vi)   the actual goals and strategies adopted will be affected by the managers themselves, their skills, competences and social capital.

This raises the possibility of latent skill deficiencies, particularly among managers – these deficiencies remain dormant until the firm attempts to or is forced to change in some way.

Notes

1   See http://www.mapnp.org/library/plan_dec/str_plan/strgzng.htm.
2   'Satisficing' implies that the outcome lies within bounds that are deemed to be satisfactory by the managers of the firm. These bounds are based upon aspiration levels that themselves may be raised (if the firm achieves a satisfactory outcome very easily) or lowered (if it proves difficult to achieve a satisfactory outcome).
3   See http://www.ethical.shares.green.net.au/.
4   See http://news.bbc.co.uk/1/hi/business/849475.stm.
5   This section updates some of the research reported by Bosworth and Jacobs (1989).
6   The direction of causality was always an issue – for a taxonomy of such models addressing this problem, see Bosworth (1983).
7   The incumbent lowers its price below the monopoly level, to exclude the new entrant, but the lower price still exceeds the level that would have prevailed after the entry of the new firm.
8   For an extensive discussion, see van Witteloostuijn (1990).
9   For reviews of this literature, see Wildsmith (1973) and Heidensohn and Robinson

(1974). See also Chapter 6, which discusses Penrose's model based upon manage-ment capacity.

10 For a brief review of this literature, see Heidensohn and Robinson (1974).

11 These two mechanisms are: (i) entrepreneur/owner manager or shareholder control; and (ii) the emergence of a 'consensual goal' of an organization that emerges through operation/practice or (small group) discussion.

12 The area of strategy and strategic management is both wide ranging and complex. For an extensive review, including Porter's work in this area, see Mintzberg *et al.* (1998).

13 For caveats about such a definition, see Mintzberg *et al.* (1998, pp. 9–15).

14 Dutta (1999, p. 195) defines a credible threat in the context of incumbents (players) facing the threat of entry by 'Coke': 'an anticipated choice in the post-entry phase is credible if, after Coke has entered the market, a player would have the payoff incentives to follow through and make precisely that choice'.

15 Of course, such a theory requires something to be said about income distribution and the sizes of the high-quality and low-price markets.

Chapter 6

Management qualities and core competences of the enterprise

6.1　Introduction

The present book attempts to place management back at the centre of the debate about the determinants of enterprise performance. Different organizational theories tend to give different degrees of scope for management choices; for example, structural contingency theory (see Part V) argues that the effect of the external environment is sufficiently strong to constrain severely the managers' degree of choice about organizational structures. However, while accepting that the external environment has a role in influencing, for example, the nature of the managers appointed and the decisions they take, the present chapter views managers as taking a much more central and proactive role. Even Donaldson (1996, p. 62) – a strong advocate of contingency theory – is willing to accept that the scope for such a role of managers is larger in smaller firms. In addition, the growth of more flexible organizational forms (which, it can be argued, itself has been contingent on changes in the environment) appears to offer management a significantly greater role.

The focus of the present chapter is on management competences and the way in which they affect performance. The characteristics and attributes of managers define the 'capacity' of particular individuals and the management team to take effective decisions that improve the likelihood of success of the enterprise. In particular, the literature has discussed the role of the CEO and the board of directors (BoD) in determining the performance of the enterprise. However, it is important to realize that management skills are not the sole domain of individuals employed in management occupations – everyone is involved in management activities of some kind and, thereby, exercises management skills (Bosworth, 2001).

The competences of the management team are viewed as being central; for one thing, their abilities are likely to determine the competences of other employees within the enterprise, as well as the efficiency with which these competences are used. Farmer and Richman (1964, p. 57) argue that:

> A country can have endless resources of all sorts but unless management is applied to these factors, the productivity of the system will be close to zero. Moreover, the better the management, the greater the output will be. Management effectiveness is the critical factor in the economic system.

Some care has to be taken with the term 'management'; in particular, it is important to make a distinction between the more general literature on management and that dealing with entrepreneurship and leadership. In the study of entrepreneurship and leadership, for example, disciplines such as psychology and sociology become extremely important. In addition, while the more general management literature tends to focus on all enterprises, the entrepreneurship literature tends to focus on small firms, indeed, often on new start-ups. However, while there may be differences in the activities and the degree of risk borne, entrepreneurial activity is likely to be important in large enterprises – this is sometimes referred to as 'intrepreneurship'. Indeed, when discussing 'management', the present chapter has something more in mind than the rather mechanistic, largely coordinating role of certain management jobs – as noted elsewhere (Bosworth, 2001), managers are viewed as being (to varying degrees) proactive, designing strategies, exhibiting leadership and undertaking entrepreneurial activities.

Section 6.2 begins with a discussion of the concept of managerial capacity, based on a model of the growth of the enterprise developed by Penrose (1959). Sections 6.3 and 6.4 then outline some of the survey results about the characteristics of managers and the linkages to enterprise performance. In particular, section 6.3 deals with management qualification levels, capacity and focus, while section 6.4 considers the discipline area of the qualifications held. While these results are interesting, they must be seen in the context of the period in which the surveys were undertaken – they are likely to be sensitive to changes in the importance of manufacturing, developments in the graduate labour market, and so on. Section 6.5 turns to the relatively separate literature on entrepreneurs and entrepreneurship. In doing so, it deals with the extremely important (and more broadly relevant) issue of social competences and social capital. Section 6.6 then briefly reviews the leadership literature. Finally, section 6.7 draws the main conclusions and discusses a number of strategic issues, such as the concept of latent management skill deficiencies.

6.2   Management capacity and firm performance: Penrose model

The discussion in Chapter 2 (section 2.6) began to sketch out a competence-based view of the firm. Not only did Penrose (1959) play an important role in developing this approach but she also emphasized the crucial role played by management capacity and competences. These management competences 'Typically ... have a social and organic quality, many depending on the shared experiences and interactions within the firm.' (Hodgson, 1998, p. 41). Penrose (1959, p. 52) argued that:

> When men [and women] have become used to working in a particular group of other men [and women], they become individually and as a group more valuable to the firm in that the services they can render are enhanced by the knowledge of their fellow-workers, of the methods of the firm, and [of] the best way of doing things in the particular set of circumstances in which they are working.

According to Hodgson (1998, p. 41):

> In sum, Penrose saw the firm as a complex and structured combination of competences and resources. Placing emphasis on organisation and managerial competences, Penrose saw the firm as undergoing a process of constrained but cumulative development.

Management 'capacity' has both 'volume' and 'quality' aspects. Thus, the main underlying principle of the Penrose theory is that the growth of the firm is limited by the capacity of management and, in particular, more rapid growth (eventually) requires the recruitment of more managers (or the improvement in the quality of existing managers), while the recruitment of *new* managers (or the upgrading of existing managers' skills) reduces the capacity of *existing* managers to manage effectively in the short term. In the Penrose model, it is assumed that firms are profit maximizers, but that this is entirely consistent with growth maximization, as long as all projects undertaken are profitable (Hay and Morris, 1979, p. 300). There in fact are various views that suggest managers might want to push the rate of growth or the size of the enterprise above the level where the rate of profit is maximized (see Marris, 1964, and the 'agency view' of the loss of control by the owners – Chapter 7). For example, there is always an incentive to grow further as there is ever-present spare capacity (i.e. unused productive services) in some resources, for instance because of indivisibilities of key assets that, at current production levels, are underused. Thus, there may be no upper limit to the absolute size of the enterprise, at least for a considerable distance above the firm's existing scale. There is, however, a constraint on the rate of growth of the enterprise, which arises from the number and quality of existing managers.

Figure 6.1 shows the basic form of the model (Hay and Morris, 1979, p. 302). The curve represented by AA shows the *potential* management growth–firm growth relationship. It is curve only of *potential* growth because it shows what would happen to the growth of the firm if all the managers could devote their time to management of production operations. In other words, AA would be achieved if the recruitment of new

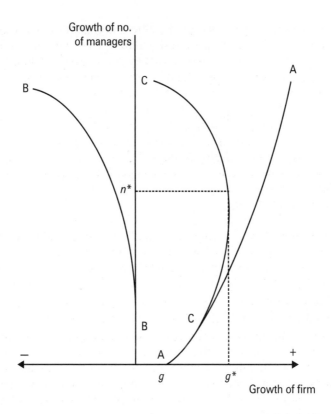

Figure 6.1 Penrose's theory of the limits to growth of the firm. Source: Hay and Morris (1979, p. 302).

managers had no adverse effects on productivity. AA starts at g, which indicates that some growth is possible with no increase in managers.[1] This can occur because existing managers have built up an expertise over time that releases some of their capacity for expansion. The curve AA becomes steeper the greater the growth in the number of managers. This is because there are diminishing returns to the appointment of additional managers, for example, because:

(i)　greater search for new management recruits is disproportionately more costly;
(ii)　the highest-quality managers are appointed first and the quality of the remaining pool falls as more managers are recruited;
(iii)　existing management capacity available for training per new recruit in any given period falls the larger is the number of recruits.

The curve BB makes it clear why AA represents only *potential* and not realizable outcomes. BB reflects the declining productivity of existing managers in current production activities: the greater the number of recruits, the more time they need to spend in the recruitment, assimilation and training process, and the less time they devote to production. Finally, CC shows the net result of these two effects. At low rates of growth in the number of managers, the effects of the new managers on growth more than offset the declining productivity of existing managers. At high rates of growth in the number of managers, however, the new managers take so much of the existing managers' time that growth falls. It can be seen that g^* is the maximum rate of growth possible.

While growth by merger or takeover appears to be an attractive option that might relax the managerial constraint, as the managerial services are already available in the target firm, there are also difficulties with this strategy. Takeovers themselves often involve problems, not least to do with differences in company ethos and culture. In addition, the brief discussion in Chapter 2 demonstrates that the empirical results suggest that post-merger/takeover performance is often weaker than that previously. Note also the link between the Penrose model and the issue of focus outlined in Chapter 2.

According to Hay and Morris (1979, p. 303):

> Penrose's work raises very significant problems for the theory of the firm. On the one hand her analysis is unrigorous yet complex. It focuses on variables which are not only relatively new to the theory of the firm, but difficult to quantify or even to formulate properly. Yet at the same time it suggests that the growth of the firm is determined by these variables and largely independent of the usual economic variables.

Nevertheless, Penrose's perspective is important to the present book because of its focus on management and the central role that managers play. In addition, there is some early empirical evidence in support of the so-called 'Penrose effect' (management capacity as a constraint on and determinant of firm growth). One final comment about the model concerns the implication that managers train new managers. If this is so, there is a real danger, where existing managers either are of low quality or do not carry out the training process properly (e.g. because of time constraints), that induction and training processes will be a way of passing on 'bad habits' from one generation of managers to another (see Chapter 13).

6.3   Selected empirical results

6.3.1   *Management qualifications and skills*

The author has been involved in exploring a wide range of evidence about the numbers, qualifications and skills of UK managers, as well as the management skill deficiencies of managers and other occupational groups (Bosworth, 1999; Bosworth and Wilson, 2004; Bosworth *et al.*, 1992). While a large number of datasets were interrogated, the Employers' Skill Survey, 1999, was a particularly useful and relatively recent source. The results provide information about imbalances in the numbers of managers supplied and demanded – the 'numbers problem'. The evidence does not suggest that there is a current numbers problem – the levels of vacancies are in line with other those for other occupations and there is a low incidence of hard-to-fill vacancies. However, the studies suggest that, taken across the board, this may be traced to the low levels of minimum qualification levels set for managers in the UK. This is a major point of contention in the research, with potentially major implications for the quality of management and enterprise performance (see Chapter 13). Bosworth *et al.* (1992) argue that, if managers were asked, for example, to have identical (or more similar) qualifications to professional occupations, the proportion of enterprises reporting hard-to-fill management vacancies would increase significantly.

Bearing in mind the relatively small 'numbers imbalance', there is the issue of the nature of the skills missing among individuals being recruited to management positions. Bosworth *et al.* (1992) indicate that only a relatively small proportion of those in managerial occupations in the UK hold a high-level formal qualification of any kind, a situation which does not compare favourably with that in many other industrialized countries.[2] In 1989, according to the Labour Force Survey, less than 27 per cent of corporate managers and administrators had a degree or equivalent professional qualification, while the figure for managers and proprietors in small businesses in services and agriculture was below 9 per cent (Elias, 1992).[3] Further confirmation for more recent years can be found in Bosworth (1999). A range of skills is required of managers and, while 'management skills' are the most frequently cited as being missing or difficult to obtain among recruits, they are by no means the only skills. In addition, although the present discussion persists with the argument that management qualifications should be brought more in line with professional qualifications, it is clear that the skills problems among managers are different to those of professional occupations. This has important implications not only for the nature of the education and training packages put together for managers, but also for professionals or other occupations if individuals located there are eventually going to move into management. The exploration of management skill deficiencies clearly shows that these problems are not restricted to those in management occupations – about 55 per cent of the problem lies in the lack of management skills in other occupational groups (e.g. professional and semi-professional occupations). Again, however, it is important to note that the nature or the level of management skills required in other occupations may be different to those needed in management posts.

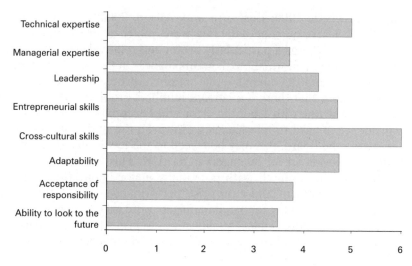

Figure 6.2 Overall rank score (1 = most important, 8 = least important) of eight management abilities by business executives (*n* = 502). Source: Savery *et al.* (1994).

6.3.2 *Which management skills?*

A study of the views of 502 Asian business executives (from Singapore, Malaysia, Indonesia, Taiwan and Japan) explored the relative importance of eight 'managerial qualities' (Savery *et al.*, 1994). Their relative importance was ranked by the respondents on a scale from 1 = most to 8 = least important (Figure 6.2). The results reflect the international context of the survey, insofar as it involved the managers of large trading and producing companies in several Asian–Pacific countries.

The survey went on to carry out a peer-group review of the perceived quality of managers in six different countries – Australia, Germany, Japan, Taiwan, the UK and the USA. Two figures are reported:

(i)   the percentage of respondents who ranked managers of the country in question as being 'best' of the six (shown by the percentage columns in Table 6.1);

(ii) the mean ranking (1 = best and 6 = worst) for managers of each country.

Table 6.1 sets out the main results by each management skill evaluated. UK managers were perceived to be poorer than their Japanese and USA counterparts in every type of skill. They scored particularly poorly in terms of their adaptability, entrepreneurial and technical skills, as well as their ability to look well into the future. Japanese managers were ranked as being the best overall, followed by US managers.

Table 6.1 Management quality by country

Management quality	Australia		Germany		Japan		Taiwan		UK		USA	
	%	Mean	%	Mean	%	Mean	%	Mean	%	Mean	%	Mean
Ability to look into future	2	4.7	11	3.4	47	2.1	6	4.4	4	3.9	30	2.5
Acceptance of responsibility	1	4.6	13	3.1	57	2.0	3	4.7	8	3.6	18	3.0
Adaptability skills	4	4.1	7	3.9	43	2.5	16	3.6	3	4.1	27	2.8
Cross-cultural skills	11	3.8	7	4.0	28	3.1	14	3.7	6	3.7	34	2.6
Entrepreneurial skills	1	4.8	8	3.7	44	2.3	16	3.4	4	4.1	28	2.6
Leadership skills	2	4.6	11	3.4	30	2.7	2	4.8	7	3.4	48	2.1
Management skills	1	4.7	12	3.3	40	2.3	2	4.9	9	3.4	37	2.2
Technical skills	1	5.0	21	2.7	56	1.8	2	4.6	2	4.0	18	2.8
Average value	3	4.5	11	3.4	43	2.4	7	4.3	5	3.8	30	2.6

Notes: % = percentage of respondents who ranked managers of countries as the best in each quality; mean = mean ranking of country (1 = best, 6 = worst).
Source: Savery *et al.* (1994).

The International Institute for Management Development (IMD) reports executives' perceptions of management quality in its *World Competitiveness Yearbook*. This survey paints a somewhat different picture of the relative international quality of managers, with Germany and the USA the highest ranked of the G7 countries in 1999/2000, and Japan the lowest ranked. One common feature, however, was the relatively low ranking of the UK. The Department of Trade and Industry (2001, p. 36) concluded that 'the UK is performing behind most of its main competitors'. A comparison of the data for 1996/97 with that for 1999/2000 suggests that the scores can change over time, which may help to explain some of the differences between the IMD work and that of Savery *et al*. (1994).

6.3.3 *Management capacity, innovation and growth*

Richardson (1964) summarized the factors limiting firm growth, based on evidence obtained from a number of managers. He reported that none of the managers felt restricted by shortages of factor inputs such as labour, materials or equipment. While two firms reported being restrained by a shortage of finance, both were small and were subsequently taken over. Another firm reported a lack of suitable investment opportunities, but this firm was setting high rates of return for potential projects. Richardson indicated that by far the most important factor restraining expansion was the lack of 'suitable' management – most of the firms in his survey highlighted the management problem 'without hesitation'. Resolving the management constraint is made more complex by the existence of management hierarchies, where individual managers need to build up expertise before being promoted.

Richardson argued that the managerial constraint would be more readily recognized by more energetic managers, who were setting higher aspiration levels for their firm. This latter finding has been shown in much more extensive and recent data for UK enterprises (Bosworth *et al*., 2001). One of the key findings of the Employers' Skill Survey was that firms that attempt to 'do more' generally have greater skills and competences problems, including those of management. Firms that set higher aspiration levels and that attempt to move 'up-market', innovate and grow are more likely to report skill problems. This result appears to be broadly consistent with Penrose's model and with the concept of latent skill shortages, and turns out to be a common finding in the present book (see Chapters 9, 13 and 14).

Shen (1970) argues that the realization of economies of scale, higher profit levels and a reduction in the price of capital relative to that of labour would tend to sustain growth. Using econometric methods, he verified this empirically, but, in the longer term, he found that, overall, growth tended to reverse in subsequent periods. In other words, plants that initially exhibit high growth rates subsequently tend to show lower growth rates. He interpreted this reversal as a result of 'Penrose effects', associated with the capacity of management. These effects allowed initially slower-growing firms to catch up with those enterprises that were initially faster growing.

6.4 Disciplines and backgrounds of managers

6.4.1 *Background to this literature*

There has been considerable interest in the literature concerning the 'ideal' background of managers, including their education and training. One part of this literature deals with the general level of qualifications of managers and the possible implications of this for company performance. For example, if top managers are unqualified two key questions arise:

(i)   Do they have the technical skills that equip them for decision making?
(ii) Does their lack of qualifications put them off employing suitably qualified managers and other workers to advise them?

A second strand of the literature stemmed from the decline in British manufacturing industry, which was argued to be associated with the lack of engineers and the undervaluation of engineering skills. This debate evolved in a way that emphasized the need to employ engineers in managerial tasks (Finniston, 1980). The lack of managers with this kind of background appeared of more importance at the time, given the greater size of the manufacturing sector in those days and the fact that individuals with science and engineering qualifications played a much greater role in management in France, Germany and Japan.

The present discussion has a somewhat broader focus, on the emerging literature concerning whether the characteristics, skills and qualifications of managers influence company performance. In order to do so, this section explores why companies decide to employ:

(i)   graduates rather than non-graduates;
(ii) graduates with different discipline backgrounds.

In addition, evidence is provided that the discipline (and other) backgrounds of managers can influence the goals adopted by companies and, thereby, performance. Finally, the discussion considers the direct evidence that the employment of different types of individuals, especially managers, affects company performance.

6.4.2 *Graduate recruitment and management*

While significant amounts of information can be found about graduate supply, less is known about the rationale that lies behind the graduate/

non-graduate decision of employers.[4] The main issue pursued here concerns the reasons for the employment of graduates. In other words, given that graduates are, on balance, more costly than non-graduates, what (additional) skills and competences do they offer that make it worthwhile for a firm to pay a premium for their services? In addition, what relationship does graduate recruitment have to management activities?

A major survey undertaken in 1988 was among the first to throw light on the factors influencing the demand for graduates in the UK (Rigg *et al.*, 1990). It revealed important differences in the extent of graduate recruitment by both sector and size of firm. At that time, for example, certain parts of the production sector, especially those towards the higher-technology end of the spectrum (such as engineering), and business and financial services were the main recruiters of graduates. In contrast, service industries, such as distribution, hotels, catering and transport, recruited much smaller proportions of graduates. Company size was also very important, with only 3 per cent of firms with under 200 employees recruiting graduates, compared with 61 per cent of firms with over 1,000 employees. Large firms were also more likely to be established recruiters and to plan their recruitment well in advance.

The decision of whether to recruit graduates rather than non-graduates was most heavily driven by business expansion/reorganization (60 per cent of respondents recruiting graduates reported this reason). In particular, the survey revealed the important positive effect on graduate employment of organizational changes, such as major diversification, financial restructuring or investment in computers or information technology (IT). In manufacturing industries, however, the importance attached to business expansion/reorganization was much lower, with correspondingly higher responses elsewhere. Technological change was specifically mentioned as the prime reason in only 8 per cent of cases. However, a general upgrading of staff and an explicit decision to recruit graduates for managerial roles was reported by 20 per cent and 12 per cent of respondents, respectively. These results can therefore be seen as generally supporting the idea that companies, at that time at least, were becoming increasingly aware of the need to place highly qualified persons in posts where long-term strategic changes were under way, but this study also revealed increased attention, in many companies, to the need to secure management succession. Thus, the employment of graduates appears likely to be strongly linked with many of the dynamic activities discussed in Part IV and the changes in organizational structure outlined in Part V of the present book.

A further interesting piece of evidence from the survey by Rigg *et al.* (1990) concerns the planning horizons of employers in the private sector. The results indicated that there was a clear link between the employment of graduates and the length of the planning horizon (although the direction of cause and effect is not entirely clear). Consistent with this,

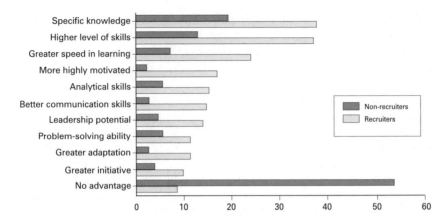

Figure 6.3 Recruiter and non-recruiter views of graduate advantages: percentage of survey respondents. Source: Rigg *et al*. (1990).

employers appear to find that graduates take much longer to be effective than other types of recruit and are prepared to allow more initial training to gain the full benefits. According to Rigg *et al*. (1990), in private sector firms, new graduates took an average of one working year to become fully effective. They received, on average, eighteen days of training in this first year, but larger firms provided almost twice as much training as small ones. These findings again appear to confirm that many firms recruit new graduates as a long-term investment rather than as high-quality staff who simply make a larger marginal contribution to the current level of output. Recruiters of graduates perceive a number of advantages other than the specific level of knowledge that graduates possess, many of which can be seen as linked to the ability to deal with change and to take initiatives (see Figure 6.3).

6.4.3 *Managers' backgrounds and qualifications*

Given differences not only in recruitment but also in the progress of individuals up the management hierarchy, it can be imagined that top managers will be heterogeneous in their background characteristics. Table 6.2 sets out the results from the Bosworth *et al*. (1992) survey with regard to the backgrounds of managing directors/CEOs within their sample of just over 700 UK companies, across all business sectors. There are issues about the dynamic nature of the stock of managers observed at any point in time, but the important feature is the diversity of backgrounds and characteristics, which may have a bearing on the goals set (and thereby performance), as well as company success in attaining these goals.

Table 6.2 Backgrounds of managing directors, by sector (column percentages)

Managing directors holding a formal qualification in:	Industry				
	Primary and transport	Other manufac- turing	Services	Engineering	All
Sciences	5.7	3.7	3.9	2.7	3.5
Engineering, technology	24.5	7.3	9.7	32.8	21.0
Social sciences	24.5	18.2	29.1	18.8	22.1
Arts	4.7	17.1	10.2	5.5	7.9
Self-made	27.4	23.2	25.2	15.0	20.4
Unknown	13.2	30.5	21.8	25.3	22.3

Source: Bosworth *et al.* (1992).

While too much should not be read into Table 6.2, it helps illustrate the considerable diversity of individuals who comprise the key strategic decision-making units of the firm. The results of the survey by Bosworth *et al.* (1992) also illustrated the diversity of goals and the possible linkages between the goals and the composition of the BoD (Table 6.3). Whether a graduate is on the board or not gives rise to interesting differences in the goals adopted. Using the revised percentages given in parentheses, the main differences are that the presence of graduates makes it much more likely that the firm has a formal goal and, where there is a goal, more likely to adopt a growth-maximizing goal than the presence of their non-graduate counterparts.

6.4.4 *Qualifications, background and company performance*

Donaldson (1996, p. 62) outlines a number of mainly US studies which argue that management characteristics influence organizational structure (although Donaldson's own view is that causality is more likely to run in the opposite direction). For example, there is evidence that the functional background of the CEO affects structure (Fligstein, 1985), although the choice of the CEO is itself influenced by the organizational structure and the corporate strategy (Fligstein, 1987). In addition, the 'actor-level' theories of Child (1972a, 1972b, 1973) see a role for managers in shaping the environment in which they operate. Child (1973) argues that the degree of bureaucratic formalization is influenced by the degree of specialization and qualifications among the administrative staff. The discussion returns to organizational structure in Chapters 11 and 12, while the present chapter concentrates on the evidence about the qualifications and background of managers and company performance. In practice, there

Table 6.3 Structure of board, background of managing director and company goals (percentages of total number of companies)

	Company goals[a]						
	Maximize market share	Maximize growth	Maximize sales/output	Maximize profit	Other	No goal	Number of companies
Technical background							
On board	29 (23)	24 (14)	19 (15)	28 (22)	13 (10)	15 (12)	466
None on board	28 (23)	22 (18)	18 (15)	23 (19)	9 (7)	21 (17)	240
Graduates							
On board	32 (24)	28 (21)	18 (14)	27 (20)	14 (11)	14 (11)	428
None on board	24 (21)	16 (14)	20 (17)	24 (21)	9 (8)	22 (19)	278
Professional scientists and engineers							
On board	31 (23)	27 (20)	18 (13)	26 (19)	19 (14)	16 (12)	309
None on board	27 (23)	21 (18)	19 (16)	26 (22)	9 (8)	18 (15)	397
Background of managing director							
Engineering and technology	28 (22)	30 (23)	22 (17)	28 (22)	10 (8)	11 (9)	148
Business and finance	36 (26)	31 (22)	17 (12)	31 (22)	8 (8)	17 (12)	131
Self-made	23 (22)	15 (14)	14 (13)	21 (20)	10 (6)	22 (21)	144

[a] Note that percentages sum to more than 100 because companies can have more than one goal; percentages that sum to 100 are given in parentheses.
Source: Bosworth *et al.* (1992).

appear to be relatively few quantitative studies that relate the performance of British companies to their managers' qualifications (see Barry *et
al.*, 1997; Bosworth *et al.*, 1992; Wood, 1992). The present section concentrates on two that extensively explored the sample of UK companies
outlined in section 6.4.3.

Bosworth et al. *(1992)*
Bosworth *et al.* (1992) studied 706 companies across all business sectors.
The authors related the qualifications of each company's board members –
executives plus non-executives – to a range of non-quantitative indicators
of its success, having controlled for other factors (such as the qualifications of the workforce). The study therefore examined the relationships
between graduate employment, as well as the employment of professional
scientists and engineers (PSEs), and various dimensions of firm performance, including:

(i)   R&D and innovation measures (see Bosworth, 1996, and Chapter
       8);
(ii)   overall firm performance measures, such as growth in market share,
       growth in profit and growth in turnover.

There was tentative evidence of a number of important links between
employment of graduates at board level and broader measures of firm
performance. First, the presence of graduates improved general economic
performance. Second, there appeared to be an optimal proportion of
graduates (and PSEs) on the BoD that was less than 100 per cent. Third,
the ratio of PSEs to other disciplines, and graduates to individuals with
a technical background, had different effects on the goals adopted, in
particular on market share *vis-à-vis* profits and turnover. Fourth, there
was an indirect linkage between the background of board members and
firm performance, via company goals. However, an important result of the
analysis was that there was little evidence that the presence of PSEs as
opposed to other types of graduates was especially beneficial to company
performance. In other words, the differential impact of graduates on
company performance (i.e. *vis-à-vis* a non-graduate workforce) was much
more clear-cut than the differential performance that could be attributed
to the employment of PSEs rather than graduates from other discipline
areas. In fact, the authors concluded that the two groups (PSEs and other
types of graduates) were likely to prove to be fairly close substitutes, a
finding broadly consistent with the survey results of Rigg *et al.* (1990).

Using the same data-set, Bosworth (1996) showed that if a company
undertook R&D it had a higher probability of adopting advanced technologies, irrespective of their source. More importantly still, from the present
perspective, it was shown that there was a closer association between R&D
and innovation in companies in which the R&D department employed

graduates. In addition, firms that utilized these advanced technologies tended to outperform non-users in a number of respects. In particular, they worked closer to full capacity but, as a consequence, tended to experience more acute skill shortages – again, a result suggesting that better-performing firms are likely to have greater problems. Nevertheless, the evidence suggests that they tend to have higher growth in turnover, profits and market share.

Barry et al. *(1997)*
Barry *et al*. (1997) constructed longitudinal information about a sub-set of the companies from the sample studied by Bosworth *et al*. (1992). They traced 263 of the original manufacturing companies over the five-year period from 1990 to 1995. The authors adopted some of the measures used by Bosworth *et al*. (e.g. whether the company undertook R&D and whether it had adopted advanced technologies) and some new measures of performance (e.g. survival of the company and EVA – see Chapter 3). In addition, rather than the somewhat more nebulous interest in the company BoD, that study focused primarily on the qualifications and background of the CEO/top executive (TE). It linked the various measures of performance to the CEO's/TE's qualifications and background. The authors concluded that:

> Within British owned manufacturing industry it is clearly beneficial to have a qualified TE. In no part of the investigation does the unqualified TE have an advantage. In every observation but one, companies with unqualified TEs come last. The performance gap between the unqualified and the qualified is so stark that this factor alone may go a long way to explain the poor performance of British industry when compared with American, French or German industry.... The fact that companies headed by qualified TEs tend to outperform those with unqualified TEs is not too surprising. What is a surprise to us is the starkness of the latter's underperformance. (p. 57)

In addition, the study gave a more considered view of the effect of the backgrounds of the CEOs/TEs:

> When we look at the British TEs who are qualified, it is difficult to escape the conclusion that companies headed by TEs with non-technical qualifications – particularly accounting – outperform companies with TEs who are qualified engineers or scientists.... What also comes as a surprise is the extent to which companies headed by TEs who are accountants and non-technical graduates outperform those headed by QSETs [qualified scientists, engineers and technologists]. This is puzzling, and frankly quite contrary to our initial expectations. (p. 57)

The authors go on to speculate about what might explain this result.

6.5   **Entrepreneurs and entrepreneurship**

6.5.1 *Nature of the literature*

Most of this literature focuses on new ventures and, hence, relates mainly to a sub-set of small firms. There are relatively few large-scale surveys and accompanying econometric work, but there is a large case study literature. The present section proceeds by summarizing the findings of a number of reviews of this literature.

6.5.2 *Definition and role of the entrepreneur*

Most students of economics are taught that there are four factors of production: land, labour, capital and entrepreneurship (Casson, 1982). In essence, it is the enterpreneur who organizes production and takes the risks of an enterprise (Knight, 1921). The concept of entrepreneurship can be traced back at least to Richard Cantillon (1680–1734) (Wennekers *et al.*, 1999, pp. 17–18). The term literally means the 'undertaker', in the sense of a person who buys at a fixed price and sells at an uncertain price (Rutherford, 1992, p. 150). As discussed below, different economists place somewhat different emphases on the characteristics of entrepreneurs with regard to their capacity for and involvement in risk bearing, organizing production, innovating and decision making in situations of imperfect information.

Taking a historical perspective, Wennekers *et al.* (1999, p. 17) identify at least thirteen distinct roles for the entrepreneur in the economics literature, as the:

(i)   person who assumes the risk;
(ii)   supplier of financial capital;
(iii)   innovator;
(iv)   decision maker;
(v)   industrial leader;
(vi)   manager;
(vii)   organizer and coordinator;
(viii) owner of an enterprise;
(ix)   employer of factors of production;
(x)   contractor;
(xi)   arbitrageur;
(xii)   allocator of resources among alternative uses;
(xiii) person who starts a new business.

From the diversity here and in both the conceptual and empirical literatures, entrepreneurship is clearly bound up with broad cultural and psychological issues.

Historically, entrepreneurs were viewed as individuals in the sense that they risked their capital in founding their own businesses. In more recent years, it has been recognized that managers in larger companies require entrepreneurial skills, as many present-day firms are run by energetic men and women who bear risks and coordinate resources. In the large public company, however, the BoD and the senior executives who take the major decisions do not necessarily bear the risk (or at least not the same risk) – insofar as there is a separation of ownership and control, such managers do not necessarily venture their capital in the business. On the other hand, such managers still undertake an entrepreneurial function insofar as they are involved in coordinating the flow of resources to produce and sell an output, they are concerned with decisions that establish and change the direction of the firm, and they deal with risks in organizing production. While the risks for the manager may be different to those of a shareholder, there may still be financial penalties for wrong decisions, including termination of contract, and today many also hold shares in the company.

Wennekers *et al.* (1999, pp. 55–56) distinguish between different 'types' of entrepreneurs (see Table 6.4). The true entrepreneurs are represented in the first row, and can be either self-employed or employees of companies. The so-called 'managerial' entrepreneurs and executive managers are not 'true' entrepreneurs. While they fulfil important roles:

> they cannot be viewed as the engine of innovation and growth, which to our opinion is the major function of the Schumpeterian entrepreneurs and intrepreneurs. Nor can they be viewed as the 'persona causa' of perception and creation, who is the 'prime mover' in the process of entrepreneurial energy and entrepreneurial behaviour. (Wennekers *et al.*, 1999, p. 56)

By implication, counts of the self-employed or, indeed, of business start-ups (see Department of Trade and Industry, 2000, p. 50) have limited use in determining the number of entrepreneurs.

Adam Smith (1776) took up the idea of the 'self-interest', in the form of the 'profit-seeking' business person. Joan Robinson's work on growth theory adopted the concept of 'animal spirits' to explain investment, which she viewed as a readiness to take risks, and argued that this was more important than the profit calculations in investment decisions (see

Table 6.4 Types of entrepreneur

	Self-employed	Employee
Entrepreneurial	Schumpeterian entrepreneurs (in both large and small firms)	'Intrepreneurs'
Managerial	Entrepreneurs in a formal sense (franchise entrepreneurs, shop-keepers and professional occupations)	Executive managers

Source: Wennekers *et al.* (1999, pp. 55–56).

Gill, 1974, pp. 64–65). Entrepreneurship is most generally used today to describe the high-risk activities to do with the dynamic growth of the firm and the economy; it was long ago recognized in this way by Alfred Marshall (1842–1924), who described entrepreneurs as 'pioneers of new paths' (see Wennekers *et al.*, 1999, p. 17). This is not too distinct from the 'self-interest' described by Adam Smith, but tends to emphasize the role of entrepreneurs in new business start-ups (small firms) and in innovation (Schumpeter, 1947) – both of which have been major foci of interest in recent years. Thus, a distinction can be made between these two entre-preneurial activities: as the business founder, 'Someone who creates and then, perhaps, organizes and operates a new business firm, whether or not there is anything innovative in those acts' (Herbert and Link, 1982); and as the innovator, 'as the one who transforms inventions and ideas into economically viable entities, whether or not in the course of doing so they create or operate a firm' (Baumol, 1993, p. 198).

6.5.3   *Entrepreneurs, dynamic competition and market outcomes*

Entrepreneurs are viewed as the principal source of dynamic competi-tion, but not the perfect competition of microeconomics texts or some desirable economic state. As quoted in Chapter 1, Robinson (1997, p. 6) argues that:

> the long-run equilibrium of perfect competition is not an appropriate policy target because it does not represent competition at all but an end-state in which competition has been exhausted. The market is at rest whereas the essence of competition is disequilibrium characterised by continuous change.

Thus, entrepreneurship lies at the heart of the competitive process, as 'It is only when entrepreneurship is introduced that we begin to appreciate how and why markets work' (Kirzner, 1997, p. 39). The role of entrepre-neurs is:

> [to] drive markets by searching for, discovering and exploiting profitable oppor-tunities which had not previously been seized. Entrepreneurial discovery is at the centre of the real-world market process. Knowledge is neither perfect nor is it available from some central pool which can be tapped: it is naturally dispersed and is uncovered by entrepreneurs competing with one another to find better ways of satisfying consumers. (Robinson, 1997, p. 6)

Hence, following Schumpeter, it can be seen that entrepreneurial discovery need not simply be in terms of some price anomaly that can be exploited for profit: it can equally be some potential quality anomaly – the discovery of some better product or process that creates an asymmetry of information (Metcalf, 1995, pp. 412–413) and, thereby, commercial advantage. In this way, market research, R&D and other discretionary investments are the tools entrepreneurs use to locate and to exploit these opportunities.

6.5.4 *Entrepreneurship and performance: indirect evidence*

According to Wennekers *et al.* (1999), the evidence to support the role of entrepreneurship in growth is primarily indirect. The nature of the indirect evidence can be found in the writings of Smith and Schumpeter. In the case of Smith, for example, it is the principle that underpins his concept of the 'invisible hand':

> Every individual is continually exerting himself to find out the most advantageous employment for whatever capital he can command. It is his own advantage, indeed, and not that of the society, which he has in view. But the study of his own advantage naturally, or rather necessarily leads him to prefer that employment which is most advantageous to society. (Smith, 1776, reprinted in Gill, 1974, p. 31)

Smith's analysis is essentially 'static' in the sense that individuals search for high-profit niches to enter, but as individuals flow into those niches, abnormal profits are forced down to normal levels, at which further entry ceases.

Schumpeter gives this a somewhat more dynamic context. Schumpeter is interested in the role of product and process innovation. These act as an important shock, which drives business investment, as the innovation creates new market niches that are potentially profitable. However, as these new lines of business and methods of production are associated with a high level of uncertainty, then the innovators require special qualities of 'character and leadership' (including the willingness to take risks) – those of 'creative entrepreneurs' (Gill, 1974, p. 219). A more 'Smith-like' process then follows, as other business men and women 'follow in a swarm, introducing their new methods and business combinations' (Gill, 1974, p. 219). Where the initial innovation is sufficiently radical, the result can be a Kondratieff cycle or long wave (Schumpeter, 1947, p. 230).

6.5.5 *Cultural conditions for entrepreneurship and growth*

Having reviewed the long-term historical evidence regarding the sources of growth, Wennekers *et al.* (1999, p. 38) state that:

> In summarising the literature at hand, we hypothesise that the following dimensions of culture are underlying causes of economic growth: open-mindedness towards other cultures; curiosity, creativity and experimentation; perseverance; valuation of wealth and savings; acceptance of risk and failure; competitiveness.

Wennekers *et al.* (1999, p. 39) go on to argue that:

> Culture and the legal or institutional framework together make up the entrepreneurial climate. This entrepreneurial climate should not be viewed in an isolated manner. Open-mindedness for instance can be conducive for both

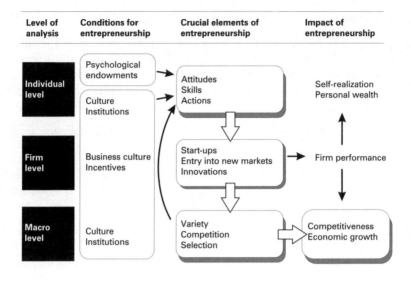

Figure 6.4 Linking entrepreneurship to economic growth. Source: Wennekers *et al.* (1999, p. 39).

entrepreneurship and a more general cultural vitality, which often go hand in hand. The same complementarity holds for innovation and invention.… These relationships between entrepreneurial climate, cultural vitality, entrepreneurship and economic growth are illustrated in Figure [6.4].

This view is consistent with that of Porter (1990, p. 125), who argues that 'Invention and entrepreneurship are at the heart of national advantage' (see also Chapters 13 and 14).

The GEM 'entrepreneurship index' suggests the existence of more favourable attitudes to entrepreneurship in the USA than in the UK.[5] The available indices also suggest that the UK may have less favourable attitudes than the rest of Western Europe. Such indicators give some feel for the extent to which society is supportive of entrepreneurs and their activities, which will determine the proportion of individuals prepared to take risks in business. While it is difficult to draw hard-and-fast conclusions, based upon this information, the Department of Trade and Industry (2000, p. 50) concluded that 'it does not appear that the UK has achieved "best practice" in terms of attitudes to entrepreneurship in society'.

6.5.6 *Entrepreneurial traits, social competences and social capital*

The discussion now turns to the characteristics of entrepreneurs that are thought to influence their actions, behaviour and, thereby, the performance of the company. The vast majority of the characteristics literature reported below relates to company start-ups. Baron and Brush (1999) identified at least three streams of the literature in this area:

(i)   *early literature* on the personal traits of entrepreneurs (Shaver and Scott, 1991), which, they argue, has provided fairly limited insights;
(ii) *cognitive processes literature*, which defines the way in which individuals think, reason and make decisions, which, they argue, provides a greater understanding of entrepreneurial behaviour and success;
(iii) *literature about 'what entrepreneurs do'*, which suggests that research should focus on 'what the entrepreneur does, not who the entrepreneur is' (Bird, 1989; Gartner, 1988, p. 21).

Social competences
Baron and Brush (1999) argue that:

> one aspect of entrepreneurs' behaviour that may well influence their success is their *social competence* – the extent to which they possess and employ discrete *social skills* that enhance their ability to interact effectively with others (e.g. venture capitalists, potential partners, employees, customers).

They go on to provide evidence linking social skills and competences to performance:

(i)   There is an extensive body of research suggesting social skills strongly influence outcomes in a range of business settings. Proficiency in impression management, social perception and persuasiveness influences the outcomes of job interviews, yearly performance reviews, negotiations and so on. High social proficiency enables entrepreneurs to interact with those outside of company, including partner networks and strategic alliances (e.g. it helps in raising finance, recruiting employees, negotiating with buyers and suppliers, etc.).
(ii) The existence of a 'team' results in more internal checks and a greater range of ideas and abilities and also helps the development of the business, and teamwork requires a high degree of social competence to facilitate face-to-face interaction within the team.
(iii) Higher levels of social competence lead to greater articulation, better communication and greater personal contact throughout the company – helping to build the internal organization and culture of the company.

The wider literature highlights a range of social skills that have proved to be important determinants of success in various business settings (again, the discussion follows Baron and Brush, 1999):

(i)   *social perception* – the accuracy with which traits, intentions, motives and so on are perceived in others;

(ii)   *impression management* – the techniques individuals use to induce a
       positive reaction on the part of others;
(iii) *expressiveness* – the ability of an individual to express emotions and
       feelings and, thereby, generate enthusiasm among other people;
(iv)   *persuasiveness* – the ability to change the views or behaviour of other
       people;
(v)   *social adaptability* – the ability to feel comfortable in or to quickly
       adapt to a wide range of social situations.

In their own work, Baron and Brush (1999) reported that entrepreneurs' ratings on a survey instrument measuring social skills, as well as the
ratings of their social skills by expert judges, were related to measures of
entrepreneurial success. They reported that:

> Results indicated that raters perceived significant differences between the
> entrepreneurs with respect to their social skills and also with respect to per-
> suasiveness, emotional intelligence, and personal appearance. In addition, one
> aspect of entrepreneurs' social skills – their *social adaptability* – was a signifi-
> cant predictor of measures of their success.

Baron and Markman (1999a) investigated two different groups of
entrepreneurs: the founders of high-tech companies and the founders of
cosmetics distribution companies. They found that two aspects of social
competence – social adaptability and social perception – were significant
predictors of the entrepreneur's financial success. Baron and Markman
(1999b) similarly demonstrated that the more favourable the entrepreneurs' personal appearance was – as rated by judges unacquainted with
them – the greater was their financial success. However, other aspects of
social competence, such as social adaptability, were also important and to
some degree mediated 'poor' personal appearance.

The literature also places considerable emphasis on the role played by
cooperation and communication, particularly between key players within
the company and those outside (e.g. venture capitalists). In addition, it
stresses both informal and formal ways of communicating, in particular,
using the venture capital company as a sounding board (Klofsten *et al.*,
1999; Landström, 1990), which is generally rated as one of the most important contributions of the venture capitalist (see section 6.6.2). On the other
hand, while venture capitalists play 'devil's advocate', they tend to be afraid
of interfering in the daily operation of the company, but cooperate either
through formal board work or, more generally, via informal contacts.

Social capital
The discussion of social competences leads naturally to the concept of
'social capital', which has been widely explored in the literature, from both
a conceptual and an empirical viewpoint. Social capital is argued to be the
non-economic knowledge that has a direct effect on economic behaviour

(Greene and Brown, 1997). It emerges from an individual's social structures and results in social norms and networks that tend to reinforce economic behaviour. It includes all forms of relationships, such as family, ethnic and political. Thus social capital is argued to be the sum of the resources (bearing in mind there may be synergies) potentially available to individuals from their relationships with others (Nahapiet and Ghoshal, 1998). In essence, higher social capital results in improved access to other resources, such as information, financial capital (Freear and Wetzel, 1992), including venture capitalist funding (Shane and Cable, 1998), and lower prices for assets and equipment (Starr and MacMillan, 1990). Higher social capital can also increase access to, and cooperation and trust among, those with whom the entrepreneur deals, including customers and suppliers. All these factors help to create a network that improves the profitability of the enterprise (Aldrich, 1987), as well as manager and CEO compensation (Belliveau *et al.*, 1996). This important concept, along with 'organizational social capital', is considered further in Parts V and VI.

6.6   Leadership, management and enterprise performance

6.6.1 *Leadership*

While leadership is often cited as one of the most important determinants of enterprise performance, it is a complex and under-researched area. It seems likely that different individuals (and groups) differ in their response to different leadership styles and that different styles may be appropriate in different circumstances. The discussion of leadership often focuses on the manner in which key managers, in particular the CEO, carry out the process of 'leading'. Clearly, this is determined by many factors. While the dominant factor seems likely to be the personality of the manager, any personal traits seem likely to be influenced by the specific role and tasks to be accomplished, as well as the expectations and behaviour of the other individuals and groups the manager deals with during the course of work.

Based upon the pioneering work of White and Lippitt (1960), which dates back to the mid-1930s, the literature suggests that there are at least three types of leader:

(i)   *Democratic leaders* are those who generally include group members in decision making. They tend to have a more original, inclusive and flexible approach to problem solving and to share the rewards from successful solutions.

(ii) *Autocratic leaders* generally make their own decisions, independently of the group they work with. They tend to supervise group members closely and, while they can be quick to praise, they can be equally quick to condemn and punish. The group consequently tends to behave in either an aggressive or an apathetic manner.

(iii) *Laissez-faire leaders* are those who minimize the directing of their
       group – providing a minimal level of leadership. The output of such
       groups tends to be low and of poor quality. Group members tend to
       place high demands on the leader, with little intra-group cooperation
       and an inability to work independently.

A study by White and Lippitt in the mid-1950s explored the effects of
these three styles of leadership on performance. First, while autocratic
leadership tended to produce the greatest volume of work (followed by
democratic and *laissez-faire*), the quality was consistently higher for the
democratic leader group. Second, democratic leadership was associated
with greater group satisfaction and cohesion, whereas the members of
autocratic-led groups tended to be more dissatisfied with their working
conditions and more confrontational. Third, members of autocratic-led
groups were much more likely to voice their discontent and their productivity tended to fall when the leader was absent; in contrast, only a small
decline in work effort occurred when the democratic leader was absent.
Fourth, absenteeism was the lowest for the democratically led group and
greatest in the case of autocratic leadership. Finally, democratic leadership
was associated with more independent and self-reliant group members,
while individuals in autocratic-led groups tended to be more submissive
and dependent.

The more recent literature appears to have coalesced around two styles
of leadership: 'defensive' and 'participative' (Gibb, 1978). Defensive
appears similar to autocratic leadership, while participatory resembles
democratic leadership. Defensive leaders are worried about their inadequacies, and feel insecure and open to attack from group members.
As a consequence, they tend to be strong willed and inflexible, highly
task focused and insensitive to the broader needs of the group. They do
not trust the group to function on their own, and take it on their own
shoulders to lead, motivate, organize and so on. As with autocratic leaders,
they are quick to discipline, but also capable of rewarding when they view
it as being appropriate. Participatory leadership, on the other hand, is
more focused on the group as a social unit and its needs. It encourages
worker participation, allows for individual and group development, and
assumes the ability of individuals to be self-motivated and self-reliant. It
equips the group to be flexible and adaptive.

There are many interesting pieces of experimental research that throw
light on the importance of leadership style, including the 'Hawthorne
experiments', the work of Likert (who established the 'Likert scale')
(Likert, 1932), and that of Coch and French (1948), who undertook a
classic workplace study. Unfortunately, space does not permit a detailed
examination of these studies. Many of the results, however, seem to be
consistent with the human relations school of thought, which concludes

that 'organizational creativity, flexibility and prosperity flow naturally from employee growth and development' (Shafritz and Ott, 1992). This literature has focused on the need to develop and maintain trust between management and group members in order to ensure organizational success (Argyris, 1973; Baird and St-Amand, 1995; Likert; 1967; McGregor, 1967). The findings have been consistent with the differences between 'traditional' (autocratic) and 'modern' (participative) styles of management leadership (Rajbhandari, 1999). It is argued that the leader has moved from a position at the 'apex' of a traditional hierarchy to a more central ('modern') position within the organizational structure. This 'apex' concept, linked to the idea of a pyramid, will be seen in Part V in the context of organizational design. In this way, modern leadership is argued to reduce the distance between policy, strategy, operation and evaluation, thereby keeping in touch with reality at each level. A key feature is that information flows become more bi- or multi-directional, with leaders acting less as a 'fount of all wisdom' and becoming instead a part of the learning process in order to increase their 'wisdom'. However, as noted above, it is not possible to view the management and the leadership style separately from the organization. The important point is that the potential benefits of 'modern leadership' will be muted or even lost entirely if there is a mismatch between management style and organizational form.

6.6.2 *Boards of directors*

Boards have been placed under increasing pressure from a number of sources, for example:

(i) litigation (Kesner and Johnson, 1990);
(ii) demand for greater participation by institutional investors;
(iii) corporate governance effects, which pressure boards to align management goals with those of the owners (Judge and Zeithaml, 1992; and Chapter 7);
(iv) green activists, who put pressure on boards to improve environmental policy (see Chapter 5).

Bearing this in mind, the BoD appears a crucial focus for research on the performance of companies. Pearce and Zahra (1991), for example, argue that boards affect organizational effectiveness in four main ways. They:

(i) provide useful business contacts;
(ii) actively contribute to the development of the organization's goals;
(iii) provide a mechanism that ensures effective 'checks and balances';
(iv) create corporate identity.

It is at the level of the BoD that venture capitalists make their most important contribution (Fredriksen and Klofsten, 1999). It is important for companies to have external sources of information and advice, in part as a 'test of reasonableness' for new ideas or actions (Bygrave and Timmons, 1997). External sources help to overcome inherent gaps or weaknesses in the entrepreneurial management team, and reduce the chances of them lapsing into an unchallenged uniformity of thought (Fredriksen and Klofsten, 1999). While venture capitalists may be used as one mechanism for overcoming these weaknesses, the same result may be achieved via a strong and independent board (Fredriksen and Klofsten, 1999). Outside directors are reported to bring a greater objectivity to decision making (Baysinger and Hoskisson, 1990).

After reviewing the largely anecdotal literature on CEO–board interaction, Pearce and Zahra (1991) suggested a fourfold typology of boards, based upon the different combinations of the power of the CEO (high/low power) and that of the BoD (high/low):

(i)   *Caretaker boards* are characterized by low board and low CEO power. Such boards comprise individuals working in the firm, and their meetings are informal and lack substance. Their existence fulfils a legal requirement, but they rarely give fundamental strategic or operational guidance. Such boards fail to make a significant contribution to dynamic performance.

(ii) *Statutory boards* are run by a powerful CEO, while the board itself is relatively weak. The CEO takes the important decisions, which the board 'rubber stamps'. Such boards do not provide a 'test of reasonableness' for key decisions and give false legitimacy to CEO decisions. CEO 'duality' – where the chair of the board is also the company CEO – can result in an unhealthy balance of power in favour of the CEO *vis-à-vis* the remainder of the board.

(iii) *Proactive boards* are dominated by members from outside the company and operate largely independently of the CEO and management. Their focus is the interests of the shareholders. Meetings are frequent and involve the board in strategic decision making. While there are strong 'tests of reasonableness', the balance of power is skewed towards those without inside information about the enterprise. Nevertheless, decision making is relatively efficient and likely to contribute to performance.

(iv) *Participative boards* have high (and balanced) levels of power for internal (CEO and managers) and external members. They debate extensively but have mechanisms for resolving differences. They have high integrity, with strong and balanced 'tests of reasonableness'. Their emphasis is on reaching consensus, which requires communication and negotiation. This is often viewed as the ideal form for dynamic performance.

There is some evidence of a positive relationship between board involvement and company performance (Baysinger and Hoskisson, 1990). According to Pearce and Zahra (1991), participative boards are likely to be the ones that contribute most to company performance from the perspective of strategic choice (followed by proactive boards, statutory boards and caretaker boards). The empirical tests, however, do not always support this ranking; Fredriksen and Kloftsen (1999), for example, analysed the role played by the relative power of the BoD in determining the economic performance of companies backed by venture capital. While the results gave some support to the hypothesis that firms perform better where decision making is equally distributed between the CEO and the board, the caretaker board type exhibited the best performance. One explanation that the authors put forward is that the caretaker type is not a formal board governance structure, but rather a mechanism for building openness and trust that is beneficial to the company.

6.7 Conclusions

This chapter emphasizes the central role that management plays in the operation of the enterprise. Within certain constraints, set by the governance rules, the market environment and so on, management decides the goals and strategies of the company. Managers are instrumental in determining almost all aspects of the company, from organizational structure through to the incentives that are designed to motivate employees. What is so surprising, therefore, is the lack of large-scale survey or econometric evidence linking management skills and competences to enterprise performance. The main evidence to date takes three forms:

(i)   tentative evidence of links between the level and type of qualification of managers and enterprise performance;
(ii) the importance of social competences and social capital;
(iii) entrepreneurial and leadership qualities, particularly participative leadership.

The present chapter, however, has also introduced the concept of latent skills shortages, which is important from both company and national policy perspectives. As already noted, consistent with the Penrose hypothesis, firms that set higher aspiration levels (i.e. adopt high-level strategies to move 'up-market', innovate and grow) are more likely to report skill problems. Those that 'do little' – in other words carry on producing the same product using the same processes and so on – may face increasing competition and risk of failure, but they may not translate this into a skills or competences deficiency. It seems likely that there is a very real danger that firms that simply repeat the same actions and operations day after day increasingly build 'decisions' into their structure and routines, and when these routines need to be changed the skills will not be available for them to do so.

Because of their own deficiencies in terms of skills and competences, managers may not even perceive the range of policy options that might be open to them if they and their employees were working from a higher skills base. Thus, causality probably runs in both directions, and becomes mutually self-reinforcing – firms that set higher product quality aspirations are more likely to appoint more highly qualified managers; and more highly qualified managers are more likely to set higher aspiration levels. Irrespective of which direction is the more important, the implications for the quality of the workforce are obvious. As a consequence, it is possible for managers to become locked into an efficiency-increasing or cost-saving strategy, as opposed to a high-skills strategy that is quality raising and EVA improving. Chapters 13 and 14 demonstrate how crucial this concept is from a policy perspective.

Notes

1 Chapters 9, 13 and 14 touch on comparative international evidence that suggests that UK managers have significantly less 'spare capacity' to be devoted to such activities than their German counterparts.

2 One issue here is that many other European countries appear to have a tighter definition of management occupations, for example requiring a manager to be responsible for some minimum number of employees.

3 While the skills required by managers in small enterprises will generally be qualitatively different from those required by managers in large concerns, it is surprising that the results indicate an almost complete absence of the use of vocational qualifications in the appointment of managers, which may be particularly relevant in smaller enterprises. Even if smaller enterprises provided on-the-job training on entry (for which there is little evidence), this would be more effective the higher the level of qualification of those recruited.

4 The mechanics of the graduate labour market are well known (Freeman, 1971, 1975, 1976, 1981) and need not concern us here.

5 The Global Entrepreneurship Monitor: www.gemconsortium.org/category_list. asp?cid=156.

Chapter 7

Agency, corporate governance and performance[1]

7.1   **Introduction**

The discussion in Chapter 6 emphasized that a positive relationship should exist between management skills and firm performance, although it was noted in Chapter 5 that so-called 'professional managers', left to their own devices, are likely to set goals out of line with those of the owners of the firm. The present chapter deals with the principal-agent literature, where the separation of ownership and control creates 'agency costs' because the owners (principals) and managers (agents) have different objective functions (Mueller and Spitz, 2002). Agency costs are those arising between the principal and the agent, and include 'the costs of drawing up and enforcing a contract, as well as transaction costs, moral hazard costs and information costs. Agency costs are major determinants of how firms are organised and how their staff are remunerated' (Rutherford, 1992, p. 10). Thus, the literature, which can be traced through Berle and Means (1932), Jensen and Meckling (1976), and Jensen (1986), addresses a 'conflict of interest problem' (Shleifer and Vishny, 1989). The principal-agent literature is concerned with the arrangements for limiting managerial discretion and, thereby, how the goals of professional managers can be more closely aligned with those of the owners (i.e. the shareholders).

If management skills are performance enhancing, then remuneration patterns should recognize this. Compensation packages, and other governance mechanisms, are an *ex ante* means of aligning management with shareholder interests. This alignment operates via performance, which is also driven by the skills/capacity of managers (see Chapter 6). Thus, there is a complex relationship between skills/capacity, governance arrangements, the goals and strategies adopted and performance. For example, the strategies and goals of a firm determine what governance and operational arrangements they choose and so what skills they look for in managers. But it also works in reverse: that is, the skills/capacity of managers influences the choice of goals/strategies and governance/operational arrangements.

157

Taking stock of the situation *ex post*, performance measurement (see Chapter 3) determines whether the capacity–governance interaction has been successful, and if not, which of the components need to be revisited.

Governance issues have always been of concern to shareholders (and other stakeholders). However, following the developments in the managerial economics literature (see Chapter 5) they have become much more topical in the last two decades or so. This new impetus has also been spurred by the increasing incidence of corporate failure and corporate fraud, against a backdrop of relatively rapid growth in the compensation packages of senior managers (Kay and Silberston, 1995). A 1994 study of Britain's top 169 companies found that their workers' average earnings increased by 17 per cent from 1985 to 1990, whereas directors' pay had increased by 77 per cent in real terms (Maclean, 1999). These developments have led to questions about the adequacy of existing governance structures and mechanisms in protecting shareholder (and stakeholder) value and, therefore, concerns about the efficiency of resource allocation. In response to these concerns, several national and international bodies have advanced best practice governance principles (e.g. Cadbury, 1992; OECD, 1999a) and efforts are being made at the firm level to comply with the new standards.

The present chapter proceeds as follows. Section 7.2 briefly highlights the main theoretical basis of the governance question and provides a context for the subsequent discussion. Section 7.3 outlines the key standards that have evolved in addressing the issues raised. Section 7.4 considers the various dimensions of corporate governance and outlines the associated empirical studies. Section 7.5 discusses the important role played by ownership structure, including the concentration of ownership, the identity of shareholders, the effects of privatization and demutualization and, finally, the effects of founder/family ownership and management. Section 7.6 undertakes a similar analysis of the role played by board structure, including board composition, size, demography, nominations committees, interlocking directorships and board entrenchment. Section 7.7 links governance issues with various organizational features or processes, in particular diversification and internationalization. Section 7.8 considers the controversial issue of management compensation, as well as management security. Finally, section 7.9 draws the main conclusions. Throughout, an emphasis is placed on the performance implications of governance structures/mechanisms and management skills/capacity.

7.2   'Theory' of corporate governance

There is no one theory of corporate governance, but a body of theories and hypotheses that describe the workings of the firm, and thereby provide a useful context for the study of corporate governance. The objective here is not a detailed elaboration of the theories, but to highlight the aspects that enhance an intuitive and meaningful discussion of their governance implications. The key theories are summarized below.

7.2.1 *Neoclassical model*

The neoclassical model is the standard theory of the firm found in the textbooks. It assumes that the firm is run by a selfless manager, who decides on input and output levels in order to maximize profit to shareholders. Inputs are sourced and output sold in respective (often competitive) markets at given prices. Profit is maximized, and cost minimized, when marginal revenue (which, under perfect competition, is equal to the price of the product) equals marginal cost. The firm faces a U-shaped average cost curve. Fixed costs do not increase with output; hence there is a tendency for unit costs to fall initially as output increases and then to rise eventually as it becomes more difficult to vary some inputs, given the firm's scale (Hart, 1996). The theory is useful for studying:

> how the firm's optimal production choice varies with input and output prices, for understanding the aggregate behaviour of an industry, and for studying the consequences of strategic interaction between firms once the assumption of perfect competition has been dropped. (Hart, 1996, p. 16)

However, Hart advances three weaknesses of the model:

(i)   it totally ignores the incentive problems that arise within the firm, in that it treats the firm as a 'black box' in which 'everything operates perfectly smoothly and everybody does what they are told' (Hart, 1996, p. 17);

(ii) it does not say anything about the internal organization (hierarchy, authority and delegation) of firms;

(iii) it does not clearly delineate the boundaries of the firm – the traditional neoclassical model does not distinguish between the firm's managers, creditors and owners, and the firm is viewed as a single homogeneous entity that maximizes value by maximizing the discounted value of expected future net cash flows.

Moreover, it is assumed that the firm does not suffer from any difficulties with corporate control or external finance (Prowse, 1994). From this discussion, it is clear that other theories must be used, since the neoclassical model assumes that corporate governance operates perfectly, whereas, in the real world, it is clear that this is not the case.

7.2.2 *Agency theory*

Agency theory explicitly addresses the incentive and internal organization issues raised above. Berle and Means (1932) laid the basis for what

later became known as 'agency theory' – they noted that while shareholders provide the funds for a firm, they leave control to professional
managers and are limited in their ability to constrain the behaviour of
management. This separation of ownership and control and the resulting
problems were formalized into the 'agency cost' model of Jensen and
Meckling (1976). Much has been written about the agency problem of the
firm (e.g. Fama, 1980; Fama and Jensen, 1983; Hart, 1995, 1996; Shleifer
and Vishny, 1997).

Goals and preferences differ between owners and managers. For
example, shareholders would seek to maximize the value of the firm's
equity, whatever of the value of its debt. That is, they would be willing
to take on more risk than that implied by a value-maximizing investment
policy (Prowse, 1994). This is because they benefit from a risky decision if
it pays off, but can avoid the full cost of a downside outcome by declaring
bankruptcy or diversifying. On the other hand, non-owning managers are
more risk averse. This is because they cannot fully participate in the gains
from high-risk decisions but they are fully exposed to employment loss
and negative reputation effects if their high-risk activities fail. The latter
would be exacerbated where managerial skills are relatively specific to
the firm. Furthermore, managers prefer policies that justify paying them
higher salaries (e.g. by increasing the size of the firm) and would also
prefer to shirk responsibilities and/or divert resources for their personal
benefit (Prowse, 1994).

More generally, diverging goals and preferences imply various forms of
misalignment between owners and managers, including risk preference,
incentive, effort and timing (Rediker and Seth, 1995). Information asymmetries exist between owners and managers that make it impossible to
write contracts that guarantee managers always act in the best interests of
owners (Prowse, 1994). The implication of separation, therefore, is that, in
the absence of effective control mechanisms, managers are likely to make
decisions that run counter to shareholders' interests. This 'managerial'
behaviour could be reflected in wasteful expenditure, perquisites, inef-
ficiencies, fraud and, ultimately, failure.

7.2.3 *Other theories*

Agency theory is clearly the dominant academic theme underlying corporate governance (Norburn *et al.*, 2000). However, other theories have
been employed in the context of governance, including transaction costs
(see Chapter 2) and property rights theories (Hart, 1996). For present purposes, the agency model is adequate to highlight the key points and is the
most commonly employed theory in empirical work, but it is worth noting
some differences between the agency model and these other theories. For
example, Williamson (1988) posits that, while the main unit of analysis in

agency theory is the individual agent, the transaction forms the basis for the transaction costs theory. Another difference is that while the agency problem involves *ex ante* costs incurred in seeking to align manager and shareholder incentives, the costs implied by the transaction cost model tend to be *ex post* ('maladaption costs' – haggling costs in correcting *ex post* misalignments, dispute resolution costs and bonding costs). Transactions and governance structures differ in their respective attributes (costs and competences); aligning them in a cost-economizing way is the main exercise in the transaction costs model.

7.2.4 *Theoretical synthesis*

Hart (1995) provides a useful reconciliation of the agency and transaction costs views. He posits that, in the absence of agency problems, corporate governance issues are irrelevant. However, the presence of agency problems does not in itself provide a rationale for the application of corporate governance. This he attributes to the fact that optimal principal-agent contracts, by definition, specify to the fullest extent possible the obligations of 'all parties' in all future states of the world, thereby precluding a role for corporate governance in 'residual' future decisions. But this optimal agency model is based on the assumption that such comprehensive contracts are costlessly written, whereas in reality only incomplete contracts can be written. Thus, given the combination of agency problems and incomplete contracting, corporate governance provides a framework for determining how decisions that could not be specified in initial contracting will be made. For a broader discussion of labour contracts (implicit contracts, incentives in contracts, efficiency wages, etc.) see Bosworth *et al.* (1996a, pp. 279–323).

7.3   **Standards of corporate governance**

The type of governance problems that led to the establishment of various panels and other bodies in the early 1990s have been summarized as:

> overly optimistic financial reporting, lack of operational and internal control within companies, questionable transactions and fraud, power in the hands of too few (particularly dominant chairman/chief operating officers), and weak boards where non-executive directors found themselves ineffectual. (Percy, 1995, p. 1)

Similarly, Short (1999) lists problems such as creative accounting, spectacular business failures, expropriation of shareholders' funds by unscrupulous directors, a limited role for audit, claims of a widening executive pay–performance gap and a short-termist corporate control market.

These concerns, both in the UK and globally, formed the backdrop for the *OECD Principles of Corporate Governance* (OECD, 1999a). These principles have the following aims:

(i)   to protect shareholders' rights;
(ii)   to ensure the equitable treatment of all shareholders;
(iii) to recognize the rights of stakeholders as established by law and to encourage active cooperation between companies and stakeholders in wealth and job creation and the sustainability of financially sound enterprises;
(iv)   to ensure timely and accurate disclosure of information regarding the financial situation, performance, ownership and governance;
(v)   to ensure the strategic guidance of the company, the effective monitoring of management by the board and the board's accountability to the company and its shareholders.

The OECD principles were no doubt informed by the UK's Cadbury Committee (1992) (which emphasized financial reporting/accountability); it pioneered the introduction of principles and standards of corporate governance, and these have been subsequently embedded in various national codes of best practice. There have been several follow-up reports in the UK, including those by Greenbury (1995) (on remuneration patterns) and Hampel (1998) (which emphasized implementation issues), and all three have been unified into *The Combined Code* by the Committee on Corporate Governance (1998) (see also Short, 1999).

The main recommended codes of best practice stemming from the above committees, as summarized from Short (1999) and from the reports themselves, are as follows:

(i)   *Board membership*
       (a) A nomination committee should be set up, comprising mainly non-executive directors, whose members should be identified in the annual report. They should make recommendations to the board on all new appointments to the company's BoD.
       (b) All directors should submit themselves for re-election at least every three years.
(ii)   *CEO duality*
       (a) The roles of the chair of the BoD and CEO should be separated.
       (b) Companies combining these roles should publicly justify doing so.
(iii) *Non-executive directors*
       (a) One-third of the board should be non-executive directors.
       (b) Independent non-executive directors should be identified by the company.

(iv) Remuneration

    (a) A remuneration committee, comprised wholly of non-executive directors, should determine the remuneration of executive directors.

    (b) The board should report annually to shareholders, giving details of remuneration policy and the remuneration package of each director.

    (c) Long-term incentive plans must have shareholders' approval.

    (d) Share options should not be issued at a discount. They should be phased in, instead of being issued in one block, and should not be exercisable in under three years.

(v) Monitoring and control

    (a) The board should report on the company's position and future prospects, including interim reports about any other price-sensitive developments (i.e. not restricted to the annual accounts).

    (b) The board should report on the soundness of the company's system of internal control.

    (c) The board should establish an audit committee, comprising at least three non-executive directors, who should be mostly independent, and who should be named in the annual report. The committee should review with management the adequacy of the company's operational and internal controls.

(vi) Shareholder involvement. Institutional shareholders should make considered use of their votes and be actively involved in seeking congruency of management's actions with set goals and strategies.

Taken together, the principles and codes outlined above seek to achieve greater congruency between owners' and managers' goals, preferences and incentives. Emphasis is placed on encouraging stewardship and accountability on the part of managers through greater transparency, disclosure and explanation of departures from codes of best practice. A greater role is given to outside directors, for example in selecting new board members, determining remuneration and monitoring operational, financial and other internal controls via the audit committee. This implies increased monitoring and oversight of the activities of managers, on behalf of shareholders and other stakeholders.

7.4 Governance tools: linking theory, standards and practice

The principles and standards discussed above are applied extensively, especially among large listed companies. A survey was commissioned in 1995 by the Cadbury Committee to assess the state of compliance with the code; it found that 97 per cent of the top 100 quoted companies had

Table 7.1 Governance reform proposals

Board roles	Structure and process
Compensation	Audit committee
Control	Nominating committee
Reporting	Insider/outsider issues
Strategy	Director pay
Evaluate senior managers	CEO/chair separation
Performance	Director education/support
	Directors' and officers' liability
	Board size

three or more non-executive directors, 82 per cent had a separate chair of the BoD and a CEO, and 90 per cent issued statements claiming compliance with the Cadbury code of best practice (Short, 1999).[2] This process has been helped by the fact that the London Stock Exchange adopted the code as a condition for listing. Thus, companies must in their annual reports describe their governance practices and explain any non-compliance (Norburn *et al.*, 2000). Norburn *et al.* (2000) list governance reform proposals under two broad headings: those setting out the roles of the board, and those addressing the structures and processes that are required to ensure that managers work in the best interests of shareholders. The list, shown in Table 7.1, offers a useful recap of the discussion in the previous section.

Governance tools have been subjected to empirical testing in the literature, especially in the context of their performance-enhancing potential. Table 7.2 lists some specific tools commonly assessed in the literature. Internal tools are those originating from within the firm and external tools reflect disciplining forces exerted from outside the firm, usually as threats of action that will be taken if the internal tools fail. Empirical studies examining the usefulness of such tools have tended to play down the role of management in the process of governance. In addition, standard setting has been viewed as a strictly one-way process, running from owners to managers, although the evolution of standards and tools is likely to be the result of a two-way interaction between owners and managers. This is where management skills and capacity are important, for example in the choice and implementation of remuneration, internal controls and organizational structure/hierarchy mechanisms. Thus, management skills and capacity are essential ingredients in determining the governance arrangements adopted, the effectiveness with which they are carried out and, thereby, the performance of the firm.

The next two sections discuss some of the studies that have analysed the empirical association between two specific classes of governance

Table 7.2 Examples of tools of corporate governance

Tools	Some contributing author(s)
Internal	
Compensation	Baker *et al.* (1988)
	Hart (1995)
	Ingham and Thompson (1995)
	Jensen and Meckling (1976)
	Jensen and Murphy (1990)
	Main and Johnson (1993)
	Murphy (1985)
	Pavlik and Belkaoui (1991)
Ownership structure	Akella and Greenbaum (1988)
	Bhide (1993)
	Cubbin and Leech (1983)
	Demsetz and Lehn (1985)
	Kay and Silberston (1995)
	Shleifer and Vishny (1997)
Management share ownership	Cubbin and Leech (1983)
	Jensen and Meckling (1976)
Internal monitoring by managers	Fama (1980)
Mutual monitoring systems	Fama and Jensen (1983)
Decision hierarchies	Fama and Jensen (1983)
Size limiting	Demsetz and Lehn (1985)
Board of directors	Fama and Jensen (1983)
External	
Market for corporate control	Fama (1980)
	Fama and Jensen (1983)
	Shleifer and Vishny (1997)
Managerial labour market	Bhide (1993)
	Fama (1980)
Debt/bankruptcy threat	Hart (1995)
	Shleifer and Vishny (1997)
Board of directors	Fama and Jensen (1983)
Regulatory control	Demsetz and Lehn (1985)
	Kay (1991)
	Kroszner and Strahan (1996)

tools – ownership structure and board structure – and firm performance. As noted, many of these studies did not examine the role of management skills directly, but instead implicitly assumed that they are proxied by other variables in the model. Where possible, however, the discussion draws skills linkages.

7.5   Ownership structure

7.5.1   *Ownership structure and control*

Ownership structure, in many ways, is at the heart of the ownership–control separation debate, and has been analysed extensively in the literature. Demsetz and Lehn (1985), for example, sought to explain the determinants of ownership structure. Most firms start from a very concentrated ownership structure, with one or very few owners, and high exit costs in such a situation provide an incentive for owners to seek an active role in governance (Bhide, 1993). In general, more concentrated ownership entails owners being involved in the monitoring and control of the firm, while greater diffuseness results in shirking by owners (Demsetz and Lehn, 1985). Free riding by individual owners translates into zero monitoring by all owners. Many of the ownership issues covered below are typically couched in terms of whether or not they lead to more concentrated ownership patterns and, ultimately, the effect of concentration on performance.[3]

7.5.2   *Ownership concentration*

There is no agreement in the literature about the direction of the relationship between ownership concentration and performance. Shleifer and Vishny (1997), for example, hypothesize a bell-shaped relationship, in which performance increases with ownership concentration up to a point, owing to improved incentives, but subsequently declines as management becomes more entrenched. Demsetz (1983), on the other hand, posits a zero relationship because market forces should tend to weed out inefficient ownership arrangements and compete away profitability differences.

Empirical work on ownership concentration proceeds on two fronts:

(i)   seeking to identify the factors influencing the degree of ownership concentration;
(ii)   explicitly testing the association with some measure of performance.

Pedersen and Thomsen (1999) provide evidence for both, based upon a study of the 100 largest non-financial companies in twelve European countries. Their results suggest that ownership concentration decreases with firm size and increases with 'noise' (volatility of profit). Institutional and national differences were also significant. However, they found no relationship between ownership concentration and performance in terms of ROE. Other authors who found no significant relationship include Demsetz and Lehn (1985), Koshal and Pejovich (1992) and Cho (1998). On the other hand, Zeckhouser and Pound (1990) and Lloyd *et al.* (1987) found a positive association between ownership concentration and performance, measured in terms of both the price–earnings ratio and the ratio of MV to sales, respectively.

Thus, the empirical evidence on ownership concentration has been mixed. Clearly, studying one governance tool in isolation from the others misses the interaction effects among the various tools. Even if ownership concentration is not directly indicated as a significant influence on performance, its role may be picked up via its influence on board structure and organizational decision processes. This is a theme that runs through the review below.

7.5.3 *Identity of shareholders*

Owners are private individuals, institutional investors and/or government. In the UK, for example, institutional shareholding of domestic market capitalization grew from 19 per cent in 1963 to about 60 per cent in 1993, with a concomitant reduction in private holdings from 59 per cent to 19 per cent (Moerland, 2000). By 1997 institutional investors owned 75 per cent of the British stock market by value, with pension funds the single largest holders (Maclean, 1999). The growth in institutional holdings leads to more concentrated ownership and so the possibility of greater involvement of shareholders in the monitoring of their companies. It is also consistent with a move away from 'exit-led' ownership to a 'voice-driven' pattern. The former is a short-termist stance, where owners sell as soon as they perceive adverse price/value movements, while the latter is a situation where owners show more loyalty and actively seek to ensure managers act in the shareholders' best interest (Ciccotello and Grant, 1999). Both McConnell and Servaes (1990) and Han and Suk (1998) find a positive relationship between institutional ownership and performance. Indeed, on balance, other empirical studies have suggested that the trend towards greater institutional ownership in the UK has enhanced firm performance.

Management share ownership is both a compensation issue and an ownership issue. Compensation is discussed in section 7.8. Management share ownership is one way of reducing agency costs in the owner–manager relationship, because, in principle, it produces a greater congruency in goals, preferences and strategies, and ultimately better performance. In practice, however, greater management ownership can also lead to

management entrenchment, thereby worsening agency problems. Entrenchment describes the situation in which managers create a position in which
they feel confident to pursue their own goals. For example, Shleifer and
Vishny (1989) argue that managers undertake manager-specific,
entrenching investments – using shareholders' money to do so – which
make the cost of replacing the manager high. As a consequence, the
manager is able to extract higher compensation from shareholders.

This suggests a non-linear relationship between insider (management)
ownership and firm performance, which has been confirmed in many
empirical studies (Han and Suk, 1998; McConnell and Servaes, 1990;
Morck *et al.*, 1988). Mueller and Spitz (2002, pp. 3, 24), for example,
studied an unbalanced panel of 1,400 German SMEs over the period 1997
to 2000.[4] Their main conclusion was that 'managerial ownership share up
to around 80% has a positive effect on firm performance and a negative
effect thereafter'.[5] Thus, there is a range in which management ownership reduces agency costs and enhances firm performance, but excessive
management ownership encourages manager entrenchment, resulting in
decisions that do not maximize shareholder value. It should be noted,
however, that the degree of management ownership is unlikely to be
entirely exogenous, as firms move to the levels of management ownership
that maximize performance. Hence, a number of studies treat the two variables as being simultaneously determined (see Mueller and Spitz, 2002).

7.5.4 *Ownership changes – privatization and demutualization*

Management entrenchment is less of a problem in the private than the
public sector because of the array of internal governance tools, as well
the corporate control market, that act to constrain management action.
Therefore, privatization implies a reduction in the threat of management
entrenchment. The same is also true of demutualization, which has been
common over recent years in the financial services sector. Mutually
owned firms are generally considered to be more diffusely held than
corporations. In line with the earlier discussion, mutuals would be more
prone to agency problems and management entrenchment, since their
owners have fewer incentives to supply the necessary monitoring and super-
vision. In empirical terms, Frydman *et al.* (1997) found that, for transition
economies, privatized firms performed better than government-owned
firms in terms of revenue growth, their preferred performance variable.
D'Souza and Megginson (1999) suggest that firm profitability (return on
sales and return on assets), efficiency (sales per employee and net income
per employee) and output (sales) show significant improvements after
privatization. Their results are based on a sample of eighty-five companies
from twenty-eight countries and twenty-one industries; fifty-eight of the
firms were from fifteen industrialized countries, including the UK.

7.5.5 *Founder/family ownership and management*

Founders are more likely than professional managers to seek to sustain firm culture, to have stronger personal stakes in the business and to behave more like entrepreneurs (Daily and Dalton, 1992; Schein, 1985). They are able to move more swiftly and act with more autonomy (Dyer, 1986). Furthermore, the combination of ownership and management in the founder(s) should substantially eliminate agency problems, and so foster performance – although that depends upon what the goals (and competences) of the founder are (see Chapter 6). One type of agency problem is when professional managers pursue goals (such as growth) that help to entrench their positions, rather than shareholder profit maximization. Willard *et al.* (1992) reported that firms led by non-founder CEOs tend to be larger and also grow faster than those led by founder CEOs. Rubenson and Gupta (1990) found a negative relationship between firm growth rates and the tenure of the founder.

It is more likely that professional managers will introduce greater objectivity into decision making and utilize strategic planning techniques (Schein, 1968; Whisler, 1988), again with the potential to enhance performance. Flamholtz (1986) posits that the reconciliation of these two perspectives may be found in firm size. Thus, founder management is optimal for small firms, and professional management for larger firms, with a cut-off point at about $10 million in sales per annum. This is predicated on the fact that the founder manager would find it difficult to maintain effective monitoring and control in larger, more complex organizations. The results of Daily and Dalton (1992) and Willard *et al.* (1992), however, suggest that whether the CEO was also the founder or a professional manager had no significant effect on performance, even when controlling for Flamholtz's (1986) size effect. This suggests that it is not founder versus non-founder management *per se* that matters, but what the leader does. Thus, performance hinges on other governance tools, strategies, internal controls and so on, and these are heavily influenced by management skills and capacity.

7.6 Board structures

7.6.1 *Control, service and resource dependence*

Johnson *et al.* (1996) identify three broad roles for the board:

(i) the *control role* refers to the board's responsibility to monitor CEOs and other senior managers on behalf of the shareholders;
(ii) the *service role* involves both advising senior management and strategy development;
(iii) the *resource dependence role* refers to the board's importance in procuring resources for the firm.

The theory and governance standards discussed in section 7.3 suggest 'best practice' board structures, which would both foster transparency and accountability and encourage the board to be relatively independent and to monitor managers, to ensure that goals, strategies and operations are in line with shareholders' aspirations. The review below emphasizes the effect of various board structures on firm performance.

7.6.2 *Board composition – internal versus external directors*

Internal directors are those who also serve as managers of the firm, while external directors are all non-management members of the board (Johnson *et al.*, 1996). The inside directors would be handicapped in the monitoring of the CEO and senior managers for at least two reasons (Johnson *et al.*, 1996):

(i)   they are likely to develop loyalty to the CEO, which may diminish their ability to give an objective evaluation of the firm's performance;
(ii) they face a conflict of interest because many decisions that they preside over affect themselves, for example executive remuneration and succession.

Thus, it is generally believed that the monitoring and control roles of the board would be best served by the appointment of external directors. The number or proportion of external directors on the board is commonly used as a measure of board independence. The empirical evidence on the performance implications of insider directors has been mixed, but for external directors the majority of studies suggest that board independence (proxied by the proportion of external directors) leads to better firm performance (Johnson *et al.*, 1996). As mentioned in section 7.4, interaction between governance tools is a strong likelihood, and it is generally expected that board independence would influence other governance decisions, for example compensation, succession and strategy (see Johnson *et al.*, 1996, for a review).

7.6.3 *Board size*

The investigation of the effect of size typically proceeds in the context of the ease of managing the number of persons involved. Thus, larger boards are hypothesized to be characterized by lower motivation, weak coordination, slow decision making and low involvement (Judge and Zeithaml, 1992). If these handicaps associated with size hold, the board will underperform in its monitoring, advisory and resource roles. Judge and Zeithaml (1992) provide evidence that board involvement is positively associated with firm performance, but they report that size is negatively related to board involvement, which suggests that larger boards would reduce performance.

7.6.4 *Board demography – knowledge and skills*

Board demography refers to the characteristics of individual board members, including education, functional background, tenure/experience and age (see Chapter 6). All these factors would have a direct bearing on the knowledge and skills that members bring to the board. A more skilled/knowledgeable board would be better equipped to understand the decisions of the CEO and to offer more effective monitoring. Further, such a board would also be more likely to appreciate and encourage skills development throughout the firm. Forbes and Milliken (1999) recognize two aspects of such knowledge and skills:

(i)   functional area knowledge (e.g. marketing, human resources, accounting and operations);
(ii) firm-specific knowledge and skills (understanding of the firm's operations and internal management issues).

Thus, the presence and use of such knowledge and skills should facilitate the board's execution of its monitoring, service and resource roles, and lead to better firm performance.

7.6.5 *Nomination committee*

The establishment of a nomination committee is one of the recommended governance instruments for fostering the appointment of members of the board who would supply effective monitoring, service and resource functions. The committee should comprise mainly non-executive directors and they should make recommendations to the board on all new appointments. Two issues are involved here:

(i)   a nomination committee with a majority of outside members should ensure relative independence in board appointments and reduce the potential for CEO influence and self-perpetuation;
(ii) such a committee, as it is not involved in day-to-day operations, should be more objective with regard to board appointments, and focus on those demographics/qualities (skills, education, etc.) that are important from a performance perspective.

However, companies appear to have been slow to implement this aspect of governance reform. Conyon and Mallin (1997), for example, found that, while 98 per cent of their sample of 298 large British quoted companies had implemented audit and remuneration committee proposals by 1995, only 51 per cent had complied with the nomination committee recommendation. This raises the concern that companies have been slow in enforcing board independence.

The empirical work in this context has mostly examined the relationship between the existence of a nomination committee and one aspect of management entrenchment – the pay of CEOs. The main idea is that where a relatively independent committee is responsible for the appointment of directors, then a relatively independent board will also emerge, and this will slow down the rate of growth of CEO pay. Westphal and Zajac (1995) found some evidence in support of this proposition, while Conyon and Peck (1998) found that the presence of a nomination committee plays little role in determining senior management pay.

7.6.6   *CEO duality*

It would intuitively seem that a firm that has the CEO also as the chair of the board ('CEO duality') is likely to be less effective in discharging its monitoring and control function, which in turn will exacerbate agency problems and lead to poorer performance. This is the basis for the governance standard that the CEO and chair of the board should be separate appointments. The effect of CEO duality on firm performance has been researched extensively. The general finding, as in many other aspects of governance, is that the relationship with performance is complex and the empirical evidence has been somewhat mixed. Finkelstein and D'Aveni (1994) and Daily and Dalton (1997), among others, argue that, while duality may lead to the problems outlined above, it can also result in unity of command and strong leadership, which can enhance performance. In seeking to reconcile these opposing theories and findings, Finkelstein and D'Aveni (1994) applied a contingency approach – they found that the risk of CEO entrenchment (and so less desirable duality) was higher when CEOs had strong informal power or when the firm was performing well.[6]

7.6.7   *Interlocking directorships*

Board interlocks is another area where the aggregate effect on performance may not be simple. Interlocks occur where the same executive is a member of the board of more than one company; in other words, the executive is a 'multiple director' (Barbi, 2000, p. 3). It could be argued that interlocking directorships compromise the monitoring and control roles of the board. At the same time, such networks would enable the board to fulfil its advisory and resource dependence roles better, since they foster interaction with key industry players and enhance access to markets. Davis and Mizruchi (1999) stress that particular interlocks, as well as the overall configuration of the interlock patterns, shape economic decisions in significant ways. Geletkanycz and Hambrick (1997) posit that knowledge acquired from such networking will feed into executive strategy formulation and implementation. Intra-industry networking tends to foster strategy conformity within the industry, while extra-industry networks can lead to 'deviant' strategies. This is an under-researched aspect of governance, at least in empirical terms. However, Geletkanycz and Hambrick (1997) find evidence that strategy and external ties (measured in several ways, including the presence of outside directors) interact to foster firm performance.

7.6.8 *Board entrenchment*

While management entrenchment is the more commonly addressed governance threat, BoD entrenchment is potentially just as important. An entrenched board would raise questions about who will monitor the monitor, as it would have the potential to diminish the effectiveness of governance (Sundaramurthy *et al.*, 1996). An entrenched board would not have the incentive to perform the monitoring, control and resource functions whose delivery helps reduce agency problems between managers and shareholders. This lack of incentive may arise when a board is not exposed to the self-scrutiny and performance pressures that are brought to bear by the presence of a significant number of independent non-executive directors and a diversity of opinions and skills. An entrenched board may be able to deploy the firm's resources as it sees fit.

Sundaramurthy *et al.* (1996) studied one action that fosters board entrenchment in the USA – the adoption of 'classified' boards. This entails the division of the BoD into three classes, with only one class standing for election each year. This means shareholders have to wait at least two annual meetings before they can replace the entire board. While its proponents see it as a tool for fostering board continuity, its contemporary prominence is as an instrument intended to provide some protection against a hostile takeover attempt judged as unfavourable to shareholders. Bebchuk *et al.* (2002, p. 2) explain that there are two key reasons why staggered boards impede hostile takeovers. First, irrespective of the date when a hostile bidder emerges, it takes at least one year to gain control of the board (and potentially up to two years). Second, the bidder must win two elections separated by a year, during which time the economic circumstances can change dramatically. They point out that the problems are accentuated further in the presence of 'poison pills'. However, the development of such boards is being actively opposed by institutional shareholders, who may be the only governance participants with the power to act where board entrenchment sets in (see Pozen, 1994). Sundaramurthy *et al.* (1996) confirm that a high level of institutional shareholding is significantly associated with a reduced adoption of classified boards.

7.7   Governance and organizational strategy

This section examines the relationship between a firm's strategy, governance mechanisms and performance. In particular, the areas of executive strategic decision making covered here are those of diversification/divestment and internationalization.

7.7.1   *Diversification*

It is often suggested that diversified firms are valued at a discount relative to their imputed values (see Chapter 2). Two hypotheses have arisen to explain this discount (see Andersen *et al.*, 2000, for a detailed discussion): first, diversification may be associated with suboptimal governance arrangements, which allow management entrenchment at the expense of shareholder value; second, diversified firms may employ optimal governance arrangements 'but may forego divestiture if the transaction costs associated with the break-up offset the expected benefit of operating a more focused firm'. Andersen *et al.* (2000) investigated 'whether governance structures are significantly different between focused and diversified companies, and whether these differences, if any, are consistent with an agency cost explanation for diversification'. They posited that if agency problems were responsible for managers engaging in value-reducing diversification strategies, then increases in diversification should be associated with smaller CEO shareholding, fewer outside directors, lower institutional or block shareholding and smaller use of share-based pay. However, they found that these governance mechanisms were largely similar for diversified and focused firms, and concluded that differences in governance structure do not explain the decision to diversify, or the discount typically associated with diversified firms.

Hoskisson *et al.* (1994) studied the effects of governance, strategy and performance on the intensity of corporate divestment. They found that relative product diversification was the primary reason for high levels of divestment activity. Their governance proxies were also shown to be important antecedents of divestment intensity. These proxies included block share ownership, independent outside directors, outside board member ownership and inside board member ownership, all of which (except the second) were hypothesized to exert a negative influence on relative product diversification. However, of the governance proxies, only outside block share ownership was found to be statistically significant.

7.7.2   *Internationalization*

Sanders and Carpenter (1998) studied the relationship between the degree of internationalization and firm governance. They posited that governance has implications for the way in which the vast amounts of complex information that accompany internationalization are processed. Furthermore, the board's role in monitoring senior management teams is made more difficult because internationalization leads to increased specialization in the firm's diffused local markets. They found evidence to support their hypothesis that a firm's degree of internationalization significantly influences its choice of corporate governance mechanisms. For example, CEO pay, top management team size, board size, CEO separation and the proportion of board outsiders were all found to be positively and significantly associated with the degree of internationalization.

7.8   Management compensation and security

This section looks at the roles of incentive pay and executive turnover in aligning the goals of managers and influencing enterprise performance. It also examines the role played by the market for corporate control, where, for example, merger or takeover allows some part of the management team of a failing company to be replaced.

7.8.1   *Compensation and share options*

The main thrust of compensation as a governance mechanism is for pay to be structured in such a way that the owners' and managers' incentives are aligned. From the control perspective, it has been recommended that, among other things, companies set up independent remuneration committees to ensure CEOs do not preside over their own pay decisions. Similar to the case of the recommendation that companies establish nomination committees, over half the British companies surveyed by Taylor (1996) had yet to comply with the key Greenbury (1995) remuneration recommendations. This is consistent with the widely held view that executive pay is 'out of sync' with firm performance. In recent years in the UK, however, there has been a trend towards the use of share options, de-emphasizing the use of fixed salaries and annual bonuses, for a proportion of total executive pay (McKnight and Tomkins, 1999). While this has incentive-aligning potential, it has also been criticized on the grounds of the high values involved.

The empirical literature on executive compensation is large. The typical question asked is whether company performance and size are related to executive remuneration. Most studies have observed a modest association between size and pay (McKnight and Tomkins, 1999). This accords with the view that senior managers focus on growth, which is pay enhancing, to the detriment of shareholder value (see section 7.1). Gomez-Mejia *et al.* (1987) argue that 'what is most intriguing in the literature investigating executive compensation is that, after controlling for size, researchers have not found the relationship between CEOs' pay and performance to be as strong or as consistent as the classical economic theories suggest'. Thus, while there are exceptions, most studies have found no distinct association between pay and performance. This has added to criticisms of UK pay governance systems and accusations regarding 'fat cats'.

McKnight and Tomkins (1999) believed, however, that the weakness of the link reported was due to how pay was measured. They said that most studies measured total pay as salary plus annual bonus, excluding share options, and in the empirical estimates they failed to distinguish between the various components of pay. In their own study, they included share options and also distinguished between the various pay components. They found that salaries and bonuses were significantly associated with firm size (measured as sales revenue). They also found that changes in the value of executive share options were strongly and significantly related to performance (shareholder returns) over both the short and long term. These results suggest that different pay categories could be employed to drive different aspects of corporate decision making. The authors suggested that share options provide performance-enhancing incentives to senior management, as intended by corporate governance reforms, and that they are consistent with a shareholder-driven view of the firm. However, it leaves questions about the size of the reward; 'small changes in performance seem to have an exponential effect on changes in executive reward' (McKnight and Tomkins, 1999).[7]

7.8.2   *CEO attrition/turnover*

Executive turnover may result from resignation or termination for performance-related reasons. The latter is a governance tool to the extent that it is based on a perceived goal, preference or strategy misalignment between owners (as represented by the board) and the executive. Thus, the stock market often responds to news of a senior sacking as an indication of a positive or negative strategic direction change or the breakdown of corporate governance. In essence, involuntary executive turnover is the end result of a failure in one or more the governance mechanisms that are intended to encourage shareholder value maximization as the central driving force of the firm.

These and other possible reasons for turnover have been analysed in a number of studies. For example, Volpin (2002) studied the effects of ownership and control structure on executive turnover and company performance among Italian firms. Overall, the evidence suggested that the lower was the sensitivity of executive turnover to performance (interpreted as reflecting poor governance and possible management entrenchment), the lower was the firm valuation (Tobin's q). More specifically, the study found that executive turnover was more sensitive to performance the larger the share of cash flow rights enjoyed by the controlling shareholder.

Furthermore, the sensitivity of executive turnover to firm performance tended to be lower for executives belonging to the family of the controlling shareholder than for other executives – indicative of management entrenchment.

Dahya *et al.* (2000) studied the effect of the adoption of Cadbury's corporate governance codes on the structure of UK corporate boards and on the linkage between top management turnover and firm performance. They observed that involuntary top executive turnover had increased, especially for firms that had adopted the Cadbury code; this they interpreted as being consistent with the view that Cadbury's recommendations had improved the quality of board monitoring and control. Further, their econometric estimates indicated that top executive turnover was significantly and negatively associated with firm performance, suggesting that poor firm performance increases the likelihood that top executives vacate their position. On the other hand, they found that equity ownership by the board reduced the likelihood that the top executive would quit. In general, they found: that compliance with the Cadbury code increased the likelihood of executive turnover, after controlling for performance; and, more specifically, that this increased sensitivity of turnover seemed to be due to the increased proportion of outside directors on the boards rather than the separation of the CEO–chair positions – two standard prescriptions of Cadbury.

7.8.3 *Market for corporate control*

In the UK and other 'Anglo models', the market for corporate control represents an important governance mechanism. It serves to impose additional (external) discipline on boards and managers. Again, its role becomes apparent in the face of governance failures within firms, as reflected in takeovers and mergers – that is, the threat of a takeover (or merger, or bankruptcy) would be occasioned by weak performance, itself the culmination of weak governance and other factors. The empirical literature has discussed the market for corporate control in two relevant contexts. The first examines the role of the corporate control market in the strategy of firms, for instance in their diversification decisions. Some empirical evidence on the connection between governance, strategy and diversification was presented in section 7.7.1. The second context focuses mainly on the disciplining of 'errant' firms. Typically, the empirical question asked here concerns the association between specific governance mechanisms and the likelihood of being taken over. Other studies, though, have focused on the activities of the CEO and the board in fighting takeover threats, either *ex ante* mechanisms (e.g. adoption of board classification, 'golden parachutes' and the use of 'poison pills') or *ex post* ones ('white knights'), and ask how these relate to performance, management entrenchment, and so on.[8] For example, Davis (1991) examined the effect of governance mechanisms on the adoption of 'poison pills', while Banerjee and Owers (1992) studied 'white knights'.

7.9   Conclusions

The above review has demonstrated the theoretical basis for the adoption of the governance reforms that have become prominent in the last two decades, but especially since Cadbury (1992). Most of the recommended reforms are consistent with agency theory. In practice, many of the ones to do with board leadership and composition have been implemented, at least by the bigger companies. However, the reforms that require independent committees for the appointment of directors and managers' remuneration appear to have been implemented by about only half the larger firms. Arguably, other proposals already implemented may substitute for the apparent non-implementation of the latter. For example, the evidence is that the majority of large firms have implemented the proposal to have the majority of the board composed of non-executive directors and to have separate CEOs and chairs of the board. These could meet the requirements for board independence, which the nomination committee is also meant to achieve. Furthermore, the adoption of share options is an incentive-aligning mechanism that could substitute for the role of the remuneration committee in empirical terms.

This possibility of substitution between governance tools may also account for the ambiguity in some studies (as well as the facts that they apply different measurements for the same phenomena and use samples drawn from different time periods, industries or countries). There are several governance mechanisms at play at every point in time, and so isolating a single one for analysis, implicitly assuming independence among governance tools, may be misleading. This view is similar to that held by Rediker and Seth (1995), who examined the possibility of linkages between alternative internal governance mechanisms and found evidence suggestive of strong substitution effects. The use of more appropriate statistical methods could address the issues of substitutability and endogeneity. A few studies have already employed these or similar models. However, Barnhart and Rosenstein (1998) also point to specification problems.[9]

In concluding, most of the above review proceeded in the context of the governance–performance association. However, as observed in section 7.1 and highlighted in several other sections above, management is clearly not a passive player. Management skills, experience, age and other factors are important drivers of the goals/preferences pursued and governance tools adopted, as well as the implementation of the resulting strategic and operational decisions.

Notes

1 This chapter was written Gregory Jobome and appeared in Bosworth and Jobome (2001). Subsequent amendments have been made by both Greg and myself. Thanks to Greg for all his work on this and for permission to include it in the book.

2 In over 85 per cent of Fortune 500 industrial companies, the chair of the board also serves as the corporation's CEO (Pearce and Zahra, 1991); similar results have been reported with regard to small corporations (reported by Daily and Dalton, 1992).

3 Ownership is typically more dispersed in the UK and USA than in continental Europe. Franks and Mayer (1997) state that in only 16 per cent of the largest 170 UK companies did one shareholder own over 25 per cent of the shares, compared with 85 per cent in Germany and 80 per cent in France.

4 A panel follows a group of firms over a number of periods. If all firm observations are available in every period the panel is said to be 'balanced'; if some firms are observed in some periods but not in others, the panel is 'unbalanced'.

5 Note, however, that Mueller and Spitz (2002, p. 24) also report a result more difficult to reconcile – that 'companies totally owned by managers do especially well'.

6 Other studies analysing the relationship between duality and performance include Daily and Johnson (1997), Davidson *et al.* (1998) and Conyon and Peck (1998).

7 Further discussions on executive compensation can be found in Gomez-Mejia (1994), Hermalin and Weisbach (1991), Beatty and Zajac (1994), Barkema and Gomez-Mejia (1998) and Aggarwal and Samwick (1999).

8 'Golden parachutes' are provisions which specify a monetary compensation to executives in the event of a displacement following a takeover. 'Poison pills' confer special rights to the target firm's owners in the event of a control change. They impose significant financial penalties on bidders. A 'white knight' is a friendly investor who acquires a company instead of the original (hostile) bidder.

9 In their own study Barnhart and Rosenstein (1998) applied 3SLS and used an instrumental variable technique in order to avoid these problems. They found, however, that the results were strongly dependent on overall model specification and the specification of the first-stage regressions, and so concluded that simultaneous equation results in this area should be interpreted cautiously.

Part IV
Discretionary investments and firm performance

Chapter 8

Research and development, innovation and performance

8.1 Introduction

The aim of this chapter, in the first instance, is to consider the link between R&D, innovation and firm performance. The literature linking R&D and innovation to organizational performance has generally focused on one of two main measures (see Chapter 3): MV and TFP (in relation to the knowledge production function). Here the empirical economics and the corresponding finance and accounting literatures are particularly strong. In carrying out this review, an attempt is made to highlight the results relating to the direct effect of the organization's own R&D and the indirect effect of the R&D activities of other firms, through spillovers and externalities. This literature says nothing about the role of management *per se*, but it does throw light on one of the most important of the strategic tools that managers can use to achieve their high-level, enterprise-wide goals. While the main literature explores the returns to R&D and innovation at the margin, across large samples of companies, it largely omits reference to the risk of R&D, innovation and NPL. This forms the focus for the latter sections of the chapter (see also Chapters 10, 13 and 14).

Section 8.2 outlines the MV approach. In this, current R&D is perceived to give rise to a stream of future profits and, therefore, should be reflected in the MV of the enterprise. Section 8.3 focuses on the knowledge production function, in which current and past R&D activities are assumed to affect the current TFP of the enterprise. Both these sections discuss the idea of spillover effects, but they are illustrated in slightly more detail in section 8.3. Section 8.4 considers R&D and innovation, focusing particularly on the evidence regarding NPLs. Section 8.5 considers the evidence concerning the risk of invention and innovation (the discussion regarding the management of risk is dealt with in Chapter 13). Finally, section 8.6 draws the main conclusions.

8.2   R&D, innovation and firm performance: the MV approach

8.2.1   *General principles of the MV approach*

While Tobin's q is essentially used as a marginal investment rule (see section 3.3.3), it was recognized from a fairly early stage that, given the way the book value of assets are measured (i.e. essentially as the tangible assets of the firm), the q also reflected the ratio of intangible to tangible assets, and would be higher the greater was the (unaccounted) value of intangible assets. While some authors, such as Lev, are now attempting to adjust the book value of assets to include knowledge capital,[1] the general approach adopted in econometric studies is to regress q on proxy measures of the intangibles or, somewhat more generally, regress the MV of the company not only to the book value of tangible assets but also to a variety of measures of intangibles (often proxied by various measures of R&D and the IP of the firm). The idea is that, using statistical techniques, it should be possible to disentangle the value that the market places upon tangible and intangible assets.

In this work, MV is measured as the sum of ordinary shares, preference shares and debt – the amount it would cost to buy the firm 'lock, stock and barrel'. The tangible assets are ideally measured as the replacement value of items such as buildings, land, plant and machinery, vehicles and so on. The intangibles are mainly proxied by R&D expenditures (or stock), patent grants (or stock) and advertising expenditures, although this list of measures is extended somewhat below. The role played by advertising, and the way it interacts with R&D, is considered in greater detail in Chapters 10 and 13.

8.2.2   *Empirical specification*

Standard MV framework
Griliches (1981) suggests that the MV is given by:

$$MV_{it} = f(K_{it}, G_{it}) = q(K_{it} + G_{it}) \qquad\qquad 8.1$$

where K is the stock of tangible assets of the firm and G is the stock of intangible assets. Estimation of specifications based on equation 8.1 normally take place using a panel data-set where i denotes the ith firm and t the tth time period. Note that while $f(.)$ represents a general functional form, q (a variant of Tobin's q) is a constant, which denotes the 'current MV coefficient' of the firm's assets (which reflects variations across firms in their risk and monopoly positions). Equation 8.1 is based on an accounting identity. In practice, however, this is reasonable only if K and G are measured by their true values – in which case q would be unity. In fact, the magnitudes of K and G are based on accounting measures or other proxies that do not necessarily correspond to their economic value. Thus, the functional form of equation 8.1 may not be appropriate. For example, if for some reason the level of K and G – as measured by accountants – somehow interact, then the marginal products of K and G are not necessarily independent and equal (as they are in equation 8.1). The literature adopts a more general functional form to allow for this.[2]

Spillovers
We now turn to the issue of spillovers, and rewrite the basic form of the model to include an additional, spillover variable:

$$MV_i = f(K_i, G_i, GP_i) \qquad\qquad 8.2$$

where K and G are as defined above, i denotes ith firm's activity (for simplicity the time period has been dropped) and GP denotes the general pool of information or intangibles relevant to the ith firm, such that:

$$\frac{\partial MV_i}{\partial GP_i} \geq 0$$

This model has been extensively tested using either R&D or patent-based measures of the pool. Despite the fact that it is difficult to define the pool, because it requires measures of distance of the technology of one firm from that of others (i.e. spillovers are more likely the closer the distance), the results of the various studies consistently suggest large and significant spillover effects. The pool exists because each firm is unable to appropriate all of the benefits arising from its own R&D and innovation activities. (The issue of spillovers is considered in more detail in section 8.3.2.)

Competitive R&D in the MV framework
There are still aspects of this model that appear to require more extensive testing in the literature – in particular, the effects of rivalry between firms. In the case of R&D, for example, greater expenditure by one company should, other things being equal, raise the MV of that company and have a deleterious effect on its competitors:

$$MV_i = f(K_i, G_i, G_j, GP_i) \qquad\qquad 8.3$$

where G_j refers to the R&D of rival j, such that:

$$\frac{\partial MV_i}{\partial GP_j} \leq 0$$

While there is an extensive literature on patent races, there is little empirical testing of this, although there is some anecdotal evidence of coincident inventions. In practice, few examples of the inclusion of competitors' discretionary investments appear in the literature – however, see Megna and Klock (1993). There is considerably more evidence of competitive effects in the case of advertising (e.g. Hurwitz and Caves, 1988; see also Chapter 10).

8.2.3 'Generic' versus 'new news' models

Two forms of the model
There are two main approaches adopted in the literature – the 'generic' and the 'new news' models. The distinction is that the 'generic' models use the observed levels of the variables, MV, K, G, and so on. The 'new news' models argue that the intangible variables have two components: first, an anticipated or expected element, G_1; and, second, an unanticipated or surprise element, G_2. Studies that distinguish the two components find the surprise variable to be the more important influence on variations in MV. However, studies that include just the *level* variable, G_1, find that this is significant in the explanation of variations in MV. Thus, the mainstream 'new news' literature is almost indistinguishable from the 'generic' MV literature, but it does help to emphasize the 'surprise' element of an announcement or event.

Natural experiments: changes in patent life, patent expiry and changes in accounting practices
There is strong evidence from natural experiments that throw light on the value of intangible assets. It is possible to provide a number of examples, based on the lengthening of patent life, patent expiry or changes in accounting practices. Many of the examples reported in this section relate to pharmaceuticals, where patent protection is strong, providing a rich source of examples. However, the general principles apply to other areas of technology.

Natural experiments: patent life. One example of the lengthening of protection is the change, in 1994, of US patent life from seventeen to twenty years (under the General Agreement on Tariffs and Trade, GATT), which, for example, meant that Glaxo's sales of Zantac (the anti-ulcer drug) would decline more slowly than had been expected. The extension of patent life resulted in Glaxo shares jumping 23p (to 663p) on the UK stock market.

A further example is provided by the Waxman–Hatch Act 1984 in the USA (the Drug Price Competition and Restoration Act 1984), which at least two studies have investigated (Grabowski and Vernon, 1992, 1996). This Act had two main effects: to restore part of the patent life lost through the drug testing period; and to facilitate the entry of generic drugs after the expiry of the patent. Grabowski and Vernon (1992) showed that the generic drugs entered the market at a significantly lower price than the incumbent, but the differential declined over time. However, their results also suggested that, following generic entry, the price of the original drug actually rose, at least in nominal terms, with generic prices rising somewhat more quickly. This rather perverse result may reflect the competitive environment of the time. Evidence that the environment was changing comes from Grabowski and Vernon (1996), who reported generic competition increasing in more recent years (which may be a result of the effects of the Waxman–Hatch Act itself), with the result that original brands would lose up to half of their market share within a year of patent expiry.

Finally, a statistical study of the effects of changes in Canadian law on pharmaceuticals companies' share prices on the New York Stock Exchange found negative effects of the establishment of the Harley Committee (which introduced compulsory licensing for pharmaceuticals), positive effects of the establishment of the Eastman Committee (which recommended less harsh treatment) and further gains of about 8.5 per cent when Bill C-22 was passed (which went beyond the recommendations of the Eastman Committee in relaxing the controls on pharmaceuticals) (Shapiro and Switzer, 1993).

Natural experiments: patent termination and expiry. It is possible to study pharmaceuticals that either get 'overtaken' by the introduction of new drugs or reach the end of their allotted patent lives. Over the period January 1993 to December 1995, thirteen key pharmaceutical patents were due to expire in the USA (in practice, the GATT provided an extension to some). For example, Tagamet (another anti-ulcer drug, produced by SmithKline Beecham) was due to expire in May 1994, but had already been experiencing major market erosion from Zantac and, subsequently, from Losec. Statistical studies by Hurwitz and Caves (1988) and Caves *et al.* (1991) show the decline in original brand share as generic entrants appeared. In Hurwitz and Caves (1988), the revised brand share was directly proportional to the age of the brand. However, market share of the original brand was increased by the company's own advertising and decreased by competitors' advertising. The revised share was also negatively affected by the number of new entrants, which was itself directly proportional to market size and age of the original brand. The continued adoption of the original brand was argued to be a reflection of brand loyalty.

Numerous other studies in this area map the growth in competition and the decline in price, revenue and profit on the expiry of patent protection (see, for example, Shaw and Shaw, 1977). Hudson (2000) investigated the effect of patent expiry and subsequent generic entry, using a comparative international approach, with results for the USA, the UK, Germany and Japan. The main findings were:

(i)   the probability of entry of generic drugs and the lag between patent expiry and the entry of generics were linked to the size of the market at the time of expiry;

(ii)   the rate of decay in the revenue from the original brand was directly proportional to the size of the market and to the price of the incumbent.

There were two main differences across countries: first, the UK appeared to be an exception, in that the price decrease was offset by a more significant growth in demand; and second, generic entry in the USA appeared stronger than in the other three countries, perhaps as a result of the Waxman–Hatch Act.

All the studies, but particularly Hudson (2000), suggest that the simple assumption that the static welfare costs of protection exist only during the lifetime of the patent is wrong.

Natural experiments: changes in accounting procedures. Changes in accounting procedures also give rise to a form of natural experiment. The new recommendations of good accounting practice (SSAP13) in 1989 led to a considerable increase in the numbers of firms reporting their R&D expenditure. The increasing number of firms that report R&D for the first time gives rise to a research opportunity, as the newly reporting firms provide 'new news' to the market – information that the market did not previously have (although it may have previously formed expectations on the firm's R&D). This form of experiment is dealt with under the 'new news' models, discussed in section 8.2.4.

8.2.4   *Overview of the empirical literature*

Archetypal MV results
This section contains a brief review of some major studies on MV and intangible assets. The work can be traced to Griliches (1981). That paper was pioneering not only in that it included intangible assets, but also because it tested 'anticipated' versus 'unanticipated' changes in assets. As such, it might more appropriately be discussed below with the 'new news' models. However, as it is the seminal paper in this area, it is dealt with here. Griliches analysed a panel of 157 US firms, which gave 1,000 observations in total. In the model, the influences on the MV of companies included R&D and patenting activity, both of which variables were entered with lags. In addition, both R&D and patents were decomposed into 'actual' and 'surprise' elements, where the latter were measured as the difference between the actual and predicted values. Other variables included the β coefficient as a measure of risk.[3] The results indicated a significant, positive relationship between the MV of the firm (represented by the original measure of Tobin's q) and the level of R&D and patents applied for by the firm. Moreover, it was the unanticipated elements that tended to determine changes in MV.

Later studies broadly followed Griliches. Connolly and Hirschey (1984) used what they called a measure of 'relative excess value' as their dependent variable (i.e. the MV of shares plus the book value of debt minus the book value of tangible assets, normalized by the value of sales). The explanatory variables included R&D per unit of sales, advertising per unit of sales, the concentration ratio, growth rate, diversification index and the β coefficient. A number of the variables were also entered interactively with the concentration ratio. The model was estimated using data for 390 US firms in 1977. The results suggested a positive effect of both R&D and advertising on relative excess value, but a negative interaction between R&D and the concentration ratio.

Ben-Zion (1984) used a panel data-set for 94 US firms over the period 1969 to 1977. The model explained the MV of the firms using the book value of their assets, a measure of earnings, R&D expenditure, firm patents, industry patents and investment. Of the various explanatory factors, earnings were probably the most important influence on the firm's value. However, the MV of the company was also affected by its R&D and investment activity – the latter reflects the introduction of technologies from outside.[4] The patenting activity of the industry had a greater effect on the firm's MV than its own patents.[5] A similar study by Johnson and Pazderka (1993) used a series of short panel data-sets for Canadian firms over the period 1985 to 1988; it found a statistically strong relationship between R&D spending and MV. The results, however, suggested a much higher rate of depreciation of the R&D knowledge stock than historically assumed in the literature (50 per cent compared with 15 per cent).[6] Cockburn and Griliches (1988) used both patents and R&D variables to represent the intangibles. However, as in a number of other studies, both variables played broadly the same role in the explanation of MV (and, of the two, R&D was somewhat stronger, with patents significant when R&D was absent). This preference for R&D over patents reflects the noisiness of standard patent count measures. The resulting estimates suggested a valuation of about US$0.5 million per patent granted.

Hall (1993a) reported the results of a similar model, but using a much more extensive database of US companies, involving 2,480 companies over the period 1973 to 1991. The independent variable was MV, with the book value of tangible assets appearing on the right-hand side of the equation. The main intangibles were R&D (expenditure or stock) and advertising expenditure (which was used as a proxy for brand value). In addition, there was a two-year moving average of cash flow (net of R&D and advertising expenditures) and the growth rate of sales in the current year. Finally, the model included several other variables, such as the investment in unconsolidated subsidiaries, year dummies and so on. The results suggested that, although the mean levels of R&D and advertising expenditures were almost the same, the associated valuation for the period as a whole was around four to five times as high for R&D as for advertising. Recent R&D appeared to have a higher explanatory power than the R&D stock, which probably reflects the standard, rather crude perpetual stock measure, based on an estimated, constant depreciation rate (but it might also reflect a 'new news' aspect – see below).

An important feature of Hall's work (not only in the 1993a paper) is that it tests the changes that have occurred to the returns on R&D and advertising. In Hall (1993a), the very high rates of return on R&D in the earlier period fell away over time and the initially relatively low returns on advertising increased in more recent years. The results appear to suggest that the value of intangible assets created by R&D had a value of between 0.6 and 1 of the tangible assets between 1973 and 1983/84, but declined significantly in the second half of the 1980s. Even the end-of-period figures, where the ratio was smaller, nevertheless constitute very large absolute amounts of IP generated by R&D. However, the study also showed that the stock market's valuation of the intangible assets created by R&D in the US manufacturing sector declined significantly over the 1980s (Hall, 1993a, 1993b). Key explanations of the changes are that:

(i)   the private rate of return on R&D fell;
(ii)   R&D assets depreciated more rapidly in the 1980s than in the 1970s;
(iii) the stock market began discounting R&D capital at a faster rate.

In a study of a balanced panel data-set of 180 UK companies over the period 1984 to 1992, Stoneman and Bosworth (1994) estimated a very similar model. The principal difference was the omission of the advertising variable, given the under-reporting of this variable in UK accounts, and the inclusion of a patent grants or a patent stock measure. In general, R&D performed more strongly than patents; when they were both included in the specification, the former tended to dominate the latter, although both had significant positive coefficients when estimated using the full panel data-set. An additional finding was that the R&D activities and patenting activities tended to be fairly stable for each firm. Thus, it made little difference to the results whether the flow or stock variables were used. By implication, when firm-specific effects were included, they tended to take up a considerable part of the explanation. This issue is considered in the discussion of the study by Bosworth *et al.* (1999b), below.

'New news' studies
The pioneering work of Griliches (1981) has already been discussed. Stoneman and Toivanen (2001) estimated an MV model using data for the UK. In this instance, in addition to the exploration of the valuation of ongoing research activities, the authors were able to use the introduction of the accounting code of conduct for reporting R&D in firm

accounts (SSAP 13) as a natural test of the 'new news' hypothesis (see section 8.2.3). The short data period (1989–1995) used by the authors reflects the relatively late start dates for the reporting of the R&D variable. The fact that firms can choose whether or not to report R&D raises a number of sample selection issues, but these were investigated by the authors. They found evidence that the market does value ongoing R&D activities, but that it places an even higher value on newly declared R&D. However, the authors also found that patents tended to carry a negative sign when included with R&D. They argued that this may reflect a number of influences, including problems of appropriability, as well as the need for further expenditure on R&D and physical capital to bring the product to market (detracting from short-term profits) and the risks inherent in the exploitation of new inventions.

There is also a closely related literature that looks at the impact of new R&D announcements on the share prices of companies (e.g. Chan *et al.*, 1990; Chaney *et al.*, 1991; Jarrell *et al.*, 1985; Zantout and Tsetsekos, 1994). These studies indicate that for the USA, *surprise* announcements of increased R&D spending have a significant and positive effect upon MV. In addition, the 'new news' literature spills over from the pure MV literature to the study of NPLs. Chaney *et al.* (1991), for example, showed that the announcement of new products increases the MV of the firm. This issue is considered further in the context of NPLs in section 8.4.

As part of their study, Blundell *et al.* (1999) explored whether 'new news' (i.e. 'surprise') in the innovation variable is the relevant indicator to use in the MV equation. Their study used R&D and patents applied for as innovation variables, but distinguished between the anticipated (projected from past trends) and unanticipated (based on the deviation from the trend). The authors found that only the unanticipated components influenced MV. In a similar vein, Connolly and Hirschey (1990) found that patenting activity (over and above the level that can be expected given the technological opportunity of that sector) has a positive and significant effect on MV. The findings of Ben-Zion (1984) also suggest that it is the unanticipated component of R&D that is important in explaining market returns.

A number of papers also throw some light on this issue insofar as they investigate the relative sizes of stock and flow coefficients for R&D or other IP measures. The paper by Cockburn and Griliches (1988), for example, contains an interesting result regarding the relative valuation of the historical R&D capital and the latest R&D activity, that 'the market values "news" in R&D much more highly than past investments or old patents and that such R&D moves are valued about 50% higher in industries where patent protection is more likely to be efficient' (p. 421). The work of Hall (1993a) also tends to suggest that more weight is placed on recent R&D than past.

However, the distinction between 'anticipated' and 'unanticipated' effects raises an important question about the extent to which the ongoing value the market places on non-surprise elements becomes embedded in the firm fixed effects (FFEs; these are the estimated constants that distinguish one firm from another). Bosworth *et al.* (1999b) used a panel data-set of 197 UK production companies active in R&D from 1990 to 1994. The R&D, patent and trademark variables were not significant when FFEs were accounted for alongside the financial variables. This conclusion was robust whether a stock flow or 'new news' model was adopted. However, a regression of the FFEs on R&D, patents and trademarks averaged over the sample period yielded a cross-sectional estimate in which the IP-related variables explained over 60 per cent of the differences in FFEs across companies.

Hall's (2000) conclusions
Drawing on Hall (2000), the results of the empirical literature may be summarized as follows:

(i)   R&D assets are valued by financial markets. A reasonable fraction of the variance in MV that remains after controlling for ordinary assets is explained by either R&D spending or the stock of R&D (with the flow coefficient averaging about four or five times the stock coefficient). However, there is still a fair amount of unexplained variance.

(ii) The R&D coefficient has not proved stable over time in either the USA or the UK. In the USA, this coefficient reached a recent peak in the early 1980s and has declined since. This result seems to vary across industries, but industry-level findings are somewhat unstable and inconclusive.

(iii) Patents are informative above and beyond R&D, although the correlation is much weaker. The average R^2 for the relationship between Tobin's q and R&D is approximately 0.15, while that for the relationship between patents and R&D is about 0.08.

(iv) Citation-weighted patents are slightly more informative than simple patent counts (see Chapter 4). The average R^2 for citation-weighted patents alone is about 0.10. When both variables are included in a regression, the citation-weighted one clearly wins.

(v)   The pattern of the patent and citation-weighted patent coefficients in the MV regression over time appears to be identical: they are measuring the same thing, but citation weights increase the precision of the estimates.

Table 8.1, based on Hall (2000), sets out the size of the coefficient estimates with regard to the coefficient on the R&D/asset ratio.[7] In the main, these parameter estimates range from around 2.5 to 8. This suggests that

Table 8.1 Market value – innovation studies with R&D and patents

Study	Country	Sample period	Functional form	Coefficient values estimated on:			
				R&D flow	R&D stock	Patents or innovation	Trademarks
Griliches (1981)	USA	1968–74	Linear (q)	–[b]	1.0–2.0	0.08–0.25[c]	–
Ben-Zion (1984)	USA	1969–78	Linear (MV)	3.4	–	0.07	–
Jaffe (1986)	USA	1973, 1979	Linear (q)	–	7.9	–	–
Hirschey and Weygandt (1985)	USA	1977	Linear (q)	8.3	–	–	–
Connolly et al. (1986)	USA	1977	Linear (EV/S)[a]	7.0	–	4.4	–
Connolly and Hirschey (1988)	USA	1977	Linear (EV/S)[a]	5.6	–	5.7	–
Connolly and Hirschey (1990)	USA	1977	Linear (MV/S)	5.7	–	5.7	–
Hall (1993a)	USA	1973–91	Linear (MV)	2.5–3.0	0.5	–	–
Hall (1993b)	USA	1972–90	Linear (q)	2.0–10.0	0.5–2.0	–	–
Megna and Klock (1993)	USA*	1977–90	Linear (q)	–	0.8	0.4	–
Bosworth and Mahdian (1999)	UK**	1986–95	Linear (MV)	0.5	–	2.4	0.1
Chauvin and Hirschey (1993a)	USA	1988–90	Linear (MV)	6.5	–	–	–
Blundell et al. (1999)	UK	1972–82	Linear (MV)	–	–	1.9	–
Stoneman and Toivanen (1997)	UK	1989–95	Linear (MV)	2.5	–	Insignificant	–
Chauvin and Hirschey (1993b)	USA	1974–90	Linear (MV)	–	–	–	–
Hirschey et al. (1998)	USA	1989–95	Linear (q)	1.7	0.2	3.3	–

[a] EV denotes the market value of equity shares and S is sales revenue.
[b] – indicates that the coefficient was not estimated or could not be derived.
[c] Patents appear to be measured in 100s.
Note: Not all of these studies are detailed in the list of references – the interested reader should refer to Hall (2000).
*Semiconductor sector only. **Pharmaceutical sector only.
Source: Adapted from Hall (2000).

the 'shadow' value of R&D is higher than investment in tangible assets. The lowest figure reported for R&D/K is by Bosworth and Mahdian (1999), for the UK pharmaceutical sector, but the resulting coefficient was significantly higher when their other two intangible assets (patents innovation and trademarks) were excluded from the specification. However, their preferred specification included R&D, patents and trademarks, all of which had coefficients that were significant at the 1 per cent level.

8.3 Knowledge production function

8.3.1 *Conceptual underpinnings*

In the knowledge production function, the output of the firm, Y,[8] is related to its inputs. Unlike standard production functions, however, the factor inputs include not only physical capital (tangible assets, K[9]) and employment (E), but also the stock of intangible assets, G (such as the R&D knowledge stock):

$$Y = f(K, E, G) = AK^\alpha E^\beta G^\gamma \qquad 8.4$$

where A is the level of technology parameter and α, β and γ are constants that reflect the change in output caused by small changes in K, E and G, respectively.[10]

For simplicity, the knowledge production function is assumed to be log-linear. Note that TFP, y, is given by:

$$y = \frac{Y}{K^\alpha E^\beta}$$

which, using equation 8.4, can also be written as:

$$y = AG^\gamma \qquad 8.5$$

and, in terms of rates of change over time:

$$\overset{\circ}{y} = \overset{\circ}{A} + \gamma \overset{\circ}{G}$$

In other words, the growth in TFP is driven by changes in the stocks of intangible assets, $\overset{\circ}{G}$ (which are determined primarily by discretionary investments such as R&D, advertising, etc.), and by autonomous technological and other changes, $\overset{\circ}{A}$. If these intangibles are generated by R&D then, clearly, it is possible to calculate the returns to investment in R&D.

8.3.2 *Externalities and spillovers*

The group of models that attempt to account for the knowledge production function has been extended to include the broader pool of R&D knowledge, in the following manner:

$$Y = f(K, E, G) = f(K, E, RS, RP) = AK^{\alpha}E^{\beta}RS^{\gamma}RP^{\tau} \qquad 8.6$$

where *RS* is the firm's own stock of R&D knowledge and *RP* denotes the wider pool and is included to pick up spillover effects (externalities). The results suggest that each company benefits from the general pool of R&D information available. If each firm is able fully to appropriate all the benefits of its own R&D indefinitely (or at least far into the future), then there will be no spillovers of this type – but it is clear that this is not the case (as in the case of basic science – Arrow, 1962 – or patent disclosures). Externalities are closely linked to the concept of appropriability. In this case, the idea is that one firm benefits from the R&D of other firms or from the body of knowledge that they develop. Griliches makes it clear that this is quite distinct from buying equipment from other firms embodying new technology or the technological change generated by the firm's own R&D, as it is a 'free good', and not something that companies pay for (Griliches, 1992, pp. 30–31).

The spillover result is extremely important from a government policy perspective. The result implies (in common with the findings of the new growth theories) that firms, taking decisions based upon their own private calculus, will invest in R&D at a level below the social optimum (see Chapter 14). In the spillover and externalities literature, for example, the firm invests only up to the point where the private return to R&D is equal to its cost at the margin. It does not take into account the fact that it would benefit from a greater industry- or economy-wide investment in R&D. Nevertheless, according to the spillover hypothesis, if there is an overall expansion in R&D, all firms benefit.

8.3.3 *Overview of empirical estimates*

The production function approach appears to have been a useful one, as it yields information about not only the private but also the social returns to R&D that arise from the unintended pooling effects:

> there has been a significant number of reasonably well done studies all pointing in the same direction: R&D spillovers are present, their magnitude may be quite large, and social rates of return remain significantly above private rates.... R&D returns account for half of the growth in output per man and about three quarters of the measured TFP growth, most of the explanatory power coming from the spillover component. (Griliches, 1992, pp. 43–44)

There have been a number of reviews of the large, international literature (Table 8.2 presents a selection of studies), and a summary of the results can be found in Mairesse and Sassenou (1991), Mairesse and Mohnen (1995) and Griliches (1992, 1995). While the results differ between countries and sectors, and so on, in the main the estimated rates of return have the following features:

Table 8.2 Selected estimates of returns to R&D and R&D spillovers

Author	Subject	Rate of return to public R&D	
Agriculture			
Griliches (1958)	Hybrid corn	35–40	
	Hybrid sorghum	20	
Peterson (1967)	Poultry	21–25	
Schmitz and Seckler (1970)	Tomato harvester	37–46	
Griliches (1964)	Aggregate	35–40	
Evenson (1968)	Aggregate	41–50	
Knutson and Tweeten (1979)	Aggregate	28–47	
Huffman and Evenson (1991)	Crops	45–62	
	Livestock	11–83	
	Aggregate	43–67	
Industry		Rates of return to R&D	
		Own R&D	Spillover effects
Case studies			
Mansfield *et al.* (1977)		25	56
Input–output weighted			
Terleckyi (1974)	Total	28	48
	Private	29	78
Sveikauskas (1981)		10–23	50
Goto and Suzuki (1989)		26	80
R&D weighted (patent flows)			
Griliches and Lichtenberg (1984)		46–69	11–62
Mohnen and Lepine (1988)		56	28
Proximity (technological distance)			
Jaffe (1986)			30% of 'within' (own) value
Cost functions			
Bernstein and Nadiri (1988, 1989)			20% of 'within' (own) value
	Differs by industry	9–27	10–160
Bernstein and Nadiri (1991)		14–28	Median 56% of (own) 'within' value

Note: Not all of these studies are detailed in the list of references – the interested reader should refer to Griliches (1992).
Source: Griliches (1992, p. 43); adapted from original manuscript of Huffman and Evenson (1993, Table 14.2).

(i)   they are almost without exception positive;
(ii)   they are often large, indicating high rates of return to R&D;
(iii)   they are often at least as large for spillover effects (i.e. the effects of the 'outside pool' of R&D) as they are for the impact of the firm's own R&D.

While the role of spillovers appears to be important, there are some issues that need to be resolved by future research. First, it is not clear that they are pure public goods in the way suggested in the literature on the knowledge production function. As noted in Chapter 4, a firm's own R&D generally has two components: one that involves searching the science and technology base, and another that involves the synthesis and creative activities based upon the knowledge garnered. Until it becomes possible to subdivide R&D into these two components, it is not feasible to determine the extent to which the contribution of the external pool is a spillover or not. Some support for the idea that not all contributions of the external pool are spillover effects can be found in the survey evidence that innovation, including the use of outside inventions, is aided by the existence of an R&D department within the company and by the existence of more highly qualified workers in R&D activities (Bosworth *et al.*, 1992). In a statistical study of UK manufacturing firms, innovation, including the adoption of outside inventions and ideas, was shown to be positively and significantly influenced by the company's own R&D activities (Bosworth, 1996).

Second, the outside pool may not be 'free' at all, but may involve companies in extensive licensing expenditures. If these licensing expenditures are not considered explicitly in the empirical analysis, then there will be a tendency to overestimate spillover effects. According to Arora *et al.* (2001):

> Technological spillovers play an important role in the process of economic growth.... However, the typical description of the mechanism of these spillovers is, in Alfred Marshall's often used phrase, one where 'the secrets ... are in the air'. Important as this ethereal mechanism may be, there are other mechanisms, more material and more amenable to economic analysis, through which technology is transferred across sectors and countries.

8.4   Innovation and NPL studies

8.4.1   *Defining new products*

First, it is important to be clear on what is meant by 'new product innovation'.[11] In marketing, new products are generally viewed as a continuum that may incorporate a minor change, such as different packaging (e.g. Yardley's rebranding of its cosmetic line), through to radical 'new to the world' products. Johne (1994) coins the phrase 'new-style product development' to denote product development that accesses quite new customer groups, such as Direct Line insurance or First Direct telephone banking. These are examples of new products that became successful because existing markets were turned into a new market via the combination of product and market developments (i.e. product repositioning and supply developments were required).

Booz Allen Hamilton Inc. (1982) outlined six types of product change:

(i)   repositionings – existing products targeted at new markets or segments, which may involve packaging changes (e.g. baby shampoo targeted at men);
(ii)   cost reductions – essentially the same product but reconfigured in order to keep prices down or improve profits;
(iii)   improvements and revisions – made to existing products (e.g. 'new improved Persil');
(iv)   new product lines – which allow a company to enter a market segment for the first time (e.g. Marks and Spencer's entry into home furnishings);
(v)   additions to existing product lines – which could be new flavours or colours (e.g. Levis' introduction of black denims) or distinct but related products (e.g. the Mr Muscle brand extending from kitchen cleaners to agents to help unblock sinks);
(vi)   new to the world – entirely new products (e.g. the first CD player).

However, only the last four can be considered to be 'new' and, even then, they appear to differ in the degree to which they are radical departures and, hence, the degree of risk involved for the company.

8.4.2   *Returns to NPLs*

While there are a large number of individual results, the present discussion focuses on a study by the management consultancy Profit Impact of Marketing Strategy (PIMS, 1998) into the role of innovation in the area of FMCGs. The authors concluded about their earlier work:

> In the work on all business types for the [European] Commission, we showed that relative innovation advantage – maintaining a higher proportion of new products and services in a business' sales mix than the competition – was probably the most powerful influence on competitive share gain. In fmcg markets … it isn't enough just to stay ahead; the rewards go to those that manage to stretch their innovation lead over rivals, gaining share as they do so. (PIMS, 1998, p. 10)

Figure 8.1 shows that the increase in the share of revenues generated by new product activity is correlated with improved relative innovation (PIMS, 1998, p. 11). Companies that experienced a rising proportion of their revenues from new products were those that had improved their level of innovation relative to that of other firms.

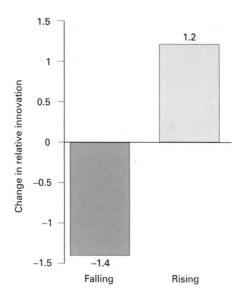

Change in percentage revenue for new products

Figure 8.1 Innovation and proportion of revenue attributable to new products. Source: PIMS (1998).

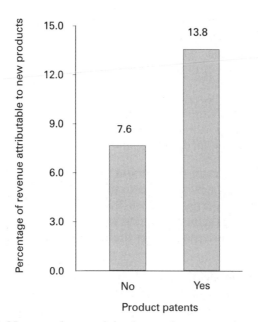

Product patents

Figure 8.2 New product activity in product patenting and non-patenting firms. Source: PIMS (1998).

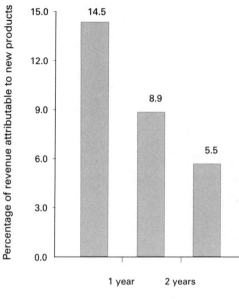

Figure 8.3 Percentage of new products and NPD time. Source: PIMS (1998).

Figure 8.2 further shows the positive link between product patenting activity and the introduction of new products. Again, it seems likely that firms that take out patents will report a higher proportion of their revenues coming from new products. This may occur because the patents indicate that they are more active in designing new products or because the patent protection allows them to charge a higher price for the products in question.

Figure 8.3 demonstrates that speed to market is also important. There are two likely interpretations of the result:

(i)   products make a greater contribution to total revenues in companies that are able to get new products to the market more quickly;

(ii) companies that undertake more NPLs are likely to gain experience in terms of getting the new products to market more quickly, and so gain competitive advantages over their competitors.

Figure 8.4 shows the link between lagged R&D intensity, subsequent NPL activity and, by implication, the likely proportion of revenues attributable to new products. While the relationship is not monotonic, it can be seen that the rate of NPL activities is almost twice as high in the most intensive R&D companies than in the least intensive companies. The authors argue that 'The causality of the relationship can be argued both

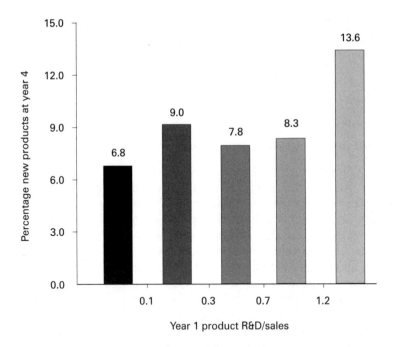

Figure 8.4 New product activity and lagged R&D intensity. Source: PIMS (1998).

ways, i.e. market growth both stimulates and is stimulated by new product introduction. The relationship is certainly powerful!' (PIMS, 1998, p. 18).

Finally, the authors argue (PIMS, 1998, p.19) that 'brands boost the value of R&D', as shown by the relationship between branded company value added per employee and that of all products (the implication is again that unbranded would appear even lower than the overall average of all companies):

> The 'extra' payback from R&D in the branded fmcg sector may be due to the dependence of businesses in this group on differentiation and quality as their key competitive advantage. Branding is a key tool in communicating differentiation to end users and in persuading them to buy new products or product improvements. If this relationship is in place, the chances of success in the process of turning development ideas into successful products which satisfy customers may be greater. The evidence suggests that the combination of branding and R&D investment (which is a key generator of potential differentiation) creates more value. (PIMS, 1998, p. 19)

In addition, the authors further investigated this relationship to see when branding is particularly effective in providing higher returns to R&D. They argue:

Branding appears to provide better returns to R&D if associated with product innovation, immediate customer focus, stable relationships, greater emphasis on communication to end users and free access to markets. It also requires a reasonably well-established market position to capitalise on the investments in new products and communication. (PIMS, 1998, p. 20; see also Chapter 10).

8.5   Invention and innovation risks

8.5.1   *Risk and discretionary investments*

One surprising feature of the mainstream economics literature on the returns to R&D is that it says little or nothing about risk. The present section therefore focuses on the private risk associated with the discretionary investments of the firm. Clearly, in the real world, decisions to invest in R&D are actually associated with uncertainty. However, many researchers are currently trying to uncover the underlying distributions that allow analysts to deal with this as an issue of 'risk' rather than 'uncertainty'.[12] This allows some insights into what the implications for investment are. Risk causes a problem for investors because, while the distribution of outcomes from any given investment may have a mean that yields a positive and acceptable return, the actual outcome may be below the mean (and even so far below that the investment is loss making). The existence of risk implies that, for any given £1 million expenditure (e.g. on R&D), say, the effect on the sum of the discounted stream of additional net revenues[13] generated might have a mean of £1.5 million, but a single expenditure drawn from this distribution can take a wide range of values about this mean with various probabilities.

What, therefore, do the results reported in the literature on the knowledge production function tell us? The results show the marginal effect of a further £1 million spent on R&D averaged across all companies in the sample. If risk is present, this will be associated with higher standard errors attached to the R&D or other discretionary investment variables, and the positive and significant estimates would be more prone to breaking down in smaller samples – which is precisely what happens. Evidence for this can be found in the preference for citation-weighted patent measures, as more highly cited patents are, on balance, more valuable (see section 4.4.3). In addition, to some extent, the effects of the risk will be observed in the error term of the regression equation. Thus, while the equations may suggest high rates of return, they say next to nothing about the degree of risk – which will be crucial to the company's views about whether to undertake the investment.

Are the discretionary investments of the firm risky activities? The degree of risk is inversely related to the extent to which the expenditures are sunk costs (Dixit and Pindyck, 1994; Pindyck, 1991). Dixit and Pindyck (1994, p. 8) argue that:

Investment expenditures are sunk costs when they are firm or industry specific. For example, most investments in marketing and advertising are firm specific and cannot be recovered. Hence they are clearly sunk costs.

In some respects this is somewhat less clear in the case of R&D insofar as the inventive outputs may have a market in other firms and even other industries (e.g. the IP may be sold or licensed). On the other hand, most research is targeted on areas of inventive activity that are of particular strategic importance to the firm and are, therefore, firm specific. While it may be possible to sell off a research unit, perhaps as a separate company, the asymmetry of knowledge between buyers and the vendor make this difficult.

8.5.2 Sources of risk

To illustrate some of the possible sources of risk, assume a simple linear model of the innovation process, in which each stage is associated with different types of risk (or different balances of these types of risk). Starting with the R&D process, two types of risk are present:

(i)   the technological risk of finding an invention – that is, of finding a solution to a problem which requires an advance in technology;
(ii) the competitive risk in the invention process – of being the first to find the solution being sought, which will depend upon the number and quality of the other fishermen at the pool.

Assume that the firm comes successfully through stages (i) and (ii) and is awarded a patent. In this simple linear example, the firm may then decide whether to proceed to product launch. This may involve further sources of risk:

(iii) appropriation risk – with regard to the strength of the patent and other IPR protection that surrounds the invention;
(iv) further development of the invention to product stage, involving R&D, which may have a risk of finding an appropriate product solution (e.g. in the UK pharmaceuticals that are rejected by the Medicines and Healthcare Products Regulatory Agency);
(v)   a further competitive risk – of being the first to develop a product that has the potential to satisfy (a substantial part of) the market.

Assuming that the firm finds a satisfactory product solution that is not pre-empted, then, in our simple linear model, it must decide whether to launch. Even after launch, there are other risks, such as:

(vi) the risk of failing to find a profitable market niche (i.e. the product is launched, but rejected by the market, as happened in the case of the Ford Edsel – see Brooks, 1971);

(vii) the risk of what initially appears to be a profitable niche being undermined by the launch of competitor products or by counterfeiting and
pirating.

8.5.3 *Evidence of risk and skewed returns*

This section provides evidence about the riskiness of innovative activities
of various types. It will become immediately clear that the distribution
of returns implied is complex and, in particular, highly skewed, with a
large number of relatively low-value (often negative-value) outcomes and
a very small number of extremely high-value outcomes. While providing
some caveats about the interpretation of these distributions as reflecting
risk, the discussion concludes with a probable explanation of why these
complex distributions emerge.

New product launches
The literature on the commercial value of NPLs largely focuses on the
risks rather the returns. The literature consistently reports a high level of
failure to progress from the original idea to a successful product in the
marketplace. In a review of seven studies, Crawford (1991) reported a
considerable range of failure rates, averaging from around 30 per cent to
as high as 95 per cent, with an average of about 38 per cent. Failure rates
appeared to be somewhat lower for industrial products and higher for consumer goods. There are many factors determining the differences between
studies, including definition and methodology, but more especially the
industries, firms and markets covered. In some areas, where there are
technological as well as market risks, success may be even more elusive. It
has been argued, for example, that around 3,000 new ideas are necessary
to produce one commercially successful product and pharmaceutical companies may require 6,000 to 8,000 ideas for every one successful product
(Stevens and Burley, 1997). Stevens and Burley (1997) interviewed eight
current or retired managing directors and patent attorneys associated with
two US chemical companies; the authors suggested that only 5–10 per
cent of the 9,000 active patents administered by the interviewees had even
marginal commercial potential and, of these, under 1 per cent earned
significant returns.

Patent values
Scherer (1996) examined the profit estimates in the early survey of the
value of 600 US patents by Sanders *et al.* (1958). Of the 600, however,
only 74 usable observations with positive profits were obtained (149 additional patents were associated with, generally small, losses). The data pose
problems at both the lower and the upper tail (the latter is open-ended,
including all patents with a value of $1 million or more). The results

indicated a highly skewed distribution of values.[14] Similar high levels of skewness were found when using information about six US universities' licence royalty incomes. Scherer and Harhoff (2000)[15] reported more recent evidence from surveys and interviews on the values of 772 patents of German origin and 222 patents of US origin on which German patent applications were filed in 1977. They concluded (p. 560) that 54 per cent of the value was concentrated in just five inventions, which exhibited values of DM50 million or higher. More importantly, however, a number of the various data-sets they were able to compile were sufficiently rich to explore the distribution of values. They concluded that, 'For all five samples, the best fitting distribution was the log-normal (surpassing, e.g., Pareto–Levy, Weibull, …)' (Scherer and Harhoff, 2000, p. 562). The log-normal is again a skewed distribution.

New ventures
Stevens and Burley (1997) also reported on interviews with more than ten mainly Californian venture capital companies. They found that as few as 10–15 per cent of the proposals which the companies financed managed to earn a return higher than the cost of capital. Scherer (1996) also summarizes evidence relating to high-technology venture start-ups, particularly proposals funded by the American Research and Development Corporation (ARDC). Scherer (1996, p. 9) reports that, during the mid-1950s, there were a few successes that fuelled an increase in the value of ARDC's portfolio. The explosion in the value of the portfolio that took place around 1966, however, was mainly attributable to one enterprise, the Digital Equipment Company (DEC). Thus, Scherer concludes:

> From the history of ARDC, we see considerable skewness in the returns from high technology investments and the volatility such skewness can impart, despite venture investors' attempts to hedge against risk by forming sizeable portfolios. (Scherer, 1996, p. 9)

A study by Venture Economics (1988) examined 383 start-up company investments made by thirteen US venture portfolios between 1969 and 1985, when they had reached the end of their main commercial lives in 1986. The results suggested that twenty-six of these start-up firms had managed to produce a return of over ten times the original outlay; these accounted for almost 50 per cent of the total terminal value of all investments, while more than a third of the investments yielded less than the original investment by the venture capitalists. Horsley Keogh Associates (1990) analysed the results of 670 separate investments made in 460 companies between 1972 and 1983 by sixteen venture partnerships. By the end of 1988, $822 million had been distributed to the various partners and $278 million had been retained. Again, however, the distribution of the returns was highly skewed: thirty-four proposals resulted in income more than ten times the original investment, accounting for around 42 per cent of the total value of the whole portfolio of investments; on the other hand, slightly over 50 per cent of the investments resulted in some loss.

Interpreting the results as risk
There are several issues that need to be considered before leaving this evidence. First, as noted above, while the distribution of 'returns' is interesting, the problem with these results is that they do not compare the resulting incomes with the initial expenditures – which would enable more to be said about the degree of risk involved.[16] Second, Scherer's results in particular appear to relate to the lifetime of earnings of a given invention and not to the annual earnings (work on income inequalities has focused almost exclusively on annual earnings). In practice, it is likely that the longevity of the flows would be an important determinant of the distributions described above. Longevity may be linked to patent life and to the appearance of new inventions that supersede older ones. Finally, the distributions are *ex post* and may throw little light on the underlying *ex ante* risks perceived by the firm at the time when the investments were made.

Simple risks, complex distribution of outcomes
Section 8.5.2 outlined the existence of many sources of risk, associated with each phase in the evolution of a new product. At each stage the firm has the option of stopping or going on and, thus, the investments should be judged using real options methods. In addition, the risk at each stage may follow a fairly simple distribution, but this does not mean that the final outcome will follow a simple distribution. Take a dice with a large number of sides, say 60 sides with values 0.5, 1.0 … 6.4 (the larger the number, the more continuous the resulting distribution looks). If you throw such a 60-sided die once (representing the next stage of the invention process), the distribution of possible outcomes is a straight line (ranging from 0.5 to 6.4), each with a probability of 1/60. If you throw two dice, each with 60 sides and multiply the numbers on each (representing two stages of the invention process), the distribution of outcomes is skewed, as illustrated in Figure 8.5. Thus, the recognition of multiple sources of risk is important to understanding the complex distributions of returns observed in the real world.

8.6   Conclusions

This chapter has reviewed the main results linking companies' inventive and innovative activities to their performance. The results of the MV and the (knowledge) production function approaches appear to be largely consistent, showing high private and social rates of return to investment in R&D. The evidence from these two models about the role that patents

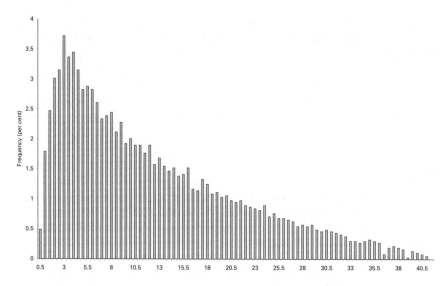

Figure 8.5 Outcome distribution: multiplicative, single throw/two dice.

play is less clear. In addition, while spillovers invariably appear to be large and significant, few studies to date have undertaken any rigorous testing of the extent to which they are truly public goods or are associated with, to date, unmeasured costs of search or payments for accessing the technology. In addition, it has been argued that the literature has not properly explored the role of the inventive activity of competitors on the enterprise's own MV. The evidence from NPLs also suggests that such activity is, on average, linked to improved firm performance.

It was noted, however, that the econometric results relate to the marginal impact of R&D (or patents or innovation) on firm performance, *averaged across all firms in the sample.* When the evidence at the level of the individual firm is considered, these high-level, discretionary investments appear to be extremely risky. One interesting aspect of Tidd and Driver's (2000) discussion relates to the observed relationships between various measures of innovation, patents, R&D, NPLs, and so on. A general finding is that, while such relationships tend to be quite strong across sectors, they are much weaker when firm-level data are used (Tidd and Driver, 2000, particularly pp. 100–101). This appears to be an important indicator of the role of risk (as well as other factors, such as differences in the propensity to patent) at the firm level. As Tidd and Driver (2000, p. 115) note, 'The weakness of the relationship [at the firm level] may be caused simply by the random unpredictability of innovation'.

The present chapter also explored the sources and nature of this risk. Despite some caveats about the interpretation of the various observed outcomes presented in the literature, the evidence does seem to point to the fact that key discretionary investments are associated with high levels of risk. In addition, the overall returns to such investments appear to be highly skewed, with a large percentage earning very little and a small percentage having a very high value. The riskiness of discretionary investments, in addition to the multi-stage nature of the process, has important implications for strategic decision making and for the decision rules that the firm should employ.

Notes

1 See www.cfo.com/printarticle/1,5317,1086,00.html. For the estimates produced by Lev, see www.strassmann.com/pubs/km/1999-9.php.

2 It is assumed that $q_{it} = \exp(m_i + d_t + u_{it})$, where, m_i is a permanent firm effect for firm i; d_t is the market effect at time t; and u_{it} is an independently distributed error term. Hence the term q allows for the fact that the market valuation may vary across firms and time, and that there may also be 'noise' in such valuations. Equation 8.1 can then be rearranged to yield,

$$\log MV_{it} = m_i + d_t + \sigma \log K_{it} + \sigma\gamma(G_{it}/K_{it}) + u_{it} \qquad 8.1a$$

where σ and γ are constants.

3 Beta values measure the movement of the price of a particular stock relative to the market as a whole. $\beta > 1$ implies that the stock is more risky (i.e. has a higher price volatility) than the market.

4 This is confirmed by a number of other studies, for example the Community Innovations Survey (Bosworth *et al.*, 1996b) and a UK study of the Tobin q model (Stoneman and Bosworth, 1994).

5 This perhaps not surprising given the inclusion of the firm's own R&D and patents. A similar result was obtained by Stoneman and Bosworth (1994). However, it is also consistent with the existence of spillover effects.

6 The archetypal MV papers often construct a stock figure for intangibles based on an assumed rate of depreciation, normally 15 per cent per annum (see Hall, 1993a). Some studies, however, estimate the depreciation rate within the model (e.g. Lev and Sougiannis, 1996).

7 Some care needs to be taken in comparing across studies; for example, in the case of Connolly and Hirschey (1990), the R&D/sales ratio is used.

8 If the price indices do not force quality into the output measure (see section 3.2), then Y is a volume (or physical measure) and the effects of R&D will be underestimated – indeed, there is likely to be a tendency for only the process innovation to be linked to these measures. However, it seems likely that in firm-level data (cross-sectional and panel data), quality is (almost by accident as much as by design) forced into the output measure. If the nominal value of the outputs of the firms from a given industry are deflated by a common price index (i.e. constant across firms in that sector), this will result in firms that charge a higher price (because they offer higher-quality outputs) retaining higher real output levels (and firms with lower price–quality combinations will have lower real output levels). The fact that

the sector-level price deflator for the average across firms is too high (because it is not quality constant) is then picked up in the industry dummies and/or the FFEs.

9 Patel (2000, p. 141) makes the point that the measures adopted need to allow for double counting of R&D – in other words, R&D needs to be taken out of the employment and capital stock variables.

10 $\partial Y/\partial K = \alpha AK^{\alpha-1}E^{\beta}G^{\gamma} = \alpha Y/K$ and $[\partial Y/Y]/[\partial K/K] = \alpha$. The other parameters ($\beta$ and γ) can be derived in a similar way. α is therefore the percentage change in output caused by a 1 per cent increase in physical capital.

11 The general approach in the measurement of NPLs is to use the information published in trade journals (see Chapter 4).

12 The *Penguin Dictionary of Economics*, for example, defines risk as 'a state in which the number of possible events exceeds the number of events that will actually occur, and some measure of probability can be attached to them'. In contrast, in the case of uncertainty, 'no probabilities can be attached for each possible outcome' (Rutherford, 1992, p. 399).

13 That is, net of all operating costs and so on, but not of the R&D investment.

14 The data showed a degree of concavity inconsistent with the Pareto–Levy distribution.

15 See also the discussion in Chapter 4 and section 8.2 on citation analysis and its links to the distribution of patent values (see also Harhoff *et al.*, 1997a, 1997b).

16 A skewed distribution of returns is not proof *per se* that the underlying processes are risky – it could be that the distribution of returns exactly matches some underlying distribution of efforts or expenditures. In practice, it is clear that a substantial part of the distribution of returns arises because of the riskiness of the associated investments – anecdotal evidence can always be located of major investments that failed (e.g. the Ford Edsel or Corfam) and small investments that make disproportionately large returns.

Chapter 9

Skills, high-performance work practices and performance

9.1   Introduction

The earlier chapters provide a variety of evidence that the skills and competences[1] of a company are a key source of competitive advantage (Pfeffer, 1994; Prahalad, 1983; Wright *et al.*, 1994). One role of the present chapter is to bring together the evidence about the effect of skills on company performance, although it also demonstrates that an increase in skills alone may not be sufficient to improve company performance. The role played by skills in the real world is complex; in particular, it is intimately related to the goals and product market strategies of the firm and, thereby, the extent to which the firm is or is not innovative. In addition, skills and strategies are bound up with the extent of exposure to risk and the ability to manage and cope with risk. While there are risks in any product market strategy – including doing nothing – the extent and nature of the risks depend upon both the strategy and the skill level of the enterprise. As throughout the book, the current discussion suggests that management (and management skills) are central to the likely performance of the enterprise.[2]

The second aim of this chapter is to explore the results of the HRM and the HPWP literature.[3] Given the widely held belief that people are a key source of an organization's competitive advantage (Pfeffer, 1994; Prahalad, 1983; Wright *et al.*, 1994), then firms' success in global markets requires appropriate investments in human resources (HR) in order that their employees are more skilled than their competitors' employees (Pfeffer, 1994). By implication, it may be argued that it is the quality of HRM that determines organizational performance (Adler, 1988; Reich, 1991; Youndt *et al.*, 1996). Thus, 'the effective management of human capital, not physical capital, may be the ultimate determinant of firm performance' (Youndt *et al.*, 1996, p. 836). There appear to be a number of different aspects to this literature, but the key focus seems to be the role of HRM and HPWPs in promoting and developing the resources available to the enterprise, and in determining the way in which such resources are organized and incentivized.

The debate about the role of HPWPs falls into one of two main strands of the literature. The first strand is termed the 'universal' or 'best practice' approach, which implies a direct relationship between particular approaches to HRM and the performance of the company (Youndt *et al.*, 1996, p. 837). The second strand, 'contingency' perspective, argues that the strategic approach adopted by the organization interacts with and moderates (i.e. either augments or diminishes) the effect of HPWPs on performance. The universal approach helps to document the benefits of HPWPs across all contexts, while the contingency perspective helps to derive theories and prescriptions for management that are appropriate to the specific situation of the organization. While the choice of one rather than the other theory is an empirical issue, the two are not mutually exclusive.

The present chapter is structured in the following way. Section 9.2 outlines a static framework to enable the reader to understand why firms face strict limits to the level of skills that they can demand. In essence, higher skills (except, in principle, firm-specific skills) incur higher wages and, in a static environment, there is a trade-off between the benefits that higher skill levels bring and the costs of employing them. Section 9.3 shows that the empirical evidence is entirely consistent with the conceptual issues developed in section 9.2. Higher levels of general skills are associated with higher wages and with higher productivity, but it is difficult to find evidence that they are linked to higher profits. However, firms have profitable investment opportunities in firm-specific skills (see particularly section 9.6 onwards). Section 9.4 argues that, in a dynamic environment, where there is technological or organizational innovation, the skill levels required by a firm depend on the firm's goals and product market strategies. Firms that 'do little', which are characterized by ageing product mixes, do not place skills high on their agenda. They are more likely to adopt strategies of increasing efficiency/cost reduction, with a focus on deskilling rather than skill enhancement. Section 9.5 then provides empirical evidence to support this hypothesis, showing the links between skills and the ability to invent, innovate, set up new ventures and increase the longevity of companies.

Section 9.6 reviews the various performance measures associated with establishing the effects of HPWPs. Section 9.6.1 explores the types of activities that comprise HPWPs, and makes the important distinction between individual work practices and 'systems' of work practices. Section 9.6.2 investigates the ways in which HPWPs can influence the performance of the enterprise. The first part of this discussion considers the role of HPWPs on the innovation performance of enterprises. The second part explores the corresponding links with a firm's overall performance, and shows how the effects of different types of HRM/HPWPs may be mediated by the goals of the enterprise, as well as linking this to the earlier discussion of risk. Section 9.6.3 reports the empirical results from a number of studies. This section begins by looking at the empirical effects of HRM practices on turnover, productivity and financial performance. The discussion then extends to examine the impact of various types of HRM/HPWPs on intellectual capital and the MV of the enterprise. Finally, section 9.7 draws the main conclusions of the present chapter.

9.2   Limits to raising skills

The present section focuses on the limits to the contribution that improvements to skills can make in a static environment (i.e. an economy without significant innovation, technological or organizational change, etc.). When it comes to the individual skills of employees, it is fairly easy to show that, on average, those with higher general and transferable skills receive greater rewards (i.e. higher salaries). On the other hand, it is less easy to show that companies that employ individuals with such skills perform better, at least in terms of their profits or MV. Indeed, if individuals are rewarded for their higher skills in terms of higher salaries, then this increases the firm's costs and, other things equal, results in lower profits. There must, of course, be other differences between a high-skill, high-salary firm and a low-skill, low-salary firm, otherwise the combination of low skill and low salary would always be more competitive. A necessary (though not sufficient condition) for the high-skill firm to compete is that it operates with greater labour productivity than the low-skill company. Mason and Wagner (2002, p. 88), for example, argue that 'German productivity ... is still large enough to help cover the relatively high labour costs (including social costs) that confront German employers'. This higher labour productivity comes about, in part, through greater capital intensity of production and, by implication, via lower capital productivity. Mason and Wagner (2002, p. 88) note that 'the key factors underpinning German industry's continued productivity advantage – and thus its ability to provide employment for relatively high cost employees – are its accumulated investments in various forms of capital'.

Equation 3.19 demonstrates that, for a firm moving to higher and more expensive employee skill levels to remain at least as competitive as before, the reduction in the number of employees must not only offset the higher wage but also the effect of any required growth in capital stock on total costs. As a higher wage is being paid than before (and assuming the price of capital does not change), this requires that TFP rises – in other words, capital productivity falls by a smaller percentage than that by which labour productivity rises (again, see equation 3.19). However, a move to more capital-intensive production tends to lower the rate of return on capital for shareholders. As a consequence, part of the increase in TFP has to be paid as interest on debt or to the shareholders in order that the rate of return on capital in the new high-skill equilibrium is at least as high as in the low-skill case.

The implications of this are extremely important – while labour productivity and TFP are likely to be greater in a more highly skilled company, the effect on profits depends on whether all of the higher productivity goes to paying higher wages and maintaining the return on capital. In other words, the extent of the move to higher skills is limited by the need to pay workers for their skill levels and by the need to maintain the rate of return on capital. This raises the question as to when profitability will rise through the employment of more skilled workers. This might occur when the following circumstances arise:

(i)   The firm does not pay the whole of the differential value of the productivity between the high- and low-skilled workers to employees. Labour economics suggests that, while employees both invest in and are paid the full value of their general and transferable skills, the firm invests in and is paid the full value of any firm-specific skills (Becker, 1964).

(ii) Synergies arise from the employment of larger proportions of more highly skilled workers (possibly linked to a more capital-intensive system of production). Such synergies reflect more than the sum of the individual productivities of higher-skilled workers. While it may be imagined that the company is the recipient of the benefits of the synergies, they may nevertheless be captured by the employees through collective action.

(iii) There are (latent) technological, organizational or other opportunities that result in higher TFP levels, that are not open to firms at current skill levels, but that can be accessed if skill levels are raised. This forms the basis of the discussion in sections 9.4 and 9.5.

9.3   Evidence on the links between skills and static performance

Before turning to the consequences of a more dynamic environment, the present section checks whether the empirical results in the literature support the three main arguments put forward so far, namely that:

(i)   more highly skilled employees are more highly rewarded;
(ii) firms employing a more highly qualified workforce have higher labour productivity and TFP;
(iii) firms that investment more in training and other HPWPs experience better performance, including higher profits and MV.

9.3.1   *More highly skilled employees are more highly rewarded*

The idea of human capital dates back at least to the time of Becker (1964), who suggested that the labour input can be decomposed into a physical dimension (numbers of workers, hours of work, effort) and a quality dimension (education, skills, knowledge, etc.). In this theory, investment in skills by the individual is associated with higher productivity and rewarded by higher future earnings. Investment takes place until the sum of discounted costs of the education or training are just equal to the (expected) sum of discounted benefits.

There is a very large and detailed literature on rates of return to education, which also incorporates human capital theory. It represents a key aspect of economists' views about the link between the acquisition of knowledge and skills and economic outcomes. The main emphasis is still probably on the returns to higher education, although there is a fairly extensive literature on the returns to training, particularly in the USA – this is considered in section 9.6.3. There are a number of reviews of rates of return to higher education in the UK (Ashworth, 1997; Skills in England, 2003; Wilson, 1986). This literature demonstrates that individuals who invest in, for example, a first degree earn a wage premium over individuals who cease their education with A levels, other things being equal. Comparing the costs and benefits of undertaking the additional education allows a rate of return to be calculated. The reviews cited suggest, for example, that the rate of return has fallen over time as more students have flowed through higher education and these individuals have borne a greater proportion of the costs of their education. Recent studies, however, suggest that the rate of return is still (surprisingly) high in the UK, especially by international standards (Skills in England, 2003). This literature, however, is generally static in approach and provides few insights when considering links between skills and organizational performance, except that the organizations that do employ (in this case) more qualified workers are, on balance, willing to pay them a premium over less qualified workers.

Growth accounting (GA) theory takes the human capital argument a step further than the rate of return to education. Although the empirical results on GA do not prove the link between skills and productivity, they are certainly consistent with it. In this approach it is assumed that an individual's wage is equal to the value of his or her contribution (at the margin) to firm revenues. In essence, the initial GA studies reported a large 'residual factor' that could not be explained by the growth of physical inputs (Solow, 1956), which suggests a major contribution for technological and other unobserved improvements. Subsequent work that accounted for the quality of inputs, such as changes in education levels of the labour force, reduced the residual significantly (Jorgenson and Fraumeni, 1992; Jorgenson and Griliches, 1967).

In a detailed GA exercise, Jorgenson and Fraumeni (1992, p. 54) decomposed the average annual growth in US output of 3.29 per cent over the period 1948–86 into the following:

(i)   rate of growth of capital, 1.31 per cent – of which, capital quality contributed 0.19 per cent and capital volume 1.11 per cent;
(ii)   rate of growth of labour, 0.96 per cent – labour quality contributed 0.23 per cent and labour volume 0.73 per cent;
(iii) TFP growth, 1.02 per cent.[4]

Thus, only about 7 per cent of the total output growth can be attributed to improvements in labour quality. This apparently small contribution of labour quality appears to be confirmed in other studies (O'Mahony, 1999), but, in part, it probably reflects the weaknesses of GA for measuring quality change. Mason and Wagner (2002, p. 93) argue strongly that it fails to take account of complementarities between production inputs, for example, that more qualified labour can squeeze more out of given plant and machinery than less qualified labour. Their arguments are discussed in more detail below.

Bosworth *et al.* (2005b) point out that, while GA accounts to some degree for changes between occupational and educational groups, it does not account for improvements within each group. Bosworth *et al.* (2005b) explored the role of labour quality change in measuring TFP in Japan. As part of this exercise they used a hedonic regression to decompose the observed changes in monthly wages over the last third of the twentieth century into pure inflation effects and payments for higher quality of workers. Quality was represented as the weighted sum of measures of education and experience, where the weights were the coefficients estimated in the wage regression. The results suggested that labour quality in Japan had risen by a factor of over 2.5 during the thirty-five-year period covered (and accounted for just over one-third of the nominal wage rise). The results of this exercise appear to show that there is a direct link between the quality of labour and earnings.

9.3.2 *More highly qualified workforces have higher productivity*

Section 9.2 indicated that high-skills, high-income outcomes would be linked with high labour productivity and (although less obviously) with high TFP. A whole series of projects run by the National Institute of Economic and Social Research in the UK that compared matched samples of companies in different countries concluded that skills differentials are linked to productivity differences. Mason and Wagner (2002, p. 20), for example, reported that 'In production areas German advantages in physical capital intensity and production scale were reinforced by higher levels of workforce skills'. The extent of the differences in formal qualifications held in corresponding plants in Germany and the UK is very marked.

A considerable number of econometric studies also link labour quality, skills and/or human capital to productivity differences between companies (Griliches and Regev, 1995; Lynch and Black, 1995; Majumdar, 1998). Castigionasi and Ornaghi (2003), for example, estimated that 45 per cent of TFP growth in a panel of Spanish firms could be attributed to improvements in the quality of labour. A number of recent studies have provided evidence linking productivity and earnings, and suggested that differences in TFP account for a significant part of the differences in international incomes (Jones, 1998; Prescott, 1998). Harrigan (undated), for example, argues that differences in TFP explain trade patterns across developed countries and 'have well understood implications for material living standards'. Thus, the evidence is fairly convincing that higher skills are linked to increased labour productivity and greater TFP, but, where these skills are general or at least transferable, most of the benefit flows to the individual, as a higher income.

9.3.3   HRM and HPWP investments increase profits and MV

The earlier conceptual discussion suggested that most of the benefits of employing transferable skills accrue to the individual in the form of higher wages and not the employer in the form of profits. It also indicated that the place to look for the benefits of skills for the firm are in its own investments in training and other HPWPs. If companies pay for the investments, they will expect a significant part of the returns in terms of higher future productivity, profitability and MV. These studies are reviewed later in the chapter, but, on balance, they provide strong support for firm-specific investments in HR and HPWPs being important in determining firm performance – not just productivity, but profitability and MV.

9.4   Skills, product market strategies and dynamic performance

The skills demanded by any company at a given point in time depend crucially on the nature of the products (or services) being produced – that is, the level of product specification and quality. In the main, lower technology and complexity, coupled with an ageing mix of products, reduce the skills demanded of employees and their remuneration levels. By implication, what happens to the demand for skills over time depends crucially on the product market strategy – that is, the changing mix of activities in terms of their technology, product specification,[5] quality and complexity, and stage of the product life-cycle (PLC) (see Chapter 13). The present discussion returns to the three broad product market strategies discussed in Chapter 5 and section 9.6.2 (i.e. cost, quality and flexibility), but a further distinction is introduced section 9.6.2 between cost reduction (through deskilling) and efficiency improvements.

In order to understand the changing demand for skills (and why skills are viewed as a comparatively low-ranked issue by many firms in the UK), it is necessary to develop a more dynamic view of the firm. To do this, the analysis builds upon the earlier discussion by Youndt *et al.* (1996), which provides a bridge between the skills and competences of the firm, HRM and the strategies adopted (see section 9.6). The bridging factor is in the degree of risk – the likelihood of success or failure – that the different skill bases produce in the adoption of different strategies. The degree of risk and perceived risk-adjusted returns to alternative product market strategies are dependent on the skills and competence base. Take, for example, a firm with a low skills base that has a corresponding administrative HR system (i.e. selection for manual skills, etc.). The risks of adopting a cost-based strategy would be low, while the risks of adopting a quality-increasing strategy would be high, other things being equal. The counterpart to this would be that high-skills firms, with a human resources system that maintains or increases skill levels, would find the quality-increasing strategy less risky than the low-skills firm (though they may not find the cost-reducing strategy more risky). This produces an asymmetry, in that low-skills firms are likely to opt for a cost-based strategy, while high-skills firms can opt for either.

The starting point is an apparently innocuous research result – one key finding of the literature is that firms that 'do little' generally report having few skills problems (Bosworth *et al.*, 2001). A second key finding is that firms that adopt efficiency-increasing/cost-reducing product market strategies (rather than moving up-market by improving quality and moving to products with higher value added) will not generally experience major skill problems, except in one regard – if they are low-paying companies, they may still find it difficult to recruit or keep certain skills.

So when do firms require higher skills and competences (and when do they not)? The first answer to this appears to be that high levels of skills and competences are likely to be required during the set-up and early growth period. In addition, it can be expected that firms will require greater skills during periods when they attempt to grow through change, particularly linked to changes in product mix and/or improvements in product quality (Skills in England, 2003). There is evidence that periods of major change, such as during NPLs or merger activities, are times of high risk and require high levels of skills to ensure success (Skills in England, 2003) – see Chapters 8 and 13.

A backdrop to all this is the underlying PLC, which has important implications for the skills and competences required. Imagine, initially, a one-to-one link between a product and a firm – thus, the firm's life-cycle becomes tied to that of the product. In the initial phases (NPL), the skills and competences required are likely to be high, while in the final phases they are likely to be low – with production eventually moving to lower-income, less-developed countries. Of course, firms will attempt to distance themselves from the effects of a single PLC, by holding a portfolio of products and changing this portfolio to a 'younger' mix. This may involve the firm in R&D, takeover and merger, divestment and other activities, which are risky activities that require higher skills, including management skills (Skills in England, 2003). The key role of management skills has been stressed elsewhere (Bosworth, 1999; Skills in England, 2003) and discussed extensively in Chapter 6. In the present context, note that the level and nature of the management skills (entrepreneurship, intrepreneurship and leadership skills) required are likely to differ between firms attempting to move 'up-market' (where greater creativity, lateral thinking, flexibility, employee involvement in decision making, etc., may be required) and those moving 'down-market' (where a more managerial, hierarchical control climate may be needed).

9.5   Evidence on the links between skills and dynamic performance

9.5.1   *High-level firm goals and product market strategies*

Bosworth (2001) used the Employers Skill Survey, 1999, to examine some of the factors related to the choice of high-level firm goals and product market strategies. The results for high-level goals of the firm produced the first indication that goals were linked to the level of qualifications of managers. For example, individuals with no qualifications are less likely to choose the 'quality of product or service' goal than the 'sales' goal, but individuals with a degree or higher degree are more likely to choose this goal than sales. Likewise, in the case of the productivity goal, individuals with a lower-level BTEC or equivalent are significantly more likely to choose this goal than sales, but this is not the case for those with, for example, a higher degree. The same study reported that managers who indicate that, in their view, the move to new, higher-quality products is a 'very important' product market strategy in their company are most likely to hold a degree or higher. On the other hand, those reporting that improvements to existing products are very important are most likely to hold A levels or BTEC Higher National as their highest qualification. Finally, managers reporting that improving efficiency is very important in their company are most likely to hold fewer than five GCSEs. Table 9.1 sets out the results of the ratio of very/not at all important across the different qualification levels of managers. The result is very similar to that reported above, except in the case of improvements to existing products. Of course, this is not proof that more highly qualified managers impose more quality-oriented goals on the firm (firms adopting such goals may appoint more highly qualified managers) – but it is suggestive of this result.

Table 9.1 Importance of various product market strategies, by qualification level of managers

Ratio of emphasis[a]	Degree or higher	A level or BTEC Higher	Five GCSEs or other BTEC	Fewer than five GCSEs
New higher-quality products				
Very/not at all	1.17	1.14	1.08	0.87
Improving existing products				
Very/not at all	1.43	1.26	1.18	0.78
Increasing efficiency				
Very/not at all	0.46	0.94	1.07	1.17

[a]Ratio of numbers of managers reporting that each of the three product market strategies is very important divided by those reporting that it is not at all important to their firm.

The results reported by Bosworth (2001) additionally show that not only do companies that emphasize product innovation set higher minimum levels of management qualifications for new recruits but also their existing managers are more likely to hold these minimum levels. Consistently, the results suggest an almost monotonic relationship between the degree of emphasis placed on product quality and the proportion of managers in the enterprise possessing at least the minimum qualification for recruits. In conclusion, there is strong evidence linking education levels with the choice of product market strategy – higher education levels are more closely linked with 'higher quality' strategies.

9.5.2 *R&D, innovation and skills*[6]

It has long been recognized that the ability to absorb new technologies is crucially dependent on the skills and competences of the workforce (Amsden, 1989; Solo, 1966). Solo (1966) argues that, in the context of economic development, the formal education of the scientific and technical elites is a necessary but not sufficient condition for development. He sees this as the important apex of the triangle. However, development begins only when the skills of the middle mass of 'mechanics and technicians' reaches a sufficient threshold. Some care is required here, as skills and competences are only a part of the broader concept of absorptive capacity – they are an element 'within the set of routines and processes by which firms acquire, assimilate, transform and exploit knowledge to produce a dynamic organisational capability' (Zahra and George, 2002). Nevertheless, skills play a central role in technology transfer and late industrialization, as in the case of South Korea. Amsden (1989, p. 9) argues that 'Salaried engineers are a key figure in late industrialization because they are the gate keepers of foreign technology transfers'. She goes on to argue that 'Turning now to production workers, late industrializations have exceptionally well educated work forces by comparison with early industrializations' (p. 10). She concludes that 'The plain fact of the matter is that Korea was a successful learner partly because it invested heavily in education, both formal and foreign technical assistance' (p. 23).

Mason and Wagner (2002, p. 93) argue that the greater skills of the German workforce – particularly intermediate skills – help to keep production moving smoothly and this frees up time for strategic incremental process improvements. In the context of the present study, this argument may be of disproportionate importance in distinguishing the strategies of ageing, medium- to low-technology production activities. Thus, the discussion returns to this issue at a number of points, including Part VI. The authors provide many other instances of the role played by skills. For example:

> the speed with which new products are transferred to full production – and indeed the 'saleability' of these products – depends in large part on the knowledge and skills of employees engaged in new product design and development. (Mason and Wagner, 2002, p. 94)

Earlier chapters have noted how such factors as speed to market and product appeal are central to success in innovation, and Mason and Wagner make it clear that such success depends upon the skills of the workforce.

9.5.3   *New ventures and skills*

One of the areas (discussed in Chapter 6) where special skills and competences are required is in setting up new ventures. Here the type/mix of skills needed is likely to be quite different to those of managing large, established concerns. Storey (1986), for example, in an analysis of County Cleveland, found that individuals working in large firms were unlikely to possess such a wide range of knowledge as similar individuals working in small firms. While the necessary skills are broad ranging, including technical skills, the literature on new ventures tends to concentrate on social skills and competences that aid in the accumulation of social capital of the enterprise, for example the ability of the enterprise to mobilize resources because of its external contacts and relationships (see section 6.5).

9.5.4   *Firm survival, skills and competences*

Teixeira (2002) points out that the issue of firm survival and its links with human capital have been given little attention in the literature. A significant proportion of empirical studies use panels of companies that are present throughout the sample period, thus avoiding issues of entry and exit from the sample (Skills in England, 2003; Teixeira, 2002). However, the few studies there are appear to support a link between skills and survival. Teixeira (2002), for example, reports that Portuguese textile plants that employed more highly qualified top managers were more likely to split up, while those that continued intact by maintaining inertia were characterized by *not* employing individuals with high levels of human capital. This result, which at first sight appears somewhat perverse in terms of the contribution of more highly qualified labour, should be interpreted against the backdrop of the decline in the textiles sector – note, in particular, that division is not the same as demise. Such divisions may be an attempt by the more highly qualified managers to save firms that would otherwise disappear, as in the case of management buy-outs.

Bates (1990) analysed a sample of 4,429 firm entrants in the USA. The entrants comprised white males entering self-employment between 1976 and 1982. Bates reported that the likelihood of business failure fell sharply for firms whose owners had four or more years of college education. The effect was mainly an indirect one – college education improved access to debt capital, which increased the probability of survival. Reid (*circa* 2000) reported on an unbalanced panel of Scottish entrepreneurs during the period 1994 to 1997. While the probability of survival depended on a range of factors, survivors were more likely to have gone on into further or higher education than the non-survivors. Reid (*circa* 2000, pp. 1 and 31) concluded that 'firms which survived generally displayed wider and deeper competencies than firms which closed. This was evident in many ways, including commercial orientation and strategic awareness.'

Hamermesh (1988) studied 2,636 US workers over the period 1977 to 1981. The results suggest that, other things being equal, additional years of schooling by workers reduced the probability of plant closure (proxied by the number of 'displaced' workers); on the other hand, tenure (a proxy for on-the-job experience) had only a small effect on the probability of closure.

Gort and Lee (2003) reported a study of 5,000 new manufacturing plants in the USA over the period 1973 to 1992. They estimated a production function in which changes in TFP are driven by organizational capital, in particular: knowledge accumulated over time (organizational learning/ managerial efficiency); initial managerial endowments; and other forms of intangible organizational endowments. They concluded that variations in managerial endowments are an important determinant of TFP performance. In addition, superior management efficiency was significantly related to the likelihood of plant survival. Of the plants that survived, the learning and superior managerial resources of the older plants helped offset the benefits of newer vintages of capital available to new entrants.[7]

9.6   High-performance work practices

9.6.1   *Individual practices and HPWP systems*

The previous sections suggested that the firm-specific investments in individuals and associated HPWPs are likely to be linked to profitability, in contrast to improvements in general (transferable) skills, which are mainly reflected in higher earnings. The present section concentrates on the largely consistent evidence that HPWPs, which are largely firm-specific, improve company performance. There are two broad types of study that link HRM/HPWPs with firm performance:

(i)   those that look at the effects of individual HR programmes or initiatives;

(ii)   those that look at the effects of bundles of HRM practices (Arthur, 1994; Boudreau and Ramstad, 1997; Huselid, 1995; Youndt *et al.*, 1996).

In the main, both sets of studies suggest that HRM initiatives have a positive effect on firm performance.

The idea of so-called 'Edgeworth complementarities' can be traced to the work of Milgrom and Roberts (1990, 1995). Their work explored the literature on internal organization and innovativeness,[8] where relatively scant attention had previously been paid to the role of new and complementary HRM practices. Their focus was on the redefinitions of strategies, organization and management among manufacturing firms over the previous few decades. They defined Edgeworth complementarities as existing if 'doing more of one thing increases the returns to doing (more of) the others' (Milgrom and Roberts, 1995, p. 181). Milgrom and Roberts' view is that the diverse characteristics of modern manufacturing are complementary elements that form an interlocking system. The emergence of this system has been driven not only by changes in technology, such as IT and 'flexible machines' (i.e. machine centres), but also by changes in consumer tastes that demand broader product lines and more frequent NPLs. Mendelsson and Pillai (1999) also take a broad view of complementarities in their so-called 'high-IQ organizations'. In these firms, complementarity occurs via the combined high level of innovativeness, widespread use of IT and 'new firm practices'. The emergence of such firms has been largely driven by the falling costs of processing information.

Laursen and Foss (2000) argue that:

> complementarities allow us to better understand what is 'systemic' about technologies and firms, and how performance is influenced by this. We argue that complementarities allow us to understand the clustering of HRM practices in firms.

Kling (1995) provides a specific example of why a *system* may be important:

participation by workers in problem-solving committees may increase productivity if workers actively participate. Guarantees of job security may be
necessary to induce workers to share the ideas that may lead to productivity
improvements – and possible layoffs. Flexible assignment of workers to jobs
might then be needed to make job security viable; assignment flexibility and
long-term employment might then make training of workers more attractive to
firms.… Thus, a system of work practices designed with such complementarities
in mind will likely result in greater improvements in firm performance.

9.6.2   *HRM/HPWPs and firm performance*

It is fairly easy to see how the adoption of HRM/HPWPs outlined above
may have direct (universal) effects on company performance, and how
these might be monitored by companies. For example, the adoption of
higher pay levels (or other improvements to a benefits package) might
result in lower labour turnover, which is easily monitored at the company
level. Improvements in incentive pay, share option schemes and the like
might improve worker effort and, thereby, labour productivity – again, this
is relatively easy to measure. Other things are more difficult to monitor
at the company level, particularly where a package of HRM practices has
been introduced at the same time. Here the larger-scale statistical studies
have a particularly important role to play.

There are at least two other dimensions that seem to be important.
These are raised by Huselid (1995) and are concerned with the 'fit' of the
various policies. In particular, the 'internal fit' is concerned with the compatibility of the HRM policies. This relates to the mix of policies chosen
and the extent to which complementarities emerge. Many studies use
some form of principal-component analysis to isolate the main elements
of such packages (see Hair *et al.*, 1995). The second dimension relates to
the 'external fit', which is concerned with the compatibility of the 'suite' of
HRM policies adopted and the company's broader competitive strategies
(i.e. goals and product market strategies – Chapter 5). In both cases, the
author distinguishes between: 'consistent' policies – meaning that the two
policies are 'in line', irrespective of their effect (i.e. are theoretically consistent); and 'moderated' policies – where there is an interaction between
the two to produce the observed outcome.

Youndt *et al.* (1996, p. 841) outline the 'behavioural', 'control' and 'competence' views of the form that mediation between the HRM system and
the strategy of the firm takes:

(i)   The *behavioural perspective* argues that the successful achievement of
      a particular organizational strategy requires particular worker atti-
      tudes and behaviour. It is the HRM that engenders such attitudes
      and behaviour.

(ii) The *control perspective* similarly argues that there is a need to match appropriate HRM practices to the administrative context associated with a particular strategy.

(iii) The *competence view* can run in either direction – competence management works to ensure that employees acquire the knowledge, competences and skills necessary for the firm to achieve its goals; alternatively, strategies are moulded to match the current knowledge, competences and skills of the current workforce; or both.

Youndt *et al.* (1996, pp. 842–847) develop a mediation model that looks at:

(i)   cost strategies;
(ii) quality strategies;
(iii) flexibility strategies.

Cost strategies are relevant to organizations that attempt to increase the value of a given product or product range through the cost/benefit ratio. In effect, the emphasis here is on reducing costs. The authors argue that:

> Since people are one of the most costly and uncontrollable resources affecting this equation, the conventional wisdom in manufacturing had been to control costs by diminishing the amount of human capital needed in the production process. (Youndt *et al.*, 1996, p. 842)

This occurs in at least two ways: substituting mechanized systems for labour and by moving from higher to lower skill levels, with given technology (i.e. deskilling). The authors argue that this strategy implies a need for:

> administrative HR systems (i.e. selection for manual skills, policies and procedures training, results-based performance appraisal, hourly pay, and individual incentives) are consistent with the requirements of a cost strategy focussed on standardising processes, reducing errors and maximising production efficiency. (Youndt *et al.*, 1996, p. 843)

In the context of the present book, it is important to view the cost reduction route in a little more detail, as the two routes proposed are very different in both their firm-level and macro implications. In essence, cost reduction can take place either through efficiency improvements or through a movement to a less skilled, lower-cost workforce. The first of these routes can allow wages to be maintained or even increased, while the second route is likely to result in lower wages (and, as Chapter 14 demonstrates, is linked to a low skills equilibrium). The first of these two routes, however, is more complex than Youndt *et al.* (1996) suggest. In section 9.2, it was demonstrated that efficiency improvements brought about by a move to greater capital intensity, holding wages constant, must also lead to increased TFP if costs are to fall. In other words, the efficiency-improvement route must involve some degree of technological or organizational change that increases TFP. Mason and Wagner (2002) argue that this is more likely to be the case with a skilled rather than an unskilled workforce. The 'deskilling' route appears to be the antithesis of the efficiency-increasing route. In this case, the level of skills demanded falls as the firm learns by doing, as skills become built into the organizational capital (see Chapters 11 and 12) and as the firm deliberately engineers out the need for skills. The result is not only that the demand for skills falls but also that these lower skill levels make it less likely the firm can locate and introduce TFP-increasing technological and organizational changes. These two routes are so very different that it seems likely that they would be associated with quite different HR policies and also a quite different management ethos.

Quality strategies 'focus on continually improving manufacturing processes to increase product reliability and customer satisfaction' (Youndt *et al.*, 1996, p. 843). The authors see the growth in the use of quality strategies as a part of the trend towards more knowledge-based production:

> employees in such environments are required to make the transition from *touch labour*, where their responsibilities are limited to only the physical execution of work, to *knowledge work*, where their responsibilities expand to include a richer array of activities such as planning, trouble shooting, problem solving, quality assurance, scheduling, maintenance and so forth. (Youndt *et al.*, 1996, p. 843)

Again, they trace the implications for the HRM system, where the goal of the firm is based upon quality improvements:

> In summary, human capital-enhancing HR systems – those with such features as selective staffing, selection for technical and problem-solving skills, comprehensive training, training for technical and problem-solving skills, developmental and behaviour-based performance appraisal, group incentives, and salaried compensation – that focus on skill acquisition and development, are consistent with the performance requirements underlying a quality strategy. (Youndt *et al.*, 1996, p. 844)

Flexibility strategies are an alternative method of seeking competitive advantage, as more and more manufacturers take up either the cost or quality strategies (Youndt *et al.*, 1996, p. 844). There are at least two dimensions: to scale the volume of production of the existing product or range of products up or down (delivery flexibility); to expand or contract the range of product offerings (scope flexibility). Flexibility strategies benefit from the development of a workforce that can deal with non-routine and exceptional circumstances that require creativity and initiative (Youndt *et al.*, 1996, p. 845). This is likely to require a comprehensive training programme focusing on problem-solving and technical skills. Flexibility strategies are also likely to be enhanced by a compensation system that supports a multi-skilled and adaptable workforce, where employee exchanges are common. Given they often involve group-based problem solving, then group-based incentives may also be appropriate. The authors conclude that:

> In short, much like quality strategies, flexible manufacturing strategies require human capital-enhancing HR systems that focus on skill acquisition and development in an effort to facilitate adaptability and responsiveness.

This discussion by Youndt *et al.* (1996), and the general principle of contingency, is of considerable importance in the context of the present book, as it provides a bridge between the skills and competences of the firm, the HRM system and the strategies that firms are likely to adopt. As noted in section 9.4, the bridge is in the degree of risk that the different skills bases produce in the adoption of different strategies – for a firm with a low skills base that has a correspondingly consistent administrative HRM system (i.e. selection for manual skills, etc. – see above), the risks of adopting a cost-based strategy would be low, while the risks of adopting a quality-increasing strategy would be very high, other things being equal. However, there are several other points to note. The first is that the relationship may not be symmetrical; for example, the degree of 'up-market' risk perceived by the low-skills firm may be significantly larger than the degree of 'down-market' risk for the high-skills firm. Second, even holding risk constant, the magnitude of profit improvements that result from moving up- or down-market may not be the same (this may depend upon technological opportunity, the actions of competitors, etc.). Third, the investment costs of shifting from being a low-skills company to a high-skills company (or vice versa) need to be compared with the risk-adjusted profit stream that accrues from the change. Such costs include not only the changes in the HRM system but also the costs associated with altering the whole culture and ethos of the workforce, as well as any changes in organizational structure. Relatedly, these investment costs may not be symmetrical; for example, one could imagine them to be greater for a shift to systems necessary for moving up-market than those necessary for moving down-market. Finally, the whole outcome is dependent on movements in the overall skills base of the economy and on changes in the perceived levels and willingness to shoulder the different forms of risk (e.g. increased short-termism might favour a cost-reducing rather than a quality-increasing strategy).

9.6.3 *Empirical results*

The present section reviews the principal empirical results of four studies that have tested individual versus systems of HRM, and/or the principle of contingency (Huselid, 1995; Bassi and Van Buren, 1999; Laursen and Foss, 2000; Youndt *et al.*, 1996). These are undertaken separately, as they have somewhat different aims, but the discussion ends with some conclusions in section 9.7 regarding common findings.

Impact of HRM practices on turnover, productivity and financial performance

As noted, Huselid's (1995) main contribution appears to have been the introduction of a systems approach to the contribution of HRM. In addition, a further focus is on two other classes of variables, the 'internal fit' and the 'external fit' of the HRM policies as well as their 'consistency' and whether they are 'moderated' (see section 9.6.2).

This is essentially an empirical study based on a large-scale survey of US companies, in which the survey responses were matched to published accounting data on financial performance. Thus, the model was able to include a number of control variables, such as firm- and sector-level trade union and market structure variables. R&D per unit of sales was also included and it was one of relatively few papers in which the Griliches extension to the Tobin q type models to include R&D also included HRM variables as well. One worry about the reported results is the inclusion of employment alongside a measure of the wage bill in the turnover equation.[9] However, the signs of all other main variables were generally as expected in all four equations explaining different aspects of firm performance, with sensible differences in the variables that were significant in each equation. The negative R&D/sales ratio in explaining the gross return on assets (GRATE) may stem from the use of the accounting (rather than economic) measure of GRATE. The variable had the expected significant positive coefficient in the MV equation.

The two latent HRM/HPWP variables derived using factor analysis were 'employee skills and organizational structures' (ESOS) and 'employee motivation' (EM). ESOS was significant in the turnover equation. Either ESOS or EM were significant in the productivity equation. There was one example in the Tobin q equation where both were significant and positive. Again, ESOS was significant and positive in the GRATE equation. The author concluded that, with regard to investments in HPWPs:

> A one-standard deviation increase in such practices is associated with a relative 7.05 per cent decrease in turnover and, on a *per* employee basis, $27044 more in sales and $18641 and $3814 more in market value and profits, respectively. (Huselid, 1995, p. 667)

Valuing investments in intellectual capital

Bassi and Van Buren (1999) report the results of a large-scale survey of 500 US establishments.[10] The data on subjective measures of organizational performance were used to construct, using factor analysis, two indices, one relating to the level of performance in 1996, the other to the change in performance from 1996 to 1997. Factor analysis was also used to identify

HRM practice clusters, which, in turn, were used to construct indices of how involved firms were with each of the practices. The classes were:

(i)   high-performance work practices;
(ii)   innovative compensation practices;
(iii) innovative training practices;
(iv)   competency training practices.

There were two sets of results. The first set is shown in Table 9.2, which reports the partial (Pearson) correlation coefficients between the two performance scales and the HRM scales across all 500 companies in the sample. All but one of the correlations is positive, and a number are significant at either the 5 or 1 per cent levels. From the present perspective, it is interesting that training expenditure as a percentage of payroll is significant in differentiating the performance of the companies, and the change in training variables and the innovative training practices variable are all significantly related to the change in firm performance variable.

The second set of results relates to the forty private sector companies for which published financial information was available. From these data, three performance measures were constructed: Tobin's q (i.e. ratio of market to book value of assets), net sales per employee and gross profit per employee. The results (set out in Tables 9.3 and 9.4) are tentative, in part because of the small sample sizes. In the case of Table 9.3, which shows the partial correlations, there are few significant correlations, even at the 10 per cent significance level. There is some evidence that commitment to training is positively related to the ratio of market to book value. Training expenditure as a percentage of payroll is significantly related (at

Table 9.2 HR/HPWP correlations with subjective measures of firm performance

	Performance versus others	Change in performance
Training as a percentage of payroll, 1996	0.138*	0.033
Percentage of employees trained, 1996	0.098	−0.047
Change in training expenditure, 1995–1996	0.071	0.165**
Change in percentage of employees trained, 1995–1996	0.030	0.110*
Innovative training practices[a]	0.148**	0.119*
High-performance work practices[a]	0.144**	0.138**
Innovative compensation[a]	0.127*	0.103*
Competency training[a]	0.064	0.025

$*p < 0.05; **p < 0.01.$
[a]Scale variables.
Source: Bassi and Van Buren (1999).

Table 9.3 HR/HPWP correlations with objective measures of firm performance

	1996			1997		
	Market/book value ratio	Net sales/ employee	Gross profit/ employee	Market/book value ratio	Net sales/ employee	Gross profit/ employee
Training as a percentage of payroll, 1996	0.431**	0.073	0.038	0.370*	0.091	-0.019
Training per employee, 1996	0.319*	0.189	0.196	0.201	0.249	0.172
Percentage of employees trained, 1996	0.259	0.115	0.210	0.324†	0.053	0.009
Change in training expenditure, 1995–96	-0.128	0.131	0.143	0.030	0.149	0.143
Change in percentage trained, 1995–96	-0.316	0.250	0.113	-0.227	0.078	-0.018
Innovative training practices[a]	0.066	-0.025	0.161	0.121	0.064	0.085
High-performance work practices[a]	-0.028	-0.121	-0.030	-0.065	0.037	0.147
Innovative compensation[a]	0.142	-0.001	0.210	0.015	-0.080	0.014
Competency training[a]	-0.013	0.026	-0.168	0.140	-0.152	-0.257

[a]Scale variables.
†$p < 0.10$; *$p < 0.05$; **$p < 0.01$.
Source: Bassi and Van Buren (1999).

Table 9.4 Regressions of Tobin's q on HR/HPWPs[a]

	Market/book value ratio, 1996	Market/book value ratio, 1997	Market/book value ratio, 1997
Training as a percentage of payroll, 1996	0.470**	0.406**	0.019
Durable manufacturing	0.310*	0.309*	0.055
Market/book value ratio, 1996			0.825**
R^2	0.280	0.231	0.720
Adjusted R^2	0.238	0.187	0.695
F	6.618**	5.248**	28.321**

[a]Standardized coefficients shown.
*$p < 0.05$; **$p < 0.01$.
Source: Bassi and Van Buren (1999).

the 1 per cent level) to Tobin's q in the same year, and the correlation persists for q in the subsequent year. There is also some evidence that training expenditure per employee is related to the market/book value ratio in 1996, but the effect falls away for the subsequent year. Finally, the percentage of employees trained in 1996 is positively correlated at the 10 per cent level with market/book value ratio in the next year.[11]

Table 9.4 sets out the results of the multiple regression equation exercises, which explore the relationship between training and market/book value ratios. All but one of the training variables are omitted because of co-linearity problems. The preferred specification includes training expenditure as a percentage of payroll and a high-technology dummy to account for high-technology sectors (in which the Tobin q was 'notoriously high'). The results correspond with the previous discussion, based upon the partial correlations. Training is highly correlated with the market/book value ratio of the same year (see first column of results in Table 9.4), and this correlation persists over time (see second column). The reason for its persistence is in part the fact that MV in one year is correlated with MV in the next (see third column). This last finding indicates why FFEs are important in the panel data-set estimates, and why the results of the present estimates are difficult to interpret in the absence of a more complete model, in which the reasons for the emergence of these FFEs are accounted for.

New HR practices, complementarities, and the impact on innovation performance
Laursen and Foss (2000) specified a simple model that allowed a test of the role of individual versus system HRM practice variables, using data for 1,897 Danish firms. The specification used a 0,1 innovation variable as the

dependent variable, and applied a maximum-likelihood probit estimation technique. The variables on the right-hand side included the HRM variables, either separately or in various combinations that reflected different systems. In addition, there were a number of other variables that traditionally enter innovation equations of this type, such as size and sector, and variables that reflect the extent to which the firm interacts with consultancies, universities and the like.

The evidence suggested that larger firms are more likely to innovate than smaller firms (although the relationship is not strictly monotonic). The results showed that external linkages (vertical and those with consultancies/universities) had positive and significant effects on the probability of innovating. When HRM practice variables were used individually in the explanation of the probability of innovating, only two (performance-related pay and firm internal training) were significant, but when the 'systems' variables were included, two entire systems were highly significant (one in which all the HRM variables were included with broadly similar weights and one in which only two systems were included, those of firm internal training and performance-related pay).

Laursen and Foss (2000, p. 1) argued that:

> new HRM practices appear to follow a very steep diffusion curve; they tend to be adopted in a system-like manner rather than as individual components; and they tend to be associated with high innovation performance.

They concluded that:

> while all HRM practices (except for firm external training) are complementary with respect to innovation performance for one group of firms, for another group of firms, complementarity between firm internal training and performance-related pay appear to be the important factor for [a] firm's ability to innovate. (Laursen and Foss, 2000, p. 14)

Further investigation shows that firms in the four manufacturing sectors and the information and communications technology (ICT) service sectors are associated with the first group, while firms in wholesale trade are associated with the second.

Summary of HPWP literature

Table 9.5 summarizes the studies reviewed by Kling (1995), in terms of the effects of three classes of HRM practices: training, compensation linked to worker or firm performance, and employee involvement in decision making (Kling, 1995, p. 29). One important conclusion is that, in line with the earlier discussion, all three practices appear to improve labour productivity. In addition, however, the author concluded that:

> these positive effects appear to be mutually reinforcing ... the impact on productivity of *systems* of inter-related practices appears to be greater than

Table 9.5 Summary of HPWP literature

Author (date)	Type/coverage	Work practice	Performance measure	Results
Bartel (1994)	All industries	Training	Net sale per employee	Productivity increased by 19% over 3 years in the firms with training
Holzer et al. (1993)	Michigan manufacturing	Training	Scrap rate	A doubling of training resulted in a 7% decrease in the scrap rate
Bishop (1994)	Literature review	Training	Wage	Wages of trainees rose between 0% and 12%
Kruse (1993)	–	Profit sharing	Various	Resulted in 3–5% increase in productivity
Kaufman (1992)	Manufacturing	Gain sharing	Relative labour productivity	15% increase in productivity over 3 years
Cooke (1994)	Michigan manufacturing	Profit/gain-sharing teams	Value added per employee	5–25% increase in value added in establishments with incentive pay
Levine and Tyson (1990)	Literature review	Participation in decision making	Various	Majority of studies showed that participation was positively correlated with productivity
Macy and Izumi (1993)	Meta-analysis	Various: job design, teamwork, training, communication, etc.	Various	Changes in work practices were associated with productivity improvements of up to 40%
Kelly and Emison (1995)	Metal-working and machinery	Decentralized responsibility, problem-solving teams	Machining time per unit of output	Production time decreased with worker participation
Ichniowski et al. (1994)	Steel	Team incentives, training, communication, etc.	Up-time, prime yield	Changes in work practices associated with productivity gains of up to 40%
Arthur (1994)	Steel	Employee involvement, team working, others	Labour hours per ton	Lines with most progressive practices had 7% more up-time

MacDuffie (1995)	Automobiles	System: teams, training, rotation, others	Standardized production time per vehicle	'Commitment' system had 12% higher productivity
Cutcher and Gershenfeld (1991)	Components manufacturing	System: problem solving, worker autonomy, others	Labour hours per standardized task	Non-traditional work groups had 17% higher productivity
Huselid (1995)	All industries	System: skills motivation, others	Sales per worker	System associated with 16% higher productivity
Ichniowski (1990)	Manufacturing	System: job design, training, others	Sales per worker	System associated with higher productivity
Hendricks and Singhai (1994)	All industries	Quality award recipient	Daily stock price	Quality award announcement coincided with a 0.6% jump in share price
Easton and Jarrell (1994)	All industries	System: training, team work, organizational structure, others	Share price, accounting profit	Firms implementing the system had 20% higher share price after 6 years

Source: Kling (1995); note that the references are not provided unless the studies are referred to directly in the text, but are available in Kling's original article.

the sum of independent impacts when each component is implemented in isolation. (Kling, 1995, p. 30)

Similar conclusions can be found in the earlier literature – according to Finegold and Soskice (1988, p. 22), for example:

a company which decides to recruit better-educated workers and then invest more funds in training them will not realize the full potential of that investment if it does not make parallel changes in the style and quality of management, work design, promotion structures and the way it implements new technologies.

HRM, manufacturing strategy, and firm performance

Youndt *et al.* (1996, p. 947) collected data in two sweeps, eighteen months apart, from a pool of 512 manufacturing plants. Usable observations from both sweeps were available for ninety-seven establishments, but they found no significant sample selection issues. The authors averaged the data over the two years and over two or more respondents from each plant, to reduce the random error component. To remove potential systematic error, the authors did not work with the operational performance variables themselves, but with constructed variables derived using principal components. This results in three stable factors:

(i)   machine efficiency (e.g. equipment utilization, scrap minimization);
(ii)   customer alignment (e.g. product quality, on-time delivery);
(iii) employee productivity (e.g. employee morale, labour productivity).

They further constructed two aggregate HRM indices:

(i)   the administrative HRM system;
(ii)   the human-capital-enhancing HRM system.

The manufacturing strategies were measured by thirty-one variables that related to one of the three strategy groups: cost, quality and flexibility. Factor analysis suggested four derived performance variables: quality, delivery flexibility, scope flexibility and cost. Finally, the estimated equations included a number of controls (e.g. plant size and industry environment).

The approach taken was to estimate separate, independent regressions for each of the four performance variables. In each case the size, environment and manufacturing strategy variables were included as the base regression, against which the universal versus contingency effects could be judged. In the next stage, the two HRM variables were included. The inclusion of these variables *without* the strategy–HRM interaction variables gives some indication that they played a positive role. Indeed, there was only one negative coefficient on the HRM variables (insignificant at the 10 per cent level), and the human-capital-enhancing HRM system variable was significant in all three performance equations at the 10 per cent level or higher. The inclusion of the strategy–HRM interaction variables (eight interaction variables, testing the contingency approach) had the effect of driving these variables negative (and apparently significantly negative at the 10 per cent level of significance in two of the performance equations). The addition of the interaction variables as a group raises the explanatory power of the regression significantly. The authors themselves were convinced of the strong role that they played, overall, in the explanation of particular measures of performance:

> Overall, … the moderation results provide strong evidence that manufacturing strategy influences the HR–performance relationship with a quality strategy interacting with human capital-enhancing HR to predict performance and delivery flexibility and cost strategies interacting with administrative HR to predict performance. In short, maximising performance appears to depend on properly aligning HR systems with manufacturing strategy. (Youndt *et al.*, 1996, p. 853)

By regressing HRM strategies on the four manufacturing strategies (controlling for size and environment), the authors concluded that manufacturing strategies are not strong determinants of HRM strategies. If this is correct, it is a powerful conclusion:

> These results suggest that, with the exception of those employing a quality strategy, firms were not making a consistent connection between the manufacturing strategies they pursued and the HR systems they employed. (Youndt *et al.*, 1996, p. 856)

9.7 Conclusions

The evidence linking skills to performance is clear – on balance, firms with more skilled workers have higher labour productivity and higher TFP – which enables them to pay higher wages. However, what is much more difficult to show is that a more skilled workforce is associated with higher profitability (and, particularly, a higher return on capital). The key to this turns on the old concept of specific and general skills (Becker, 1964) – if individuals invest, they (rather than the firm) receive the reward in terms of higher wages, while if the firm invests (rather than the individuals), it receives the reward in terms of greater profits and higher MV. This is confirmed by the empirical results of the HPWP literature. It gives considerable support to the view that individual HRM practices can be important in driving firm performance. There is also growing evidence that *systems* of such practices, which exploit complementarities, may be more important than individual practices. Synergies appear to be extremely important – while there may be performance improvements from the introduction of one HRM practice or HPWP, the gains from a package of such practices seems to be disproportionately larger. Then there is the

issue of what comprises each 'package' and how this might affect performance. There is some evidence, for example, that different systems may be
best suited to different sectors (see Laursen and Foss, 2000).

The product market strategy appears to play a central role in explaining
the behaviour of companies (see Chapter 5). The present chapter has
emphasized that the strategy that a firm can reasonably adopt is not
independent of its skills base, including its management skills (see Chapter
6) or the HRM and HPWP systems in place to generate and maintain
those skills and competences. The present chapter demonstrates that quite
different HRM practices/HPWPs are required for different strategies.
A firm with a low skills base would find moving 'up-market' in terms of
product quality (involving R&D, innovation and NPL) a high-risk venture.
Indeed, the degree of risk associated with such a strategy, other things
being equal, moves inversely with the level and skills of the enterprise. If
the discounted, risk-neutral increases to profits of moving down-market
are exactly equal to those of moving up-market, the difference in the calculation when risk is accounted for will induce low-skilled firms to take
the down-market option. Which route the high-skilled firms will take is
less certain, but they are significantly more likely to take the up-market
option than the low-skills enterprise. In essence, the lower the skills base,
the higher will be the risk and the lower will be the risk-adjusted rate of
return to the 'up-market' (high-quality/high-value-added) strategy.

Contingency appears to be a remarkably important issue, although it
is almost entirely absent from the literature in other areas, such as the
R&D literature. There is an urgent need to explore firms' invention and
innovation activities (basic and applied development; product and process,
and so on) in the context of the company's goals, as well as in terms of
the HRM/HPWP activities that best support them. Contingency implies
that, once companies start down a lower-skills trajectory, they are likely
to get locked there. In particular, the investment costs of shifting from
being a low- to a high-skills company (or vice versa) need to be compared
with the risk-adjusted profit stream that accrues from the change. Such
costs include not only the changes in the HRM system, but also those of
altering the culture and ethos of the workforce, as well as any changes in
organizational structure. In addition, note that these relationships need
not be symmetrical, and the balance of choice will depend on the overall
skill levels in the economy and the overall degree of risk aversion (i.e.
the degree of short-termism). Thus, while all firms can effectively follow
a low-skills strategy towards higher profit, only firms with high skill levels
can effectively follow an 'up-market' strategy and, as will be demonstrated
in Part VI of this book, this becomes increasingly difficult the higher the
proportion of firms that move down-market. This gives an asymmetry that
increases the likelihood of the majority of firms adopting a 'down-market'
strategy.

Notes

1   In the present chapter, 'skills' and 'competences' are largely used interchangeably, even though they have slightly different meanings.

2   A number of the arguments here were developed by the author in Skills in England (2003).

3   The present chapter deals with the literature on both HRM and HPWPs without making any clear distinction between them. In practice, however, HPWPs, which generally subsume HRM practices, may include activities which are not directly related to HRM.

4   Note that the 1.31 per cent, 0.96 per cent and 1.02 per cent sum to give the overall growth of 3.29 per cent.

5   The literature has tended to talk about 'low specification' rather than 'low quality' (Hogarth and Wilson, 2003). While the potential importance of this is clear, in associating high-skill demand with higher-specification products, it is difficult to compare specifications where some attributes are better and some worse. Thus, the present discussion largely sticks with the idea of higher quality – measured by the consumers' willingness to pay for alternative specifications, as outlined in hedonic theory (Berndt, 1991, pp. 102–149). This also avoids the problem of necessarily thinking that the product with the highest specification is necessarily the 'best'.

6   In addition to the present discussion, Chapter 8 covered a number of studies, including Bosworth *et al.* (1992) and Bosworth (1996), linking the adoption of external technologies to internal R&D and the presence of more highly qualified employees.

7   The link between plant survival and skills may be a two-way process. Quintin and Stevens (2003), for example, develop a model which they believe is in accord with empirical observations – workers in firms that are more likely to survive devote more time to human capital accumulation and, therefore, have steeper wage seniority profiles; this investment in human capital also helps firms to survive longer.

8   The work of Milgrom and Roberts (1990, 1995), Aoki and Dore (1994), and Holstrom and Rogers (1998) is important in the context of the policy conclusions of Part VI of the present book, as is the early work of Burns and Stalker (1961) regarding the link between 'organic' organizational structures and innovation performance.

9   The two variables show + and – signs, respectively, both highly significant, with almost equal absolute magnitudes. The estimated wage rate might have been preferred to the wage bill, which is effectively the wage rate times employment.

10 Note, however, that the authors achieved only a 5 per cent response rate in obtaining the sample of 500.

11 There is an important question of the direction of causality. While MV is a forward-looking indicator, current profit is an important determinant of MV, and it could be argued that the volume of discretionary investments, such as training, depends upon the size of current profits. The inclusion of a lag between the HRM variables and the market/book value ratio does not entirely resolve such issues – the evidence of persistence of correlation between these variables and Tobin's q in both years suggests that q is itself quite strongly correlated over time.

Chapter 10

Advertising, marketing and brand development

10.1 Introduction

The initial aim of this chapter is to establish the more immediate effects of advertising (and other forms of market promotion) on product demand, and in particular its ability to shift the demand function for a brand or product outwards at a given price.[1] Standard microeconomic texts view advertising as an expenditure or cost that is incurred period after period if the higher position of the demand function is to be maintained. This short-lived 'investment' needs to be reconciled with the existence of brands. In some way, the persistent use of advertising creates (and helps to maintain) something which is much longer lived, and may form a major intangible asset of the company. As such, advertising and market promotion can truly be viewed as investments in future monopoly power (Cowling and Mueller, 1978, 1981), although, again, the social welfare implications are not addressed in the present book. The problem with the concept of a 'brand' is that it has at least three meanings:

(i)   a particular good (or category of goods) produced by a particular firm;[2]
(ii) a 'name, term, symbol, sign or design used by a firm to differentiate its offerings from those of competitors' (Czinkota and Ronkainen, 1998, p. 320) – the word 'brand' comes from the Norse *brandr* (meaning 'to burn'), when it was applied to the marking of livestock (Runkel and Brymer, 1997, p. 4);
(iii) and, finally, something almost 'ethereal' – an intangible that is associated with a particular good (or a range of goods) produced by a particular firm under a particular brand name or mark.

The meaning in the text should be clear from the context in which the word is being used.

The present chapter, therefore, develops a number of themes. Section 10.2 provides a definition of advertising and makes a distinction between advertising, other forms of market promotion and marketing. Section 10.3 outlines the largely comparative static economic presentation of how advertising shifts the market demand curve, leading to the Dorfman–Steiner condition for optimal advertising expenditure. The discussion extends to consider the empirical specification of product demand functions in the face of own and competitor advertising activity. Section 10.4 explores the results of the empirical work looking at the role of advertising in influencing consumer demand, in particular, empirical evidence of the advertising elasticity of demand. Despite the fact that some of the product demand models allow for short- and long-term impacts of advertising, their heritage is essentially the comparative static model in which advertising shifts the demand curve. Section 10.5 attempts to move toward a somewhat more dynamic model, based on the use of advertising in building brand value, which forms a key intangible asset of the company. Finally, section 10.6 draws the main conclusions.[3]

10.2 Advertising, marketing and brands: concepts and definitions

Advertising has been defined as: 'mass paid communication, the ultimate purpose of which is to impart information, develop attitudes and induce action beneficial to the advertiser' (Colley, 1961, p. 51); and as 'A communication activity used to influence potential buyers, voters or others who can "help" the advertiser to reach defined goals' (Rutherford, 1992, p. 8). The precise nature of advertising, in particular whether it is informative or persuasive, is probably of secondary importance from the perspective of the firm (although of prime importance from a social welfare perspective). As with the other discretionary investments of the firm, the present study views advertising as an investment in future monopoly power, which, further, is associated with a significant degree of risk, relating to the 'quality' or effectiveness of the campaign in terms of the consumer impact. In effect, advertising expenditure is risky in much the same way as R&D. Given the industrial specificity of R&D and patents, it is perhaps not surprising that studies tend to suggest that, in many sectors, advertising is a more important influence on product demand than R&D (Bresnahan *et al.*, 1996; Levin and Reiss, 1984).

Marketing comprises a much broader set of activities than advertising and other forms of market promotion. It includes, at least, the four 'p's – decisions about price, place, promotion and product. Dibb *et al.* (2001, p. 5) define it as 'activities that facilitate and expedite satisfying exchange relationships in a dynamic environment through the creation, distribution, promotion and pricing of goods, services and ideas'. Marketing efforts are sometimes categorized into two types: the 'prepositional' and the 'creative'. Prepositional efforts are somewhat more focused and seen as being more scientific, while creative efforts are more diffuse in nature. The idea of the prepositional approach is to isolate a 'unique selling proposition' – in essence, a single, substantive 'claim' about the product or service, which is thought to be the most persuasive argument that will attract new and retain existing customers. This is often justified on the grounds that the high degree of focus of a unique selling proposition aids both consumer memory and the credibility of the claim. The creative approach is more generally linked to developing and maintaining the brand and the associated brand image.

An important focus of the present chapter concerns the investment aspects of advertising and market promotion – more closely linked with the creative type of advertising – that are associated with building and maintaining brand image. It has been argued in the MV literature (see Chapter 8) that, for example, advertising is a mechanism for building intangible assets – the brand name or brand image, often linked with key trade names and marks of the company. Brands are a more nebulous concept, associated with a lifestyle or image, and, thus, may require a wider range of stimuli than a unique selling proposition. Branding often involves all four of the 'p's and for some companies, at least, branding has become the central focus of the marketing effort – 'the glue that holds the broad range of marketing functions together' (Ries and Ries, 2002, p. 2). The principal objectives of an advertising campaign for a given brand are argued to be:

(i)   to create awareness;
(ii)   to inform customers of the attributes and benefits;
(iii) to create desired perceptions;
(iv)   to create a preference;
(v)   to persuade customers to purchase (Bendixen, 1993, p. 19);
(vi)   and, perhaps, to persuade consumers to adopt a certain 'lifestyle', synonymous with the brand (Runkel and Brymer, 1997, p. 4).

10.3   Advertising decision

10.3.1 *Effect of advertising on demand*

The standard economic model argues that advertising shifts the demand curve for the product or service outwards. The effect of advertising, as shown in Figure 10.1, is that the firm can charge a higher price for a given output or sell a larger output at a given price. At advertising level A^0, the demand curve for the product is D/A^0 (and marginal revenue, MR^0), but, when advertising rises to A^1, the demand curve shifts outwards to D/A^1 (and marginal revenue to MR^1). In Figure 10.1, the shifted demand curve is parallel to the original demand curve, but this issue is considered again later in the chapter. In addition, for simplicity, Figure 10.1 assumes marginal costs remain unchanged (although total costs rise because

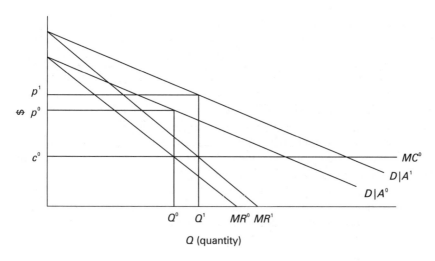

Figure 10.1 Standard economic representation of the effects of advertising. (See text for explanation.)

of higher advertising expenditures and higher output). Given that the change in advertising raises total costs, the profit of the firm changes from $(p^0 - c^0)Q^0 - A^0$ (setting $MR^0 = MC^0$) to $(p^1 - c^0)Q^1 - A^1$ (at $MR^1 = MC^0$). Thus, the profit-maximizing firm searches across different values of advertising expenditure to find the largest profit.[4]

10.3.2 *Advertising elasticity of demand and the advertising decision*

The preceding discussion suggests that the optimal extent of advertising for any given firm depends on the sensitivity of the demand function to small changes in advertising expenditure at the margin. The degree of sensitivity is measured by the advertising elasticity of demand, which is defined as the percentage change in demand for the product (holding price constant) caused by a small (unit) percentage change in advertising expenditure. It is generally argued that there are diminishing returns to advertising – as the level of advertising rises from a low level, the position of the product demand curve is initially quite sensitive to changes in advertising, but as advertising increases further and further the outward shifts become smaller and smaller at the margin.[5]

A fairly simple rule for determining the optimal amount of advertising was established from a very early stage (Dorfman and Steiner, 1954). This was termed the Dorfman–Steiner (DS) condition, which establishes the profit-maximizing level of advertising within a single period (i.e. static profit maximization). The proof of the DS condition can be found in a number of texts, and the equilibrium condition can be written as:

$$\frac{A}{S} = \frac{\varepsilon_A}{\varepsilon_P} \qquad\qquad 10.1$$

where A is advertising expenditure, S is sales, ε_A is advertising elasticity and ε_P is own-price elasticity of demand. In other words, in static profit-maximizing equilibrium, the advertising/sales ratio (advertising intensity) can be written as the ratio of the advertising elasticity to own-price elasticity of demand. The very large differences that exist in advertising intensity across product areas suggest that the ratio of the two elasticities will also vary in the same way. However, the real world is more complex in at least two respects. First, the simple model that leads to the DS condition does not account for rivalrous behaviour – the presence of and response to change by other competitor firms in the sector. Second, in addition to the issue of the optimal extent of advertising activity by the firm, there is also the question of the optimal marketing mix.

10.3.3 *Advertising pool and effects of competitor advertising*

In principle, analogous to the role of R&D in Chapter 8, it would be easy to expand the underlying model both to allow for the effects of the overall level of advertising that promotes demand for all products in that market (a 'pool effect') and to account directly for competitor advertising:

$$Q_{it} = a + bX_{it} + cA_{ij} + dA_{jt} + eAP_t \qquad\qquad 10.2$$

where i denotes the ith firm, j the jth competitor and t is time; Q is the quantity demanded; X is a variety of control variables, including prices; AP is the total expenditure of advertising by all firms in the market; and a–e are constants. In general, the following signs can be expected:

$$\frac{\partial Q}{\partial A_i} > 0; \quad \frac{\partial Q}{\partial A_j} < 0; \quad \frac{\partial Q}{\partial AP} > 0$$

A one-shot game theoretic model representing the prisoner's dilemma certainly seems consistent with the outcome perceived in the literature. Table 10.1 shows the firm-level payoffs (for firms I, J) in terms of the change in demand associated with two advertising strategies (low, high). It can be seen that if I chooses low, firm J will choose high (a gain of $40 million, compared with only $20 million); if I chooses high, J still chooses high (a gain of $0, compared with a loss of $40 million). A symmetric result occurs for firm I's choices in the face of what firm J chooses. Thus, both firms choose high, even though they both would be better off (if they colluded) if they chose a low advertising strategy. This suggests that, where competition between firms is intense, advertising is pushed to high levels and, with diminishing returns to advertising, the marginal returns may be low.

Table 10.1 Firm payoffs ($million) from different advertising strategies

		Firm J	
		Low	High
Firm I	Low	20,20	−30,40
	High	30,−40	0,0

Contrast this with the results in Table 10.2, where the firms still choose a high–high strategy, but for different reasons. Here, high levels of advertising by one firm benefit the other – in effect, the pool effect (AP) more than offsets the competitive effect (A_j) from equation 10.2 – thus, J is better off if I plays high, even though it does not play high itself. However, both companies are better off if they both play high. This might occur during the early phases when a new market is being established, and the size of the market itself is sensitive to the level of advertising.

Table 10.2 Firm payoffs ($million) from different advertising strategies with pool effects

		Firm J	
		Low	High
Firm I	Low	0,0	40,30
	High	30,40	50,50

Much more complex game theoretic models exist to establish optimal advertising strategies. For example, Grossman and Shapiro (1984) analyse the optimal level of advertising of the company under oligopolistic rivalry. While such models give interesting results, they depend quite heavily on the assumptions that they make.

10.3.4 *Short- versus long-run elasticities and the link to branding*

Section 10.3.1 suggested that, if advertising increases from A^0 to A^1, then demand shifts outwards – but only as long as this new level of expenditure is maintained. If expenditure were to fall back from A^1 to A^0, then the position of the demand curve would also fall back to its original position. In effect, advertising is a current cost and has an immediate and transitory effect. However, the building of brand value suggests that at least part of advertising expenditure is an investment – with an effect lasting longer than one period. This can be shown by the lagged effects of advertising on current output (in much the same way that the effects of R&D were discussed in Chapter 8, although the rate of decay of the effect of past advertising might be higher):

$$Q_t = a + bX_t + cA_t + c(1-\delta)^1 A_{t-1} + c(1-\delta)^2 A_{t-2} + \dots \qquad 10.3$$

where a, b and c are constants, and δ is the (constant) rate of decay of the influence of past advertising. The present equation ignores competitor and 'pool' effects. Setting $A^* = A_t = A_{t-1} = A_{t-2} \dots$ and collecting terms in $(1-\delta)$, it is possible to rewrite equation 10.3 as the new long-run equilibrium:

$$Q_t = a + bX_t + \frac{c}{\delta} A^* \qquad 10.4$$

By implication, a change from a long-run equilibrium at, for example, $A = 0$ to that at $A = A^*$ results in a gradual adjustment of demand over time to a new asymptotic value given by equation 10.4. An implication of this discussion is that there is a need for current advertising to make up the depreciation of past advertising in order to maintain demand and, thereby, profit, MV and brand value at their current levels. Hence, as an investment, the costs of advertising have to be weighed against their effect on the revenues of the firm. Thus, in the same manner as with any investment (bearing in mind the issue of the risks involved), advertising will be undertaken up to the point where the addition to the discounted stream of future profits at the margin is zero.

10.3.5 *Real-world setting of advertising budgets*

The early evidence suggested that firms do not appear to use very sophisticated methods in setting their advertising budgets – often adopting some form of 'ratio of sales' or 'competitive parity' approach (see Mitchell, 1993, pp. 6, 8, 9) – or in allocating the agreed budget across markets. This view continues to prevail, although a few studies have suggested that the degree of sophistication used by companies may be higher than these early studies suggested (Aaker and Myers, 1982; Piercy, 1987). While some authors argue that they can discern a narrowing of the gap (Blasko and Patti, 1984), the balance of the literature suggests a significant difference between 'best practice' as seen by academics and 'actual practice' as evidenced in day-to-day decision making (Mitchell, 1993, p. 9).

Mitchell (1993) reported on a study of UK marketing practices, based upon a variety of data-collection techniques resulting in fifty-two usable responses. The findings were broken down into three inter-related decisions: first, whether to advertise or not; second, if yes, then the scale of advertising; third, the distribution of the spend across markets, regions, and so on. Mitchell found evidence that top-level managers are involved in all three types of decision – confirmation of the strategic importance of the marketing decision. However, there was some evidence of the greater involvement of lower-level managers in the third area, concerning the distributional aspects – a reflection perhaps of the more detailed knowledge needed to reach appropriate decisions.

Mitchell (1993, pp. 16–17) found that the most frequently used method of setting overall marketing budgets was 'task and objective' (40 per cent of the sample – similar to a finding of Blasko and Patti, 1984). This method is argued to have a theoretically sound and logical basis, with a strong marginal component (i.e. comparing the costs and benefits of advertising undertaken in order to attain some strategic objective). The second most important method comprised various forms of 'percentage of sales' (27 per cent of the sample – somewhat higher than the 21 per cent of Basko and Patti, 1984). However, the author makes two points about the second method. First, what appears to be a simple 'rule of thumb' often conceals quite complex calculations and deliberations of the firm with regard to achieving profit targets (Mitchell, 1993, p. 16). Second, even where this is not the case, Mitchell (1993, p. 19) argues that the use of apparently arbitrary rules of thumb (e.g. percentage of sales) may not indicate that the firm is behaving in a suboptimal manner. Companies are often willing to justify their use of such rules in terms of 'a well established product, stable markets, knowledge and experience' (Mitchell, 1993, p. 19; see the discussion of routines in Chapter 11).

Mitchell (1993, pp. 17–18) pointed to a range of other influences on the decision process, including organizational factors. While centralized (top-down) processes dominated in terms of marketing decisions (52 per cent of the sample – again consistent with the high-level, strategic importance of marketing), it is difficult to interpret this in the absence of information about how companies behave in areas of decision making other than marketing. The other two alternative organizational effects in that study were the allocation of budgets by bargaining (21 per cent) and 'other' (unspecified) processes (14 per cent). Other interesting results involved differences in approach when dealing with new as opposed to established products and differences over the business cycle.

10.4 Advertising in empirical estimates of demand functions

10.4.1 *Advertising and total market demand*

There is a vast literature providing original econometric estimates of demand functions for products and services[6] (most of which include the role of advertising), and also subsequent meta-analyses of the results of these studies.[7] The econometric work faces important conceptual and estimation problems, including issues of simultaneity (i.e. while advertising may determine sales, sales may also be a determinant of advertising) and problems arising from the fact that the purchase of the good in question should be seen as part of a demand system (because it is only one of a number of products that the consumer may purchase from a limited income). The estimated advertising elasticity of demand for a particular brand (or range of brands owned by a particular company) can have important implications for that firm's decision making, as it is crucial to the price it sets. It is, however, an area where firms feel they face a considerable lack of information (see Chapter 4). The main problem with the economic literature is that it is generally undertaken at the product group level (e.g. the demand for alcohol) and the effect of advertising on demand, while a marginal concept (the change in demand caused by a small change in advertising expenditure), is averaged across companies in the market or sector. Hence, it is possible to establish the advertising elasticity of demand for automobiles, but this does not throw light on the advertising elasticity of particular brands of automobiles. From a marketing perspective individual company (or brand-level) estimates would be, subject to their reliability, much more valuable than the overall elasticity associated with all companies (or brands) in a particular product market.

However, such studies provide information about:

(i)   the combined effect of advertising (of all companies or that spent on all brands) on the overall size of the market, which is clearly also extremely important to the performance of firms in that market;
(ii) the need to defend market share.

While some studies find evidence of positive advertising effects, this is not the case with regard to the work of Duffy in the areas of food products (Duffy, 1999) and cigarettes (Duffy, 1996, 2003a, 2003b). In an exhaustive review of the literature on cigarette advertising, he concluded that the studies 'have found in general that advertising, and advertising restrictions (including bans), have had little or no effect upon aggregate consumption of cigarettes' (Duffy, 1996, p. 21). Although Duffy (1996) was critical of the methodology of earlier studies, when he applied the most recent, advanced techniques, he found similar results for food consumption and alcohol: 'they do confirm the finding of many previous studies that advertising appears to have no significant effects upon the product composition of total drink demand or upon the total demand for other non-durable products' (Duffy, 2003b). Bishop and Yoo (1985, p. 408) similarly concluded that the small positive effect of advertising on the demand for cigarettes 'confirms previous studies which suggest that in the industry as a whole, advertising was not very effective in inducing more demand, but perhaps caused a change in intra-industry market share'.

10.4.2 *Advertising elasticity of demand at the brand or firm level*

The previous section suggested a low market-wide value of ε_A, with the implication that the effects of advertising, at least in some sectors, must

lie at the brand or firm level. This view of the role of advertising in determining (maintaining) market share is often quoted in the product demand
literature. The implication drawn is that, if the aggregate (market-wide)
elasticity is close to zero and firms in the market expend considerable
amounts on advertising, then the returns to advertising must lie in the
gains from increasing (or the losses avoided by maintaining) market
share at the firm level. It is possible to develop several alternative game
theoretic models of this outcome (see the first example in section 10.3.3).
This hypothesis about market share does not appear to have been tested
properly in the economics literature. The issue is much more complex than
using the overall ε_A to indicate what would happened to market shares
if one firm increased its relative share of advertising. The reason for this
is that the individual firm or brand elasticities could be potentially significantly larger than the market-wide elasticity, but, to some degree, the
larger changes in market share that this can give rise to do not occur,
as changes in advertising expenditures by one firm are offset by similar
changes by another firm. It might be argued that, to a limited extent at
least, the US MV studies that include advertising expenditures go some
way towards doing this (see section 10.5.4), but these are far from a complete answer to the problem posed here.[8] The way forward would appear
to be to estimate the product demand functions using a panel data-set
of brands across a given market, using an equation similar to 10.2. Some
steps seem to be being made to move in this direction, but the results are
very specific to the product area involved (Cotterill and Haller, 1997).

Partial-adjustment models of product demand potentially enable some
insights into the 'carry-over' effects of advertising. These provide estimates both of the lagged adjustment of demand to its optimal level and
of short- and long-run ε_A values (see section 10.3.4). Thus, rapid adjustment of demand to its desired level in the face of changes in advertising
expenditures (and little or no difference between short- and long-run coefficients) is an indication that advertising is not an 'investment' activity in
the normal sense of the word and gives some justification for its treatment
as a cost in economics and accounting. McGuinness and Cowling (1975),
for example, concluded that the coefficient of adjustment, λ, is close to
unity and, therefore, adjustment is close to being instantaneous. Other
studies that provide evidence of the short- and long-run elasticities generally indicate a difference of around 1 percentage point or less, suggesting
that there is a small investment component (e.g. a 10 per cent rise in
advertising expenditures leads to a rise of less than 1 per cent in long-run
sales – see, for example, the papers reviewed by Duffy, 1996). Given that
advertising warnings and bans are in some way the opposite of positive
advertising campaigns, their effects are therefore also potentially short
lived. Duffy's review of the effects of advertising bans on the consumption
of cigarettes suggests that, almost irrespective of country, the impact is, if

anything, small and, where any reduction in demand results, this decays with time. However, again, these studies are at the market level and may give few insights about the longevity of advertising at the brand or firm level.

10.4.3 *The literatures on SCP and the persistence of profits*

Even the early SCP literature recognized a potential two-way relationship between advertising intensity and seller concentration and, thereby, profitability[9] (Cable, 1972; Comanor and Wilson, 1974; Ferguson, 1974; Strickland and Weiss, 1976; Vernon and Nourse, 1973). Thus, the effects of advertising on profitability became an increasing focus of the literature, particularly in the USA, although, again, not all the models tested the simultaneity of the relationship. Overall, the results suggested that higher levels of advertising were associated with higher profit (Comanor and Wilson, 1974; Ferguson, 1974; Strickland and Weiss, 1976; Vernon and Nourse, 1973).[10] Devine *et al.* (1985, p. 262) note that:

> The force of the ... argument has been widely acknowledged, and studies by Comanor and Wilson (1974), Vernon and Nourse (1973) and Strickland and Weiss (1976) have attempted to distinguish the main elements in the two-way relationship between advertising intensity and profit margins. Each of the studies indicates both that advertising intensity influences profit margins and that profit margins are a determinant of advertising intensity. However, in certain instances the former relationship is relatively weak, and further evidence is needed before this relationship can be confirmed.

Lambin (1976) was among the first to note that current advertising influences both current and future sales. This suggests that advertising has an investment quality similar to that of R&D, although perhaps not as long lived. This result can also be interpreted as an indication that the goodwill 'capital' created may form a barrier to entry into the market. Thus, even the early literature was giving some support to the hypothesis that advertising had the capacity to reinforce existing barriers and imperfections in the market. Given that, broadly speaking, higher levels of market power (below monopoly) give rise to greater advertising intensity and that advertising is an investment in future monopoly power (Cowling and Mueller, 1978, 1981), this is a potential forerunner of the more recent work on the 'persistence of profit' models (Goddard and Wilson, 1999; Mueller, 1992; Waring, 1996).

There are a wide range of such empirical models at the firm and sector levels; these suggest that profit differentials tend to be maintained for significant periods of time. The underlying empirical model generally has a form such as:

$$\pi_{it} = \alpha_i + \beta\pi_{it-1} + \gamma X_{it} + \mu_{it} \qquad 10.5$$

where π denotes profit, X is a set of variables reflecting influences and shocks on profit and μ is the error term; α, β and γ are parameters estimated in the regression, where β reflects the speed of adjustment of profit (i.e. persistence of profit) in the face of shocks. The conceptual underpinnings of the model are open to question. It has been argued that equations of this type may be viewed as a reduced form of a more complex structural model that involves threatened and actual entry and exit of firms, a number of features of which are difficult to model explicitly.

Rigby (1991) reports the results of an autoregressive model and concludes that, in Canada, there is no evidence of any pronounced tendency for profit rates to converge to industrial or regional averages, which suggests a relatively high degree of persistence. Benito (2001), using an extensive (1975–98), unbalanced panel (2,129 companies) data-set of UK companies, argues that persistence is more marked for high- than for low-profit companies.[11] One possible interpretation is that 'competitive forces act less swiftly to eliminate superior returns than inferior returns' (Benito, 2001, p. 5).

10.4.4 *Advertising, relative performance and market share*

In order to gain some insights into the brand- or firm-level effects, it is necessary to turn to the marketing literature. In an early paper, Peckham (1976, p. 1), for example, argued that 'it is the *combination* of product and advertising that produces value for the consumer and, hence, influences consumer purchases'. This forms the focus of section 10.5, while the present analysis concentrates on the findings with regard to advertising and market share.

Peckham (1976) examined a series of US products that had been on the market for at least twenty-five years. He began by looking at the post-war performance of thirty-four brands over a fifteen-year period (p. 2). Of these, 65 per cent maintained their leadership position over this period. The firms that made the leading brands all consistently made frequent product and packaging improvements and 80 per cent of them maintained a share of advertising consistent with the brand's share of consumer purchases – continually reminding consumers of the brand. The 34 per cent that lost their lead had the common characteristic that the manufacturer failed to keep the product up to date (see section 10.5). Peckham (1976, p. 3) argues that:

> Both store and consumer promotions, although often important factors in consumer purchase trends, generally have a temporary or short-term influence and thus tend to average out over time under the impact of competitive promotional activity which inevitably takes place.

Over time, market advertising patterns can be built up for particular brands. These patterns are based on the year-to-year relationship between

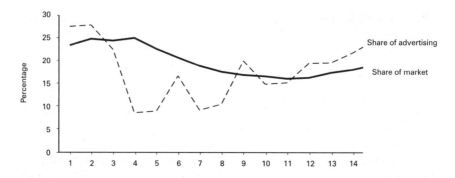

Figure 10.2 Long-term trends in market share of a particular brand. Source: Peckham (1976, p. 4).

the differences in advertising share and changes in market share. The difference in advertising share is the share of advertising (this year) minus the share of the market (last year) (Peckham, 1976, p. 4). The change in market share is this year's market share minus last year's. Given the need to cope with attrition of consumers because of various factors, the market share would erode if nothing was done about it. Peckham (1976, p. 4) argues that it is necessary to maintain advertising share in excess of last year's market share to offset the inherent attrition. Peckham (1976, p. 4) gives the example shown in Figure 10.2 of the relationship between advertising share and market share for an established US food brand. It can be seen that when advertising share slips below market share, market share tends to fall and vice versa. In addition, a simple regression of market share on advertising share in the previous year yields the following result:

$$MS_t = \; 15.6^{**} + \; 0.24^{\dagger}AS_{t-1} \qquad\qquad \bar{R}^2 = 0.15; F = 3.28^{\dagger} \qquad\qquad 10.6$$
$$(6.49) \quad\;\; (1.81)$$

where ** denotes the coefficient is significant at the 1 per cent level and † at the 10 per cent level (*t* values given in parentheses). Peckham (1976, p. 5), however, is more interested to show that it is the leverage of the differential between advertising share to market share that produces improvements in market share. In essence, he looks at the effect of $AS_t - MS_{t-1}$ on MS_t.

The estimated equation is:

$$MS_t - MS_{t-1} = \alpha + \beta\,(AS_t - MS_{t-1}) \qquad\qquad\qquad\qquad 10.7$$

Which is similar to equation 10.6 but, in effect, with a lagged market share term, as shown in equation 10.8:

$$MS_t = \alpha + \beta(AS_t) + (1- \beta)MS_{t-1} \qquad\qquad 10.8$$

The results of estimating 10.7 are as follows:

$$MS_t - MS_{t-1} = \begin{array}{c} 0.00 + 0.11^{**}(AS_t - MS_{t-1}) \\ (0.0) \quad (3.15) \end{array} \bar{R}^2 = 0.41; F = 9.94^{**} \quad 10.9$$

Thus, the advertising differential levers the market share, which Peckham refers to as the 'ad-share leverage', associated with the slope coefficient of 0.11 (Peckham, 1976, p. 6). Peckham (1976, p. 10) also produces some data supporting short-run relationships between changes in advertising share and share of consumer purchases. The results of equation 10.9 can also be interpreted in the form of equation 10.8 (bearing in mind that 10.9 imposes a restriction on the lag coefficient when interpreted as 10.8). Reworking 10.9 suggests that adjustment is slow and that current advertising has a significant impact over a considerable number of periods.

10.5 Advertising as an investment

10.5.1 *Expense or investment – revisited*

Section 10.1 highlighted a potential difference between the standard economic and the brand-development approaches to advertising and other market promotional activities. Economics tends to view advertising as a cost – while a given level of advertising expenditure shifts the demand curve outwards (see Figure 10.1), this shift is reversed within the period if expenditure is reduced. Indeed, the empirical results on the advertising elasticity of demand, *based on market-level data*, discussed in section 10.4.2, gave considerable support for this view, with little evidence of significant periods of adjustment of actual consumption to desired levels. Only equation 10.9, at the individual brand level, began to suggest otherwise.

The marketing literature also generally suggests that the effects of an advertising campaign are often short lived – a matter of months rather than years. However, even this limited effect of advertising may increase brand value, as, for each additional $1 spent up to the optimal level of advertising the firm adds more to revenue than the cost of advertising and, thereby, generates higher profit. This results in a flow of profits into the future as long as the advertising continues – a flow that is reflected in MV. This can be interpreted as a capital good that will be reflected in brand value:

> consumers tend to forget brands and continuous advertising is needed to maintain a given rate of sales. Thus advertising expenditures can be viewed as a capital good that depreciates over time and needs maintenance and repair. (Hirschey, 1982)

The branding literature, however, has something more fundamental and long lived in mind than this suggests (though still subject to depreciation in the absence of advertising support for the brand). One question is whether there is a distinction between the effects of an advertising campaign and the effects of a sequence of campaigns over time. It is possible that a succession of (successful) campaigns has two related effects:

(i)   brand loyalty is cumulatively built, and it may take some years to be entirely eroded in the absence of advertising;
(ii)   coupled with a shift in the demand curve outwards, the product differentiation that advertising creates also has the effect of pivoting it – making the demand for a given brand less elastic.

The second of these arguments seems potentially important. While the advertising elasticity of demand is an interesting and important phenomenon, it has the potential to miss one important aspect of advertising and market promotional expenditures. In particular, it fails to explore the interaction between advertising and the own-price elasticity, in other words, the potential for advertising to pivot the demand curve, making it less elastic in the relevant price interval (at least, compared with what it otherwise would have been). If this is the case, then advertising truly is an investment in future monopoly power, not because it shifts the demand function outwards at a given price (which may itself alter the own-price elasticity), but because it pivots the demand function, making it less own-price elastic than it would otherwise have been. This seems to be the real way in which brand value is likely to be built.

Investment in advertising, coupled with the associated product differentiation, creates consumer loyalty, which acts as a barrier to entry. This loyalty may be accentuated by consumer uncertainty about the quality of new brands that appear on the market and, thus, even if quality is identical in practice, consumers may be prepared to pay a premium for the incumbent firm's brand. There now appears to be some debate over what factors truly constitute a barrier to entry and, in particular, whether scale economies and capital costs should be considered to be barriers (McAfee *et al.*, 2003). McAfee *et al.* show, however, that brand loyalty, if sufficiently strong, deters entry in its own right; it also tends to interact with scale economies to raise barriers, even though the scale economies would not deter entry in their own right.

Advertising is often viewed as an archetypal sunk cost, particularly for a new entrant. Faced by a first advertising campaign on entry, the failure to launch a successful new product may result in withdrawal from the market, with all the initial advertising expenditure lost. Advertising campaigns also have a degree of risk for firms established in the market; this is likely to be even greater for new entrants with no experience of that market (although this might be reduced by the use of professional advertising agencies experienced in both the market and in NPLs). Again, brand spreading may be important here, with a well known company in one sector using its reputation to establish itself in other sectors (Virgin is an example). While the literature often refers to the deterrent effect on entry of economies of scale in advertising, this may be a secondary consideration to the volume and period of advertising necessary to break down existing brand loyalties and build new ones.

10.5.2 *Marketing activities of manufacturers of branded and unbranded goods*

This section provides further evidence that advertising is an investment in brand value by demonstrating the significant difference between the extent of advertising activities for branded and non-branded goods. Figures 10.3 and 10.4 make the link between branding and advertising and other market promotional activities absolutely clear. Figure 10.3 shows that almost 70 per cent of the unbranded businesses spend less than 10 per cent of their revenues on any form of sales or marketing activity (i.e. sales force, advertising, promotion and other marketing). In the case of branded companies, 80 per cent of them spend more than 10 per cent of their revenues on these activities. Figure 10.4 provides information about the distribution of advertising and promotional activities within the total of selling and marketing. Here the distinction is even clearer, with 80 per cent of unbranded companies indicating that they spend less than 5 per

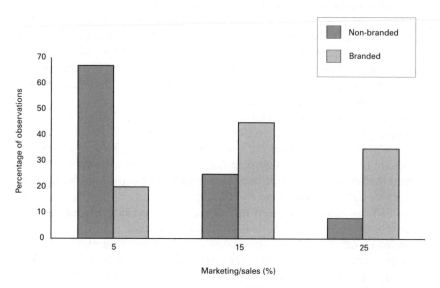

Figure 10.3 Marketing expenditures as percentage of sales. Source: PIMS (1998, p. 38).

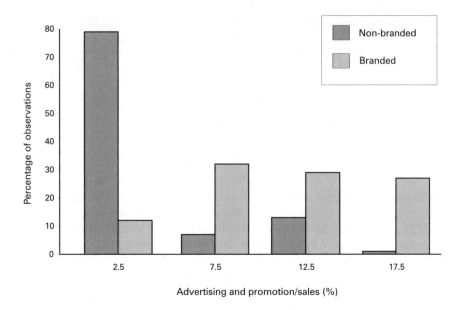

Figure 10.4 Advertising and promotional expenditures as percentage of sales. Source: PIMS (1998, p. 38).

cent of their revenues on this activity, compared with almost 90 per cent of branded businesses reporting over 5 per cent of sales and around 25 per cent reporting spending over 15 per cent of the value of their sales. While this higher level of activity undertaken for branded goods may simply be a reflection of the need for brand maintenance, the literature on trade-marks suggests that it may be a consequence of the more dynamic nature of branded than unbranded producers – in other words, their higher com-mitment to new product innovation.

Companies will review the support for particular brands over their life-cycle (Wild and Scicluna, 1997, p. 96). This is not to say the deci-sion to withdraw support for the brand is not rational, for example where particular product/technology platforms become dated or obsolete (this is discussed below). While it may be possible to keep up with changing product design for some time by making modifications to the platform, there may come a stage when this is no longer economic and the only viable route is an entirely new product. Peckham (1976, p. 7) gives examples of what happened to market share for a number of US brands for which advertising was severely curtailed or stopped. The estimates from equation 10.9 would suggest an annual 11 per cent fall in market share as advertising share sinks to zero. For one food brand for which support was withdrawn, Peckham (1976, p. 8) shows that the first-year loss

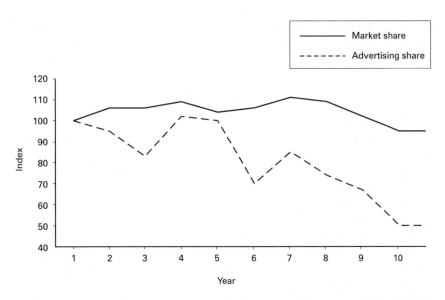

Figure 10.5 Advertising and market shares, firm 1. Source: Peckham (1976, pp. 8–9).

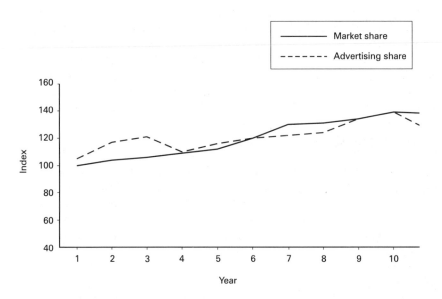

Figure 10.6 Advertising and market shares, firm 2. Source: Peckham (1976, pp. 8–9).

was 15 per cent of market share and the average loss over the subsequent six years was 4.5 per cent per annum (i.e. market share fell to just under 65 per cent of its original, supported value in seven years). Other examples showed annual losses of 5.5 per cent and 3.5 per cent per annum.

Figures 10.5 and 10.6 show the contrasting fortunes of two firms in the same market, one which advertises strongly and one which reduces its share of advertising (Peckham, 1976, pp. 8–9). Peckham argues (p. 8) that while all other factors seem to be favourable for firm 1, things began to go wrong for this sixty-year-old brand when the firm failed to maintain its advertising share (see Figure 10.5). Firm 2, in contrast, benefited not only from its own advertising but also from the reduced advertising of its competitor (see Figure 10.6).

Some product platforms age more quickly than others. A classic example is that of products protected by fixed-term IPRs, such as patents, where, in the absence of other major barriers to entry, the product becomes generic at the end of the patent life. However, some products can have extremely long-lived platforms, based around copyright or, more particularly, trademark protection. Table 10.3 provides an example of some long-lived brand names; it illustrates the point that, if they are maintained, existing (even very old) brands can command large sales and be extremely valuable. All the brands shown in Table 10.3 were owned by Diageo (formerly GrandMet) during the 1990s. At that time, GrandMet

Table 10.3 Valuable brands owned by Diageo in the 1990s

Brand	Date of origin	Sales rank	Cases[a] (million per annum)
Smirnoff	1860s	2	15
J&B Rare	1760s	5	6
Baileys	1974	15	4
Popov	–	20	3
Gilbey's London Gin	1872	33	>2
Black Velvet	–	38	>2
Malibu	1981	70	1.5
Christian Brothers Brandy	–	74	>1
Metaxa	1888	100	>1
Croft Port	1678	–	–
Delaforce Port	1868	–	–
Ouzo 12	1880	–	–
Dreher Brandy	–	–	4
Cinzano Sparkling Wine	1757	–	2

–, data not available.
[a]Global sales for nine-litre-equivalent cases.
Source: Corbett (1997, p. 17).

had net assets of over £3 billion – almost entirely intangible. In 1994/95 its advertising, marketing and promotional expenditures topped £1 billion for the first time. More recent data are available on the Diageo website (www.diageo.com).

10.5.3 *Strategic protection of brands: anti-counterfeiting and anti-piracy*

Counterfeiting and piracy relate to the actions of one company in attempting to pass off their goods (or services) as those of another company. According to the UK-based Anti-Counterfeiting Group, for example, counterfeiting is:

> The deliberate attempt to deceive consumers by copying and marketing goods bearing known trade marks, generally with packaging and product configuration, so that they look like they are made by a reputable manufacturer when they are in fact inferior copies. (http://www.a-cg.com/info.html)

The agreement on Trade-Related Aspects on Intellectual Property Rights (TRIPs) distinguishes counterfeiting and piracy as follows:

> a) 'counterfeit trademark goods' shall mean any goods, including packaging, bearing without authorisation a trademark which is identical to the trademark validly registered in respect of such goods, or which cannot be distinguished in its essential aspects from such a trademark, and which thereby infringes the rights of the owner of the trademark in question under the law of the country of importation; b) 'pirated copyright goods' shall mean any goods which are copies made without the consent of the right holder or person duly authorised by the right holder in the country of production and which are made directly or indirectly from an article where the making of that copy would have constituted an infringement of a copyright or a related right under the law of the country of importation. (OECD, 1998, p. 5)

While the English term 'counterfeiting' technically refers only to cases of trademark infringement (OECD, 1998, p. 5), in common parlance its use has evolved such that:

> [it] encompasses any *manufacturing of a product which so closely imitates the appearance of the product of another to mislead a consumer that it is the product of another*. Hence, it may include trade mark infringing goods, as well as copyright infringements. The concept also includes the copying of packaging, labeling and any other significant features of the product. (OECD, 1998, p. 3, original emphasis)

It is not difficult to see why trademark rights are so central to the counterfeiting and piracy debates, as they are used to prevent others from using a confusingly similar or identical mark, although not to prevent others from selling goods or services under a clearly different mark.[12] Packaging and product configuration, referred to as 'trade dress', is also subject to counterfeiting:

When a product configuration identifies the source of the product, a subset of trademark law, called trade dress law, prevents copying of the configuration in a manner that is likely to cause confusion about the origin of the product. (European Economics, 2000)

One further important feature of the relevant IPR legislation is that, in the main, there is an onus of proof on the plaintiff to a trademark, as under US federal trademark legislation (the Lanham Act 1946). Thus, the plaintiff must prove that the use of a mark by the defendant is likely to cause confusion about the origin of the defendant's goods or services. However, a distinction is made in the case of the 'dilution' of well known marks. The laws in a number of countries have been extended to protect famous and distinctive trademarks further (e.g. as under the US Federal Trademark Dilution Act 1995, which extended the rights defined by the Lanham Act). In the case of well known marks, the argument of 'dilution' differs from normal trademark infringement because the plaintiff does not have to prove that there was a likelihood of confusion, but simply has to show that the defendant's use of a 'famous' mark dilutes the 'distinctive quality' of that mark.

10.5.4 *Advertising, brands, marketing and firm performance*

Advertising and firm performance
Martin (1996, p. 18) asks provocatively, 'Who is more important to the company: the marketing director or the head of R&D? To put it another way: in a business downturn should you slash the advertising budget or shut the labs?' The answer to both questions is almost certainly *neither*; however, the questions do address an important issue – the returns (on average and at the margin) to expenditure on advertising and on R&D, or indeed on any other discretionary investment of the firm. A number of studies of firm performance have used advertising as an indicator of intangible assets, or the effort being made to build such assets. All these found advertising to have a positive and significant effect on MV (Connolly and Hirschey, 1984; Hall, 1993a; Hirschey, 1982). The present section focuses on the results of Hall (1993a), which throw some light on this issue. However, the inter-relatedness of R&D and advertising as joint activities of the enterprise are considered in greater detail in Chapter 13.

The basic approach used by Hall (1993a, 1993b) was a straightforward application of the standard Tobin q model to the valuation of intangible assets (see Chapter 8). There are several features of Hall's work that are important in the present context. In particular, the empirical specification adopted by Hall distinguishes the roles of R&D and advertising. The derivation of the empirical specification of the model from the underlying accounting tautology means that the effects of advertising and R&D are linearly separable. In addition, Hall allowed the coefficients on these two variables to change from year to year – the extensive US database used in her estimation allows comparisons of the changing effect of both R&D and advertising over a substantial period of time. The general form of the model was set out in Chapter 8 and, for ease, is repeated here:

$$\log MV = \log q + \sigma \log K + \gamma_1 \frac{G_1}{K} + \ldots + \gamma_n \frac{G_n}{K} \qquad 10.10$$

where the G_i denote the various intangible assets, one of which is R&D (flow or stock) and another advertising – the respective γ_i for advertising and R&D are calculated for each year of the sample.

The coefficients reported in Figure 10.7 are not the rates of return to the discretionary investments *per se* – the values reported are the ratios of the MV of advertising relative to R&D. While these are relative marginal values, they are effectively averages across all companies in the sample. Hall argues that:

> The figures show that the value of R&D capital relative to ordinary capital was somewhere between 0.6 and 1.0 until about 1983 or 1984, at which time it declined precipitously, reaching a level of almost 0.2 by 1989–1990. This is in stark contrast to advertising expenditure; the ratio between the two flow coefficients (R&D and advertising) is plotted in Figure [10.7], and this ratio is roughly zero until 1983, when it starts rising towards unity in 1989 and 1990. (Hall, 1993b, p. 21)

Hall (1993b, p. 27) further argues that investigation of why these results might be spurious gave negative results, and subsequent work using productivity-based equations confirmed them.

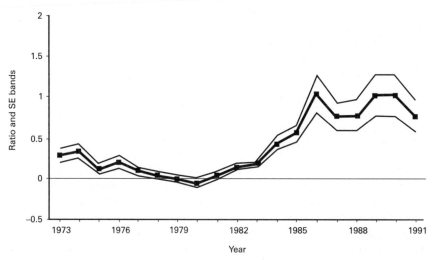

Figure 10.7 Ratio (mean and SE) of the effect of advertising on MV to the effect of R&D on MV. Source: Hall (1993a, 1993b).

Table 10.4 Role of trademarks in explaining market valuation

Variable	Without trademarks	With trademarks
LnK	1.10**	1.11**
$R\&D/K$	0.37**	0.40**
P/K	0.43**	0.61**
T/K	–	0.72**
$\bar{R}^2$	0.85	0.84

Note: K denotes tangible assets; $R\&D$ is R&D expenditure (or stock); P is the number of patent grants; T is the number of trademark applications.
** denotes coefficient is significant at the 1 per cent level.

A number of econometric studies are now beginning to emerge that explore the value of trademarks that have been built up through advertising and marketing activities. In the UK, data on advertising are not published in firm accounts and trademarks have been used as a proxy for this, as well as an indicator of product modification and NPL activities. Using a panel data-set of UK pharmaceutical companies, Bosworth and Mahdian (1999) found that trademarks could have a significant positive effect on firm valuation (using Tobin's q). While patents appear somewhat stronger in the explanation than trademarks, trademarks are often significant when both variables are included and are always significant where patents are excluded from the model (see the estimates from the random-effects model in Table 10.4). At least in the case of the pharmaceutical industry, trademarks appear to add to the explanation of MV over and above the roles of R&D and patents.

Branded goods and performance
A PIMS (1998) survey examined a sample of 168 businesses in the area of branded FMCGs. To be included in the sample, these businesses:

(i) had to sell consumer non-durable goods (low-value, frequent-transaction goods) to households through a variety of distribution channels (and not through a third party, as in the case of medicines);
(ii) had to spend a minimum threshold percentage of revenue on both advertising and market promotion.

The key measures of performance were: the gain in relative market share, reflecting the effectiveness of firms in competing for customer preference; growth in value added; and return on capital employed (ROCE) – as a reflection of their ability to compete in capital markets.

In the analysis of ROCE PIMS (1998) concluded that profitability for branded businesses was significantly higher than that for non-branded businesses (see Figure 10.8). This greater profitability was strongly associated with the following for branded goods:

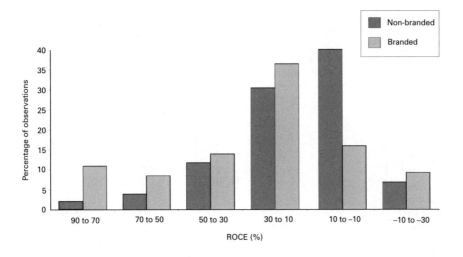

Figure 10.8 Return on capital employed (ROCE, %). Source: PIMS (1998, p. 33).

(i)   both market share and change in market share;
(ii)   high quality and image;
(iii)   good value for money;
(iv)   relatively low direct costs;
(v)   and, to a lesser extent, real growth in value added.

While the PIMS (1998, p. 35) results suggest that a significant proportion (around 55 per cent) of companies experience changes in market share, the distribution was similar for branded and unbranded companies, but, on balance, the branded increased their market share relative to the unbranded. The PIMS database tracks the relative quality of products, based on 'key non-price purchase criteria' (p. 36). The results show that branded businesses were 'marginally more likely to have competitive advantages in product and/or service quality' (p. 36).

There is little difference in the distribution of 'capital intensity' – capital employed per unit of value added – between branded and unbranded companies. If anything, the unbranded companies appear to be somewhat more capital intensive than the branded. This may reflect the lower value added of the unbranded companies (i.e. higher volumes and lower margins are associated with the more 'mass market' activities of the unbranded companies). The alternative 'capital intensity' measure – of capital per employee – shows a quite different picture, however, with the branded companies, on balance, having a higher capital intensity. The two sets of results are perfectly consistent, if the value added of the unbranded

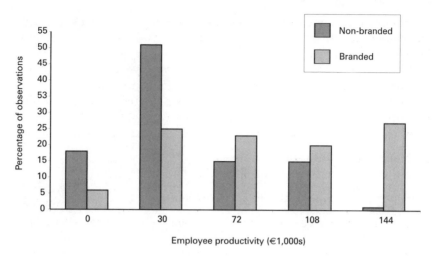

Figure 10.9 Employee productivity (€1,000s). Source: PIMS (1998, p. 35).

companies is sufficiently low or if the labour productivity of the branded companies is sufficiently high. Figure 10.9 demonstrates that labour productivity among the branded companies is, on balance, significantly higher than that among the unbranded.

Marketing effectiveness and firm performance
There are a variety of studies that link organizational performance with 'marketing excellence' (e.g. Ghosh *et al.*, 1994; Hooley *et al.*, 1988; Hooley and Lynch, 1985). In the study by Ghosh *et al.* (1994), for example, the authors collected information about 'self-perceptions' of performance and the degree of marketing competence in the firm in a survey of Australian, New Zealand and Singapore companies. The perceptions of performance for the Australian and Singapore companies were collected using a scale of 1 (much better than other companies) to 3 (worse than other companies) for the following variables:

(i) profitability;
(ii) sales volume;
(iii) market share;
(iv) brand awareness;
(v) return on investment (ROI);
(vi) coverage of market segment.

In order to be classified as 'top performers', companies had to be classified as 1 in *all* of the above categories. The New Zealand survey used a somewhat different classification, requiring companies to be ranked 1 on the basis of profits, sales, market share and ROI. This less restrictive requirement perhaps explains why 21 per cent of New Zealand companies were identified as 'top performers', compared with 11 per cent in Singapore and 12 per cent in Australia.

The authors were able (subject to the above caveat) to compare 'top performers' with 'worse performers' across the board and separately by country. Here the discussion concentrates on the overall results, rather than the country comparisons. The surveys were sufficiently similar to allow them to focus in detail in two broad areas relating to marketing:

(i)   attitudes towards marketing;
(ii) organizational structure and marketing.

The authors concluded that better performers:

> claimed a much stronger marketing, as opposed to production or selling, orientation than their less successful counterparts [and] ... a stronger commitment to marketing's role within the organization, by adopting marketing as a guiding philosophy for the whole organization. (Ghosh *et al.*, 1994, p. 42)

Consistently, the authors argued that a significantly higher proportion of the successful companies saw marketing as identifying and meeting customer needs and exhibited a stronger commitment to marketing among their chief executives (Ghosh *et al.*, 1994, p. 42).

With regard to organization, the results were somewhat less clear cut. While 'More than half of the better performers ... indicated the existence of a separate marketing department' (Ghosh *et al.*, 1994, p. 42), a significant minority did not. In addition, marketing was only marginally better represented at board level among the better-performing companies than the others. The results for the organizational structure of the marketing function were also mixed, although perhaps somewhat more consistent within a particular country. In Australian and New Zealand, there was a preference among the better-performing companies to organize marketing under a single manager, but this was not the case in Singapore. Thus, taking the overall results relating to company organization, the authors were not able to demonstrate that the more successful companies were organized along product lines rather than functional lines.

10.6   Conclusions

This chapter has outlined a wide range of empirical evidence that indicates the important role that advertising and market promotion play in determining firm performance. From the outset, it was made clear that what might be good for the enterprise might not necessarily be good for the consumer or for society at large. The analysis has explored advertising as a current cost, with immediate and short-lived effects, but expressed a preference for viewing advertising as an investment, through which the company attempts to develop a brand image and, thereby, long-term brand value. It was argued that the effects of this may not only be to shift the demand curve for the brand outwards, but also to pivot the curve, making it more inelastic and creating consumer loyalty. Consumer loyalty was argued to be a potentially important barrier to entry, which might augment other barriers. Tentative empirical evidence was presented to show that the effects of advertising may be quite long lived at the brand level. Much more substantive evidence was provided for a link between advertising, brand formation, profitability and MV.

Notes

1　More importantly, advertising may not only shift the demand curve outwards, but also pivot it, making it steeper in the relevant price range.
2　For example, Chaudhuri and Holbrook (2001, p. 82) note that 'We use brands – that is specific branded versions of particular product classes – as the units of analysis in this study'.
3　The issue of the inter-relationship between advertising and product innovation, in particular with regard to the development of synergies between different forms of discretionary investment – which is largely underdeveloped in the existing literature – is dealt with in Chapter 13.
4　Of course, professional managers might search for other optima (e.g. revenue maximization subject to a minimum-profit constraint), if their salaries or perks are linked to factors other than profit (e.g. to size).
5　Chamberlin (1933) argued that the returns to advertising would be 'U'-shaped. The idea was that the shift in the demand curve would become increasingly pronounced from low levels of advertising expenditure, as at this stage advertising expands both the demand for the firm's own product and the size of the market. At high levels of advertising expenditure, however, the returns to a further increase in advertising begin to fall, because the overall size of the market is roughly given and advertising works by taking consumers from competitors.
6　Two of the key categories of product that have been investigated are cigarettes and alcoholic drinks, where there is a double welfare issue associated with the fact that advertising may persuade individuals to consume a harmful drug (Duffy, 1996, 2001, 2003a, 2003b).
7　Meta-analysis generally involves a wide-ranging review of the literature in which, in this particular instance, various econometric estimates of the advertising elasticity are averaged to produce some overview of likely magnitudes (see Andrews and Franke, 1991; Assmus *et al.*, 1984; Tellis, 1988).
8　The US MV studies that include advertising expenditures are far from a complete answer to the problem posed in at least two respects: first, the dependent variable is MV and not product demand (although in some respects MV may be viewed as a more appropriate 'performance' indicator); second, they rarely estimate MV across companies in a particular market (which is anyway difficult given that large companies may have many lines of business and many brands).
9　This summary of the early literature is based upon Devine *et al.* (1985, p. 262).

10 As Devine *et al.* (1985, p. 262) point out, however, the reliability of this result is undermined by the fact that advertising expenditure should be treated as an investment and not a current cost of production. In addition, where a simultaneous model is not estimated, the assumed direction of causality from advertising to profit may be incorrect.
11 Note that issues of entry and exit from the panel can be extremely important when dealing with profit persistence.
12 See www.uspto.gov/main/trademarks.htm.

Part V
Management, routines and organizational structure

Chapter 11

Organizational structure and design

11.1   Architecture, management hierarchy and routines

The foundations for the present discussion were laid in Chapter 2, where the concept of an enterprise was defined, the rationale for the existence of firms was provided, and consideration was given to their size and scope. In addition, scanning the internal and external environments (Chapters 3 and 4) cannot be viewed as a stand-alone activity – it is intimately related to the communications within and, thereby, the structure of the firm (Kourteli, 2000). While 'structure' is used generically, the present chapter takes the discussion of 'structure' a considerable way further in terms of the company's 'architecture', 'management hierarchy' and 'routines'. It addresses the following types of question:

(i)   *How* does each company organize itself? What kinds of features of the company can be utilized in an examination of company organization?

(ii) Is it possible to *classify* the form of organization (like a plant genus) and produce some kind of *taxonomy* of organizational forms (that differentiates between the 'genera')?

(iii) Is it possible to link company structure to performance and, in particular, are some structures better than others for the performance of certain tasks?

The structure of the company is a principal way in which the organization not only stores knowledge but levers this to give it 'distinctive capability' (Kay, 1995, p. 66). According to Kay:

> The value of architecture rests in the capacity of organisations which establish it to create organisational knowledge and routines, to respond flexibly to changing circumstances, and to achieve easy and open exchanges of information. Each of these is capable of creating an asset for the firm – organisational knowledge, which is more valuable than the sum of individual knowledge,

flexibility, and responsiveness which extends to the institution as well as to its members. (Kay, 1995, p. 66)

The idea of a 'distinctive capability' is important. It is one which other firms, competitors in particular, find difficult to copy and, hence, can be the source of lasting competitive advantage. However, it seems less likely to lie in the formal and codified architecture of companies (which is more easily observed and replicated), and more likely to be embedded in the tacit and informal routines (which are more difficult to replicate).

Section 11.2 provides definitions of architecture, hierarchy and routines. Section 11.3 continues with a discussion of the organizational structure from a legal perspective. Section 11.4 considers the insights into the links between organizational structure and performance offered by structural contingency theory. Section 11.5 explores the corporate structure both in terms of the management hierarchy and from the hierarchical nature of the organization itself, setting out a taxonomy of different organizational forms that are suited to different types of activity. Section 11.6 then explicitly addresses the issue of the management hierarchy in terms of an 'organogram' of the organization. This leads naturally to a discussion of designing the structure for efficient flows of information in section 11.7. Section 11.8 outlines the role played by routines as a store of information. Finally, section 11.9 sets out the main conclusions.

11.2   Architecture, management hierarchies and routines

In the present book, 'architecture' refers to the shape or configuration of the company. At the highest level, this relates to the 'corporate architecture', in other words, for a group of companies, the existence of subsidiaries, parent company and, possibly, an ultimate parent. Where ownership is concerned, such relationships are generally formal and codified (i.e. set out in legal contracts), but the boundaries of the firm are fuzzy in the sense of the existence of unconsolidated subsidiaries, alliances, joint ventures and so on. In addition, the architecture in this formal sense is generally tangible – parents and subsidiaries have physical locations, buildings and plant, for example. At the lowest level, this refers to the 'production architecture', which relates to the 'layout' of the establishments or plants. The production architecture is generally codified and tangible when designed and first installed, but it may develop a greater tacitness (or even degree of intangibility) over time. The various levels of architecture are closely related, as, at different stages of production, a product or service is passed between different parts of the group.

A second aspect of company structure is the management hierarchy. Given that management involves individuals (teams or groups) and inter-personal (inter-group) relationships, this form of structure will have both codified and tacit elements. The codified part will be set out in the various documents and formal rules that govern the management and control of various aspects of the company, including the job descriptions of individual employees. The formal parts include recorded rules and evidence of actions, behaviour, performance and so on of different individuals and groups within the company. However, the management hierarchy will inevitably build up tacit rules and informal relationships and routines – some of which may be essential to the smooth running of the company.

'Routines' can be thought of as sequences of actions (or thoughts). At one level these relate to how an individual undertakes a given task, which may not involve other individuals directly. They may also relate to the way in which a group of individuals undertakes a given task, involving both individual routines and intra-group routines. Finally, they may relate to the relationships and processes that link different individuals and groups within the organization (inter-group, intra-organizational interactions) and, as demonstrated in Chapter 12, may link individuals and groups in different organizations (inter-individual, inter-group and inter-organizational interactions). While some routines may correspond to codified rules and regulations, their essence is that they are mainly tacit in nature.

The architecture and routines will be intimately related. The layout of an establishment (production architecture) will reflect the sequence of routines to be followed in the production process. The corporate architecture will reflect the sequence of routines to be followed in strategic planning, monitoring, accounting and reporting procedures, and so on. When a new company is established (e.g. a greenfield subsidiary), its initial design and operating systems may be largely formal and codified, but, over time, the overall design and systems will be modified through the development of routines. Importantly, the architecture and routines will interact over time – the initial architecture may be an important influence on the nature of the routines that emerge and, as routines develop, they may result in evolutionary adaptations being made to the architecture. The interactive and evolutionary processes help to establish and reinforce social skills, social capital and an identifiable corporate culture:

> Each [high-performing] company has established a structure, a style, a set of routines, which operates to get the best out of relatively ordinary employees, and these routines have continued to produce exceptional corporate results over many years and through many changes in the economic environment. (Kay, 1995, p. 67)

These routines are crucial; for example, Donaldson (1996, p. 51) argues that 'The recurrent set of relationships between organisational members can be considered to be the structure of the organisation'. However, Donaldson's phrase 'between organisational members' should be extended to include 'between organisational members and members of other organisations'. The *external structure* is taken to refer to the corresponding formal and codified/informal and tacit relationships with suppliers and customers, regulators, professional bodies and so on outside the company. The *external architecture* of the company relates to the number and nature of its formal relationships and contracts with other organizations, such as licensing and franchizing (in Chapter 2, one view of the company was as a 'nexus of contracts'). In other words, the *external structure* defines the boundaries of the firm, but such boundaries are often somewhat 'fuzzy' in nature.

11.3   Corporate architecture: legal structure

Eastman Kodak is one of the world's leading companies in the area of taking, sharing and storing pictures. The 'ultimate parent' resides in the USA (i.e. Eastman Kodak), while its global reach means that individual 'parent' companies are set up in the domestic markets in which it operates (e.g. Kodak UK). Each domestic parent may have 'wholly owned' subsidiaries in the sense that the parent owns more than 50 per cent of the company (or controls the composition of its BoD). Because of their separate jurisdictions, both Eastman Kodak (USA) and Kodak UK are accounting and reporting units, but Kodak UK's subsidiaries in the UK will generally not be.

In addition to the parts of the company outlined above, each part of the company may have partially owned unconsolidated affiliates, where the company owns 50 per cent or less of the affiliate.[1] Even this list omits the wealth of 'external contracts', with buyers, suppliers, licensees, franchisees and so on. Such linkages often make the boundaries of the organization 'fuzzy' in the sense that 'there is a pattern of relationships variously within firms, around firms, and between firms, which is complex, subtle, and often hard to define precisely or to replicate' (Kay, 1995, p. 68).

11.4   Structure and performance: structural contingency theory

Contingency theory takes the environmental imperative as given; this governs the strategy of the firm and, thereby, the most appropriate organizational structure. The environmental imperative may be formed in part from a slowly changing set of economic and social factors, but also key elements – such as competitor actions – that are shifting in a manner that affect the firm's performance (i.e. the contingency). Thus, the aim of structural contingency theory is to identify the 'contingency factor or factors' (e.g. contingencies such as a radical new technology) that, given other aspects of the environment, will drive the organizational structure. The extent to which the organizational structure is appropriate to the (changed) environment is termed the 'fit' of the organization (Donaldson, 1999, p. 51). A large number of studies address the degree to which organizations are 'fitted' to the contingencies they face (Donaldson, 1999, p. 63; Drazin and Van de Ven, 1985). While the early literature tends to focus on a particular contingency, more recent work has seen the development of multicontingency models (e.g. Donaldson, 2001).

The literature deals with a wide range of contingency factors, in particular firm size (Donaldson, 1999, p. 58); for a list of contingencies found in the literature, see Klaas (2003, p. 3). Uncertainty can be identified as a second important factor – often linked to changes in technology (innovation) or changes in the market (the entry of new products, etc.). These influences may be linked to the PLC – where the different phases of the life-cycle require different structures. In addition, single-product and diversified companies need different structures (i.e. U- versus M-form companies – see section 11.5). Likewise, diversified companies operating in multiple geographical markets – typical of many multinational companies – may also require different structures (i.e. matrix form – see section 11.5). It is possible to think of many other contingencies that lead to the adoption of quite different structures.

The seminal work by Burns and Stalker (1961) in the UK used case-study evidence to argue for a dichotomous framework, where the distinguishing feature is the degree of uncertainty (caused by technological or market factors). The authors argued that, in a stable environment, a mechanistic structure is effective, but where a company faces a high level of technological and market change then an organic structure is required. The 'organic structure' is one in which 'organizational roles were loosely defined and arrived at by mutual discussion between employees, with knowledge being dispersed among the employees who possessed varieties of expertise germane to the organizational mission' (Burns and Stalker, 1961, p. 53). Woodward's seminal empirical work (Woodward, 1958, 1965) was based on survey evidence from 100 UK manufacturing companies. The results suggested a threefold classification:

(i)   relatively primitive craft production technology, where the organization is informal and organic;
(ii) large-batch and mass production, where the more formalized work patterns accord with classical management theory;
(iii) high-technology operations, where the organization is a composite of work teams that operate along more organic lines (Donaldson, 1999, p. 53).

The results suggested that the 'optimal' span of control[2] is 21–30 employees for the unit and small batch, 41–60 for the large batch/mass production and 11–20 for the process enterprises (Woodward, 1965, p. 69). However, Woodward concurred with Burns and Stalker that technological changes were making the 'organic–human relations' the form of the future (Donaldson, 1999, p. 54).

There are other important contributions, particularly from the USA. Lawrence and Lorsch (1967) recognized that different functional areas within the firm would be subject to different degrees of uncertainty (e.g. the R&D and production functions), and that this would lead not only to different structures but also to potential conflicts in management. In addition, Perrow's (1967) argument provides another link with the nature of knowledge and optimal organizational design:

> knowledge technology was a contingency of organizational structure. The more codified the knowledge used in the organization and the fewer the exceptions encountered in operations, the more the organization could be centralized in decision making. (Donaldson, 1999, p. 54)

Structural contingency theory, in its pure form, is rather deterministic in nature – similar to the SCP models of industrial economics. This has produced considerable debate in the literature, with some authors arguing that the organization plays a more proactive role. Child (1972b), for example, focuses on the potential diversity and inventiveness of intervening strategies – the so-called 'strategic choice theory' – that may be used to delay the need to change the organizational structure, or may be used to vary the contingency, while keeping the structure unchanged. It is quite easy to think of examples where firms have managed to change the environment (e.g. networking between companies to establish product standards or the changes to patent life as the result of lobbying by pharmaceutical companies).

11.5 Taxonomy of company types

The present section explores the categorization of companies. The important point here is that the architecture and routines are organized in discernibly different ways, depending on the nature and mix of the products and activities undertaken by companies. In addition to implying something about the nature of the management hierarchy and the location of various management tasks, the taxonomy also implies something about the ethos and *modus operandi* of the company.

11.5.1 *U-form*

The U-form refers to the *unitary* form of business enterprise. This is viewed as the 'traditional form', often associated with the larger, single-product firms operating at the end of the nineteenth century. These companies were organized around functions, such as production, marketing, sales and R&D. Figure 11.1 outlines an organization with a 'span of control' of four; that is, each manager has (an average) of four employees for whom they take responsibility. This is generally argued to be an appropriate structure

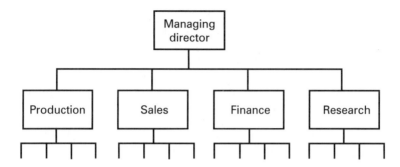

Figure 11.1 U-form enterprise (span of control = 4). Source: Adapted from Ferguson *et al.* (1993, p. 32).

for small and even medium-sized enterprises in the modern economy, but is viewed as being inefficient for larger organizations because of its associated high communication costs. In addition, the U-form suffers an increasing risk of opportunistic behaviour (a major consideration of transaction cost theory) with increases in size, but particularly in the extent of diversification. Lower-level managers act opportunistically in dealing with higher-level managers (who do not fully understand the particular product or market) in determining firm strategy or investment.

11.5.2 *M-form*

The M-form refers to the *multidivisional* form of enterprise. This form of organization, discussed extensively by Williamson (1975), was pioneered by companies such as DuPont and General Motors. It is reported that, by the end of the twentieth century, the M-form had become the predominant form of organization among the largest companies (Whittington *et al.*, 1999a, 1999b). In the UK, around 95 per cent of the top 100 firms were M-form, compared with 75 per cent in France and 70 per cent in Germany. In this form of enterprise, the operating divisions are separated from those that take the strategic decisions of the company. Figure 11.2 outlines the nature of an M-form organization. Below the level of the head office, the structure *for each division* effectively replicates that of the U-form organization. Thus, the functional activities shown for division 1 in Figure 11.2 are also replicated for divisions 2 and 3 (not shown).

The role of the head office is, in part, a response to the need to manage distinct divisions. The structure occurs as a consequence of growth through diversification, and is arranged in the form of different profit centres for different products, brands or geographical markets. In effect, the M-form enterprise develops an internal financial market, based on retained profits, reserves and external borrowing, such that profits from

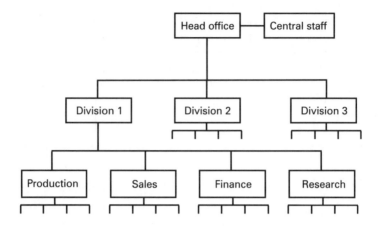

Figure 11.2 M-form organization. Source: adapted from Ferguson *et al.* (1993, p. 35).

one area can be used to invest in another area. Each division is able to focus on and develop specialist knowledge about the product or geographical area for which it is responsible. Thus, the firm is organized into largely self-contained operating divisions or 'quasi-firms', which 'enables the M-form structure to economise on intra-firm transaction costs' (Chi and Nystrom, 1998, p. 142). In effect, the independence of the divisions saves on costs of inter-divisional bargaining and the need to reach compromises that will prove suboptimal (Chi and Nystrom, 1998, p. 143). What inter-relationships there are can be handled by the head office. As the divisions effectively operate as 'quasi-firms', their performance, and that of their managers, can be measured by means of standard operating results (revenues, costs, profits, etc.). This saves on the costs of monitoring and eases the issue of designing special incentive schemes. The head office, therefore, is largely freed from operational responsibilities and is able to concentrate on developing and exploiting the synergies between the different divisional activities. Thus, the head office is responsible for the strategic direction of the company, allocating scarce capital to the different divisions.

11.5.3 *H-form*

The H-form type of enterprise is organized in the form of a *holding company*. The holding company is effectively the 'ultimate parent' and each of its *divisions* is itself a 'parent', where each 'parent' potentially has its own set of subsidiaries. Thus, the H-form is similar to that of the M-form, but the staff of the 'ultimate parent' in this case are mainly concerned with financial evaluation of the divisions' activities, using similar criteria to stock market analysts. Thus, the main strategic influence is through merger, takeover and divestment. It is not clear that the various branches below the ultimate parent need to be organized according to any one of the above forms – it seems possible for there to be a wide mix of arrangements. Thus, subject to the 'divisions' meeting various financial criteria, they are largely left to their own devices and the holding company has little or no involvement in their strategic decision making.

11.5.4 *Matrix form*

According to Chi and Nystrom (1998, p. 141), the matrix form (MX-form) generally combines two (or more) layers of M-form structures. The matrix is organized along at least two dimensions, for example spatial and product (Chi and Nystrom, 1998, p. 141), where geographical groupings are important from a marketing perspective and product divisions from an R&D viewpoint (Ferguson *et al.*, 1993, p. 36). This implies that each manager will report to at least two superiors, as shown in Figure 11.3. Chi and Nystrom (1998, p. 141) argue that:

> a firm's operation in a specific country (e.g. Singapore) formally reports to an area command center (e.g. the Asian Regional Headquarters) as well as reporting to one or more product-based command centres (e.g. the Consumer Product Division and the Industrial Product Division).

This produces a problem – each intersection of the matrix, where the responsibilities of the product and area manager coincide, is a point of potential dispute for the managers involved.

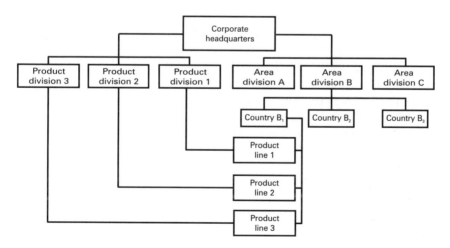

Figure 11.3 Matrix structure. Source: Chi and Nystrom (1998).

11.5.5 *N-form*

The N-form denotes the *networked* form of enterprise. This is often argued to be *flatter*, with the various components linked together by an information system (IS). Indeed, the rationale for various 'outposts' is often the need to access spatially dispersed information that is fed to other parts of the enterprise. The N-form organization is of particular interest in the context of a knowledge-based society, and has its strengths in 'exploration' rather than 'exploitation'. The structure is suited to gleaning information, which is disseminated within the enterprise and combined into new forms of information and knowledge. The N-form is more organic in nature, with temporary constellations of people – a heterarchy rather than a hierarchy, in which individuals are given more independence and responsibility.

11.5.6 *Project-based organizations (PBOs)*

Hobday (2000) outlines the role of project-based organizations (PBOs) in the production of complex products and services (CoPS), which are defined as 'the high-technology, business-to-business capital goods used to produce goods and services for consumers and producers'. The production of CoPS involves high levels of creative and innovative activity, in some cases during the production process itself and even after installation. While they may not comprise the core activities of large manufacturing firms, they are adopted to carry out non-routine, complex tasks, including R&D, NPD and NPL, and marketing campaigns. There is no functional division of labour and no formal functional coordination across the different projects. Thus, all major business functions are subsumed and coordinated within each project. Project managers have a very high degree of direct control and are given a very high status. As projects are flexible and fixed term in nature, the PBO is flexible and reconfigurable, in contrast to the large integrated, hierarchical organizations. Thus, the PBO is 'organic' rather than 'mechanistic' in the definition of Burns and Stalker (1961). However, the PBO has inherent weaknesses – as might be expected given the lack of functional specialization, it is weak in coordinating processes, resources and capabilities across the organization as a whole. Because many functional activities are subsumed within projects, various management rules, procedures and systems can vary from project to project. Inconsistencies may develop that make overall management of the company difficult. In addition, PBOs can lack structures or incentives for cross-project learning, causing a significant 'knowledge loss' when particular projects are completed.

11.5.7 *X-form*

The X-form has been suggested as a category covering structures that cannot be classified as one of the more standard forms outlined above

(Williamson and Bhargava, 1972), and thus would include the hybrid of the H- and M-forms proposed by Williamson (1986).

11.5.8 *Overview*

It is clear from this discussion that each organizational form has both strengths and weaknesses. While particular functional forms may be strong in, for example, the direction and control of employees' actions, they may be weak in, say, the transmission of information or in the encouragement of enterprise. Thus, as economic and technological factors change (e.g. globalization and ICT), it is not surprising that there is a shift from one form of organization to another.

11.6   Lines of reporting and responsibility

Figure 11.4 provides an example of an organogram for a bank.[3] Numerous other examples are available, both in company reports and on the web. An organogram is a stylized and much simplified view of the lines of

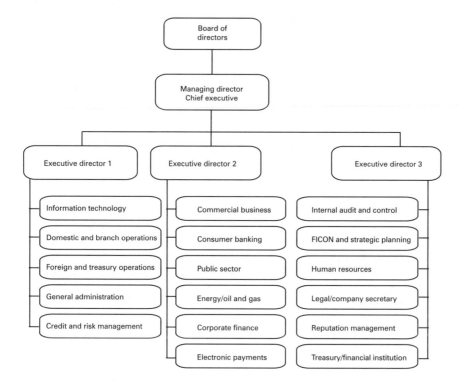

Figure 11.4 Organogram: lines of reporting.

responsibility and reporting within a given organization, where the 'top' of the organogram represents where ultimate responsibility resides. Organograms form a useful starting point for understanding information flows through the company, although many other factors come into play in determining such flows, as will be demonstrated below.

Ferguson *et al.* (1993, p. 32) discuss the concept of the 'span of control'; this may be thought of in a number of different ways, such as the number of distinct functions supervised by a manager (as in the organogram shown in Figure 11.4), the amount of resource falling under the control of the manager or the number of people supervised (as in Figure 11.1). The narrower the span of control, the greater the number of levels in the hierarchy, other things equal, leading to a trade-off between the breadth of control (i.e. horizontally) with the depth of control (i.e. vertically). The greater the breadth of control of a manager, the more pressure is placed on that person's (limited) management capacity, while greater depth has implications for the extent of delegation of various tasks. Each new level in the hierarchy introduces new 'managers', although the level and nature of the management skills are likely to differ between the top of the 'pyramid' and those lower down. In particular, a change in balance is likely, away from leadership and entrepreneurship and towards more basic administrative skills, from the upper to lower echelons in the hierarchy (see Chapters 2 and 6 for a discussion of these issues). In essence, the 'flatter' the organization, probably, the less difference between top and bottom.

11.7 Structure and efficient flows

11.7.1 *Introduction*

In the age of IT and the growth of the knowledge-based company, it is perhaps not surprising that the ease with which information flows within the company has come centre stage. There is a very good reason for this focus. A good MIS is part of the core competences of a business:

> With all the knowledge and skills inherent in a core competence system, managers must be able to access and distribute quickly product and process developments, as well as a wealth of marketing information. The systems need to be flexible, timely, readily accessible, accurate, and compatible with other systems in both cross-functional and cross-organisational capacities. (Unland and Kleiner, 1996, p. 8)

11.7.2 *Technology and physical organization: links to production concepts*

The recognition of the interaction between 'factory' design and organizational performance can be traced back at least to the work of Adam

Smith (1776), who considered 'division of labour' to be a major factor in economic growth:

> Indeed, he favored capital accumulation in part because he felt it would lead to increased division of labor. Smith argued that as the size of the productive operation was increased, the producer would be able to increase the skill and specialization of his workers, to save time in moving from one part of the productive process to another, and to develop more effective and more specialized machinery to increase output. (Gill, 1974, p. 417)

This link between skills and capital intensity was discussed in Chapter 9 and is considered again in Chapter 14.

The main point of the present section is to argue that part of the organizational knowledge of the enterprise is built into the design of the production or service facility.[4] The design of such a facility may be contracted out to a specialist designer, rather than undertaken by the organization itself. The design will depend on the line of production and the locational specificities, as in the case of a shipbuilding facility or a car assembly plant. At this stage, the design may include codified and formal information on how individual pieces of equipment and the system as a whole operates, which will be modified by subsequent tacit knowledge. The website of the Arab Heavy Industries shipbuilding facility, for example, gives details of all the major items of capital in the yard and their layout.[5] The precise layout and capital of the shipbuilding yard will not only govern the size of vessel that can be built or refurbished, but also the efficiency of the process. Efficiency will depend upon the availability of the correct pieces of equipment, raw materials and workers being available at the times and in the locations that they are required. There are clearly links here with the management of production efficiency, including the use of MRP and JIT methods. The appropriate design and fitting of factories, offices and shops is of crucial importance to allow the organization to operate efficiently.

The reader can find many examples on the web of the implications of plant design for efficiency. For example, a report on a new bottling plant argues as follows:

> Most functions, including the all-important sweep of bottles from the pallet onto a mass-flow discharge conveyor, are performed at or below eye level. Operators can easily see machine status without climbing to observe an overhead operation. That gives an operator time to pitch in on tasks that might otherwise have to be handled by a second operator.[6]

These types of issues are clearly fundamental to the efficiency of the firm. They range from the layout and style of shops in attracting consumers and enticing them to buy, through to the planning of locations and routings to the optimal design of the factory. However, the main interest of the present discussion concerns information flows within the company.

11.7.3 *Architecture and information flows*

This section begins with a stylized view of the issue of designing an organization to optimize the efficiency of information flows. It is important to view this discussion against the background of the organizational learning literature, which forms the subject of Chapter 12. In particular, Brown and Duguid (1995, p. 60) introduce the concept of the canonical and non-canonical practices of the organization. The distinction is one between 'espoused practice' – according to rules, regulations, training manuals and so on – and 'actual practice' – what is observed in the day-to-day operations of the firm. The initial discussion in this section deals more closely with canonical practice; later (section 11.8.4) the discussion turns to the question of actual practice and, in particular, Brown and Duguid's (1995) discussion of 'communities of practice'.

Transmission network
The physical structure discussed above does not make explicit the associated position of employees, who will be taking decisions and transmitting information, although the two will be related. While the physical design of the establishment or enterprise will affect the efficiency with which tangible items are moved and dealt with (e.g. ships in a shipyard or customers in a supermarket), the overlay of information flows is at least as important. The issues here are wide ranging and involve, for example, the following questions:

(i)   How does one employee or group communicate information necessary to the efficient running of the enterprise to another?
(ii)   Is the information accurate and timely?
(iii) Does it give rise to the required response by the next employee?
(iv)   Is the transmission network itself efficient in ensuring movement of information, prioritizing it and signalling its importance?
(v)   Is the organization efficient in storing such information for future use?

Efficient hierarchies and information flows
Radner (1992) explores a rather mechanistic problem of the design of an organization for efficient processing of information. Radner argues that in all companies, although particularly the larger and more diversified ones, information processing has become highly decentralized. Thus, the efficiency with which information is processed is a natural focus of attention. Radner's (1992) paper has some surprising findings with regard to the possible nature of efficient hierarchies. Figure 11.5 shows a typical (regular/symmetrical) hierarchy, with:

(i)   fifteen processors (nodes, managers, etc.) – shown by the various circles or dots in the hierarchy;

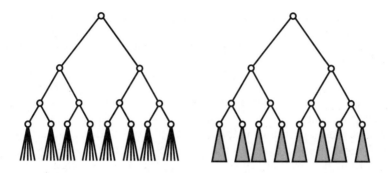

Figure 11.5 Symmetric hierarchical structure. Source: Radner (1992).

(ii)   forty items (i.e. pieces of information) – shown at the very base of the hierarchy;

(iii)   a delay of eleven periods in information transmission from top to bottom (the delay of eleven periods occurs because processing of information takes one period at level 1, two periods at level 2, three at level 3 and four at level 4).

The diagrammatic representation is simplified in the right-hand side of the figure.

Radner (1992) explored the changes to the architecture that help minimize the delay in the system in processing forty items (pieces of information), by reducing the amount of idleness in the network. The algorithm to minimize idleness used by Radner eventually produced the architecture shown in Figure 11.6. Radner (1992, p. 1396) concluded:

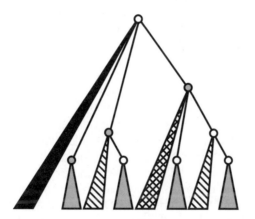

Figure 11.6 Final outcome of all reductions of the symmetrical information hierarchy shown in Figure 11.5. Source: Radner (1992).

> There is ... something odd about Figure [11.6], at least as a picture of an organisational hierarchy. It can be seen that the top ranking processor has immediate subordinates at all levels. In fact, a similar phenomenon is repeated at each lower level.

He further notes that, 'At AT&T this is called "skip-level reporting"'.

One interesting variant on the rather mechanistic view of the information processing and transfer activities can be found in the applied psychology and operations management literatures (Buzacott, 2000). The underlying concept is that different workers or groups of workers not only vary in their performance of their tasks in the sense outlined above (different nodes have different processing times), but also vary around the mean time at each mode. In other words, each individual or group has a mean time, but also a standard deviation around the mean. Thus, in a sequence of tasks, the extent of the deviation from the mean at each stage will affect the overall mean speed of the operation. It will also have implications for the design of the operating system in terms of the manning of different nodes as a whole, buffer stocks held at each stage, and so on (Buzacott, 2000; Hurley and Kadipasaoglu, 1998).

11.7.4 *Computer investments and organizational change*

The returns to investments in computers could have been discussed in Chapter 8. However, it seems appropriate to consider the issue now because the literature on the returns to computers makes a link between this investment and the organization of the company – though the links remain rather tentative. Clearly, computer investment will have contributed to economic growth in the normal manner that arises from the growth in the use of a particular factor (Jorgenson and Stiroh, 1995, 1998). This growth in usage has been driven, in part, by the falling quality-constant price of computers (see Chapter 4). However, other authors have argued that computers act as a facilitating technology, enabling other more important changes within firms, across a wide range of activities and sectors (Helpman, 1998).

There is clear evidence in the literature of a link between computer adoption and productivity growth (Brynjolfsson and Hitt, 1993, 1995; Lichtenberg, 1995). In a paper linking MV and investment in computer capital, Brynjolfsson and Yang (1999) report a significant role for IT investments. In brief, based on a similar but smaller sample of companies to that used by Hall (1993a), they found a large and highly significant coefficient associated with the IT variable – the explanation for which is discussed below. The empirical specification tested included a range of other, control variables, including R&D. When the IT variable was included alongside R&D, the coefficient on IT fell somewhat, but it was the R&D variable that became insignificant (Brynjolfsson and Yang, 1999, p. 25). The authors concluded:

The main finding of the paper is that the financial market puts a very high value on installed computer capital. Market valuations for each dollar of installed computer capital are in the order of ten times greater than the market values for each dollar of conventional assets ... in both manufacturing and services industries and in both the 1980s and the 1990s. (Brynjolfsson and Yang, 1999, p. 26)

The model allowed for the capitalized adjustment costs of investments,[7] which can differ between types of capital and with the magnitude of the investment (IT investments were growing particularly quickly). While this is difficult to disentangle from other effects linking IT investments to the generation of other intangible assets, the authors present some results that favour the 'intangible asset' hypothesis over the 'short-term rent' hypothesis (Brynjolfsson and Yang, 1999, p. 20).

What, then, are the likely sources of computer-related intangible assets? The most obvious source is software – neither internally generated nor purchased software can be allowed for directly in the empirical specifications. In addition, both investments are associated with potentially performance-enhancing organizational changes, but generally appear as a non-separable expense that is written off in the firm's accounts. For example:

some software-related costs such as person-hours of outside consultants and internal employees are sometimes hard to disentangle from costs to re-engineer the firm's business processes. Finally, the costs of computer-associated business process redesign, organizational restructuring and strategic repositioning include not only outside consultants' time but also significant management effort and employee retraining. Again, these costs are typically treated as expenses even when they are expected to create long-lived revenue streams. (Brynjolfsson and Yang, 1999, pp. 26–27)

Making a qualitative attempt to allow for the costs of internal and external software, the authors conclude that:

To summarize, even when using the most generous estimates for the size of software ... [t]he majority of the computer-related intangible assets remain to be explained. Our deduction is that the main portion of the computer-related intangible assets comes from the new business processes, new organizational structure and new market strategies, which each complement the computer technology. (Brynjolfsson and Yang, 1999, p. 29)

In addition, studies by Brynjolfsson and Hitt (1998) and Bresnahan *et al.* (1999) suggest that computer use is 'complementary to new workplace organizations which include more decentralized decision making, more self-managing teams, and broader job responsibilities for line workers' (Brynjolfsson and Yang, 1999, p. 30). According to the authors, it is not Wal-mart's software and hardware *per se* that are the main assets of the business, but the intangible business processes that are founded upon their computer systems. Likewise, they suggest that Amazon's website and associated hardware and software form only a part of that company's assets – it is the associated business models and processes that are really valuable.

Brynjolfsson *et al.* (2000) argue that the early applications of computers were mainly directed at factor substitution, for example affecting low-skilled clerical activities. However, more recent uses of computers and flexible manufacturing technologies have not only enabled but also necessitated organizational redesign (Brynjolfsson *et al.*, 2000, p. 1). Their review of the literature suggests that:

> Collectively, these papers argue for a complementarity between computer investment and organisational investment, and specifically a relationship between information technology use and increased demand for skilled workers, greater decentralisation of decision rights, and team oriented production. (Brynjolfsson *et al.*, 2000, p. 2)

Their work purports:

> analytically [to] explore the hypothesis that new intangible organisational assets complement information technology capital just as factory redesign complemented the adoption of electric motors ... and memos and filing systems complemented the printing press: (Brynjolfsson *et al.*, 2000, p. 2)

Their research moves beyond a simple attempt to show that the coefficient on IT capital is large (as it reflects a broader range of unmeasured investments in organizational change), to measure directly some of these organizational changes, using survey information for large US firms. Their questions regarding organizational change were adapted from earlier surveys, including one by Huselid (1995) (see section 9.6.2). The questions included ones on topics relating to 'the allocation of various types of decision-making authority, the use of self-managing teams, the breadth of job responsibilities and other miscellaneous characteristics of the workforce' (Brynjolfsson *et al.*, 2000, pp. 14–15). The result was a cross-sectional sample of organizational variables for 416 firms during 1995–96 (although the estimates as a whole are based on an eight-year panel), which was used to estimate MV equations of the type discussed by Brynjolfsson and Yang (1999) (Brynjolfsson *et al.*, 2000, p. 15). In many respects, the results are very similar to those reported in Chapter 9 and, hence, it is possible to concentrate on the role of organizational structure. In this respect, the authors concluded that:

> Consistent with our argument that IT and organisation are complementary, we confirm that across multiple measures of IT and multiple measures of organisation, firms that use more IT differ statistically from other firms: they tend to use more teams, have broader job responsibilities, and allocate greater authority to their workers, even after controlling for firm size and industry. (Brynjolfsson *et al.*, 2000, p. 23)

Factor analysis produced a single principal component that was more closely correlated with the various IT measures than any of the organizational variables taken individually. This composite organization variable ('ORG') was also significant in the explanation of the MV of companies. This remained true when the interaction variables between ORG and the various capital variables were included, although none of the other ORG–capital interactions were significant. However, the ORG–computer interaction was highly significant. The authors concluded that 'The magnitude of the interaction term between IT and ORG is about 6 in the pooled estimation, suggesting large complementarities between computers and organisational structure' (Brynjolfsson *et al.*, 2000, p. 26). Thus, they concluded that not only do IT investment and organizational structure contribute to performance independently, but also 'Firms with higher levels of *both* computer investment and these organisational characteristics have *disproportionately* higher market valuations than firms investing heavily on only one or the other dimension' (Brynjolfsson *et al.*, 2000, p. 29).

11.7.5 *Management and strategic information systems*

One point at which IT (including ICT) comes together with organizational change is in the adoption of MIS. Ward and Peppard (2002, pp. 3–4), for example, describe the integrated system utilized by Dell Computers:

> Some information systems are totally automated by IT. For example, Dell Computers has a system where no human intervention is required, from taking customer orders, to delivery of components to the Dell factory for assembly, to shipment to customers. With this build-to-order model, perfect information and tight linkages match supply and demand in real time. The company can receive an order for a personal computer (PC) directly from a customer via its own website (www.dell.com). Indeed, Dell has built in an element of 'intelligence' into its site to help the customer in making decisions regarding the configuration of components, ensuring that 'non-optimal' configurations or configurations not technically possible are not selected. Customers can also choose from a variety of delivery options. Once a customer order has been confirmed, purchase orders for components are automatically generated and electronically transmitted to suppliers. This has enabled Dell to build exactly what the customer has ordered, resulting in a stock turn of 56–60 times per year compared with 13.5 for Compaq and 9.8 for IBM's PC business. Dell also feeds real-time data from technical support and manufacturing lines directly through to suppliers on a minute-by-minute basis.

Information systems existed well before IT and, even today, many companies have some form of IS, but no IT (Ward and Peppard, 2002, p. 3). The discussion of Chapter 4 made clear, however, that one of the principal problems likely to face inquisitive companies is information overload. Thus, the modern enterprise has to give serious consideration the MIS that it adopts and how this is best facilitated using IT. Ward and Peppard (2002, p. 4) make clear the importance of this decision, as:

> organisations may fail to realise any benefits from their investments in IT – investments are often made in technology without understanding or analysing the nature of the activities the technology is to support – either strategically or operationally – in the organisation.

However, one of the conclusions of Brynjolfsson and Yang (1999, p. 30), more generally about IT and organizational change and performance, was that 'Not only are the costs of IT-enabled organizational change large, but there is a very real risk of failure'. Champy (1995) has suggested that up to 70 per cent of major computer-enabled re-engineering projects fail. This is consistent with arguments about the riskiness of key firm investments presented in Chapter 8. A related issue is that in developing an IT IS, the company rarely starts with a clean sheet – it will have existing systems that have developed via learning by experience, and it may not make sense to replace the whole system at one go (Ward and Peppard, 2002, pp. 3–4).

Ward and Peppard (2002, pp. 14–17, 22–25) outline three stylized phases in the development of ISs:

(i)   Data processing (DP) and database management can be traced back to the mid-1960s. Thus, by the mid-1970s, many companies had quite sophisticated IT systems in operation, which, for example, could monitor transaction handling and control, and trigger the reporting of exceptional events or actions. These systems primarily collected, collated and reported data to management, allowing management more control over the production process and, thereby, increasing efficiency. The applications were largely pre-defined and inflexible.

(ii) In the second phase, MISs required the more powerful and sophisticated machines that began to emerge during the 1970s. Thus, by the early 1980s, the developments in personal computers and software were such that the IT system could be productively used by a much wider range of employees (i.e. significantly beyond just those who entered data or transactions).

(iii) Ward and Peppard (2002, p.15) argue that the final phase of advances added at least three new functions of the IT IS: flexible access to data or information initiated by request; decision support, involving flexible processing of data and information; and strategic information systems (SISs), which began in earnest in the mid-1980s.

The authors make the point that the latest functions are often the same as in the case of DP or MIS, but their impact on the business is different (Ward and Peppard, 2002, p. 24). SISs use information to improve the competitiveness of companies, but in new and innovative ways (e.g. linking the company to customers via the internet). Early examples include

American Airlines' SABRE reservation system and the computer-based ordering system of American Hospital Supplies.

Ward and Peppard (2002, p. 26) argue that SISs take four main forms:

(i) sharing information with buyers and/or suppliers;
(ii) integrating information in the firm's value-adding processes;
(iii) aiding the development of new or enhanced products and services;
(iv) providing management information that improves strategic decision making.

Venkatraman (1991) argues that an IT IS enables:

(i) business process redesign – changing the activities and the relationships between activities to improve performance;
(ii) business network redesign – changing the information set of the company and its buyers and suppliers, to improve performance;
(iii) business scope redefinition – changing the product or service portfolio, or changing the role of the organization in the industry.

The empirical literature suggests that SIS innovations afford firms at least temporary competitive advantage. Based upon thirty well known examples of SISs, 40 per cent of the adopting firms still had above average performance ten to twenty years later and 10 per cent of adopters sustained an advantage for about ten years (Kettinger *et al.*, 1994). Such advantages cannot be sustained indefinitely, as new technological opportunities arise and the innovations are generally fairly easily imitated. Thus, Ward and Peppard (2002, pp. 52–58) talk of a 'fourth era', in which firms seek IS/IT capabilities that lead to sustainable competitive advantages. This aspect of the literature suggests that it is probably not the 'technical wizardry' of IS and IT, but a combination of IS and IT competences and the way in which the company manages its IS and IT processes.

11.8 Routines

11.8.1 *Routines defined*

Within the *internal* structure are the informal and formal business models that define the company's operations. The distinction between informal and formal is similar to, though perhaps somewhat broader than, that between the 'procedural' and 'declarative' knowledge put forward in psychology (Cohen and Sproull, 1996, p. x). Here procedural refers to individual knowledge or competences arising from well practised cognitive and motor skills. They are tacit in nature, often taking some time to form and are less easily forgotten. Declarative refers to knowledge of facts, propositions, concepts and so on, which is often gained by more formal types of study and learning, but which may be informed or stimulated by the day-to-day operations of the firm. While procedural memory is extremely valuable in economizing on repeated tasks, declarative knowledge is more important in solving problems where traditional routines break down.

Thus, the distinction between procedural and declarative is linked to the difference between tacit and codified information and to that between 'actual working routines' and an organization's 'official standard operating procedures' (Cohen and Bacdayan, 1996, p. 406). Cohen and Bacdayan note that such distinctions are often highlighted when employees 'work to rule', or when current 'actual' routines result in accidents or other kinds of failure. At any point in time, a company may be said to be characterized by a particular set of 'routines' that govern various aspects of behaviour. Cohen and Bacdayan (1996, p. 406) define organizational routines as:

> patterned sequences of learned behaviour involving multiple actors who are linked by relations of communities and/or authority.... We use 'routine' to designate established patterns of organisational action and we distinguish routines from 'standard operating procedures' which are more explicitly formulated and have normative standing.

Cohen and Bacdayan (1996, p. 406) reserve 'routines' for organizational actions. This is certainly a much richer area, encompassing the inter-relationship between individuals or between 'communities' within an organization. Figure 11.7 sets out a routine involving four actors or communities. The sequence is fairly obvious, set out as a series of tasks from 0 to 4, which are then passed on elsewhere within the organization (Cohen and Bacdayan, 1996, p. 410). In such routines, the action of one community triggers the action(s) of another:

> As individuals become more skilled in their portion of a routine the actions become stored as procedural memories and can later be triggered as substantial chunks of behaviour. The routine of a group can be viewed as the concatenation of such procedurally stored actions, each primed by and priming the actions of others. (Cohen and Bacdayan, 1996, p. 410)

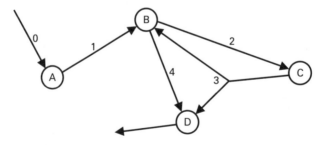

Figure 11.7 Routines for four actors. Source: Cohen and Bacdayan (1996, pp. 410–411).

The routing is, to some degree, important (see sections 11.7.2 and 11.7.3), as individuals or groups come into direct contact with each other and these points of contact are likely foci for information transfer and, as a result, innovation. However, this should not be taken as the only points of contact, as individuals and groups build up social networks and capital through less direct mechanisms within the enterprise and between enterprises. Such social mappings may be influenced by procedural sequences, but they are unlikely to be anywhere near one-to-one mappings.

11.8.2 *Routines as a store of information*

This section investigates the fundamental idea that knowledge becomes embedded in the organization in terms of the routines adopted. Nelson and Winter (1982, p. 99) argue that:

> It is easy enough to suggest that a plausible answer to the question 'Where does [the] knowledge reside?' is 'In the organisation's memory'. But where and what is the memory of an organisation? We propose that the routinisation of activity in an organisation constitutes the most important form of storage of the organisation's specific operational knowledge.

According to Nelson and Winter, therefore, a routine is an efficient mechanism for 'recording' and 'retrieving' operational information. They argue that organizations 'remember by doing', which is achieved largely through exercise – the repetition of particular tasks. In other words, 'the situations confronted replicate ones that were confronted the previous day ... and are handled in the same way' (Nelson and Winter, 1982, p. 100). Thus, the type of organization they have in mind is 'engaged in the provision of goods and services that are visibly "the same" over extended periods' (p. 97).

According to Nelson and Winter (1982, p. 104), 'Information is actually stored primarily in the memories of the members (individuals or groups) of the organisation'. However, they recognize that organizational knowledge is broader than the collective individual memories, and argue that 'It typically includes, first, a variety of forms of *external memory* – files, message boards, manuals, computer memories, magnetic tapes – that complement and support individual memories' (p. 105, emphasis added). Note that information stored in other places, such as rules of thumb or computer software, may be lost from individual memory but still be important to the operation of the company.

Doing the right thing at the right time depends on the transmission and receipt of (correct) 'messages' (Nelson and Winter, 1982, pp. 100–101). The sending and receipt of messages takes place partly through the routine of the organization – a semi-finished product moves from one workstation to another, and its appearance at the next workstation acts as a signal to the workers at that station to undertake their task. It may also involve the sending of a verbal or written message (e.g. a requisition order). Thus, in steady state, 'There is, indeed, an internal equilibrium "circular flow" of information in an organisation in routine ... operation, but it is a flow that is continuously primed by external message sources and time keeping devices' (p. 103). Whatever the source of the messages, 'What is crucial to a productive organisation's performance is coordination; what is central to coordination is that individual members, knowing their jobs, correctly interpret and respond to the messages they receive' (p. 104).

Nelson and Winter (1982) also touch upon the question of the size and scope of the company. For example, they note that 'The capabilities of a particular organisation are ... associated with the possession of particular collections of specialised plant and equipment, and the repertoires of organisational members include the ability to operate that plant and machinery' (p. 103). What is also interesting, however, is that such equipment embodies the organizational knowledge of the company that supplied these capital goods. In many cases, no one in the user company may fully understand the equipment in use (as many drivers do not fully understand the workings of a car). Even if members of the user company understand the technology of the capital equipment, it may still not pay the company even to repair the capital – it may well call an 'expert' from outside the company. Broadly the same argument applies to the purchase rather than production of materials and components used in the production of the company's product or service. The absence of sufficient organizational knowledge of the user company may be a deliberate strategy, enabling the company to control its scale and scope and, thereby, its efficiency and performance. This issue essentially concerns the focus of the company (see Chapter 2).

11.8.3 *Procedural memory and suboptimal routines*

Cohen and Bacdayan (1996, p. 408) discuss the lack of research developing the theory of routines. They argue that, 'For the most part, the concept of routine has been applied to mop up the "residuals" of rationality, i.e., as *post hoc* explanation of apparently non-rational behaviour'. Nelson and Winter (1982), however, argue that routines may not be ineffective or irrational and, in addition, can change. The experimental results of Cohen and Bacdayan (1996), based upon learning while playing new games, throws some further light on these assertions by Nelson and Winter. It is difficult to see anything in their results that suggests any kind of irrational behaviour – on average both the speed and reliability of actions increase. Their findings, however, suggest that the routines that develop may not be 'optimal'. While this would not disturb Nelson and Winter, who do not subscribe to the notion of optimality, it is interesting that, against the background of improvements in performance from 'routinizing' behaviour, a number of suboptimal routines emerge and persist. Cohen and Bacdayan (1996, p. 420) note one example, in which 'we have a case where an approach to the problem that left all of the action to one individual would actually be better than the more organisationally balanced one, but the groups use the approach they have learned [i.e. in which the pair both play a part]'.

Tolbert and Zucker's (1999) review of institutional theory of organizations adds significantly to our understanding of the process by which routines and structures emerge and their likely economic efficiency. It appears that, in the early years of the development of sociological studies of organization (the functional analyses of organizations) there seemed an inherent link between organizational design, performance and survival. This is linked to two assertions of functionalist theory (Tolbert and Zucker, 1999, pp. 170–171):

(i)   that the components of the organizational structure should be integrated if the system is to survive – since the various components interact to produce the product or service and, by implication, changes in one component require changes in others;

(ii) that existing structures should, on balance, make a net positive contribution to the functioning of the organization as a whole, otherwise changes would be introduced to remove net dysfunctional components.

These two assertions encouraged the direction of research, which consequently focused on whether the design of formal structures reflected the managers' efforts to ensure coordination and control, thereby maximizing efficiency.

Given this background, it becomes clear why the seminal paper of Meyer and Rowan (1977) was such a radical departure. In addition to adding to the current discussion of routines and structure, this contribution also links closely with the issues of brand development, discussed in Chapter 10, and to the literature on HRM/HPWPs, examined in Chapter 9. The discussion in the relevant literature focuses more closely on formal structures, but it may equally be applied to the issue of routines. At the heart of Meyer and Rowan's (1977) contribution is a key insight, that 'formal structures have symbolic as well as action-generating properties' and, more particularly, that 'structures can become invested with socially shared meanings, and thus, in addition to their "objective" functions, can serve to communicate information about the organisation to both internal and external audiences' (Tolbert and Zucker, 1999, p. 171). The implication is that the formal structure can exist quite independently of the problems of coordination and control that the organization faces. Thus, the organizational form of the company may not necessarily be the best in terms of day-to-day productive efficiency, but nonetheless be one that is broadly accepted by the various actors in society. Hence, Meyer and Rowan (1977, p. 340) argue that:

> Organizations are driven to incorporate the practices and procedures defined by prevailing rationalized concepts of organizational work and institutionalized in society. Organizations that do so increase their legitimacy and their survival prospects, independent of the immediate efficacy of the acquired practices and procedures.

Tolbert and Zucker (1999, p. 172) argue that day-to-day behaviour and formal structures are, at best, only loosely coupled. This relates directly to the distinction, outlined in section 11.8.1, between 'actual working routines' and an organization's 'official standard operating procedures' (Cohen and Bacdayan, 1996, p. 406). Meyer and Rowan (1977, p. 342) suggest that:

> formal organizations are often loosely coupled ... structural elements are only loosely linked to each other and to activities, rules are often violated, decisions are often unimplemented, or if implemented have uncertain consequences, technologies are of problematic efficiency, and evaluation and inspection systems are subverted or rendered so vague as to provide little coordination.

However, it is not clear why society comes to prefer certain structures as 'efficacious and necessary' when, in fact, there is no tangible evidence that they are linked to any particular measure of performance (Tolbert and Zucker, 1999, p. 173).

11.8.4 *Communities of practice*

As was mentioned briefly in section 11.7.3, Brown and Duguid (1995) made the important distinction between formal descriptions of work (canonical practice) and the actual practices of members of the organization (non-canonical practice). The link with the earlier discussion of organizational design that aids information flow is that a divergence can develop between the formal organizational practices, including the practices as perceived by management, and the informal practices that help to keep the firm operating smoothly. Thus, the organization becomes blind to the actual practices of its members, and an attempt to enforce canonical practice can be counterproductive and reduce performance. Brown and Duguid (1995) utilize a sequence of papers by Orr in which he describes the ethnography of service technicians, whose job it is to maintain and repair machines on the clients' premises. The evidence indicates how problems with the machines arise that cannot be solved by reference to repair manuals or through skills imbued through the training programmes attended by the technicians. Faced by such a case, the service technician (rep) and specialist engineer are forced to solve a problem *in situ*, without losing face in front of the client. As the canonical practice is of no use, they resort to a number of discussions of the past experiences of problems faced by the rep and the specialist, where they encountered similar types of problems. Through the story telling, their separate experiences lead to a shared diagnosis of previously experienced symptoms that lead to a solution, even though the new problem is novel (Brown and Duguid, 1995, pp. 63–64).

Thus, Orr's description leads to at least three key dimensions of non-canonical practice that appear to be of considerable importance to organizational performance:

(i) *Narration* – which relates to the dissemination of experience through the mutual telling of and listening to stories relating to the experience of clients and members of the organization. These stories can be handed down from rep to rep, and they act as a repository of accumulated wisdom, in much the same way as in ancient tribes which had no access to writing and reading.

(ii) *Collaboration* – which occurs through the communal nature of the activities and from the social networks built up at work.

(iii) *Social construction* – which has two main facets:
  (a) the reps' non-canonical model of the machine, which differs in many important respects from the canonical view;
  (b) the development, in part through the narration process, of a 'community of reps', which interacts with (and learns from) other communities, both within and outside the enterprise.

This idea of social construction has a number of implications for organizational structure. Brown and Duguid (1995, p. 70) argue, for example, that 'a specialist cannot hope to exert hierarchical control over knowledge that he or she must first construct cooperatively. Occupational communities ... have little hierarchy; the only real status is that of member'. In addition, the idea of formal, canonical, bounded groups within the organization is undermined by the presence of and need for non-canonical practices. The authors argue that:

> The communities that we discern are, by contrast, often non-canonical and not recognised by the organisation. They are more fluid and interpretive than bounded, often crossing the restrictive boundaries of the organisation to incorporate people from outside.... Indeed, the canonical organisation becomes a questionable unit of analysis from this perspective. (Brown and Duguid, 1995, p. 70)

Finally, in the context of organizational design, the authors argue that the issue is not so much the creation of new organizational groups but 'the *detection* and *support* of emergent or existing communities' (pp. 70–71).

11.9   Conclusions

This chapter has focused on the role played by a number of dimensions of organizational structure – including architecture, management hierarchy and routines – in determining enterprise efficiency. All three are related to one another, but also to the range of products or services produced and the functional activities (such as R&D and HPWPs) carried out. Different architecture, hierarchies and routines are required in different areas (e.g. for simple or for complex products) and activities (e.g. routine production and R&D). In a number of places, as in the case of the discussion of routines, which build up through repeating the same actions time and again, the issue arises as to what might happen in the face of an external shock or from the build-up of internal pressure as the company grows. These issues are considered in detail in the context of a learning organization in Chapter 12.

Notes

1   In September 2002, Kodak's unconsolidated affiliates included: SK Display Corporation (34 per cent ownership interest); Kodak Polychrome Graphics, a joint venture (50 per cent ownership); and NexPress, a joint venture between Kodak and Heidelberg (50 per cent ownership). See http://biz.yahoo.com/e/l/e/ek.html.
2   See section 11.5.1 for a discussion of this concept.
3   Such organograms were a principal focus of research in the pioneering work of Woodward (1958, pp. 96–124).
4   There is a long history of work on the efficient internal organization of the production process, which can be traced back to Adam Smith's (1776) 'pin factory', through the introduction of *mass production* methods (i.e. the Model-T Ford), through Joan Woodward's (1965) seminal work *Industrial Organization* and Bell's (1972) analysis of the implications of computer numerical control machines in the 1960s.
5   See www.ahi-uae.com/faci1.htm.
6   See www.packworld.com/articles/Features/14685.html (reports an article on 'Clever layout enhances bottling efficiency' from *Packaging World Magazine*, July 2002).
7   The marginal q should be equal to 1 plus the marginal adjustment costs, and values of q in excess of unity reflect the '"short-term rents" that are earned by the installed capital and persist until the installation completes' (Brynjolfsson and Yang, 1999, p. 4). Note that investment in hardware (as opposed to software) is likely to be capitalized in the firm's accounts.

Chapter 12

Organizational learning and performance

12.1 Introduction

This chapter takes a brief look at organizational learning. In doing so, it begins with a fairly traditional definition of learning, which is said to occur when the organization becomes:

> able to respond to task-demand or an environmental pressure in a different way as a result of earlier response to the same task (practice) or as a result of other intervening relevant experience.... The sign of learning is not a shift of response or performance as a consequence of a change in stimulus-situation or in motivation, but rather a shift in performance when the stimulus-situation and the motivation are essentially the same. (English and English, 1958, p. 289)

While this gives a particular instance of when learning is likely to have occurred (as in learning by doing), it is a fairly restrictive definition – at least if it is used to define the only times when learning can occur (Weick, 1995, pp. 163–165).

The present chapter takes a more pragmatic view, examining the sources of learning using a framework developed by Huber (1995), based upon his extensive review of the organizational learning literature. The rational for using this framework is that it enables the analysis to bring together many of the approaches and pieces of empirical evidence from earlier in the book. In the present chapter, even if organizational structure is not perhaps viewed as a design for organizational learning (Stinchcombe, 1990), the two are seen as closely intertwined. In addition, it allows a discussion of what Simon (1995, p. 180) terms a 'major topic' in organizational learning, that is, 'an understanding of the mechanisms that can be used to enable an organisation to deviate from the culture [technology, line of business, etc.] in which it is embedded'.

Section 12.2 outlines a range of different forms and types of learning. Section 12.3 continues with a discussion of various sources of knowledge within the firm. It deals with: 'congenital learning'; individual and organizational appraisal schemes; formal experiments within the enterprise; and natural experiments primarily caused by shocks external to the enterprise, with a focus on those that are sufficiently large to prompt radical innovations in company structure. Section 12.4 deals with various forms of learning from others, including grafting, noticing and vicarious learning. Section 12.5 outlines the literature on the learning curve and distinguishes it from the literature on the experience curve. Section 12.6 examines the concept of organizational memory. It is clear, for example, that without organizational memory there can be no organizational learning. Section 12.7 deals with the strategic issues of managing the rate of growth of organizational learning to give competitive advantage. Finally, section 12.8 draws the main conclusions of the chapter.

12.2   Nature and sources of learning

12.2.1 *Types of learning*

Even a casual glance at the relevant literature reveals that learning is a heterogeneous activity. Many of the articles make a distinction between 'learning by doing more' and 'learning by doing longer' (see, for example, Sheshinski, 1967). While these two concepts are, in principle, quite distinct, it is not always easy to disentangle them, given that doing something for longer usually means doing more of it as well. Equally, the later discussion makes it clear that the empirically observed 'learning' and 'experience' effects range from the almost involuntary acquisition of knowledge (like 'manna from heaven') through to the results of focused and intensive search.

At various times the present chapter touches on the distinction between task (labour), capital and organizational learning (Bahk and Gort, 1993):

(i)   *Labour learning* is generally associated with semi-skilled and skilled manual tasks. One of its main features is the gains in speed and reliability of action as workers become better adjusted to the jobs they perform – a form of manual dexterity, which seems more important in more labour-intensive processes and industries (Hartley, 1965; Hirsch, 1952, 1956). However, it is also easy to see how this can be extended to non-manual activities (e.g. the speed of adding up a darts score or calculating the score required to finish).

(ii) *Capital learning* refers to the improvement in knowledge about the firm's capital stock. Bahk and Gort (1993, p. 575) argue that 'It encompasses engineering information that accumulates through experience on the tolerances to which parts are machined, on the use of special tools and devices, and on improvements in plant layout and the routing and handling of materials. Such knowledge allows firms to improve their utilisation rates and maintenance procedures' (see also section 11.7.2).

(iii) *Organizational learning* is a concept that can be traced back at least to the work of Conway and Schultz (1959), who argued that productivity change is the result of changing the tasks of individuals – a concept which appeared in the literature in various guises in the 1980s (Gort *et al.*, 1985; Prescott and Visscher, 1980; Tomer, 1981).

Bahk and Gort (1993, pp. 575–576) outline four examples of organizational learning:

(i) improved matching of individuals to tasks;
(ii) accumulation of interdependent or team-based knowledge;
(iii) employee-based 'knowledge networks' (i.e. knowing whom to ask for what);
(iv) better coordination between departments, and with suppliers and buyers.

Malerba (1992, p. 848) adopts a somewhat different taxonomy of learning processes:

(i) learning by doing – internal to the firm and related to production activity;
(ii) learning by using – internal to the firm and related to the use of products, machinery and inputs;
(iii) learning from advances in science and technology – external to the firm and related to the absorption capacity of the firm (see also section 9.5.2);
(iv) learning from intra-industry spillovers – external to the firm, related to what competitors and other firms in the industry are doing;
(v) learning by interacting – external to the firm, related to upstream or downstream sources of knowledge, alliances and so on;
(vi) learning and searching – internal to the firm, related primarily to formalized activities such as R&D, aimed at generating new knowledge.

The last of these, in particular, introduces more proactive forms of learning.

Huber (1995, p. 124) suggests four key dimensions for understanding organizational learning, which the analysis of the present chapter largely follows:

(i) knowledge acquisition;
(ii) information distribution;
(iii) information interpretation;
(iv) organizational memory.

The first of these, in particular, brings the earlier chapters together, and the other three enable the discussion to be rounded off. As the knowledge acquisition literature is so large and diverse, Huber suggests that it should be broken down into six main 'sub-constructs' or 'sub-processes', namely:

(i)   congenital learning;
(ii)   experiential learning;
(iii) learning by observing other organizations;
(iv)   vicarious learning;
(v)   learning by 'grafting';
(vi)   learning by searching and noticing.

12.2.2 *Exploration versus exploitation*

Huber (1995, pp. 125–126) notes that not all learning need be conscious or intentional. He argues that academics, because of the inquiring nature of their jobs, tend to concentrate on the intentional search for information and knowledge. Huber argues that organizations make 'explicit' and 'implicit' choices between exploration and exploitation. The explicit choices involve 'calculated decisions about alternative investments and competitive strategies', while the implicit choices are 'buried in many features of organisational forms and customs, for example, in search rules and practices, in the ways that targets are set and changed, and in incentive systems' (p. 102).

   March (1995, pp. 104–105) suggests that exploitation may drive out exploration. The problem arises because the returns from exploration, in comparison with the returns from exploitation, are generally less certain and take longer to have a positive effect on the firm. Basic research is a longer-run and more risky business than applied research; NPD and NPLs are more risky than the modification of existing products. March (1995, p. 104) describes the processes by which 'Reason inhibits foolishness; learning and imitation inhibit experimentation'. Exploitation is the mechanism that generates economic surplus, which may be reinvested to fund exploration. At particular points in the life-cycle, however, the returns to exploitation may be significantly higher than the returns to exploration. Thus, the former tends to drive out the latter. March's worry therefore has a very real basis, and one that is discussed further in Chapters 13 and 14. Thus, March makes the important point that, 'Since long run intelligence depends on sustaining a reasonable level of exploration, these tendencies to increase exploitation and reduce exploration make adaptive processes potentially self-destructive'. It is worth adding that exploration processes develop a learning dimension of their own, which cannot be efficiently switched on and off at short notice. However, the balance is a fine one – too much learning may be unproductive if it cannot be effectively exploited or if the period of exploitation is insufficient to reap the rewards of earlier exploration. Lant and Mezias (1995, pp. 273–274) note that some organizations fail to learn how to balance change with stability, either changing too often or not often enough. In a similar way, Dutton and Freedman (1985) argue that the optimal balance between imitation and internally sourced learning is likely to depend upon the particular situation in which the company finds itself – a topic that is considered in Chapter 13.

12.2.3 *Learning and improved performance*

Before moving to the main thrust of the chapter, several other comments are in order. Huber (1995, p. 126) argues that learning does not necessarily increase an individual's or organization's effectiveness, for a variety of reasons. For example, what is learnt may not be correct. As Huber (1995, p. 126) puts it, 'Entities can incorrectly learn, and they can correctly learn what is incorrect'. In the socialization and acclimatization process, new management recruits may adopt the bad practices of their new employer, only to contaminate other firms with such practices when they move on. Organizational slack may allow routines to evolve that reduce efficiency and which require stricter policing or new incentives to remove them. March *et al.* (1995) make the slightly different point that success and failure are a consequence of distinct individual events and are the result of risky and uncertain processes, which makes it very difficult for companies to draw hard and fast lessons from 'small histories'. They conclude:

> Many of the ways in which organisations treat small histories are difficult to justify as leading to shared beliefs, exhibiting intelligence, or producing competitive advantage. Learning processes sometimes result in confusion and mistakes. (March *et al.*, 1995, p. 14)[1]

12.3 **Knowledge acquisition**

12.3.1 *Congenital knowledge*

Huber (1995, p. 128) defines congenital knowledge as the inherited knowledge brought to bear by the organization's creators, plus knowledge learned by the latent organization before its formal birth. Key to this will be the entrepreneur or the entrepreneurial team (see Chapter 6), including the non-executive directors. In addition to the technical skills of the entrepreneurial team, as in the case of biotechnology start-ups, the social capital of the enterprise is important. One potential problem is that those with a highly technical background may not have the social competences to develop a sufficient level of social capital for the organization (and those with the social competences may not have a sufficiently innovative idea). As noted in Chapter 6, the nature of this early team is crucial to the potential success of the enterprise, in terms of convincing venture capital partners and other backers, and in terms of acting as means of suggesting, rebuffing and refining ideas. The literature also suggests that this latent organization sets the foundations for the future trajectory of the enterprise. Huber (1995, p. 128), for example, argues that:

> The nature of an organisation is greatly influenced by the nature of its founders and its founding.... What an organisation knows at birth will determine what it searches for, what it experiences, and how it interprets what it encounters.

In other words, enterprises exhibit an important history dependence in their search and learning processes.

12.3.2 *Individual and organizational appraisal*

Appraisal is a further form of experiential learning. This often occurs at the individual level, for example the monitoring of each employee's performance in the task and assessing the person's career development. But it can also occur at the team, section, department and company levels; for example, did the unit involved meet the targets set? Such activities sound more reactive than proactive, but they can be built into a more inclusive (management and worker) network, for the analysis of various performance issues. Such research enables the sharing of information and the establishment of mechanisms for discussion of joint action to improve outcomes. Based upon the information gathered, the organization can learn from its successes and mistakes and realign its strategies – raising or lowering aspiration levels, changing priorities of actions and so on, along the lines suggested by Cyert and March (1963). This is a way of viewing the tensions between stability and change (Lant and Mezias, 1995, p. 279). Depending on the size of the problem, the change required may be sufficiently large to require the firm to alter its frame of reference. Lant and Mezias (1995, p. 290), for example, refer to periods of 'convergence and re-orientation' – 'normal organisational routines sometimes provide the equivocal experiences which lead to second-order learning and change'. Argyris (1983, p. 116) makes the distinction between the relatively minor resolution of mismatches, which do not require a change in governing policies or values ('single-loop learning'), and those that require changes in the organization's frame of reference, which demand longer, more strategic and perhaps even cultural shifts ('double-loop learning').

12.3.3 *Formal experiments*

Huber (1995, p. 129) argues that relatively few formal experiments tend to be authorized by organizations. The more obvious ones considered in earlier chapters are R&D (Chapter 8) and market testing of new products (Chapters 4 and 10). There are other examples of experimentation, such as new forms of training programmes, or shop display layouts. However, Huber (1995, p. 129) argues that the need for managers to appear decisive often militates against undertaking such experiments and that, even if they are undertaken, their subsequent evaluation is often coloured by the need to put as positive a spin on events as possible. Given that experiments are often going to involve new activities with a fairly high degree of risk, then the organization requires a culture that, to some degree, accepts and learns from failure. However, in many instances there are a variety of ways of designing such activities as multi-stage experiments – with evaluation and learning taking place at each stage – that reduce the all-or-nothing costs of some of these actions (Huber, 1995, p. 130; see also section 8.5 and section 13.2.2).

Chapter 9 discussed the advantages of organizational flexibility (as a supplement to, for example, either efficiency-increasing or quality-increasing product strategies). This has proved a long-lived theme in the literature. For example, Boulding (1978, p. 111) argued that 'Adaptation to a particular niche ... while it leads to short-run survival, is never adequate for survival in the long run.... Adaptability is the capacity to expand niches or find new niches'. Based on this, some researchers, probably fuelled with some of the ideas from evolutionary theory, suggest that organizations should experiment with themselves by 'maintaining themselves in a state of frequent, nearly-continuous change in structures, processes, domains, etc., even in the face of apparently optimal adaption' (Huber, 1995, p. 131). Such a state would maintain a high skill requirement among its employees and may equip the firm to manage change better, even if the experiments were not close to the change required. However, experimentation is costly in terms of management time, worker uncertainty about the rational for change and so on, and seems to run against March's (1995) discussion of the optimal balance between experimentation and exploitation. Levitt and March (1988, p. 334), for example, argue that continuous experimentation is more likely to result in 'random drift' than improvement. Nevertheless, Huber (1995, p. 132) notes that 'there may be instances or conditions in which experimenting organisations do or might thrive and survive'.

Huber (1995, pp. 132–133) reports on both laboratory-based and natural experimental learning situations. He notes that the early studies led to observations that have not been subsequently contradicted, in particular that 'group or organisational learning is often haphazard and multi-faceted'. He argues that, in the main, more recent work has been 'decidedly non-cumulative', not allowing broadly based conclusions to be drawn. However, one interesting and somewhat more substantiated result appears to be that 'fast learning is sometimes disadvantageous' (p. 133). This point has already been made in several contexts – an example is that a reduction in the period allowed for an R&D programme disproportionately increases the cost of invention. In the present context, it is equally relevant to the trade-off between learning new things and allowing a sufficiently long period to exploit existing knowledge profitably.

12.3.4 Natural experiments, shocks and radical versus non-radical innovations

Section 11.8.4 touched on the ethnographic work of Orr, on the problem-solving activities of service technicians (Brown and Duguid, 1995). That discussion considered the evolution of 'communities of practice', drawing on the experience of members in solving unusual or unique problems. It covered the transmission of information across members of each community and (with greater difficulty) across communities. This concurs with Simon's (1995, p. 176) view that:

> an important component of organisational learning is internal learning – that is, transmission of information from one organisational member or group of members to another. Individual learning in organisations is very much a social, not a solitary, phenomenon.

Such communities of practice are:

> inherently innovative. 'Maverick' communities of this sort offer the core of a large organization a means and a model to examine the potential of alternative views of organizational activity through spontaneously occurring experiments [i.e. finding workable solutions to machine malfunction and failure] that are simultaneously informed and checked by experience. (Brown and Duguid, 1995, p. 73)

Brown and Duguid (1995, p. 73) argue that such non-canonical practices are important to company efficiency and that 'The potential of such innovation is ... lost to an organisation that remains blind to non-canonical practice'. Indeed, supposed improvements to canonical practice may have the effect, at best, of driving non-canonical practices further underground and, at worst, disrupting and even largely eliminating them.

It seems interesting to explore some of the implications of more radical shocks, during and following which learning occurs and routines change. Again, this relates to the question of whether there is a need to change the company's frame of reference. Simon (1995, p. 185) makes the distinction between the cases where:

(i)   the learner is 'presented with an appropriate problem representation, and has to learn how to use it effectively';

(ii)   the situation is entirely new and the organization 'must create a problem representation to deal with it'.

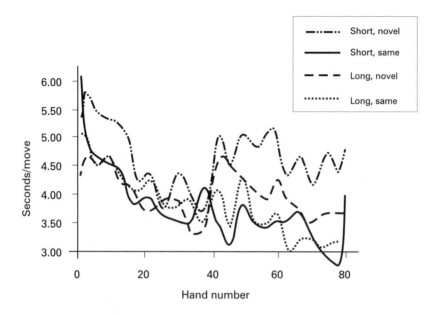

Figure 12.1 Evolution of routines over time. Source: Cohen and Bacdayan (1996).

Most obviously, shocks and changes to the environment often produce a need to modify or, *in extremis*, to redesign the company – to change its structure and its routines. The company's own success (or failure) can produce a stimulus for such changes as it grows and/or diversifies (see section 11.4).

The results of a radical change – being asked to 'play a new game' – suggest a significant learning period in which routines continue to evolve. In a game of the type considered by Cohen and Bacdayan (1996), there is a probabilistic lower limit to the eventual efficiency of the players – similar limits have often been argued to exist in learning curve effects (e.g. when physical capital is held constant – see below). Figure 12.1 shows the distinction between two 'same' curves, where the players are able to continue with their developing routines, and two 'novel' curves, where the players are asked to adapt to a change in the rules half way through the experiment. In both cases there are two curves – one where the mid-point is associated with a short and the other with a long break.[2] Cohen and Bacdayan (1996) suggest that more radical changes of this type – where the rules change – may require declarative rather than procedural responses, before the new environment settles and procedural routines again emerge.

The institutional literature on organizations links major changes with the emergence of new organizational forms. Tolbert and Zucker (1999, pp. 174–178) describe the effects of an innovatory shock that might arise as

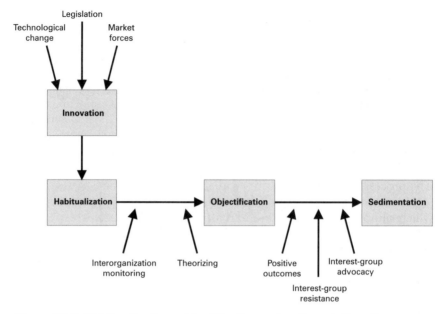

Figure 12.2 Habitualization, objectification and sedimentation: the process of organizational structural change in response to changes in technology, legislation or market forces. Source: Tolbert and Zucker (1999, pp. 174–178).

a consequence of a significant change in technology, legislation or market forces (see Figure 12.2). As a consequence, key players within the firm are forced to rethink the organizational structure – the process of habitualization. The authors note that:

> In an organizational context, the process of habitualization involves the generation of new structural arrangements in response to a specific organizational problem or set of problems, and the formalization of such arrangements in the policies and procedures of a given organization, or a set of organizations that confront the same or similar problems. These processes result in structures that can be classified as being at the pre-institutionalization stage. (Tolbert and Zucker, 1999, p. 175)

Note that the new structure might be 'borrowed' from elsewhere (i.e. imitated). Objectification denotes the processes that lead to a proposed structure taking on a more permanent and widespread status (Tolbert and Zucker, 1999, p. 176). The process can involve product champions as well as groups resisting the change. It also, however, involves building social consensus among decision makers about the value of a particular emergent structure. Finally, sedimentation (i.e. the full institutionalization of a structure) occurs as the structure becomes both widely accepted and attains a continuity and duration that make it well established. Again, actors who are likely to be adversely affected by the changes may still resist. The authors conclude:

> Hence, full institutionalization of a structure is likely to depend on the conjoint effects of relatively low resistance by opposing groups, continued cultural support and promotion by advocacy groups, and positive correlation with desired outcomes. Resistance is likely to limit the spread of a structure among organizations identified by theorizing as relevant adopters, and continued promotion and/or demonstrable benefits are necessary to counteract entropic tendencies, and to thus ensure perpetuation of the structure over time. (Tolbert and Zucker, 1999, p. 178)

The process has many similarities with the adoption of industry standards.

Henderson (1995) develops the concept of 'architectural innovation', which, although not the most radical form of innovation, can creep up and take a firm unaware. This type of innovation changes the relationships between the component parts of a product but leaves the core components and the core design concepts unchanged. The idea is that many products require knowledge of both their component parts and the way in which they are configured or 'linked together into a coherent whole' (Henderson, 1995, p. 361). Thus, architectural innovation occurs where (largely) the same components are used but in some novel way – though it may be triggered as some chain event caused by modification to a single component (e.g. miniaturization of a computer chip). Henderson argues (1995, p. 363) that, 'Since architectural knowledge is usually stable during long periods of incremental innovation, it tends to become embedded in the communications channels, information filters, and problem solving strategies of the organisation'. More fundamentally, she posits that the architecture of the organization is itself often a reflection of the architecture of the product – 'the organisation and the products that it builds will mirror each other in very specific ways' (p. 371). In particular, many companies may evolve into separate units, each responsible for a particular component or group of components, where the relationship between them is determined by the stable architecture of the product. While each unit has a remit to look after and develop a component of the product, no one has the responsibility for the evaluation and construction of the architectural knowledge (Henderson, 1995, p. 372). Thus, major organizational barriers to change develop from long-established and widely held assumptions (i.e. the architectural knowledge) about the way in which the different units in the firm are required to work together to ensure the performance of the enterprise as a whole – and such barriers are difficult to break down.[3]

12.3.5 *Experiential learning, learning by doing (and experience) curves*

The discussion of radical innovation arising from some cultural shock brings the discussion to the issue of learning (or experience) curves. In this instance, the 'shock' arises from some important act by the firm, such as establishing a new plant or replacing its plant and machinery by new equipment. The issue concerns how the firm learns to use this new capital more efficiently and the effects that this learning or experience has on enterprise performance. Note that, while the experience literature is associated with an extensive range of empirical estimates, this is undermined by a lack of precision about the causes of the gains in learning. The more sociological literature on experiential learning is far richer, at least conceptually, though, at this stage in the development of the subject, many of the interesting hypotheses lack rigorous testing (Huber, 1995).

Two quotes from Berndt (1991) help to show how important experience effects may be. The first argues that:

> The effect itself is beyond question. It is so universal that its absence is almost a warning of mismanagement or misunderstanding. Yet the basic mechanism that produces the experience curve effect is still to be adequately explained.... Our entire concept of competition, anti-trust and non-monopolistic free enterprise is based on a fallacy if the experience curve effect is true. (Boston Consulting Group, 1973, p. 2; quoted in Berndt, 1991)

The second quote gives some explanation for the reference to anti-trust:

> The learning curve creates entry barriers and protection from competition by conferring cost advantages on early entrants and those who achieve large market shares. (Spence, 1981, p. 68; quoted in Berndt, 1991)

While there is a very large empirical literature on learning and experience curves, the following review is somewhat sceptical about how much can be learnt about the nature and causes of learning. There appears to be an important distinction between learning and experience curves, although these terms are often used interchangeably in the literature. Berndt (1991, p. 66) notes that:

> The literature on the cost effects of learning has occasionally differentiated learning curve from experience curve effects; the former was confined to the learning and increased effectiveness of workers, while the latter incorporated the complete effects of experience, from workers' training to technical improvements to better management.

Hodgson (1998, pp. 40–41) summarized Penrose's work as showing that, 'Typically, growth also involves change and development within the firm itself: both an automatic increase in knowledge and an incentive to search for new knowledge are, as it were, built into the very nature of firms possessing entrepreneurial resources of even an average initiative'. Thus, while 'pure learning by doing' is seen as an unintentional by-product of the provision of goods and services and essentially free ('manna from heaven'), the experience curve also includes the effects of purchases of the services of human capital, investment in training, expenditure on R&D

and so on (Bahk and Gort, 1993, p. 562; Ferguson *et al.*, 1993). As intentional learning is considered in section 12.5, the present section, as far as possible, focuses on unintentional learning (although it is often difficult to make a clear distinction either in theory or in practice).

Penrose (1959, p. 53) stressed the tacit and elusive nature of skills, arguing that much of a company's knowledge is neither formal nor can be taught:

> It is the result of learning, but learning in the form of personal experience ... experience itself can never be transmitted; it produces a change – frequently a subtle change – in individuals and cannot be separated from them. This learning through experience shows itself in two ways – changes in the knowledge acquired and changes in the ability to use knowledge.

Learning by doing can be defined as 'The increase in productivity [or reduction in unit costs] which results from repeated performance of a particular activity' (Rutherford, 1992, p. 264). As noted in section 12.2.1, a distinction is sometimes made in the literature between 'learning by doing more' and 'learning by doing longer'. The former is widely researched in terms of standard production efficiency; the latter has been much less widely researched, but there are references to it in the literature.

In its pure form, the learning process is often defined against a background of a given stock of fixed capital – where the workforce operate existing equipment more effectively. For example:

> in numerous assembly line operations in which tasks are performed in a repetitive manner, it has frequently been found that workers tend to learn from their experiences, thereby reducing the time and the labour costs required to perform prescribed tasks. (Berndt, 1991, p. 62)

Thus, in the classic case, the tangible assets of the firm remain unchanged – the phenomenon takes place with given plant and machinery, and the improvements are embedded either in the skills and competences of the workforce or in the routines and organizational structure of the company. The important point here is that, in the pure form of learning, the tangible assets of the firm remain unchanged and the improvements are embedded in the intellectual capital of the company.

The expectation would be that new learning processes are initiated by various key events, such as the purchase of new equipment, after the redesign of the establishment layout, for example. The corollary is that the magnitude of pure learning effects is likely to decay over time as further improvements become more difficult to find with existing equipment. Indeed, from an early stage it was suggested that learning effects would follow a sigmoidal curve, accelerating at first (as teething problems are overcome) and tailing off later (Svennilson, 1963). Certainly it was thought that such effects would approach zero within some finite period unless a new stimulus came along (Matthews and Hahn, 1966, p. 68). In practice,

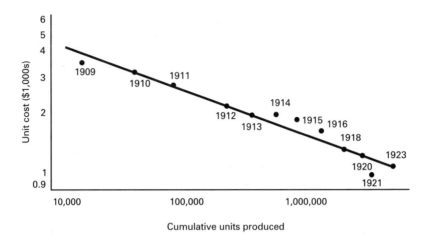

Figure 12.3 Learning effects: the example of the Ford Model T. Source: Abernathy and Wayne (1974); reported by Berndt (1991, p. 67).

the empirical literature suggests that the effects persist into the medium if not the long run. In a study of the Horndal steel plant in Sweden, for example, Lundberg (1961) discovered that, despite the absence of any new investments, productivity improvements took place at an average rate of 2 per cent per annum over a period of fifteen years as a result of incremental modifications and improvements. This became known as the 'Horndal effect'. Empirical researchers recognize, however, that, in many production contexts, it becomes increasingly difficult to hold other things constant as the period of study is extended further and further (and, thus, some of the observed improvements may not be true learning effects).

Figure 12.3 sets out the central importance of learning by doing (Abernathy and Wayne, 1974; reported by Berndt, 1991, p. 67), although it is not clear what proportion of the improvement can be attributed to pure learning effects. It can be seen that the unit cost of producing Ford Model Ts was approximately log-linearly related to the *cumulative* output of the cars (the axes are in logs). The costs are in $1,000s per car over the period 1909 to 1923. The general shape of the learning curve suggests

Table 12.1 Approximate numerical relationship between α and d in the example of Ford Model T production

α	−0.50	−0.33	−0.25	−0.16
Progress rate, d (%)	0.71	0.80	0.84	0.89

α is the slope of the unit cost line (see Figure 12.3); d is the ratio of new costs per unit to original costs per unit, when cumulative output is doubled.
Source: Berndt (1991, p. 67).

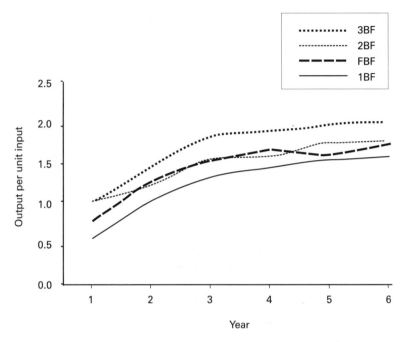

Figure 12.4 Learning curves: efficiency gains (output/input) over six years for four Korean blast furnaces. Source: Amsden (1989).

that a 1 per cent rise in output produces a less than 1 per cent rise in cost efficiency and, if the relationship is log-linear, then a 1 per cent rise in output always produces a fixed α per cent ($\alpha < 1$) fall in unit costs.[4] In the example of the Ford Model T, the slope of the unit cost line is about −0.25 and, thus, doubling cumulative output reduces costs to around 85 per cent (d) of their initial level (for details see Table 12.1).

Figure 12.4 provides data from the operation of four furnaces (named 3BF, 2BF, etc.) over a six-year period in South Korea (Amsden, 1989). The measure of performance is output per unit of input, which rises by 94 per cent (3BF), 73 per cent (2BF), 119 per cent (FBF) and 177 per cent (1BF) over the period. While there are clearly month-on-month deviations, the increases are very large over the period as a whole.

Amsden (1989) also reports the rejection rate for wire rods being produced by a Korean factory – the lower the rate, the higher the average quality of the output of the factory. The rejection rate fell from just under 1 per cent of output to around 0.1 per cent over a five-year period. This implies that not only was quality increasing, but also that the effective output of the plant was rising from given inputs and therefore input productivity was growing. Similarly, Amsden (1989) reports on the acceptance/inspection ratio (the counterpart of the rejection rate) of jobs

Table 12.2 Summary of the learning curve results

Learning curve elasticity (α, absolute value)	Learning curve slope (percentage of original costs)	Number of products
0.63–0.74	0.60–0.64	3
0.52–0.62	0.65–0.69	3
0.42–0.51	0.70–0.74	10
0.33–0.41	0.75–0.79	23
0.25–0.32	0.80–0.84	30
0.16–0.24	0.85–0.89	26
0.08–0.15	0.90–0.94	6
0.01–0.07	0.95–0.99	1

Average learning curve slope = 0.85.
Source: Ghemawat (1985, exhibit II, p. 146), reported by Berndt (1991, p. 80).

inspected on ships being built by the Hyundi Corporation. The acceptance ratio on tasks associated with the hull rose from just under 84 per cent in 1978 to around 95 per cent in 1985; the ship outfitting activities showed a similar rise, if somewhat less dramatic. Again, the reduced need to redo work meant TFP was rising and that ships could be produced more quickly.

There is a long tradition of empirical work in the area of learning by doing (bearing in mind that many of the estimates are not pure 'learning by doing' curves). The seminal paper examined the relationship between productivity growth and cumulative output in the aircraft industry (Wright, 1936). On the basis of these results, Wright proposed the '80 per cent rule' – that a doubling of output causes average total costs to fall to 80 per cent of their original level (i.e. to fall by 20 per cent – see Table 12.1). Since that time, there has been an enormous range of empirical research in this area, including work on the machine tool industry (Hirsch, 1952, 1956), a steel plant (Lundberg, 1961), a rayon plant (Hollander, 1965), capital- and labour-intensive industries (Baloff, 1966), chemical products (Lieberman, 1984) and an electronics firm (Alder and Clark, 1987). Several reviews of the literature pull together the empirical results. Table 12.2 outlines the distribution of findings on the slope of the learning curve reported by Ghemawat (1985) (reported by Berndt, 1991, p. 80). The modal value of d is between 80 and 85 per cent (see Table 12.1), hence α lies in the range –0.25 to –0.32.[5] The distribution reflects the different product groups, specifications, methodologies and so on. In general, the larger learning curve elasticities are associated with manufacturing rather than other product areas, and 'manufacturing costs decline particularly steeply in industries with standardised product ranges and complex labour intensive production processes such as the airframe assembly or machine tool businesses' (Berndt, 1991, p. 80). Nevertheless, the diversity of results suggests there is no golden rule for learning – different activities and functions in different industries give rise to a various types and degrees of learning.

12.4 Learning from others

12.4.1 *Grafting*

There are a variety of levels and forms of 'grafting', from the recruitment of individual employees through to the merger and takeover of whole organizations that give firms access to new knowledge. All forms of grafting may have both an intentional and an unintentional effect on the stock of knowledge (and on subsequent learning). For example, the growth of foreign R&D capacity among multinational enterprises may be the result of an intention to acquire specific knowledge, but also a by-product of a takeover of foreign production capacity (when the foreign production unit has its own R&D activities).

Wherever the foundations of corporate competences are viewed as being located in the individuals employed (Stinchcombe, 1990; see also Chapter 9), then turnover becomes a potentially crucial issue. Personnel turnover has the effect of losing corporate knowledge – especially when key employees leave the company (Brooks, 1971). An example was the disquiet caused to General Motors when its CEO left to head Volkswagen. In the extreme, such cases raise questions about the loss of trade secrets by a company to an arch rival. In addition, the need to recruit individuals who operate in a manner consistent with the goals and ethos of the enterprise means that higher turnover increases the socialization costs to the firm (Simon, 1995, pp. 178–179).

Recruitment, on the other hand, is a chance to improve the skills, competences and knowledge base of the organization. March (1995) sees recruits as a potential source of variation in the workforce that reduces the tendency of a static, long-tenured workforce to stagnate and fail to explore rather than exploit.

Carley (1995) investigated the effect of turnover on the rate and level of learning between teams and hierarchies. She concluded that, while teams generally learn faster and more completely than hierarchies, the latter are less affected by higher rates of turnover than the former. She argued that 'two organisations in the same industry (and hence facing similar tasks with comparable complexity) can have different structures and yet similar performance if they use [experience] different turnover rates or employ different types of personnel' (Carley, 1995, p. 258). She added that, 'For ease of learning, start up companies may be formed of a loose group of more or less equivalent individuals but will (or should) move to a hierarchical structure as they are faced by personnel turnover'.

The net effect of wastage and recruitment of course depends upon the quantity and quality of the individuals lost and the corresponding quantities and qualities of their replacements. Virany *et al.* (1995), for example, looked at the importance of CEO succession – particularly when associated with the need for strategic reorientation – as a potentially critical element for revitalizing the performance of the firm. Their study of fifty-nine mini-computer firms, founded in the period 1968 to 1971, suggests that succession has a positive influence on company performance. They distinguished two principal modes of change:

(i)   the more common has both a change of CEO and sweeping changes to the senior management team, linked to strategic reorientation;
(ii)   the less common but, the authors claimed, more effective in the long term is associated with changes to the executive team, but retention of the CEO (as this allows organizational learning to occur while key organizational competences are maintained).

One company may take over another in order to acquire information and knowledge. Huber (1995, p. 136) reported that 'A well-known example is General Motors' acquisition of Ross Perot's corporation, EDS, in order to obtain the information systems expertise possessed by EDS'. As Huber noted, grafting of this kind can be faster than learning through experience and more complete than learning by imitation. On the other hand, it can also be a risky way of moving forward, for a number of reasons, including differences in structures and cultures. It may be that, in some instances, 'grafting' would be better handled by various forms of collaborative ventures. Certainly, there is evidence to support Huber's (1995, p. 136) contention that, as the need for knowledge accumulation accelerates, these forms of grafting are becoming increasingly important.

12.4.2 *Noticing*

The concept of pure spillovers (see section 8.3.2), as perceived by Griliches (1992), perhaps fits best under the present heading of 'noticing', because, despite falling like 'manna from heaven', they are quite distinct from internally generated learning or deliberately acquired grafting, and they are not the result of deliberate R&D search. They are the natural consequence of the (relevant) R&D undertaken by all companies that generates some (difficult to define) pool of public knowledge that the firm can draw upon. The present discussion takes the view – which is broadly consistent with that of the main body work on R&D spillovers (Griliches, 1992) and new growth theory (NGT) (see Solow, 1991) – that external sources of 'knowledge' are important to the performance of the company. The focus of NGT is the externality that R&D or education gives rise to – while each firm cannot individually influence the size of the R&D pool, each company benefits from a larger pool. Thus, individual companies, in deciding their invest-ments in human capital, do not take into account the beneficial effects that arise from the growth in the pool of more qualified labour in the economy. As a consequence, private investment in human capital is less than the social optimum (see Chapter 14).

12.4.3 *Vicarious learning*

Chapter 4 dealt with attempts by the enterprise to learn about the strategies, technologies and practices of other firms, especially, though not exclusively, their competitors. Different schools of thought would see the rationale for such behaviour in different ways; for example, the insti-tutional theorists would argue that it is a way in which the firm is able to imitate others, as well as to legitimize its structures and behaviour, thereby avoiding sanctions from a variety of stakeholders. While searching for information may be a means of facilitating imitation, however, it may also be a way of fuelling internal developments that enable the firm to leapfrog its competitors, or make strategic moves into new or alternative niches.

It is clear, however, that economic theories of diffusion, as rich as they are (Stoneman and Karshenas, 1993), may be too abstract for many organizational theorists. 'Epidemic' models, for example, view each step in the diffusion of a new technology as simply being the consequence of a (chance) contact between two organizations, at which point information is transmitted about the new technology. Attewell (1995, p. 207) argues that this appears inappropriate whenever 'adoption is not a single event, and when complex organisational processes rather than individual decision-making come to the fore' Moreover, he makes the important distinction between two different types of communication: *signalling* – which provides information about the existence of some 'better' technological solution; and *know-how* – the more important transmission/learning of knowledge about how to introduce and utilize the new technology (Attewell, 1995, pp. 208–209). Hence, he argues, while 'one can readily buy the machine that embodies an innovation, the knowledge needed to use modern produc-tion innovations is acquired much more slowly and with considerable more difficulty' (p. 209). The efficient utilization of such technology requires both individual and organizational learning, such that 'individual insights and skills become embodied in organisational routines, practices, and beliefs that outlast the presence of the originating individual' (p. 210).

While essential to performance, the principal learning is not generally transferred by the supplier of the technology (except perhaps in the case of turnkey projects), although some training by the supplier or other external bodies may help initiate or stimulate this learning. Nevertheless, according to Attewell (1995, p. 223), the supply side is important in overcoming barriers to innovation – 'supply-side institutions have to innovate, not only in their design of products, but especially in the development of novel institutional mechanisms for reducing the knowledge or learning burden upon end users'. In the early history of business computing, for example, the supply-side organizations did more than simply sell equipment – they also provided key services, which, while often expensive, enabled buyers to overcome otherwise insuperable barriers to entry. As such technologies evolve, they become more 'user-friendly', with more of the skills embodied in the 'machine', thus reducing the barriers to and costs of innovation. Attewell (1995, p. 225) sees this as a recurring dynamic – technologies shift from complex and service supported to simpler and supported internally by the buyer.

12.4.4 *Diffusion, learning and performance*[6]

In her discussion of the industrialization of South Korea, Amsden (1989, ch. 1) argues the importance of learning in the process of economic development. For example, 'If industrialisation first occurred in England on the basis of invention, and if it occurred in Germany and the United States on the basis of innovation, then it occurs now among "backward" countries on the basis of learning' (Amsden, 1989, p. 4). A hint of the mechanism that Amsden sees for newly industrializing countries can be found in the highly developed countries' focus on R&D, and on the focus of the 'backward countries' (Amsden's phrase) on shopfloor learning:

> The shopfloor tends to be the strategic focus of firms that compete on the basis of borrowed technology. The shopfloor is the focus because it is here that borrowed technology is first made operational and later optimised. Because products similar to those that the company produces are internationally available, the strategic focus is necessarily found on the shopfloor, where the achievement of incremental, yet cumulative, improvements in productivity and product specification are essential to enhance price and quality competitiveness. (Amsden, 1989, p. 5)

This shopfloor learning takes place on the back of information and technology transfer from more developed countries, which she sees as an integral part of the overall 'learning' process in the developing world (Amsden, 1989, p. 3). She argues that:

> Economies commencing industrialisation in the twentieth century transformed their production structures and raised their incomes *per capita* on the basis of borrowed technology. They produced using processes conceived by unallied economic and political units. The means by which they managed to compete will be referred to here as learning.

The knowledge base is an essential determinant of the ability to learn – a feature which may also be true of the more mechanistic forms of learning outlined above. It determines the 'level' and the 'range' of learning to be found in each company (or country). In an early paper, Solo (1966, p. 480) asked 'what determines the capacity of the developing society for incorporating … advanced technology into its own operations and, thereby achieving high productivity?' The answer he gave (p. 487) was as follows:

> A society's capacity to adapt itself to the requirements of advanced technology and to adapt the advanced technology to its own circumstances and objectives, as well as the capacity to innovate,[7] will depend in part on the intellectual skills, the acquired knowledge and know-how, the problem-solving competencies – in a word, on the cognitions possessed by those who constitute that society.

He argued that the 'required structure of cognition' could be viewed as a pyramid:

> At its base … would be simply a sense of the machine, of its logic, of its manipulability, of its limits, … i.e. cognition of mechanism … a middle mass of mechanical and technical skills occupying the centre part of the pyramid.… Merging with and emerging out of the middle mass of technical skills is another sort of cognition which comprehends the interrelationship of machines, materials, labour, and information in processes in producing goods and services. And at the apex of the pyramid, interacting with the cognition of process, are the cognitions of science, of a development-oriented science, and a science-based development engineering. These are necessary in order to 'apply' research method and the world accumulations of scientific knowledge to problems impeding technical advance. (Solo, 1966, p. 487)

Solo argued that sufficient of the pyramid needs to exist even to 'evaluate the feasibility of transferring science-based technology or to adapt science-based technologies for assimilation' (p. 487). However, the pyramid needs to be complete and pervasive if companies are (or society is) to attempt the 'higher level' learning activities, such as R&D, with any chance of success. There are immediate parallels between these country-level observations and those applicable from a company perspective.

The above suggests that research-based learning is primarily the domain of companies (and countries) in which the cognitive pyramid is most highly developed. This gives such 'high level' companies a potentially significant advantage, as 'indigenous R&D not only improves world best-practice, it also enables the assimilation of outside technology' (Patel and Pavitt, 1995, p. 17). Much more broadly than this, in-house R&D raises new questions, informs about where to search and what to search for, and how the resulting data, information and/or knowledge may be productively utilized. In essence, their own R&D augments firms' 'scientific and technological competencies to learn about knowledge, products and processes developed elsewhere' (Patel and Pavitt, 1995, p. 18). The role played by the interaction of companies' own R&D and the broader outside pool of 'R&D knowledge' has been investigated in only a few of the papers reporting on spillover. For example, Griliches (1992, p. 37) states:

> In some models ... the amount borrowed [of outside 'knowledge'] depends also on the level of own R&D expenditures, allowing thereby for an interaction and potential synergy between the two flows of R&D expenditures: 'inside' and 'outside'.[8]

12.5 Search, learning and experience curves

12.5.1 *Search and scanning*

Huber (1995, pp. 136–141) considers:

(i)   scanning, which he defines as a 'relatively wide-ranging sensing of the organisation's external environment';
(ii)   focused search, which involves the organization searching in a restricted area of the external environment, generally in reaction to either threats or opportunities;[9]
(iii) performance monitoring, which may be narrow or wide ranging and which addresses the issue of whether the organization is fulfilling its goals;
(iv)   noticing, which involves information and knowledge that the organization unintentionally picks up (see section 12.4.2).

As Huber (1995, p. 137) points out, scanning can range from 'high vigilance' through to 'passive search'. Tidd and Trewhella (1997) suggest that, although firms are increasingly drawing on external sources of innovation, few currently systematically scan for these outside of their own sector. Despite the different degrees and foci of scanning, the empirical literature generally concludes that scanning contributes to performance (Daft *et al.*, 1988; Dollinger, 1984; Tushman and Katz, 1980).

Huber (1995, pp. 138–139) argues that focused search is a quite different activity to unfocused search, and is not undertaken without adequate reason – 'for search prompting signals to have an effect they must be very "loud" and received from multiple sources'.[10] Chapter 8, in particular, argued that such search (in R&D) would be induced by strong technological opportunity, competitor search, stock market expectations and so on, but also noted the need for such searching to account for the risks or uncertainties of finding profitable outcomes.

The literature has also attempted to elucidate the nature of the search process, for example the returns from searching locally (generally for more minor changes) or 'jumping' to more radical solutions. It is important to remember that firms can experiment with different forms of search, directions of search and so on, and, in doing so, learn how to search. Search also can be seen as ranging along a spectrum from reactive to proactive (i.e. in response to a perceived problem, through searching in response to a known opportunity, to searching for currently unknown problems or opportunities). In relation to the mix of proactive and reactive activity, Huber (1995, p. 139) argues:

> My speculation is that in organisational sub-units and at lower organisational levels search is largely reactive to problems, but that in autonomous organisations and at higher levels a significant proportion of search is a consequence of pro-active management initiatives.

12.5.2 *Proactive learning*

As noted above, the empirical literature on learning curves suggests that learning effects persist in the long run. This may be because, in practice, other things do not remain constant when estimating the empirical relationships and, in particular, some of what appear to be learning effects involve deliberate acts that require a degree of investment, at least of time and effort. Porter (1985), for example, argues that:

> Learning does not occur automatically, but results from the effort and attention of management and employees. Attention to learning should not be confined to labour costs but also to the costs of constructing facilities, the cost of scrap, and other significant value activities. Every premise and every practice must be examined for possible revision.… Management must demand learning improvements and set targets for them, rather than simply hoping that learning will occur. When setting targets, the rate of learning should be compared across facilities and regions as well as to industry standards.

Insofar as learning is not costless, it involves an investment of resources that should be paid back through higher quality and therefore price, and/ or lower unit costs of operation in later periods. Where this is the case, however, it becomes more difficult to distinguish learning effects from dynamic investments, such as R&D. In addition, following the discussion of Chapter 9, the need to offer incentives to learn can mean that it is possible for learning to take place with significant TFP gains, without this being reflected in real unit costs (Bahk and Gort, 1993, pp. 562, 575). The way in which the learning effects are manifested depends on which of the stakeholders appropriates the returns. As noted in several places in the present book, economic theory does have something to say about the possible outcomes; in particular, learning which results in improvements to general skills is more likely to be appropriated by the individual in the form of higher wages, while more firm-specific skills and knowledge will be appropriated by the company in terms of lower costs (Becker, 1964).

Thus, it seems important to consider a variety of more proactive models of learning and their implications for firm performance. In this context, learning implies '(possession of) knowledge got by study' (*Oxford Concise English Dictionary*). This definition implies an active 'seeking' of knowledge (i.e. 'by study'). The seeking of knowledge is formalized in activities such as:

(i)   market research;
(ii)   monitoring of best practice with a view to imitating it;
(iii) scientific research, design and development.

In this sense, a clear distinction can be made between (proactive) learning of this type and the type of 'learning by doing' outlined in section 12.3.5, in which it was broadly defined as 'The increase in productivity which results from repeated performance of a particular activity'. The latter sounds 'manual' and almost 'accidental', falling like 'manna from heaven'.

12.5.3 *Intentional search and the experience curve*

In place of the standard additive learning term, suppose that cumulative output is allowed to enter multiplicatively – more in keeping with the log-linear functional form – and allows for the depreciation of past learning (a similar suggestion is made by Epple *et al.*, 1995). The result is shown in equation 12.1:

$$Y_t = AK_t^{\alpha}E_t^{\beta}\ \{\prod_{i=0}^{\infty}(Y_{t-i-1})^{(1-\delta)^i}\}^{\rho} \qquad\qquad 12.1$$

where Y is output, K is the capital stock (fixed in the case of the learning curve, but variable in the experience curve) and E denotes employment; A, α and β are technology constants; δ is the rate of depreciation of the past stock of knowledge and ρ is the impact of cumulative past learning on current output; t is the current time period and i is a lag that allows the model to explore the contribution of learning $i + 1$ periods ago. Suppose, however, that R&D expenditure, R, is proportional to output; then equation 12.1 can be written in terms of output or, as in 12.2, TFP:

$$\frac{Y_t}{K_t^{\alpha}E_t^{\beta}}\ =\ A'\ (\prod_{i=0}^{\infty}R_{t-i-1}^{(1-\delta)^i})^{\rho}\ =\ A'\ (R_{t-1}R_{t-2}^{(1-\delta)}R_{t-3}^{(1-\delta)^2}...)^{\rho}\ =\ A'\ R^{\rho/\delta} \qquad 12.2$$

In the final part of equation 12.2 it is assumed that R&D is constant over time. It can be immediately seen that the flow coefficient, ρ/δ, exceeds the stock coefficient, ρ, unless $\delta = 1$. It can be seen that the role of R&D in equation 12.2 is identical to the role that was outlined for R&D (search) activity in Chapter 8.

To take this one step further, equation 12.3 adopts a functional form in which both search and learning effects appear. To simplify the exposition, current (or one-period lagged) R&D enters the equation directly, but prior R&D is assumed to enter via the learning effects. Such a function does not appear to have been estimated to date in the literature. Thus, again assuming inputs are constant over time:

$$Y_t = A K_t^{\alpha} E_t^{\beta} R^{\rho} \left\{ \prod_{i=0}^{\infty} (Y_{t-i})^{(1-\eta)^i} \right\}^{\gamma}$$

$$= A' K_t^{\frac{\alpha(\eta + \gamma(1-\eta))}{\eta}} E_t^{\frac{\beta(\eta + \gamma(1-\eta))}{\eta}} R^{\frac{\rho(\eta + \gamma(1-\eta))}{\eta}}$$

12.3

The stock of learned knowledge is now assumed to depreciate at a constant rate η ($0 \leq \eta \leq 1$)and γ reflects the effects of learning. It can be seen that, if there is no learning (i.e. there are no effects of past output on the current period), then $\eta = 1$ and each of the coefficients collapses to give the standard production function with coefficients α, β and ρ. However, if $\eta < 1$, then the effects of past learning depend on the sizes of both η and γ. The implication is that, unless learning appears explicitly in the empirical specification, the effects of learning shifts some of the parameter estimates in the standard knowledge production function upwards.

12.6 Organizational memory

Organizational learning is not possible without organizational memory (also see the discussion of MIS in section 11.7.5). While Simon (1995, p. 180) argues that 'turnover of personnel is a great enemy of long-term organisational learning', the preceding discussion has made it clear that organizational memory is much more than just the sum of the individual human memories, although these are clearly an important component. The discussion of labour turnover noted that it was important that firms minimize the effects on the knowledge base – particularly with regard to tacit knowledge (and take advantage of the improvements to the knowledge base during recruitment), and it was noted that different forms of organization are likely to be differentially affected by such events.

Huber (1995, p. 148) also points to problems caused to the knowledge base of the failure of the organization to predict future events and, thereby, to ensure that the required knowledge is contained in corporate memory in advance of their occurrence. He argues that, while key knowledge may be stored in corporate memory, the members who require it need to know where it is and how to access it. As Huber (1995, p. 150) puts it, 'that which has been learned must be stored in memory and then brought forth from memory'. Efficiency in learning must be paralleled by the efficiency of the memory, in both storage and retrieval.

The discussion of canonical practices suggested that organizations tend to be *relatively* good at storing routine, formal information and knowledge in a variety of forms, such as rules, regulations, standard operating procedures, blue prints and so on. Huber (1995, p. 149), however, notes that it is not clear to what extent non-routine information is deliberately stored – information or knowledge that might be needed under certain non-routine operating conditions. Chapter 4 suggested that, in general, companies operate with a broader memory set than is strictly required for their day-to-day operations. Indeed, in the case of 'integrating firms' they hold a wide range of, often, non-routine information that could be called into play to solve a broad range of problems both within the firm and in their operating environment (e.g. within the buyer–supplier chain). The efficiency with which this is carried out depends on the extent to which the company can effectively predict its future environment, and the extent to which it is willing to pay to hold the option of operating in non-standard (i.e. non-core) areas.

In addition to human memory, clearly there are a variety of other forms of storing knowledge, such as routines, which are triggered automatically by some stimulus (see Chapter 11). Of these, computer-based memory has become increasingly important. Huber (1995, p. 149) argues that:

> Information concerning the times necessary to complete fabrication of certain products, to receive shipments of ordered materials, to recruit various types of employees, or to deliver certain types of services are more and more frequently resident in computers as transactions artefacts.

The increasing user-friendliness and capabilities of such systems (at least some time after their first introduction) have increased their take-up across companies, along with their abilities in terms of their completeness and precision in carrying out various tasks, which often make them superior to the human equivalent. The combination of 'soft information' lodged in specialists who use computer systems has led to the development of 'expert systems'.

As Brown and Duguid (1995) suggest, non-canonical knowledge may be extremely important and may have very different forms of memory and knowledge transmission to canonical knowledge. They emphasize the individual and, more particularly, community memories of knowledge, where the generation and diffusion of new knowledge – and thereby its storage in organizational memory – involve extensive story telling and narration. The canonical/non-canonical distinction also throws up the fact that many senior managers often do not realize either what the company knows or its importance to the smooth running of the firm. While not addressing this formal/informal issue directly, Huber (1995, p. 149) argues that, 'As a result of specialisation, differentiation, and departmentalisation, organisations frequently do not know what they know'.

12.7 Some strategic issues

The present section turns to strategic issues associated with the learning process and, in particular, with learning by doing. According to some authors, the improvement to the speed and content of routines, as well as the efficient switching between routines, are major sources of competitive advantage (Stinchcombe, 1990). Kay (1995, pp. 116–119), for example, discusses the performance gained by early entrants via learning and experience effects under the heading of a 'strategic asset'. As the Boston Consulting Group noted (see section 12.3.5), 'It is so universal that its absence is almost a warning of mismanagement or misunderstanding'. Despite the potential competitive effects of learning, Figure 4.5 (p. 77) suggests that only 29 per cent of managers feel well informed about learning curve effects (Dolan and Simon, 1996, p. 47). This echoes the worry, reflected throughout the present chapter, that academics themselves do not fully understand learning and experience effects. Nevertheless, the literature asserts the strategic value of learning and experience. The present section, therefore, outlines the implications of learning curve effects for pricing, as a barrier to entry and, relatedly, in developing firm specificities.

12.7.1 *Pricing*

Tirole (1990, p. 72) demonstrates that learning effects influence the firm's optimizing behaviour. He sets up a two-period profit-maximization problem for a monopolist, in which there can be learning. The solution to this problem, given period 2 is the last year of production, requires the monopolist to set marginal revenue equal to marginal cost for the second period. However, given that unit costs fall with the output of period 1, because of the presence of learning, then overall (i.e. the two-period) profit is maximized by setting marginal revenue less than marginal cost in the first period. The intuitive explanation is simple. The monopolist charges less than the instantaneous profit-maximizing price in the first period in order to sell more units of output. While there is a cost to doing this (as marginal revenue is not equal to marginal cost), this is more than offset by the gain in profit during the second period, which stems from the cost reduction attributable to learning. Intuitively, bearing in mind the role played by discounting, the marginal opportunity cost of this strategy in period 1 should be equal to the marginal benefit in period 2. In the absence of learning, the model collapses to a standard profit-maximization problem and the monopolist sets marginal revenue equal to marginal cost in both periods.

Barriers to entry
Learning effects raise a potential barrier to new entrants, because incumbents, by definition, must have produced a greater output and experienced learning effects. As noted in section 12.3.5, the Boston Consulting Group (1973, p. 2) argued that 'Our entire concept of competition, anti-trust, and non-monopolistic free enterprise is based on a fallacy if the experience curve effect is true'. Spence (1981, p. 68), for example, argues that 'The

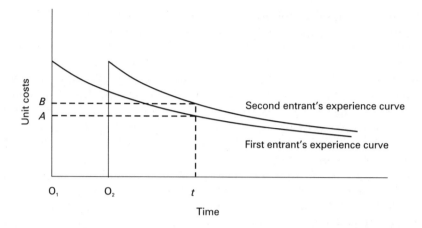

Figure 12.5 Barriers to entry: first-mover barrier persists. O_1 indicates the first firm's time of entry into the market and O_2 the second firm's. *A* and *B* are the unit costs of the two firms at time *t*. *B* is always higher than A, which is the barrier to entry. Source: Ferguson *et al.* (1993, p. 64).

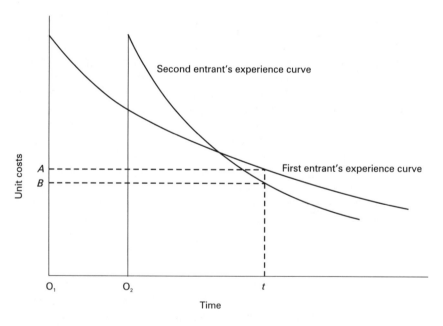

Figure 12.6 Barriers to entry: first-mover barrier negated. The notation is as in Figure 12.5, but here *B* becomes less than *A*, and the barrier to entry is negated. Source: Ferguson *et al.* (1993, p. 65).

learning curve creates entry barriers and protection from competition by conferring cost advantages on early entrants and those who achieve large market shares'. Ferguson *et al.* (1993, pp. 64–65) illustrate the problem as shown in Figures 12.5 and 12.6. Figure 12.5 demonstrates the 'first-mover advantage', in other words, the advantage of being first in the market, rather than the potential entrant. Under the conditions shown in Figure 12.5, learning produces a disincentive to others to enter the market – a potential barrier. Figure 12.6 demonstrates that, in principle at least, this does not have to be the case. Higher unit costs than the incumbent firm's at the time of entry into a new market – which make the investment look unprofitable – may be transformed over time via learning to make entry viable. This might occur by producing a higher volume of output per period than the original incumbent or through more efficient learning per unit of cumulative output.

Learning, innovation and specificity
It has been argued that, in order not to make the discussion of learning effects too sterile, it is important to admit the possibility that learning results in innovation. Malerba (1992, pp. 847–848) notes that:

> because there are several different sources of knowledge, the type of learning highly affects the type of stock of knowledge that firms have. Firms then become characterised by different levels and types of knowledge capital; accumulated through time … firms' specific stock of knowledge generates mostly local and incremental innovations. This is because most new products and processes are the result of modifications and improvements of existing products and processes and build up cumulatively on firms' existing stock of knowledge. Because of the diversity in the stock of knowledge accumulated by firms and fed by the variety of learning processes the directions of incremental technical change pursued by firms may differ.

Thus, Malerba is arguing for the development of 'knowledge specificity'.

A consequence of Malerba's argument is that, if a different knowledge base is relevant to each area of learning, in general it results in a particular (history-dependent) 'trajectory' of technical change. In particular:

(i)   learning by doing, learning by using and learning by interacting with equipment suppliers all tend to stimulate trajectories of yield improvements (e.g. TFP increases and RUC reductions);
(ii) learning by searching results in trajectories of vertical product differentiation in terms of the reliability, performance or compatibility of products – such as ship construction, farm tractors, forms of transportation, as well as the automobile, aircraft, electronics and construction industries.

12.8 Conclusions

It is clear that the concept of a 'learning organization' is more than the cumulative, individual improvements in employees or other inputs. Indeed, it means something more than the emergence of innovative forms of organization. A learning organization is one that:

(i) effectively monitors the internal and external environments;
(ii) efficiently moulds information into relevant knowledge;
(iii) can efficiently store and retrieve this information and knowledge;
(iv) disseminates this knowledge to the appropriate individuals and communities within the organization at the appropriate time;
(v) fully harnesses the performance improvements that come from learning from experience, recognizing the contribution of the results of spontaneous experimentation, particularly in non-canonical practices;
(vi) maintains an ongoing explorative dimension, even when exploitation is more profitable than exploration (Huber, 1995);
(vii) is able to innovate in the conventional manner, reactively, but efficiently to changes it detects in its environment (Brown and Duguid, 1995, p. 73);
(viii) is an 'enacting organization' that is 'proactive and highly interpretive', not only responding to the environment, but 'reaching out' into the environment, partly to mould the circumstances to which it must respond (Brown and Duguid, 1995, pp. 73–74);
(ix) sets up mechanisms to enable it to reconfigure itself proactively, in such a way that it (always) works with the 'optimal' architecture and routines, bearing in mind the contribution not only of canonical but also of non-canonical practices to organizational performance.

Notes

1 Nevertheless, March (1981, p. 575) concludes that, typically, 'it is not possible to lead an organisation in any arbitrary direction that might be desired, but it is possible to influence the course of events by managing the process of change, and particularly by stimulating or inhibiting predictable complications and anomalous dynamics'.
2 It is not clear why the short break seems more disruptive to the performance of the players than the long break.
3 The real-world example Henderson provides is that of Xerox, which failed to respond to the architectural innovation in plain-paper photocopiers (Henderson, 1995, pp. 359–360).
4 The learning curve is potentially quite distinct from economies of scale because a firm of given size can still experience learning by producing the same level of output period after period, with cumulative output rising with time. Clearly, however, in the presence of economies of scale, larger firms will experience both greater

learning by doing and greater scale economies. The relative importance of the two effects must be unpicked statistically (Berndt, 1991).

5 Dutton and Thomas (1984) undertake a survey of more than 200 'learning by doing' studies and, consistent with Wright's 'rule of thumb', suggest a modal progress rate of $d = 80$ per cent.

6 There are links here with the efficient transfer of skills and knowledge at the individual level and, hence, with the role of training and HR development that were considered in Chapter 9.

7 Here Solo is referring to 'local' innovation (i.e. first use in that country or firm) rather than 'global' innovation (i.e. first use anywhere).

8 Somewhat contrary evidence has often been noted in the literature – organizations that are good at inventing may not be good at taking those inventions through the innovation process to commercial success (Stinchcombe, 1990).

9 Some care needs to be taken with this concept of narrow focus, as some companies – termed 'systems integrating firms' – maintain an ability for focused search over a wide range of technologies and areas (Prencipe, 2000, 2004).

10 Huber (1995, pp. 138–139) makes the link here with Cyert and March's (1963) behavioural theory, where the company does not act upon problems until they reach some threshold level of importance, at which time management attention gives them a high priority.

Part VI
Private and public policy issues

Chapter 13

Private policy and enterprise performance

13.1 Introduction

The present chapter draws together parts of the earlier discussion in a more holistic way. The first part focuses on the pervasive theme of the management of risk, both in terms of each area of activity and holistically across all the company's operations. It is perhaps helpful to begin by referring back to key parts of the earlier discussion. Chapter 2, for example, noted that the very existence of companies might be attributed, in part, to the risks of operating through the market (i.e. because of opportunistic behaviour). Chapter 5 discussed the different degrees of risk attached to different goals of the enterprise (e.g. increasing product quality versus cost reduction). Chapter 6 touched on the ways in which higher levels of management qualifications and competences are required during periods of significant change, when levels of risk are greater. Chapter 7 indicated how the governance structure could be designed to influence management decisions, and how it might be designed to penalize or reward various levels of risk taking. The discussion in Chapters 8–10 focused on a variety of investments (R&D, advertising, training, etc.), and emphasized that they are discretionary, dynamic and often associated with high levels of risk or uncertainty. In a similar vein, Chapters 11 and 12 indicated that changes to the organization of the enterprise also entailed risk.

Management is seen as attempting to maximize the opportunities posed by risk, as much as to minimize the potential for adverse consequences. The extent to which a firm might expose itself to risk depends upon the potential benefits, in other words, whether there are commensurate potential rewards from doing so: 'risky courses of action are undertaken because the relevant actors perceive the *possibility* of abnormally high returns. The risk must be matched by the prize' (Branscomb and Auerswald, 2000, p. 7). It may be added that the risk must also be matched by the ability to withstand failure – while much can generally be done to minimize the downside, there is invariably a downside. The risky, discretionary

331

investments, often associated with various forms of technological or organizational innovation, are crucial decisions, because they determine the dynamic performance of companies and, thereby, the economy as a whole.[1] However, what may be socially desirable from a national perspective may not be privately optimal from a company perspective – such individual decisions are sculpted by companies in the context of the institutional settings of the national innovation system (NIS), broadly defined (see Chapter 14). It is important to note that it is not always possible to say as much as desired about the extent and nature of risk, or about the best methods that can be employed to make decisions or manage risk. Until recently, perhaps even now, this has simply not been the focus, at least in the work of economists:

> Applied economists are interested first and foremost in identifying statistical regularities, not in exhaustively analysing factors that might have been responsible for a statistical 'outlier' – a rare event that deviates from the norm, of which exceptional profits from an innovation are an example. (Branscomb and Auerswald, 2000, p. 8)

The second theme of the present chapter is that, in order to be successful, the company must take a more integrated approach that accounts for the inter-relationships between investments such as R&D, advertising, human resource development, and so on. Likewise, it cannot consider such investments in isolation from the 'design' of the company itself, for example whether the company is M-form or N-form, the nature of the management hierarchy, the extent and role of canonical versus non-canonical processes or, indeed, the ethos and culture of the company. The integrated approach is linked closely to the issue of decision making under risk. While the invention and innovation process is not linear in nature, it nevertheless involves a sequence of investment decisions. At each point in the decision-making process, the firm has the choice of making a risky investment or withdrawing from the investment project. A further feature that arises from the more holistic discussion of the inter-relationships between discretionary investments is that potential synergies arise not only within each area of investment (e.g. through the adoption of more than one HPWP) but also between discretionary investments (e.g. between R&D, advertising, HPWPs, etc.). Finally, the analysis demonstrates how the relationships between discretionary investments, and the rates of return to the associated investments, vary over the product life-cycle (PLC) and brand life-cycle (BLC).

Section 13.2 continues with a discussion of the new forms of investment rule that can be found or developed to make rational decisions in the face of risk. Section 13.3 turns to the various methods open to the firm to manage risk. It covers some of the management technology literature about systematic differences between successful and unsuccessful innovators, and the role of design for manufacturing (DFM) processes, as well as pricing strategies for new products. Section 13.4 begins the discussion of managing risk in a more holistic framework, based upon the firm's PLC (or, more accurately, the firm's portfolio of BLCs and PLCs). It makes the important point that the risk-adjusted rates of return to various discretionary investments vary over each product's life-cycle (this is related to the discussion of explorative and exploitative activities in section 12.2.2). Section 13.5 takes the move to a holistic picture a step further and discusses the likely synergies both within particular functional activities (such as HPWPs) and between such functional activities. Finally, section 13.6 draws the main conclusions.

13.2   Investment rules under risk

13.2.1 *Issues in the application of standard DCF rules under risk*

Cost–benefit and net present value
The costs and benefits of technological change can be diverse, and it might be argued that investments in R&D and innovation, and so on, should be the subject of 'cost–benefit' (C–B) analysis, which generally implies a broader evaluation of the costs and benefits of a given project than, say, analyses of net present value (NPV) or internal rate of return (IRR). While company decision makers may feel more comfortable with the narrower and generally more quantitative NPV and IRR analyses, they should begin with a broader C–B study. Private decisions tend to focus on the more quantifiable aspects, and to concentrate on the costs that they incur and the net revenues that accrue directly to the company. Evidence exists, however, that the qualitative aspects of some investment decisions often prove more important than those quantified by managers before the investment (Stoneman *et al.*, 1992). If these qualitative influences have a positive effect on the performance of the firm, it implies that the normal investment criteria may lead to underinvestment.

Even as a standard NPV calculation, investments such as R&D have a number of special features. In particular, it is argued that R&D often has high 'up-front' costs and a long period before the revenues from the investment occur. This is particularly true of key areas of technology such as pharmaceuticals, where the invention period is followed by a period of drugs testing (under the regulation of the Medicines and Healthcare Products Regulatory Agency in the UK) before new compounds can be marketed. In addition, innovatory investments are subject to a relatively high degree of risk, and the question then arises as to how the existence of risk can be incorporated into the DCF framework. One suggestion is that, in the NPV calculation, the discount rate can be increased to allow for the degree of risk. Alternatively, in the IRR calculation, some increase could be made to the stream of costs, to reflect a charge for insuring against the risk. Clearly, these adjustments to the DCF lower the likelihood of undertaking the investment – the more so, the higher the risk.

It is important to be clear what the returns to the investment are. Often with investments such as R&D, the counterfactual is not that existing profits would continue into the future whether or not the R&D expenditure takes place. In many instances, for example, coming second in a race to invent does not leave the profits of the 'loser' unchanged. A firm that chooses not to race still has to face the consequences of its competitor being first and, thereby, capturing some or all of its own market. This is fundamental to the investment decision – the counterfactual is not that existing profit streams will be maintained, but that profits will be eroded. The loss of profit in the absence of the investment should be taken into account in the DCF calculation deciding on the investment – making it more likely that the investment will occur. Nevertheless, more emphasis is needed in the empirical literature to test the importance of this factor.

Bias in the calculation
Before attempting to cope with risk in discretionary investment decisions, the decision maker needs to ensure that the estimates used in the calculation are unbiased. Marshall and Meckling (1959, p. 3) report some cost estimates of delivering new military technologies that involved operational development rather than basic research. They point out the issues in judging the outcomes, as it is possible, during the R&D phase, to trade off costs, performance, time of availability and utility. This is important, as the initial cost estimate is based upon certain performance parameters, while the finished technology may have inferior characteristics. This problem appears to be reasonably well controlled for in their data, as the authors report that 'degradations in performance are seldom tolerated ... though estimates of performance tend to be slightly higher than what is finally achieved, they are much more nearly fulfilled than are predictions of cost and availability' (Marshall and Meckling, 1959, p. 21).

Table 13.1 sets out the ratio of the final available estimate of the average cost of production to the earliest estimate available (Marshall and Meckling, 1959, p. 10). The overall mean factor is about 6.5; even when the extreme missile case is excluded, the value is about 4. It is clear that the mean ratio differs significantly across areas (although sample sizes are small), and the authors go on to state:

> The accuracy of estimates is a function of the stage of development (i.e. estimates improve as development of the item progresses). This also means that estimates for development projects representing only 'modest advances' tend to be better than for more ambitious projects. (Marshall and Meckling, 1959, p. 2)

Table 13.1 Total factor increases in costs of production

Fighters	Factor	Bombers	Factor	Cargoes and tankers	Factor	Missiles	Factor
1	5.6	1	8.7	1	1.7	1	57.6
2	3.6	2	3.5	2	1.6	2	20.7
3	3.1	3	1.5	3	1.0	3	11.1
4	2.1			4	1.0	4	10.3
5	1.9					5	1.5
6	1.5					6	1.3
7	1.4						
8	1.2						
9	1.2						
Mean	2.4	Mean	4.5	Mean	1.3	Mean	17.2[a]
All classes	6.5[b]						

[a] 9.0 and [b] 4.1 when excluding missile case 1.
Source: Marshall and Meckling (1959, p. 11).

However, the important point is that the cost estimates do not appear to be some random draw from a distribution, but biased. The authors conclude:

'Early' estimates of important parameters are usually inaccurate. First, such estimates are strongly 'biased' toward over-optimism. Second, aside from the bias, the errors in estimates evidence a substantial variation. That is, even if estimates were multiplied by an appropriate standard factor to eliminate the bias, a non-negligible source of error remains. (Marshall and Meckling, 1959, pp. 1–2).

The authors report slippage information for ten of the developments for which they had information (see Table 13.2). Their estimates are based on conservative dates, which may lead to some underestimation; nevertheless, they found an average of two years' slippage and that projects took 50 per cent longer than planned (a slippage factor of 1.5).

A study of eighty-four electricity-generation research projects revealed a similar picture (Allen and Norris, 1970). The researchers had access to the initial estimates of cost (broken down into person-days, etc.), as well as two reviews of the costings during the project's life, and the outcomes. The authors report that:

Except for the abandoned and curtailed projects, nearly all the mean outcomes show a substantial increase over the initial estimates, but by far the most striking increase is in duration. For all projects and for normal projects, this increase is about 200 per cent. In contrast, in the same two categories, the increase in total cost is only about 41 per cent, made up from a smaller increase in purchases (about 30 per cent) and a larger increase in labour cost (about 85 per cent). (Allen and Norris, 1970, p. 277)

Table 13.2 Slippage in completion of projects

System	Slippage (years)	Slippage (factors)
1	5.0	2.5
2	3.0	1.6
3	3.0	1.5
4	3.0	1.5
5	2.0	2.0
6	2.0	1.5
7	1.3	1.3
8	0.7	1.2
9	0.5	1.2
10	0.3	1.1
Mean	2.0	1.5

Source: Marshall and Meckling (1959, p. 19).

The reviews of the costings enable an investigation of the learning processes in each project. The authors report a linear reduction in the error of the costings as the completion date was approached, which indicates that:

> the progress of the project is proportional to the lapse of time, and that the uncompleted part of the project is estimated with a constant proportional error. If the knowledge gained in the earlier stages of the projects had enabled the remaining stages to be estimated more accurately, the sides would have been concave [remaining error less]. (Allen and Norris, 1970, p. 281)

The important point here is not that research is risky, but that there are important mechanisms at work that lead to a systematic bias – underestimating the overall costs of producing certain performance characteristics. Allen and Norris (1970, p. 271), for example, argue that 'The estimates show considerable errors, and a bias towards underestimation'. Marshall and Meckling (1959, p. 24) argue that 'Steps can and should be taken to improve the estimates, especially to remove the bias'.

13.2.2 *Optimal waiting rules*

Resolving uncertainty and the returns to waiting
Options pricing theory suggests that waiting is an activity with an economic value, though this may be positive or negative. In the simplest case, if some uncertainty is resolved by waiting, then there is likely to be a positive value attached to delay. An illustration is provided by Dixit and Pindyck (1994, pp. 27–30). Suppose it is possible to place some intrinsic value on inventive output in each period. Assume that the value for the current period

is known, but for the next period is uncertain (which introduces risk), but whatever happens in the next period is propagated infinitely far into the future. The going 'price' (or value) in the current period (0) is $P_0 = 200$, but the price in the next period (1) is either 300 (with probability q) or 100 with probability $(1 - q)$, and these values continue infinitely far into the future (2, ..., ∞). Suppose the cost of R&D needed to generate this flow is 1,600. The NPV at time zero uses the expected future flow of returns, $E(P_t)$, and if $q = 0.5$ then $E(P_1) = E(P_2) = \ldots = 200$, and is calculated as:

$$NPV = \sum_{t=0}^{\infty} \frac{200}{(1 + 0.1)^t} - 1,600 = 2,200 - 1,600 = 600 \qquad 13.1$$

where the discount rate is 10 per cent. However, what happens if the investment is delayed by one year (i.e. the payment of 1,600 occurs at time $t = 1$ rather than $t = 0$), by which time the uncertainty resolves itself? At that stage, which of the two possible streams occurs will be known; if it is the 300 stream, the investment will be profitable and the firm will invest, but if it is the 100 stream it will be unprofitable and abandoned. The NPV for the delayed project can now be written,

$$NPV = 0.5 \left[\sum_{t=1}^{\infty} \frac{300}{(1.1)^t} - \frac{1,600}{1.1} \right] + (0.5)0 = 773 \qquad 13.2$$

The NPV associated with one year's delay is 773 compared with only 600 for immediate exercise of the option to invest. As Dixit and Pindyck (1994, p. 28) note:

> if our choices were to invest today or never invest, we would invest today. In that case there is no option to wait for a year, and hence no opportunity cost to killing such an option, so the standard NPV rule applies. We would likewise invest today if next year we could disinvest and recover our $1600. Two things are necessary to introduce an opportunity cost into the NPV calculation – irreversibility, and the ability to invest in the future as an alternative to investing today.

Thus, the difference between the two NPVs, 773–600 = 173, measures how much the firm would be willing to pay for the flexibility of waiting – the option to invest has an economic value (which disappears if the investment is made). The value of the option is derived from avoiding the downside risk from not waiting.

Marshallian and Dixitian triggers
The idea is that there comes some point, the 'trigger point', at which the future flows become sufficiently certain to make the firm 'jump'. Song

(1993) provides a neat comparison of the standard NPV (Marshallian) and options (Dixitian) trigger points. The traditional Marshallian trigger point, R_M, can be derived from the following inequality:

$$\frac{R}{\rho} \gtreqless K \tag{13.3}$$

such that the trigger revenue occurs at $R_M = \rho K$, where R is the (constant, zero variance) stream of future revenues, K is the capital cost of the project and ρ is the discount rate. Revenues less than R_M result in no investment and revenues greater than R_M trigger the investment. Investing straight away gives a yield of $R/\rho - K$, and not investing gives a yield of nothing at all. However, if R follows a random walk, the investor can choose to wait – waiting has value as the passage of time reduces the risk, but it has a potential cost from the loss of profits during the waiting period. Thus, if the current expected profit reaches a sufficiently high level, it then does not pay to wait any longer. This results in a corrected discount rate that includes the variance of the stream of returns:

$$\rho' = \frac{\beta}{\beta - 1} \, \rho \tag{13.4}$$

where β reflects the variance ($\beta > 1$, where higher values are associated with lower variance) and, thus, $\rho' \to \rho$ as $\beta \to \infty$. Thus, the Dixitian trigger occurs at $R_D = \rho'K$ and investment takes if $R > R_D$.

Song (1993, pp. 13–14) illustrates the magnitude of the difference between the two trigger points, or the corresponding difference between the modified and the risk-free discount rates, using a numerical example. If initially a variance in the return of 0.04 is assumed, then, with a risk-free discount rate of 5 per cent per year, $\beta = 2.15$, and the modified discount rate is 9.35 per cent. This implies that the current net returns have to take a value of nearly double that which ensures a positive net worth before waiting is no longer the optimal strategy. If the variance is raised to 0.15, while the risk-free discount rate is maintained at 5 per cent, then $\beta = 1.43$ and the modified discount rate rises to 16.6 per cent, and the current net returns need to be more than triple that which ensure a positive net worth, otherwise waiting remains the optimal strategy.

Dixit and Pindyck (1994, pp. 394–427) provide several examples of empirical applications of this 'options' approach, relating to the value of waiting. One which appears in the innovations literature concerns the decision of patent holders whether to continue to pay the renewal fee or to allow the patent to lapse. The continuation of the patent right maintains an option to exploit the patent in the future:

> An agent who acts optimally will pay the renewal fee only if the sum of the current returns plus the value of this option exceeds the renewal fee.... An optimal sequential policy for the agent has the form of an optimal renewal

(or stopping) rule, a rule determining whether to pay the renewal at each age. (Pakes, 1986, p. 756)

13.2.3 *Optimal stopping*

The earlier discussion addresses the value of 'waiting', that is, allowing new information to emerge that enables risk to be reduced. In the case of R&D, waiting has both a cost (a competitor may invent first) and a benefit (some uncertainty in the invention process is resolved), such that the net benefit may be very small or even negative. In addition, the analysis above misses an important element of the investment decision – the problem faced by the company is not so much 'when' should it start the research (although this may give rise to the potentially interesting though indirect result of 'never'), but how much resource should it 'throw' at solving the research problem, and 'when' should it stop undertaking a particular line of investigation. These issues concern some form of 'optimal stopping rule'. The present section begins to develop this idea in the context of a risky investment such as R&D. It begins by developing the idea of a 'reservation return' on R&D, then introduces a simple sequential investment model that copes with the various stages that NPD and NPL might go through and, finally, tentatively introduces the idea of learning in the context of optimal search/optimal stopping.

'Reservation return'
A way of approaching the problem is to set up a sequential search model, in which the firm considers the profitability of undertaking one more trial, having undertaken n trials to date. The discussion follows McKenna (1990, p. 38), who illustrates the basic concepts in the somewhat different context of the extent of job search activity. In the present model, the firm attempts to set some reservation (gross) return to R&D given the costs per unit of sequential search. In other words, at the end of each trial, the firm asks the question – do the discounted benefits of undertaking one more trial exceed the (discounted) costs of this trial? There are three possible outcomes to this question:

(i) stop – and exploit the (latest or even some earlier) technology which has been discovered;
(ii) continue to search – in the expectation of finding some improved technology with a higher NPV;
(iii) stop – and accept that there is no commercial value in continuing this line of investigation.

Assume that the firm in question has only the resources to exploit a single invention. The question addressed here, therefore, is whether the firm can specify some optimal outcome (return to search) at which it should cease the R&D process and exploit the invention or continue to search for a 'better' (i.e. more profitable) invention. The minimum return to search that the firm would find acceptable (and for which it would exploit the invention) is RS^{min} but an attempt is made to isolate the RS^{min*} at which it becomes optimal to stop looking. For the moment, assume that each time the firm decides that it does not wish to exploit an invention, the knowledge loses its commercial value (i.e. it becomes public knowledge). The probability of finding an invention with $RS < RS^{min}$ is:

$$Pr\,(RS < RS^{min}) = 1 - Pr(RS \geqslant RS^{min}) \hspace{3cm} 13.5$$

Thus, for simplicity ignoring the need to discount, the expected returns to searching once are V, where:

$$V(RS^{min}) = E(RS \,|\, RS \geqslant RS^{min})Pr(RS \geqslant RS^{min})$$
$$+ V(RS^{min})[1 - Pr(RS \geqslant RS^{min})] - c \hspace{1cm} 13.6$$

The equation has an entirely intuitive interpretation. $V(RS)$ is the (present) value of the expected returns to searching once. The first term on the right-hand side comprises the expected value of returns from the range of the distribution that the firm would find acceptable, multiplied by the probability of drawing an outcome from this range. The second term on the right-hand size is the (present) value of the returns to continued search if the first does not provide an acceptable return, multiplied by the probability of not achieving a high enough outcome at the first stage. The third and final term, c, denotes the cost per search, which, for simplicity, is assumed to be constant ($c = \$2$ million). The cost of exploiting the invention, once found, is \$100 million. It is now possible to rewrite equation 13.6 in the following way, but imposing the need for the net revenue to be as large as possible:

$$V(RS^{min*}) = \max \left[E(RS \,|\, RS \geqslant RS^{min}) - \frac{c}{Pr(RS \geqslant RS^{min})} \right] \hspace{1cm} 13.7$$

which gives the optimal R&D outcome. Note that $E(RS|RS \geqslant RS^{min})$ is not generally the mean of the overall distribution. Using the data from Table 13.3, it is only the mean of the overall distribution if RS^{min} is set at the lowest possible value, \$120 million, in which case:

$$E(RS \,|\, RS \geqslant 120) = \frac{\sum_{RS \geqslant 120} RSPr(RS)}{\sum_{RS \geqslant 120} Pr(RS)} = E(RS) = 141.2225 \hspace{1cm} 13.8$$

Note that all possible returns are greater than or equal to \$120 million and, hence:

$$\sum_{RS \geqslant 120} Pr(RS) = 1$$

However, for higher values of RS^{min}, different results are obtained:

$$E(RS \mid RS \geq 125) = \frac{\sum_{RS \geq 125} RSPr(RS)}{\sum_{RS \geq 125} Pr(RS)} = \frac{139.6745}{0.9871} = 141.4998 \qquad 13.9$$

Continuing this process for ever higher RS^{min} gives the results shown in Table 13.3. It can be seen that RS^{min*} occurs at $145 million. The revenues minus variable costs are given in the penultimate column and the net revenues minus total exploitation costs, which are assumed to be $100 million, are given in the final column. The inverse 'U-shaped' nature of the distribution of returns is caused by the fact that the initial increases in RS^{min} cause disproportionate increases in $\Sigma RSPr$ *vis-à-vis* ΣPr (note the shape of the underlying distribution, as the low values of RS have very low probabilities); later, however, this is reversed.

Table 13.3 Optimal (minimal) R&D commitment ($million)

RS^{min}	Relative frequency	$E(RS \mid RS > RS^{min})$	$c/Pr(RS > RS^{min})$	$V(RS^{min})$	$V(RS^{min})$ – exploitation costs
120	0.0129	141.2225	2.0000	139.2225	39.2225
125	0.0452	141.4998	2.0261	139.4737	39.4737
130	0.0903	142.2916	2.1234	140.1682	40.1682
135	0.1806	143.5950	2.3485	141.2465	41.2465
140	0.2581	145.9083	2.9806	142.9277	42.9277
145	0.1677	149.6016	4.8438	144.7678	44.7678
150	0.1290	152.7588	8.1566	144.5922	44.5922
155	0.0968	155.8003	17.2117	138.5886	38.5886
160	0.0194	160.0000	103.0928	56.9072	–44.0928

Source: Adapted from McKenna (1990, p. 46).

The main feature is that the optimal stopping rule suggests a higher R&D outcome than the mean of the distribution of returns. McKenna (1990, p. 36) demonstrates that the expected gross return is a weighted average of each possible outcome, where the weights are the relative frequencies with which the corresponding outcomes occur:

$$E(RS) = \sum_{i=1}^{9} [RS_i Pr(RS = RS_i)] \qquad 13.10$$
$$= 0.0129(120) + 0.0425(125) + \ldots + 0.0194(160) = 141.2225$$

Thus, according to the traditional decision rule, the firm will invest in R&D if the trial costs and exploitation costs are less than $141 million. Given the values assumed here, the NPV would be $141 million – $2 million – $100 million (= $39 million). In the case of the optimal stopping rule, the firm would invest in R&D with a view to not accepting any invention with a gross return of less than $150 million, which net of search costs is $145 million, which yields an expected profit after exploitation of $45 million.

Sequential investments and optimal stopping
Large R&D investments can be viewed as a sequence of stages (see also Dixit and Pindyck, 1994, pp. 319–356, and section 8.5). Kellogg and Charnes (2000, p. 2), for example, argue that, in the case of new drugs:

> The development process is composed of several stages, during which the drug company gathers evidence to convince government regulators that it can consistently manufacture a safe and efficacious form of the compound for the medical condition it is intended to treat.

The authors, drawing on Myers and Howe (1997), identify seven distinct phases, with associated costs, durations and probabilities of success (Table 13.4).

Indeed, Weitzman *et al.* (1981) argue that it is crucial to see large R&D investments as a sequence of stages, because, seen as an all-or-nothing decision (i.e. ignoring the separate phases), it is possible to reject a research project that could have significant value. To show this, Weitzman *et al.* (1981) set up a two-stage model in which the net rewards are NR_1 and NR_2 respectively, such that the total reward is $NR = NR_1 + NR_2$. However, NR_1 and NR_2 are random variables with the following probabilities:

$$NR_1 = \left\{ \begin{array}{l} \overline{NR}_1 + \sigma_1 \text{ with probability 0.5} \\ \overline{NR}_1 - \sigma_1 \text{ with probability 0.5} \end{array} \right. \qquad 13.11$$

$$NR_2 = \left\{ \begin{array}{l} \overline{NR}_2 + \sigma_2 \text{ with probability 0.5} \\ \overline{NR}_2 - \sigma_2 \text{ with probability 0.5} \end{array} \right. \qquad 13.12$$

Table 13.4 Pre-tax cost of development, duration and conditional probabilities of success

R&D stage	Total cost ($1,000s)	Years in stage	Conditional Pr(success)
Discovery	2,200	1	0.60
Pre-clinical	13,800	3	0.90
Phase I	2,800	1	0.75
Phase II	6,400	2	0.50
Phase III	18,100	3	0.85
FDA filing	3,300	3	0.75
Post-approval	31,200	9	1.00

FDA, Food and Drug Administration.
Source: Myers and Howe (1997).

Ignoring discounting and assuming $\sigma_1 > \sigma_2$, NR is also a random variable with a mean value of $\overline{NR}_1 + \overline{NR}_2$ and a variance of $\sigma_1^2 + \sigma_2^2$. The costs are denoted as K_1 for the first stage and K_2 for the second stage. Viewing the problem as a single all-or-nothing decision, the investment would not be undertaken if:

$$E[NR] = \overline{NR}_1 + \overline{NR}_2 < K_1 + K_2 \qquad 13.13$$

However, treating the problem sequentially, the investor can stop at the end of the first round if $NR_1 - \sigma_1$ is drawn, allowing the net return to be written:

$$E[NR] = -K_1 + (0.5)(0) + 0.5\left[-K_2 + 0.5(\overline{NR}_1 + \overline{NR}_2 + \sigma_1 - \sigma_2) \right.$$
$$\left. + 0.5(\overline{NR}_1 + \overline{NR}_2 + \sigma_1 + \sigma_2)\right] \qquad 13.14$$

and investment should occur if $E[NR] > 0$. It is possible to show that the investment is profitable as long as:

$$\overline{NR}_1 + \overline{NR}_2 + \sigma_1 > 2K_1 + K_2 \qquad 13.15$$

Undertaking stage 1 is like buying an option to undertake stage 2, where the cost of the option is K_1. It can be seen that for sufficiently large σ_1 and sufficiently small K_1 the investment should proceed. Weitzman *et al.* (1981, p. 57) point out that:

> *Ex post* it may look as if R&D costs of K_1 were wasted under such circumstances [if $\overline{NR}_1 - \sigma_1$ occurs], but that would be the wrong way of viewing the problem. It is exactly the possibility of termination before the end which encourages a sequential decision maker to go forward even though the standard cost–benefit criterion … looks discouraging.

Learning in an optimal stopping environment

The optimal stopping model outlined above is extremely naïve in the sense that it simply takes a number of random draws from a known probability distribution. There is considerable scope for introducing learning processes into such a framework; for example, researchers might learn about the parameters of the distribution as either time or cumulative research expenditures increase, or they might learn about the technology landscape in a way that helps them to decide where to search for profitable inventions. One way forward is to attempt to model the technology landscape in which the firms are researching. Some of the tools for empirical work in this area have started to emerge. Chapter 4 outlines the concept of technological distance and explores some measures of distance (e.g. based on the IPCs in which firms operate, with science and technology 'mappings'). It also explores how patent data throw light on the richness of the vein in which search is taking place – indicating how particular lines of research are opening up or are being 'mined out'.

Theoretical models are also being developed in which technology land-scapes are simulated, enabling optimal search patterns to be established. The uncertainty now comes from the terrain in which the researchers find themselves. Sampling various terrains and, in doing so, moving uphill or downhill, discovering gullies, ravines, foothills and peaks, have some similarities to the sequential search models with uncertainty described above. However, the idea of technological distance makes this more 'real world', as there are locations involved, and time and effort are required to move from one to another. Locations may reveal part of a story that, when a bridge is built to another location, provides the basis for a solution. The richness of this approach is that the theory is attempting to get at a 'strategy' linked to a technological landscape, which could be based upon the researcher's knowledge of the terrain, and determines where it might be rewarding to look and where it might be unproductive.

Kauffman *et al.* (2000) established a measure of distance between tech-nologies that enabled them to distinguish between evolutionary change (small distance) and revolutionary change (large distance). Technological search was modelled as movement in the technological possibilities space, constrained by the cost of search. The authors were interested in the relationship between the firm's current location in the 'space of techno-logical possibilities' and the distance of search that the firm should undertake. They related the optimal search distance to the firm's initial productivity, the cost of search, and the correlation structure of the tech-nology landscape. They found that, if the firm's initial technological position is poor early in the search for technological improvements, it is optimal for the firm to search far away on the technology landscape. However, as the firm succeeds in finding technological improvements, it is optimal to confine search to the local region. They also obtained the familiar result that there are diminishing returns to search, but without having to assume that the firm's repeated draws from the space of possible technologies are independent and identically distributed. Note, however, that the authors did not explicitly model the learning processes that drive the location of search.

13.3   Methods of managing risk

13.3.1 *Aims and scope of the present discussion*

This section focuses mainly on the discussion of managing risk in ways that help to optimize firm performance. While some of the early contribu-tions to these issues tended to focus on specific areas of investment, such as R&D or NPL, more recent contributions have become increasingly holistic. At one level, this more inclusive approach has provided convincing evidence that, for example, R&D decisions and processes must be allied to compatible decisions and processes in other functional areas, such as marketing and HRM. At another level, it is increasingly showing that the success of 'good' management practices in one area, such as R&D, are compounded through internal synergies and spillovers from 'good' (and compatible) management practices in other areas.

13.3.2 *Investment portfolio*

While risk is often attached to each possible investment, it may be possible to reduce the overall level of risk faced by the company by diversifying its portfolio of investment activities. Note, however, that diversification to reduce risk may have costs of its own because of a decline in the degree of focus of the enterprise (see Chapter 2). In addition, a broader portfolio is potentially something which is more readily accessible to large, multi-product companies that are able to finance a range of different research projects than to SMEs. However, it is also possible for companies to adopt collaborative and cooperative strategies which reduce various aspects of risk. This may be particularly important in non-core and high-risk technology areas.

Using simulation techniques, Scherer and Harhoff (2000, p. 564) indicate that portfolio averaging can partially even out the returns to R&D. They argue that:

> Even with a skew log normal distribution it remains true that the more observations over which one samples, the more stable the year-to-year averages (or totals) are. Thus, recent mergers among pharmaceutical companies, motivated in part by a desire to create larger portfolios spreading the risks of individual R&D project investments, undoubtedly do reduce the year-to-year variability of outcomes. (Scherer and Harhoff, 2000, p. 564)

The idea of a portfolio of R&D projects finds some resonance in the literature. For example, Matheson and Menke (1994) argue that, in order to maximize returns, key decisions need to be made in terms of building up a portfolio of projects, with a mix of high-risk, high-potential R&D and low-risk projects that produce more immediate returns through incremental improvements to products and processes. However, portfolio selection is much more complex than even this suggests. It has long been realized, for example, that project selection models, including R&D projects, should in principle account for the inter-relationships between projects in terms of both the value generated and the utilization of resources (Baker and Freeland, 1975; Weingartner, 1966).[2]

Scherer and Harhoff's (2000, pp. 563–564) experiments, however, suggest that there are strict limits to the effectiveness of portfolios:

> even at the extreme of merging the entire industry into one hypothetical firm, year-to-year standard deviations equal to roughly 8 per cent of industry quasi-rent totals remain. For individual firms much smaller than the pharmaceutical industry aggregate, substantially larger year-to-year variations cannot be

escaped through portfolio strategies. Thus, given skew-distributed outcomes, appreciable risk-taking cannot be avoided. And in judging the innovative performance of individual firms, a long time perspective is essential, since short-run returns can be dominated by particularly favorable or unfavorable draws from a skew distribution. (Scherer and Harhoff, 2000, p. 564)

13.3.3 *Success and failure in innovation*

There is a large literature that attempts to identify the factors that increase rather than reduce the chances of successful innovation. As might be expected, there is some common ground between the literature on the success and failure of innovation and the management of risk in the NPL literature. Freeman and Soete (1997, p. 203) argue that the characteristics of successful innovating firms in the twentieth century were:

> (i) strong in-house professional R&D; (ii) performance of basic research or close connections with those conducting such research; (iii) the use of patents to gain protection and to bargain with competitors; (iv) large enough size to finance fairly heavy R&D expenditure over long periods; (v) shorter lead times than competitors; (vi) readiness to take high risks; (vii) early and imaginative identification of a potential market and substantial efforts to involve, educate and assist users; (viii) entrepreneurship strong enough effectively to coordinate R&D, production and marketing; (ix) good communications with the outside world as well as with customers.

Project SAPPHO was designed in 1968 and undertaken by the Science Policy Research Unit at Sussex University during the 1970s. The methodology was to use fifty-eight pairs of firms in the chemicals and scientific instruments sectors, where one firm was a successful innovator and the other was unsuccessful. The idea was that, by comparing the activities and behaviour of the successful and unsuccessful, it should be possible to isolate the factors that lead to success. There are clearly important problems with the matching process, as the firms were not identical twins and, while it is possible to designate innovations as successes or failures, there is an issue concerning the degree of success or failure. A number of factors stood out as important:

> those that came through most strongly were directly related to marketing ... [including the] greater attention to the education of users, to publicity, to market forecasting and selling ... and to the understanding of user requirements ... [of which the] single measure which discriminated most clearly between success and failure was 'user needs understood'. (Freeman and Soete, 1997, pp. 207–210)

Thus, the results highlight some composite influence of technological and marketing competences:

> The fact that the measures which discriminated between success and failure included some which reflected mainly on the competence of R&D, others

Table 13.5 Success factors in industrial innovation

Project execution factors	Corporate factors
Good internal and external communication; accessing external know-how	Commitment of top management and visible support for innovation
Treating innovation as a corporate-wide task; effective inter-functional coordination; good balance of functions	Long-term corporate strategy with associated technology strategy
Implementing careful planning and project control procedures; high-quality upfront analysis	Long-term commitment to major projects ('patient money')
Efficiency in development work and high-quality production	Corporate flexibility and responsiveness to change
Strong marketing orientation; emphasis on satisfying user needs; development emphasis on creating user value	Acceptance of risk by top management
Providing a good technical service to customers; effective user education	Innovation-accepting, entrepreneurship-accommodating culture
Effective product champions and technological gatekeepers	
High-quality, open-minded management; commitment to developing human capital	
Attaining cross-project synergies and inter-project learning	

Source: Rothwell (1992, 1994).

which reflected mainly on efficient marketing, and some which measured characteristics of the business innovator with good communications, confirms the view that industrial innovation is essentially a coupling process. (Freeman and Soete, 1997, p. 216)

Rothwell (1992, 1994) provides a summary of the work of the 1970s and 1980s in this area (see Table 13.5). In addition to the factors brought out by Project SAPPHO, his listing places somewhat greater emphasis on management planning and control procedures (Freeman and Soete, 1997, p. 222). As 'technology' and other factors (ICT, company structures, globalization, etc.) change, so too will the influences on success.

13.3.4 *Success and failure in NPL*

General factors
Given the riskiness of new product activity, many studies have attempted to identify the factors that influence product success and failure (Calantone

and Cooper, 1979; Cooper, 1980; Cooper and Kleinschmidt, 1988, 1990; Rothwell, 1972). The mismanagement and poor execution of the NPL itself is often suggested to be a major determinant of new product failure (Cooper, 1979; Dwyer and Mellor, 1991). Craig and Hart (1992) reviewed the literature and, using content analysis, identified the following as being crucial for success:

(i)   management – including in terms of authority, support, technical aspects and communication;
(ii)   organizational structure – mechanism and style;
(iii) strategy – orientation, objectives, synergy, product characteristics;
(iv)   information – general, marketing, external, communication;
(v)   people – multi-functional, coordination, product champion, communication;
(vi)   process – timing, pre-development activities, development activities, marketing activities, launch activities.

They concluded that developing successful new products is 'a task of cross functional information management and decision making' (Craig and Hart, 1992, p. 38).

Balachandra and Friar (1997), however, argue that trying to uncover success factors is more complicated than was previously thought and trying to provide prescriptive models is even more problematic. They undertook a review of the literature across disciplines, covering the previous thirty years, to investigate factors critical to the success or failure of R&D projects and NPLs. They found that:

(i)   even with a conservative approach to listing factors, the list is very long;
(ii)   the magnitude, significance and the direction of influence of a given factor varies across studies;
(iii) given differences in context, the meanings of similar factors differ.

The contradictory findings led the authors to propose a contingency framework for NPD and R&D project models.

Kleinschmidt and Cooper (1995) used a sixteen- page pre-tested questionnaire to gather data on 103 major new product projects over a two-year period from twenty-one large UK, German, US and Canadian chemical firms. A single industry was chosen to reduce inter-industry, inter-market effects. The chemical industry has the advantage of being science- and technology-based with a long history of NPD activity, with high R&D spending. The survey looked at various aspects of NPD and found that:

(i)   about 66 per cent of products were rated a commercial success;
(ii)   as with previous findings, managers tended to view marketing factors as being far less important than technical ones (including

pre-commercial business analysis, test market or trial sell, detailed market studies/market research, etc.).

The authors concluded that 'this tendency to over-rate technical activities and under-rate marketing/business actions may help to explain why industrial new products continue to be plagued by high failure rates and why deficiencies in marketing actions … remain the main reasons for failure' (Kleinschmidt and Cooper, 1995, p. 21).

Cooper and Kleinschmidt (1988) also emphasize that industrial NPD tends to be dominated by technological considerations – only twelve person-days of marketing activity are allocated for every seventy-eight days of technology-related issues (based on a benchmark of 100 person-days). In addition, of the twelve person-days, 80 per cent is devoted to launch activities (i.e. only 20 per cent is spent on activities such as customer analysis and product advantage). Biemans and Setz (1995) studied NPLs in the telecommunications sector, which had been growing by about 10 per cent per annum, with firms typically spending around 4–5 per cent of their total costs on new products. The authors looked at fourteen firms and interviewed manufacturers, customers, dealers and consultants, as well as looking at formal/informal announcements and internal/external sources of information. Like other authors, they concluded that the process is long term and complex, but that a key factor is the networks of personal relationships that help to facilitate the process.

Planning for new products
Dolan and Simon (1996, pp. 306–307) set out the nature of the management process, as shown in Figure 13.1, although their discussion is perhaps too heavily focused on pricing issues. They suggest that this process should begin (phase 1) with a workshop aimed at getting the whole of the project team involved in the price-setting process, in order to ensure that they 'buy into' the research methodology used for establishing the price. Phase 2 involves a study of other firms in the market, their prices, their market shares and so on, with a view to assessing their response to the entry of the new product. Phase 3 (which largely runs in parallel with phase 2) is intended to collect data from potential consumers and in phase 4 these are interpreted (see section 4.3 for a discussion). Phase 5 develops a variety of scenarios based upon alternative pricing and marketing options. Phase 6 relates to the development of an implementation plan that is put forward to the top managers about seven months before the new product is due for launch. The top managers may consider this for up to one month, which leaves about six months to put all the agreed plans into action.

Design for manufacturing processes
The DFM process is normally undertaken towards the end of the development of new products and concerns the 'product architecture'. In essence,

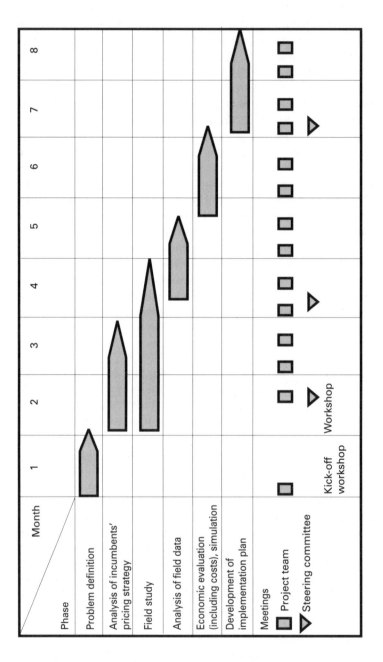

Figure 13.1 Planning for new products. Source: Dolan and Simon (1996).

the designing company looks for commonalities in the product design that can lead to economies in production. While this is perhaps most obvious in manufactured products (e.g. all rotor blades in an engine are designed with the same shape and materials), it applies equally to services (where the sequence of steps in dealing with one customer are made as similar as possible to those for other customers). In addition, the firm seeks commonalities in product components, so that one product contains some of the same components as another. The ability to locate such commonalities will increase both economies of scale in certain areas of production and learning effects (see Chapter 12).

Pricing decisions for new products
This area receives little attention in the mainstream technology management literature, but Dolan and Simon (1996) argue that the pricing decision is an important determinant of the success of new products. They view it as a key strategic issue, because this price 'marks the reference point for future prices' (pp. 315–316). The authors suggest that, if the price set seems too high, it is better to offer discounts than to lower the official list price, as this maintains the reference list price, and discounts can be reduced as the market accepts and takes up the product. They also argue that one strategy for the innovator is to make an early price announcement – testing the water, and leaving time for adjustments before the product launch:

> For example, the maker of a new sports car announced a preliminary price two years before the introduction. This price was seen to be very low by the public and by the press, leading to a well-accepted introductory price that was 10% higher. (Dolan and Simon, 1996, pp. 315–316)

The authors give a further example of the importance of this process at the time of NPL:

> Glaxo introduced its ulcer medication Zantac after market incumbent Tagamet. The conventional wisdom was that as the 'second one in' Glaxo should price 10% below the incumbent. However, Chief Executive Sir Paul Girolami understood that Zantac had superiority over Tagamet in featuring fewer drug interactions and side effects and more convenient dosing. If adequately communicated to the marketplace, this performance superiority provided the basis for a price premium over Tagamet. Thus, Glaxo introduced Zantac at a significant price premium over Tagamet and still gained the market leadership position. In addition, as the product established itself in the market and became more proven, price was increased with the increase in perceived customer value. (Dolan and Simon, 1996, p. 13)

Firms tend to adopt either:

(i) a 'skimming' strategy, where prices are initially set low and gradually increased – which may be appropriate where, despite the newness of the product, competition is strong (initially, profits are low, but the strategy has a low risk of failure on entry and profits should rise over time);

(ii) a 'penetration' strategy, where prices are set high and reduced over time – which may be appropriate where competition is weak (while this is a higher-risk strategy, profits can be high throughout).

13.4   Product life-cycle and dynamic performance

13.4.1 *Basic principles*

The present section explores the idea that R&D and advertising (and, in principle, other discretionary investments, such as training) interact in a synergistic manner to produce improvements in firm performance. The rationale can be found in Chapters 8–10, where studies were shown to come from different discipline backgrounds and, hence, R&D *or* HPWPs *or* advertising variables were included, but not all of them. Even where two of the variables appeared in the same model (e.g. HPWP and R&D in the work of Youndt *et al.*, 1996), they did so additively and were not included interactively to investigate synergies between investments. There are many suggestions in the literature that this is likely to be an important area, for example Brutinni's (1975) discussion of the advertising used to promote new products during the early stages of the Industrial Revolu-tion. Brutinni (1975, p. 94) provides many examples of patented inventions that were advertised, including Thomas Savery's steam pumping machine. An advertisement from the *Gentleman's Magazine* (1735), describing a patented threshing machine, stated that:

> a gentleman ... in Scotland has invented a Machine for threshing Grain, which in a Minute gives 1320 strokes, as many as 33 Men threshing briskly.... The inventor has a patent and can make them of smaller sizes to do the work of 8 or 10 men.

In order to illustrate some of the issues, the discussion below outlines the ways in which R&D and advertising are likely to be related over the PLC – the argument is simplified by omitting discussion of other dis-cretionary investments. According to Grantham (1997, p. 4), 'The product life cycle represents a core element of marketing theory and has done so for four decades ... how this [the life-cycle] is managed is key to survival in business'. Note that not all authors accept the PLC as a realistic construct for many products (e.g. Dhalla and Yuspeh, 1976; Grantham, 1997, p. 4; Polli and Cook, 1969). Some of the arguments put forward for scepti-cism about a 'fixed' or 'standardized' PLC are precisely the reasons why the concept has been adopted in the present chapter. Grantham (1997, p. 5), for example, points out that 'a product's life cycle differs to that of a human being's as it is usual for products to attain a second life or to be "reincarnated" as a result of promotion'. Likewise, numerous brands have been seen to go from maturity back to rapid growth (Dhalla and Yuspeh, 1976; see also Hiam, 1992).

13.4.2 *Product life-cycles and discretionary investments*

The traditional PLC is characterized by four phases (assume initially a single-brand, single-product firm):

(i)   introduction;
(ii) growth;
(iii) maturity;
(iv) decline.

According to marketing theory, each phase requires a different strategy to maximize the product's profitability (Grantham, 1997, p. 4):

(i)   During the introductory stage, it is important to create and raise product awareness. Marketing costs are likely to be high relative to sales as the firm tests the market, carries out promotion linked to product launch and establishes distribution channels.
(ii) During the growth phase, increases in output lower costs through economies of scale and learning effects. As these are passed on as lower prices, this further stimulates demand. The firm adopts marketing strategies to maximize market share and to benefit from the overall growth in the market.
(iii) In the maturity phase, competition is intense and the strategy is to maximize profits while defending market share in a stagnant market. Advertising offensives are likely to be countered by competitors. There is some recognition in the literature that R&D is likely to focus on product modification and enhancement or process innovation to reduce costs and improve price competitiveness.
(iv) In the decline phase, the market is shrinking and there is generally a need to reduce expenditures and 'milk the product'. Firms search for extension strategies to prolong the life of the product. Decline may be partly offset by competitors exiting, but the company itself may be forced to stop production by competition in a falling market. By this stage, there is intense pressure on prices and an incentive to transfer production to lower-cost locations (see Chapter 14).

This suggests that the rate of return to discretionary investments (R&D, advertising, etc.) vary both in absolute terms and relative to one another over the PLC. The following offers a possible scenario. At the pre-product stage, the returns to market research are high compared with those to

R&D because, in the absence of strategic information about the potential market and competitors, the likely returns to R&D are relatively low (i.e. because of the high risk in the absence of market information). As the firm builds more extensive market information, its knowledge about potentially viable new products increases and the returns to collecting further market data decrease at the margin. The potential returns to R&D rise as the knowledge of potentially viable alternatives increases. As R&D reveals potential technological solutions, this information can be collated with existing and (if the returns suggest it is useful) new market information (i.e. market testing). As the R&D search continues and begins to yield solutions, so the return to R&D begins to fall at the margin. The reader can image how this process continues through the various stages of the life-cycle, until the final decision is taken to withdraw support for the ageing product and cease production. The process has been described in a rather linear fashion, while, in practice, many feedbacks and other factors can be envisaged.

This story, if left at this stage, paints a fairly gloomy picture for firms whose product life is given, at the end of which the firm ceases to exist. However, the dynamics of the firm suggests that, at some stage, it should begin searching for a new product. This is perfectly consistent with the concept of different rates of return to different forms of investment. If the earlier argument is extended to its natural conclusion, as the life-cycle unfolds, not only is the rate of return to various activities *in support of that platform* changing (e.g. the returns to advertising may decline as the platform approaches obsolescence) but so too are the returns of staying with that platform *vis-à-vis* developing a new platform (i.e. the returns to R&D are rising – see the discussion of exploration versus exploitation in section 12.2.2). The choice of the timing and extent of such new activities depends crucially on a wide variety of influences, including:

(i)   the competences of the firm;
(ii)   the extent of technological opportunity;
(iii) the potential for product differentiation in the market.

13.4.3 *Sequencing of NPLs and inter-related investments*

The discussion now moves to a multiple-brand or multiple-product firm. Figure 13.2, taken from Granstrand (1999), demonstrates a technologically based company building a stock of valuable IP. While the 'total value of IP' line is smoothed, it will exhibit various lumps and bumps because of the discrete nature of innovations. The line comprises growth in trade secrets and know-how, patented inventions and building up trademarks (i.e. brand value); however, it is not a simple arithmetic sum of these because of inter-actions between them in determining IP value. The sequence of patenting

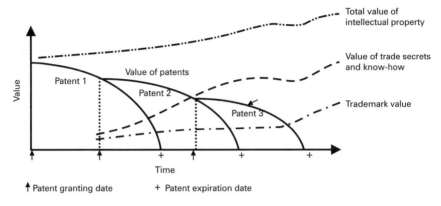

Figure 13.2 Building the value of intangibles. Source: Granstrand (1999).

activity for technologically based firms is seen to be accompanied by trademark activity and, implicitly, by associated advertising and market promotional activity, as well as anti-counterfeiting activity.

Section 8.4.2 demonstrates that, consistent with the above story, branded businesses are more active and more successful in the area of NPLs. There is evidence that they are significantly more likely to report that a higher proportion of their revenues are driven by new products or services. The present section examines the associated information regarding R&D expenditures. Figure 13.3 shows that product R&D in FMCGs is largely

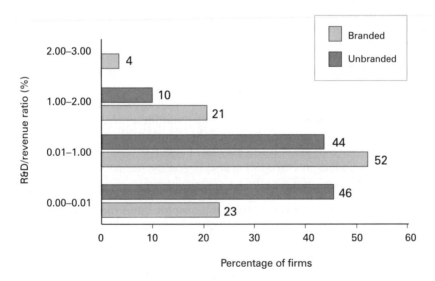

Figure 13.3 Product R&D/revenue ratio for branded and unbranded products. Source: PIMS (1998).

undertaken by branded companies. Indeed, 'Almost half the unbranded businesses have no budgets at all for product R&D, and almost none spend more than 1% of sales revenue' (PIMS, 1998). However, PIMS (1998) also provides tentative evidence that, where the unbranded companies do R&D, they are more likely to be involved in process than product R&D. The relative emphasis on process R&D among the unbranded reflects their need to compete on price rather than quality.

Evidence of a significant link between R&D, advertising (branding) and performance is entirely consistent with the earlier discussion of innovation in sections 13.3.3 and 13.3.4, where communication between marketing and R&D functions was important to the success of NPLs. This finding is also consistent with the broader marketing and firm performance literature. In a survey in three countries:

> among Australian companies, the better performers tend to have a closer working [marketing] relationship with most other functional areas, especially production, sales and R&D. A similar situation is evident in New Zealand and Singapore, but with the latter these relationships appear to be even stronger for the better performers.... the more successful companies display stronger links between marketing and R&D, resulting more often in market-led than technology-driven innovation. (Ghosh *et al.*, 1994, p. 45)

One interesting piece of statistical work on the joint role of advertising and R&D in developing brand value focused on the market for PCs in the late 1980s (Bresnahan *et al.*, 1996). This market 'offered almost laboratory conditions to examine winners and losers' (Martin, 1996, p. 18). The market was differentiated by level of technology (high/low, termed frontier/non-frontier, respectively) and by branding (branded/non-branded), resulting in four market clusters:

(i)   branded/frontier – which, at the time, were based on the 386 chip, and included machines made by companies such as Compaq and IBM;
(ii) non-branded/frontier – again, based upon 386 technology, but made by relatively small high-technology manufacturers;
(iii) branded/non-frontier – based on the 286 chip, but produced by companies such as AT&T and Hewlett Packard;
(iv) non-branded/non-frontier – also based on the 286 technology, but by 'unknown' makers (the so-called 'clones').

Prices were ranked (i) to (iv), that is, highest for those machines with both 'brand' and 'high-technology' advantages (averaging US$7,577) and lowest for those with neither advantage (US$2,924). Bresnahan *et al.* (1996) undertook statistical analysis of 120 different brands (i.e. makes and models) of PC in 1987 and 1988. They found that competition tended to be relatively strong *within* a given cluster, but relatively weak *between* different clusters. Thus, a new entrant into the branded/high-technology market at this time might take market share from, say, IBM, but not from the other market clusters. The authors argued that IBM's loss of market share was not due to the emergence of a large number of 'clones', as has often been argued, but was the result of IBM's loss of status within its own market cluster, as Compaq and others began to reposition themselves at the frontier and to invest heavily in marketing their products. The results suggest that marketing and brand image played a crucial role in IBM's decline and the rise of other PC producers. Bresnahan *et al.* (1996) concluded that 'Having a brand name conferred a large advantage in the sense of shifting out the demand function, whereas being early at the technological frontier did not'. As Martin (1996, p. 18) points out, however, 'being a technology leader can itself be a powerful reinforcer of brand identity'. And Compaq's emergence as a powerful competitor occurred because 'the brand was also better because Compaq was now setting the technological pace' (Martin, 1996, p. 18). Thus, Martin draws three conclusions:

(i)   there is more potential to raise prices if markets are more clearly clustered (i.e. where competition between clusters is low);
(ii) technology spending is most valuable when it helps to differentiate the firm's product from those of (potential) competitors (i.e. allowing brand image to emerge);
(iii) 'creating a true brand is one of the most powerful things any company can do to enhance its market power'.

13.4.4 *Strategic management of PLCs and firm performance*

The discussion returns to the important difference between model life-cycle, PLC and BLC. In the main, a particular model (such as an Austin 7 or Mazda RX8) will be built on a design and technology platform. While it is possible to vary and improve this platform, the returns to major changes appear to be higher if this is presented as a new model – marketed as a significant improvement on the older 'vintage'. Insofar as a brand is tied closely to a particular product and, in effect, cannot be separated from that product, then the PLC determines the limits of the BLC. However, insofar as the brand can be separated from the product, then in general the brand might be expected to outlive a particular model or even product platform. There is no reason why a brand name such as Virgin or Diageo should have any relationship with a particular model or product platform's life-cycle. It has already been demonstrated that brands can be very long lived (and may be sold by one firm to another). Mercer's (1993) work on BLCs examined 929 brands in 150 market segments from 1969 to 1989, using British Marketing Research Bureau data. The main result was that the majority of brand leaders in 1969 were still brand leaders in 1989. Of those that had not maintained their leadership, the vast majority were still in the top three brands – only 7 per cent of all brand leaders in 1969 had declined below fourth place by 1989 and only 1 per cent had been discontinued. This should not be interpreted as an indication that PLCs do not exist, but that brands are quite distinct from products and the concept of a BLC may have very different attributes to that of a PLC.

While platforms often depreciate and eventually become obsolescent, the longevity of a particular model, brand or product is not predetermined and fixed – it can be modified by the discretionary investments of the firm. In particular, the PLC is not independent of the firm's marketing practices (Grantham, 1997, p. 8; Polli and Cook, 1969). Equally, it is possible to demonstrate that investments in R&D (product modification) and advertising can be used jointly to support the product and increase longevity. Peckham (1976, p. 2), in discussing the differences between successful long-lived brands and those that fall by the wayside, argues that the successful ones not only maintained their advertising, but, in addition, 'All made consistent product and packaging improvements ... not once but many times' (see also Chapter 10). The 34 per cent of companies in his sample that lost their lead had one major common characteristic – they had failed to keep the product up to date, in line with consumer requirements (advertising alone cannot maintain market leadership). Data from a long extinct book about the Austin Seven illustrates how product modifications are linked with sales.[3] Figure 13.4 shows the number of modifications made to the car after its initial launch in 1923 and the sales of the Austin Seven. The cumulative curves that can be constructed from Figure 13.4 are both sigmoidal – 'accelerating' in the early phase after introduction and 'falling away' towards the end of the product's life. The data suggest

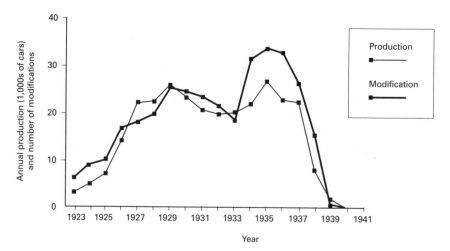

Figure 13.4 Product sales and technical modifications for the Austin Seven. Note that the two series have been scaled to lie on top of each other (units for modifications, thousands for cars sold).

that the initial growth in cumulative sales was more rapid in the early years than the cumulative product modifications, but when the Austin Seven platform became dated, the opposite was true.

The literature suggests that the PLC, at least as it was originally portrayed (i.e. as given and fixed), took on such a stature among managers that any slowing of growth was interpreted as the onset of maturity and any downturn in sales was considered as the onset of decline, to be followed by demise. Thus, a number of authors argue that the concept of the PLC became a self-fulfilling prophecy (Dhalla and Yuspeh, 1976) – as in the US case of Iparla toothpaste (Grantham, 1997, p. 6). This product was marketed until 1968, when it was dropped and replaced by new products. A year later two businessmen obtained the brand name, created a new formula but kept the original packaging and, within three years, the product was being purchased by more than a million people. Thus, brand and product deletion are important strategic decisions (Hart, 1989). The PLC route tends to imply that product deletion occurs at a stage when, based upon a variety of performance criteria, the product has become 'weak', but the literature indicates that there are alternative reasons (Avlonitis and James, 1982; Hart, 1989). Hart (1989) reported a study of British manufacturing companies involving thirty-one 'in-depth' interviews and 166 complete postal questionnaire responses. The author examined the influences on product deletion among companies according to whether the firm was concerned with:

(i)   strategic financial issues;
(ii) strategic growth-related issues;
(iii) strategic marketing-related issues.

Often the various influences differed in importance across the three strategic influences. As might be expected, NPD and the availability of new products influence the deletion decision in (ii) and (iii) above. Across firms with a strategic growth-related focus, a fairly wide range of influences were important in the deletion decision, including: competitive activity; NPD; third-party decisions; poor product quality; poor fit with company capabilities or strategic goals; poor fit with company image; and parent company decisions and policies.[4] Again, it is clear that the buying and selling, development and deletion of brands are an integral part of broader firm strategies (e.g. strategies for growth or strategies to move up- or down-market).

13.5 Towards a more holistic approach

13.5.1 *An overview of the drivers*

This section further develops the more holistic picture of the management of the assets of the company and the way in which the different drivers interact. The PIMS (1998) survey of 168 businesses in the area of FMCGs is again used to illustrate the arguments. The key measures of performance adopted were:

(i)   gain in relative market share – an indicator of the firm's effectiveness in competing for customer preference;
(ii) growth in value added – representing its contribution to GDP;
(iii) ROCE – reflecting the firm's ability to compete in capital markets.

The relationships found to be significant drivers of market share are shown in Figure 13.5 (PIMS, 1998, p. 5):

(i)   product R&D, product know-how and speed to market were the main drivers of increased rates of innovation – giving innovation advantages, greater competitiveness and market share;
(ii) product and process R&D did not appear to lead to significant improvements in cost or quality advantages over competitors (presumably because they were cancelled out by their rivals' R&D);
(iii) however, quality and cost advantages had a positive effect on firm performance, also resulting in better image and reputation – leading to improved competitiveness and market share;

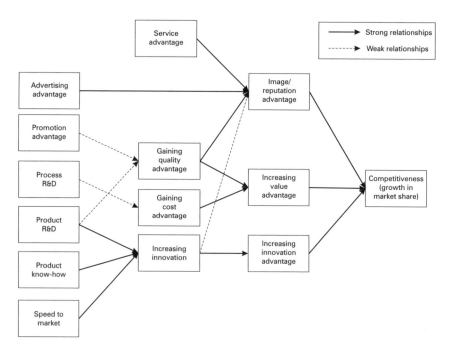

Figure 13.5 How branded businesses grow in their markets. Source: PIMS (1998).

(iv) image and reputation advantages were themselves driven by adver-
      tising, quality and service advantages (e.g. better displays, leading to
      higher consumer awareness).

The authors report that 'the three key drivers of competitive growth –
value, innovation and reputation – are closely linked' (PIMS, 1998, p. 5).

   Figure 13.6 shows the PIMS (1998) view of how the intangible (discretionary) investments of the firm generate capabilities, and, thereby,
intangible assets, which lead to improved competitiveness and market
share, as well as resulting in growth of value added, employment and
labour productivity. It can be seen how differences in the level and balance
between the various discretionary investments influence the abilities of
the firm to deliver low costs, high product quality and so on. Setting the
drivers out in this way provides something approaching the holistic vision
that the present study argues to be so important. The over-arching link
between the various discretionary investments and the performance
measures are largely confirmed by the analysis of firm-level panel data
set out in Chapters 8–10. However, the earlier discussion in the present
chapter would probably give more emphasis to the complementarities and
synergies between the discretionary investments.

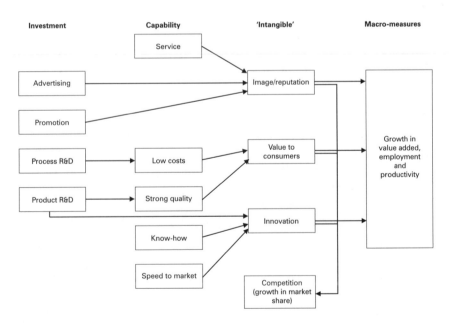

Figure 13.6 Discretionary investments, intangible assets and growth. Source:
PIMS (1998).

13.5.2 *Complementarities and synergies*

The concept of so-called 'Edgeworth complementarities' was introduced in section 9.6.1. Over time, the view of complementarities has broadened to encompass not just parts of the HRM system, but a variety of different activities and functions within the enterprise. Mendelsson and Pillai (1999) also take a broad view of complementarities. In their so-called 'high-IQ organizations', complementarities occur via the combined high level of innovativeness, widespread use of IT and 'new firm practices'. The emergence of such firms is largely driven by the falling costs of processing information. Similar conclusions can be found in the earlier literature. For example, according to Finegold and Soskice (1988, p. 22):

> a company which decides to recruit better-educated workers and then invest more funds in training them will not realize the full potential of that investment if it does not make parallel changes in the style and quality of management, work design, promotion structures and the way it implements new technologies.

Section 9.6.2 reviewed the work of Youndt *et al.* (1996, p. 853), in which:

> [the] results provide strong evidence that manufacturing strategy influences the HR–performance relationship with a quality strategy interacting with human capital-enhancing HR to predict performance and delivery flexibility and cost strategies interacting with administrative HR to predict performance. In short, maximising performance appears to depend on properly aligning HR systems with manufacturing strategy.

In Chapter 14, the discussion broadens the scope of synergies further, examining the way in which firms interact within and with the NIS.

13.5.3 *Multidimensional management 'best practice'*

Sampson (2000, p. 91) argues that the management books that advocate a particular formula, recipe or approach (which have grown exponentially in number) are misguided: 'What is nearly always missing is a strategic and holistic view and approach of long-term, sustainable and systemic management fundamentals that is implementable and that increases shareholder value'. Sampson (2000, p. 92) reports to have undertaken 'worldwide reviews of excellent companies and their management activities'. While none of the companies was seen as doing everything in a 'best' manner, 'These "best companies" could demonstrate a clear link between managerial action and customer satisfaction, business growth, environmental management, safety performance, unit cost, employee satisfaction and shareholder value'. On the basis of this experience, 'it is both possible and very useful to develop a view of what "best practice" looks like in order to plan progress towards that state' (Sampson, 2000, p. 92). Best practice revolves around the adoption and use of a set of management principles that leads to 'success of firms in introducing improved practices, and ultimately, their ability to profit'. He makes two further important points about these principles (p. 93):

(i)   they are not a fad, but sustained over time;
(ii) they are not separate ideas, but form a *system* used in combination.

Sampson (2000, p. 95–96) identifies eight elements of 'alignment', which are argued to be important influences on the activities and behaviour of employees and of organizations. These concern the alignment of:

(i)   employees' values with those of the company;
(ii)   employees' needs and expectations with the stated company direction;
(iii) the direct value chain of an organization (i.e. the functions, departments and processes) to act in the interests of the whole company rather than their own interests;
(iv)   the support units (e.g. accounting and information systems) that enable the direct value chain to operate efficiently;
(v)   goals and performance measures at all levels of the organization, driving effective behaviour in the workplace;
(vi)   the organization with its suppliers, ensuring efficient buyer–supplier relationships;
(vii) products and services with customer requirements, in order to retain/ improve relevance in the market;
(viii) working conditions and rewards with desired employee behaviour (i.e. 'well designed jobs and roles, skills development processes and career progression systems').

Sampson (2000, pp. 96–103) outlines his 'fourteen principles of best companies' (these are summarized in Table 13.6). He also tests whether companies with more of these 'good characteristics' out-perform those with fewer of them. The empirical evidence he provides is based on a survey of Australian companies, matched to financial information from the IBIS database.[5] The performance variable was net profit after tax per employee. The extent of utilization of each of the 'good characteristics' was measured on a Likert scale from 1 (low) to 5 (high). The responses with regard to each characteristic were cumulated, producing a score for each company, which ranged from 35 (lowest use) to 65 (highest use). The correlation between the 'principles sum' (i.e. the extent of good characteristics) and net profit after tax per employee was 0.321, with a probability of 0.019 (one-tail test). The author reports that the strength of the correlation was higher among better than poorer performing companies. Thus, the study provides tentative evidence of broadly based synergies in best working practices.

Table 13.6 Fourteen principles of best companies

Principle	Description
1 Alignment	There is good alignment of employees' behaviour with stated company values and direction at all levels of the organization
2 Distributed leadership	Individuals and work teams are assigned, and accept, responsibility for operational decision making and performance improvement
3 Integration of effort	The organization is focused on value creation and process management, not functional needs and hierarchies
4 Out front	The business proactively strives to lead the pack in all industry standards and practices: safety, customer service, product and process design, environmental management etc.
5 Up front	All employees demonstrate integrity and openness in all areas of their work and dealings with others
6 Resourcing the medium term	The business is able to balance short-term operational and medium-term development and growth issues and requirements
7 Time based	Time is developed as a critical organizational value. The business practises the principles of time-based competition
8 Bias for action	All employees demonstrate a willingness to embrace and accept change as an essential part of doing business. The organization excels at implementing new ideas
9 Learning focus	All employees demonstrate a willingness to develop skills and knowledge and are involved in a learning/development programme
10 Enabling disciplines	The organization invests in policies, procedures and standards and applies a strong systems perspective in everything it does
11 Measurement and reporting/ publication	The business measures/reports to all employees, and publishes the financial and non-financial performance information needed to drive improvement
12 Customer value	All employees understand the set of order winners and actively strive to enhance customer value creation
13 Capabilities creation	Business and organizational capabilities are defined and prioritized and drive critical development and investment decisions
14 Micro to macro	All employees know how their particular activities and individual efforts contribute to the 'big picture' of business success

13.6 Conclusions

This chapter has presented a wide-ranging discussion of the policy issues facing private sector firms. One theme has been the need to manage risk – not to remove risk *per se*, but to manage the firm in such a way as to give it the greatest chance of being successful. This requires not only new decision techniques but also new attitudes and approaches by senior managers to risk taking and to both success and failure. From an academic perspective, it has also been shown (Chapter 8) that there is a need for econometric work to refocus, away from the marginal effects of particular activities *averaged across companies*, to examine what drives the small proportion of really successful activities. Perhaps the most important theme, however, is the need for a holistic approach, among both academics and company policy makers. It is clear from reading the literature that academic research remains too narrowly discipline based, which is reflected in the choice of variables and the specification of models: those in the HRM area examine the role of HPWPs, those in labour economics explore the influence of skills, and those interested in technological change investigate the effects of R&D and patents. Even where variables are included from different discipline areas – which is all too rare – they do so in a separable form which does not allow for the role of cross-functional complementarities. The HPWP literature has at least made it clear that the role of such practices should be viewed in the context of the goals (and strategies) of the enterprise – a topic on which most of the econometric work in other discipline areas has been remarkably silent.

Notes

1 Based on the US experience of the late 1980s, Branscomb *et al.* (2000, p. 1) reported that 'There was evidence that firms were systematically under-investing in leading edge technologies and failing to commercialize the products of their own research activities effectively'.

2 A wide range of potential internal interactions might be considered: (i) resource interactions, for example, when knowledge or equipment is shared; (ii) value interactions, when there are synergies from the mix of projects developed (e.g. development of new software and hardware); and (iii) outcome interactions where doing one project has a beneficial impact on the probability of success of other projects.

3 There are no data on advertising, although it is reported that the various modifications were promoted by the company.

4 All seven factors had a positive effect on deletion (significant at 10 per cent or higher).

5 The survey response was low and restricted to quoted companies, which resulted in forty-two usable replies.

Chapter 14

Public policy and enterprise performance

14.1   Introduction

The present chapter examines whether government policy can create a virtuous cycle of economic growth leading to increased income levels in the economy. Discussing the role of government is not an easy task, partly because of the number and diversity of areas where government can intervene. The present discussion focuses primarily on government interventions that enable firms to perform better, which, outside the present book, need to be balanced against broader welfare implications relating to the consumer interest. The minutiae of policies that a particular government can apply are not considered, but an attempt is made to explore more general lessons from the earlier chapters that may have relevance to a range of economies.

Again, it is worth emphasizing that the government's goals may not correspond with those of private sector companies. Chapter 5 raised the issue that the performance of the private sector has to be seen against the goals and product market strategies that enterprises set for themselves. Chapter 5 also demonstrated that these private sector goals set by managers may not be in line with those of shareholders, and Chapter 7 that, even if aligned with shareholders, they still may not lead to the socially optimal outcome. In particular, it has been argued that, on balance, companies may find it more profitable to adopt a low-skills, low-wage trajectory, rather than a high-skills, high-income trajectory. Just as it is the role of governance structures to align the goals and strategies of managers to maximize the benefits to owners, it is the role of government to align the goals and strategies of companies to maximize social welfare.

A second theme of the present chapter concerns the idea of synergies, particularly, though not exclusively, where these are associated with externalities with implications for government intervention. Examples include the results from Chapters 8 and 9, such as R&D, education and training externalities. Finally, the present discussion also returns to the concept of latent skill shortages, drawing on Chapters 5 and 9, with respect to the inter-relationship between skill demands and the goals and strategies of the firm.

Virtuous (or vicious) circles leading to the growth (or decline) of both the economy and income levels are intimately related to the skills and competences within society and, thereby, the education and training systems in place to generate those skills and competences (see, for example, Finegold and Mason, 1999). However, Chapter 9 provided considerable evidence of the likely failure of any policy that focuses on skills alone. The analysis demonstrated that, in a static economy, the move to higher transferable and general skills tends to result in higher salaries and greater capital intensity, which also requires the firm to maintain the rate of return on capital. Thus, the improvements to labour productivity and TFP are absorbed by higher costs, with profit rates and MV left largely unchanged. The enterprise is left indifferent between low- and high-skill trajectories, and other factors, such as ageing products, draw the firm into a low-skills trajectory. The present chapter argues that, for society to make progress in the growth of productivity and incomes, it must provide an environment that stimulates a larger proportion of enterprises to choose a high-skills, high-quality trajectory. Chapters 9 and 13 suggested that this requires the adoption of systems of HPWPs, consistent with these 'up-market' goals, resulting in improvements in firm-specific skills, innovation, productivity, value added and more profitable products and services.

Thus, the discussion of Chapter 9 indicated the need for skills improvements to be accompanied by an expansion of incentives for firms to move 'up-market' rather than 'down-market'. Following Finegold and Soskice (1988), this is viewed as a 'systems problem' in which a wide range of factors impinge on the opportunities and incentives that firms face. The government plays a central role in this because, to a large degree, it sets the environment – in effect the NIS – within which companies operate (Lundvall *et al.*, 2002). It seems that the NIS is a crucial determinant of the likely success and, thereby, the extent of innovation in a given country. Popper and Wagner (2002, p. ix), in discussing the USA's relative success in scientific and technological innovation, argue that:

> The system that supports this process [the NIS] has emerged as one of our most important national assets, as [an] important source for growth today and in the future as have been in the past the nation's natural resource endowment, the talents and dedication of its workforce, and the accumulated stock of capital goods.

Section 14.2 examines the idea of a 'systems failure', looking at the concepts of 'low-skills equilibrium' and 'low-skills trajectories'. Section 14.3 provides a discussion of some of the key features of NISs, as well as some of the strengths and weaknesses of this concept. Section 14.4 considers the empirical evidence that throws light on how well the UK economy is performing in terms of the desired 'virtuous circles'. The picture painted is not all black, but the evidence points to many areas of weakness, where the UK's dynamic performance appears less than acceptable given its status as one of the largest industrialized countries. Then, section 14.5 examines a range of possible government interventions – both demand and supply side – that would simultaneously improve a number of different strands of the 'system'. Finally, section 14.6 draws the main conclusions of the policy debate.

14.2   Consequences of a systems failure

The whole point about a system is that it is not governed by rules of strict proportionality or constant returns to scale. Popper and Wagner (2002, pp. 7–8) argue that:

> relatively small innovations and developments of new technology may lead to results almost beyond our imagining, as we have witnessed only in the last decade with the advent of the internet and the world wide web. Relatively small investments in knowledge creation may lead to large dividends in more familiar form such as enhanced productivity, more sustainable economic activity, and richer, healthier, and more fulfilling lives.

Equally, however, when systems fail, they have important consequences and can be difficult to remedy. There are at least two principal consequences of a systems failure – the economy may be characterized by:

(i)   low skill levels (low-skills equilibrium) or falling skill levels (low-skills trajectory);
(ii)   low rates of innovation (technological stagnation) or falling rates of innovation (technological slowdown).

Finegold and Soskice (1988, p. 22) portray the UK, as the result of such systems failure, as being trapped in a low-skills equilibrium 'in which the majority of enterprises [are] staffed by poorly trained managers and workers produce low quality goods and services'. They argue that, by this, they mean a systems failure arising from a 'self-reinforcing network of societal and state institutions which interact to stifle the demand for improvements in skill levels' (p. 22). Chapter 9 argued that shareholders and firms have no preference *per se* for a high- or a low-skills route – or if they have, the choice is nevertheless dominated by which is the more profitable. Individuals and firms act rationally in terms of the incentives they face and, as a consequence, if the low-skills route is the more profitable, it is possible for the economy to gravitate to a low-skills equilibrium – even though society would prefer a high-skill/high-income trajectory. In coming to this rational decision, however, many diverse influences play a part – the 'system' – and the low-skills equilibrium can be viewed as the outcome of a 'systems failure'. A systems failure offers a complex policy problem – the message of dynamical systems is that changing any one element of the system may not, indeed probably will not, bring the required policy outcome – it may even produce a perverse or chaotic result (Kaplin and Glass, 1995).

While the concepts of high- and low-skills equilibria help to focus the mind, it is difficult to think of the UK as being in a low-skills equilibrium, for a number of reasons. First, the UK economy has much higher skill levels than many other economies, although perhaps not as high as it would like *vis-à-vis* its main competitor nations. Thus, the concept is diluted by the fact that a low-skills equilibrium must be a relative concept (Hogarth and Wilson, 2003). Second, the concept cannot be applied across the whole of the UK, at least not to the same extent. There are clearly pockets of very high as well as very low skills levels within the UK. The issue is one of balance between high and low skills, and this issue is crucial in the sense of matching the demand for and supply of skills at any given point in time and, in doing so, providing gainful employment and incomes for the mix of skills that exist within the economy. Third, equilibrium has static connotations, whereas individuals and firms are changing their skill levels over time – some upwards and some downwards. Again, from society's viewpoint, it is the *changing* mix of skill levels that is important – 'skills trajectories', which makes the 'systems' concept even more relevant.

14.3 National innovation systems

14.3.1 *Skills and innovation literatures*

The focus of the NIS literature is generally somewhat different to what the commentators on the low-skills equilibrium have in mind (e.g. Ashton *et al.*, 2003; Finegold and Soskice, 1988). For example, while Ashton *et al.* (2003) discuss many of the elements of the NIS likely to raise the demand for skilled labour, they do not focus on the institutions that raise innovation activity *per se*. Equally, while individuals writing about NISs from a technology management perspective discuss the issue of education and skills, their focus tends to be on the institutional framework that raises innovation activity. What is needed is a synthesis of the two; for example, the aim of the system is not innovation for innovation's sake, but the maintenance and creation of employment opportunities, alongside growth in real incomes. The NIS literature errs on the side of exploration/innovation and the skills literature errs on the side of exploitation (see Chapters 12 and 13). Exploitation allows firms to earn profits from earlier innovations, which in turn fund exploration of new innovatory activities, which offer higher future incomes and profits (Chapter 8). Thus, while the present chapter has something broader in mind than the traditional view of the NIS, the term is well established and helps the present discussion focus on the key issues.

14.3.2 *Institutions, agents and their inter-relationships*

Metcalfe (1995, pp. 462–463) defines a NIS as follows:

> [the] set of distinct institutions which jointly and individually contribute to the development and diffusion of new technologies and which provide the framework within which governments form and implement policies to influence the innovation process. As such it is a system of interconnected institutions to create, store and transfer the knowledge, skills and artifacts which define new technologies.

Popper and Wagner (2002, p. ix) argue that:

> this system constitutes a dense and complex network of interconnected parts. The major actors in this system – the private sector, government agencies and labs, universities, the non-profit research sector – relate to each other in complex ways neither easy to describe nor trace through the system.

Branscomb and Auerswald (2003) outline the burgeoning growth and diversity in the USA of:

> institutions specializing in supporting the commercial development and marketing of new technologies. These include venture capital firms, corporate venture funds, incubators of various types, niche law firms, university and government offices of technology transfer, and networks of individual private angel investors.

Branscomb and Auerwald (2000, p. 3) had earlier argued that:

> The pace of development is accelerating and is changing the innovation system. With advances in science and engineering, increased global competition, and decreasing product cycle times, innovators must learn to reduce market and technological risks concurrently. Thus the linear model of innovation, known to be inappropriate for the evolutionary process that characterises most of industry, is increasingly inappropriate for science-based innovations as well.

Popper and Wagner (2002, p. 7) also see the NIS as not only as complex, but also as dynamic and adaptive:

> The system is characterized by the self-organization of its own structure. Rather than being crafted according to any previously planned design, the network of institutions and linkages has arisen through myriad actions taken by the system's constituent agents.

Thus, company behaviour and the institutional framework co-evolve over time (Coriat and Weinstein, 2002; Nelson and Nelson, 2002, p. 271).

Smith (1996) notes that the performance of an NIS depends on both the performance of the individual institutions that comprise it and on their interaction as part of a collective system of knowledge creation and use, as well as their interplay with social institutions (e.g. values, norms, legal frameworks).

Johnson and Jacobsson (2000, pp. 3–4) propose five functions of the NIS:

(i)   to create new knowledge;
(ii)   to guide the direction of the search process;
(iii) to supply resources (capital, competence, etc.);
(iv)   to facilitate the creation of positive external economies (e.g. in the exchange of information, knowledge and visions);
(v)   to facilitate the formation of markets.

Rickne (2000) outlines the functions of the actors in the NIS:

(i)   to create human capital;
(ii)   to create and diffuse technological opportunities;
(iii)   to create and diffuse products;
(iv)   to incubate (i.e. provide facilities, equipment and administrative support);
(v)   to regulate technologies, materials and products that enlarge the market and enhance market access;
(vi)   to legitimize technologies and firms;
(vii)   to create markets and diffuse market knowledge;
(viii) to enhance networking;
(ix)   to direct technology, market and partner research;
(x)   to facilitate financing;
(xi)   to create an appropriate labour market.

Edquist (2001, p. 19) argues that there are a number of sources of systems failure:

(i)   functions in the system of innovation may be inappropriate or missing;
(ii)   organizations and institutions may be inappropriate or missing;
(ii)   interactions or links between these elements in the system of innovation may be inappropriate or missing.

14.3.3 *Scope of the NIS*

Nelson and Rosenberg (1993) note that the underlying NIS concept can be attacked because it is both too narrow and too broad:

(i)   it is narrow in that technology and business is increasingly transnational (see also Chesnais, 1992, pp. 267–268; Chesnais, 1995);

(ii)   it is too broad in that the innovation system for a sector does not involve the whole NIS, and sectors use different parts of the NIS to different degrees (see also Malerba, 2002, p. 261).

According to Branscomb and Auerwald (2000, p. 3):

> Innovation systems exist on intersecting scales – including the corporation, the city/region, the nation, and the transnational region – and may be quite different for different technologies. This is why institutions (stable [but evolving] networks of incentives/contracts/trust) are important.

Finegold (1999) introduces an analogous concept of spatially delimited skills 'eco-systems', comprising a network of actors who propagate a virtuous cycle of skill development. Freeman (2002, p. 209), however, concentrates on:

> developments at the *national* level in the belief that the major phenomena of forging ahead, catch-up and falling behind ... can most plausibly be explained in terms of national systems, albeit in an international context and recognizing uneven development at the sub-national level.

He adds, however, that this may not be the case in the future and, later in the present chapter (see section 14.5.7), the discussion turns to policies at the sub-national level (i.e. spatial and technological clusters).

14.4   Empirical evidence for the UK

14.4.1 *Nature of the empirical evidence*

In the present section, it is possible to give only the briefest overview of the comparative position of the UK (for further information see Department of Trade and Industry, 2003). Given that the UK has been suggested to be in a low-skills equilibrium, this section begins by providing a range of evidence relating to skills and the workforce, as well as scientific and technological activities, to see if there is unambiguous evidence that this is the case. The discussion then turns to the related (and crucial) issue of whether UK products are of a lower specification than those of the country's main competitors. While the discussion is couched in terms of the UK, some comparative international data are presented. Care is needed in considering the position of each country, as these positions change over time (as government policies change).

14.4.2 *Evidence of education and skills*

The starting point for understanding low-skills equilibrium must be the education system. It is important to note, however, that educational qualifications are only tenuously related to skills. The analysis then turns to a brief discussion of international differences in skills.

Educational differences

The UK ranks about tenth out of twenty-one OECD countries for which data were provided in terms of the proportion of young people completing tertiary education in 2002/03 – about the same as the average (21 per cent of young people) across all OECD countries. The UK is ranked fourth among the nine countries listed in Table 14.1 in terms of the proportion of students completing upper secondary education, but fifth out of nine in terms of both the proportion completing tertiary education and average years of schooling (see Table 14.1).

Table 14.2 provides data for expenditure per student for the same set of key European countries and the USA. It can be seen that the UK's performance with regard to primary school pupils is extremely poor, with a rank of eighth out of the nine countries. UK expenditure per student is only just over half that of the USA. The rank for secondary and tertiary education is not much better, at seventh out of the nine. In the case of tertiary education, in particular, the UK spends less than half the amount per student than the USA.

Measures of the extent to which each country's education system meets the needs of its economy in terms of maintaining or improving competitiveness are reported by the IMD (see Figure 14.1). While the rankings here may be something of a surprise, they reflect the match between the position of the economy (i.e. the needs of the economy given its present economic and technological position) *vis-à-vis* the supply of educated labour. The USA and, to some degree, Germany as technological and economic leaders require a higher contribution from their education systems. It can be seen that the UK (ranked seventh) still does quite poorly by this measure.

Table 14.1 Students' completion rates (percentage of all students) and years of schooling

	Upper secondary or higher	Rank	Tertiary	Rank	Years of schooling	Rank
USA	86	1	33	1	13.5	1
Germany	84	2	23	3	13.4	2
Netherlands	61	6	22	4	12.7	3
Switzerland	82	3	21	5	12.6	4
UK	76	4	21	5	12.1	5
Belgium	53	7	25	2	11.7	6
France	68	5	19	8	11.2	7
Ireland	47	8	20	7	10.8	8
Italy	35	9	8	9	10.0	9

Table 14.2 Expenditure per student, 2003

Country	Primary		Secondary		Tertiary	
	US$	Rank	US$	Rank	US$	Rank
USA	6,995	1	8,885	2	20,358	1
Switzerland	6,631	2	9,780	1	18,450	2
Netherlands	4,325	3	5,912	8	11,934	3
Belgium	4,310	4	6,889	5	10,771	6
Germany	4,198	5	6,826	6	10,898	5
Italy	5,973	6	7,218	4	8,065	9
France	4,486	7	7,636	3	8,337	8
UK	3,627	8	5,991	7	9,657	7
Ireland	3,385	9	4,638	9	11,083	4

Source: OECD, *Education at a Glance*, 2003 (www.oecd.org).

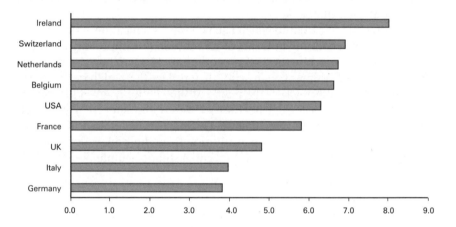

Figure 14.1 Extent to which the national education system meets the needs of a competitive economy. Source: IMD (2004).

Skills

It is more difficult to obtain statistical information about the skills and competences of the workforces *per se*, or even the amount of resources devoted by government, companies and individuals to training. According to Finegold and Soskice (1988, pp. 22–24), the evidence at the time they were writing was fairly unambiguous, in that the UK exhibited an education and training failure. They argued that 'Workers' lack of initial qualifications is not compensated for by increased employer-based training; on the contrary, British firms offer a lower quality and quantity of training than their counterparts on the Continent' (p. 23). One of the most important sources (the earlier elements of which Finegold and Soskice used in their analysis) is the large volume of case-study evidence from the National Institute for Economic and Social Research (NIESR). This work, based upon matched pairs of case-study companies in the UK and Germany (as well as other advanced countries), has been a continuing cause for worry regarding the level of education and skills of the UK workforce (see also Chapters 6 and 9).

The UK also has an extremely poor record on vocational qualifications (Learning and Skills Council, 2003). Although, according the Learning Skills Council (2003, p. 17), 'the UK has one of the highest levels of workers participating in training', the Department of Trade and Industry (2001, p. 35) found that:

> about one third of employees report never having being offered any kind of training by their current employer during the last year. And, despite a broad definition, the National Adult Learning Survey found that 26% of respondents (or 8 million) said in 1997 that they had done no learning in the previous three years, or since leaving full-time education if that was more recent.

While the International Adult Literacy Survey shows that adult education and training have become the rule rather than the exception in the UK, countries divide into three broad groups (Department of Trade and Industry, 2001, p. 34):

(i)   the Nordic countries – where overall participation rates in lifelong learning reach over 50 per cent;
(ii) a middle group of countries, forming the majority (including the UK), with participation rates of around 40 per cent;
(iii) countries where lifelong learning is less common, with participation rates generally between 20 and 30 per cent or less.

There are other elements to the story – the more qualified are much more likely to receive training and acquire skills in later life than the less qualified. According to the Department of Trade and Industry (2001, p. 35), 'Current levels of training are unlikely to raise the qualification levels of the significant number of adults with no or low level qualifications or improve the vocational qualifications[1] at levels 2 and 3 in the UK relative to its competitors'. In addition, the duration of training in the UK is shorter than in most other comparable countries, which implies that it is likely to have a higher informal (possibly off-the-job) content, which may be less effective. The Department of Trade and Industry (2001) reported that the UK ranked seventh in terms of the average hours of training per person out of the thirteen OECD countries for which information was available.

The UK has fewer formal, certificated, intermediate-level qualifications than most other OECD countries (OECD, 1998). The differences between the UK, France and Germany (Department of Trade and Industry, 2001, p. 33) at level 2+ are clear enough, but the differences at level 3+ are particularly marked. The Department of Trade and Industry (2001, p. 33) concluded:

> Compared with Germany, at least, the main reason for this deficit is the lower proportion of the UK workforce with intermediate level vocational qualifications. The deficit is even greater when considering that continental Europe takes longer to gain qualifications, particularly vocational ones. The gap in intermediate vocational qualifications for the 25–28 year old group remains considerable. Additional research also suggests that over 90% of 25–28 year olds in Japan are qualified to level 3 or above.

The implications in terms of Solo's (1966) pyramid of skills for the absorption of innovations are clear (see sections 9.5.2 and 12.4.4).

Support for the role of both generic and vocational skills can be found in the literature – Layard *et al*. (2001), for example, suggest that basic literacy and numeracy, as well as intermediate vocational and technical skills, may be an important source of low productivity in the UK *vis-à-vis* its main competitors. According to the Department of Trade and Industry (2001), the UK was ranked tenth out of the twelve countries shown (the USA did little better, and only the Ireland and Poland were lower). While the position may have improved significantly in the UK, with the proportion of the workforce with no qualifications falling from about 50 per cent in 1979 to 10 per cent in 1999, it is reported that 'over 50% of the workforce still have either a low level of qualifications or none at all. Although poor qualification levels do not necessarily mean poor basic skills, there is a strong correlation between the two' (Department of Trade and Industry, 2001, p. 30). Finally, the Moser (1999) report estimated that around 7 million adults in the UK are functionally illiterate (i.e. about 20 per cent of adults read less well than the level expected at age eleven; in addition, nearly 50 per cent have numeracy skills below that level). Compounding this, as noted above, those with lower literacy are less likely to receive training to upgrade their skills (Department of Trade and Industry, 2001, p. 30).

Broader labour market issues and systems failure
Given that the low-skills equilibrium is purportedly the result of a systems failure, it is important to consider other labour market factors – see Table 14.3 for some comparative international results. The IMD reports that in terms of worker motivation the UK ranked seventh out of nine European countries and the USA. Its view of the compliance of British trade unions was somewhat more positive, as on this measure the UK ranked

Table 14.3 Broad labour market issues: an international comparison

Country	Worker motivation		Trade union compliance		Most likely to succeed in knowl-edge industries	
	Score[a]	Rank	Score[b]	Rank	Points[c]	Rank
Switzerland	7.90	1	8.29	1	52	1
USA	7.20	2	6.93	4	40	2
Ireland	7.16	3	7.26	3	38	3
Netherlands	7.08	4	7.46	2	33	4
Germany	6.42	5	6.33	6	26	7
Belgium	6.40	6	5.69	7	29	5
UK	5.78	7	6.61	5	28	6
Italy	5.28	8	4.87	8	10	9
France	4.72	9	3.63	9	15	8

[a]Worker motivation is high (maximum = 10) or low (minimum = 1).
[b]Labour relations are hostile (most = 1) or productive (least = 10).
[c]Most likely to succeed (maximum = 100), least likely (minimum = 0) (Marsh, 2001).
Source: IMD (2004).

fifth out of the nine countries reported. In analysing the extent to which these countries are likely to succeed in the knowledge-based economy, Marsh (2001) ranks the UK sixth, but a long way behind the USA and Switzerland.

14.4.3 *Scientific and technological activities*

Key indicators of long-term dynamism include scientific publications, R&D and patenting activity (see Chapter 4), as well as NPLs (see Chapter 8). It is clear that many of these themes are closely related, and it is interesting to see if a consistent picture begins to emerge *vis-à-vis* the discussion of education and skills outlined above. Based upon the number of publications, the UK appears to be well placed in terms of its scientific activity in many discipline areas. The UK was ranked second, behind the USA (out of twenty-five countries reported),[2] in terms of the total number of scientific and engineering papers published in 1990–94 (Department of Industry, Science and Technology, 1996). While the UK was only seventh in terms of science and engineering papers per head of population, it was sixth in terms of the effect of those publications, based upon citation counts.

Chapter 8 demonstrated that R&D activities have important implications for government investment, because of the major externalities/spillovers that arise from the common pool of R&D knowledge. What is surprising, however, is the apparently low extent of government support for R&D in the UK (Department of Trade and Industry, 2001) – both the UK and the USA are below the OECD average, and in the same group of countries

Table 14.4 Investment in research and development, 2000

Country	Total expenditure on R&D[a]				Business R&D[b]		Competitive role of basic R&D[c]	
	as % of GDP	Rank	*per capita* (US$)	Rank	as % of GDP	Rank	Score[d]	Rank
Switzerland	2.731	1	1,143.20	1	2.32	2	8.13	2
USA	2.687	2	936.80	2	2.36	1	8.54	1
Germany	2.460	3	559.90	3	2.17	3	6.94	4
France	2.143	4	471.80	6	1.85	4	6.44	6
Netherlands	2.024	5	509.80	4	1.46	7	6.81	5
Belgium	1.961	6	481.00	5	1.70	6	6.11	8
UK	1.849	7	453.20	7	1.75	5	7.14	3
Ireland	1.608	8	302.20	8	1.34	8	6.28	7
Italy	1.040	9	213.20	9	0.73	9	3.76	9

Sources: [a]IMD – see http://www.geneva.ch/research_development.htm#ancre3; [b]OECD (2002); [c]IMD (2004).
[d] Extent to which basic research enhances long-term economic development (maximum = 10 and minimum = 1).

as Poland, Hungary, Turkey and Mexico, among others. Table 14.4 sets out information about total R&D intensity (R&D per unit of GDP[3] and per capita) for nine countries for the year 2000. While the two series give slightly different rankings, the conclusions for the UK are broadly the same – the UK is ranked seventh out of the nine, but, more importantly, is significantly below the corresponding ratios for Switzerland and the USA. In the case of R&D per capita, the UK spends well under half the amount of Switzerland. Further evidence is provided in Table 14.4, which shows business R&D as a percentage of GDP and the extent to which basic R&D is viewed as contributing to future competitiveness. In both cases, the UK does better than on the other measures, being ranked fifth in the former case and third in the latter.

Figure 14.2 shows business R&D intensity broken down according to whether the area is high- or low-technology manufacturing. Results for four other countries are reported relative to the UK (UK = 100). While some reassurance might be found in the fact that the UK performs better relative to the other four countries in the high- than in the low-technology areas, it still only just keeps up with Japan and Germany in the high-technology areas and is worse than the USA and France. Where the UK appears to be failing is in the medium-high and particularly the low-technology areas. This result may be particularly insightful – competition in these areas tends to come from less radical product innovation and increased efficiency (fewer workers, with the potential to maintain wages) or from lower costs (i.e. moving to less skilled workers and lower

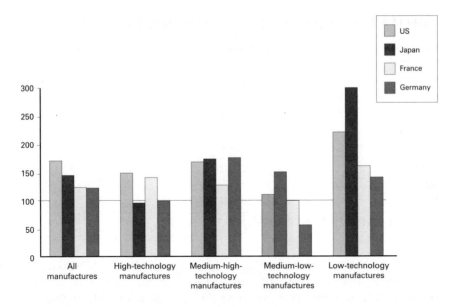

Figure 14.2 Business enterprise R&D intensity by level of technology (relative index of R&D as a portion of value added, UK = 100). Source: OECD reported by Department of Trade and Industry (2001, p. 50).

wages) – see Chapter 9 and section 14.4.4. The result implies that the UK has opted for (or been forced into) cost-reducing (rather than efficiency increasing) strategies in these low-technology areas. It is likely that the lower skill levels in the UK in these technology areas not only make the 'up-market' route unviable, but also its adoption of a cost-reducing (rather than the efficiency-increasing) route makes it difficult to maintain skill and income levels.

According to Metcalfe *et al.* (2003, p. 17) studies suggest that differences in R&D expenditures account for around a quarter of the productivity gap between the UK and the USA and a sixth of the gap with France. The authors conclude that innovation is one of the most important influences on productivity, with a significance comparable with investment, capital intensity, skills, enterprise and competitive markets.

The UK does not perform well in terms of patenting activity (measured by the extent of patenting activity in the USA) – it lies sixth among the G7 countries reported by the Department of Trade and Industry (2001) and way behind other countries in terms of patents per head (Table 14.5). Given the relative strength of the UK science base, this seems to be consistent with the long-held belief that the UK is better at 'inventing' than 'innovating'. In addition, over the period 1994–96, the UK ranked

Table 14.5 Patent applications per million inhabitants

Country	Patent applications	Rank
Switzerland	249.5	1
Netherlands	151.7	3
UK	74.2	7
USA	90.0	6
Belgium	110.0	4
France	102.7	5
Germany	209.9	2
Ireland	34.6	9
Italy	54.2	8

Source: OECD (2002), 'Patent database, May 2001'.

only tenth among European Union countries in terms of introducing technologies that are new not only to the firm but also to the market (Department of Trade and Industry, 2001). Figure 14.3 shows that, in terms of the share of manufacturing turnover that arises from the sale of new or improved products (Department of Trade and Industry, 2001), the UK ranked only eighth in the list of European Union countries in 1996, with a figure well below the overall Union average (with a share around half that of Germany).

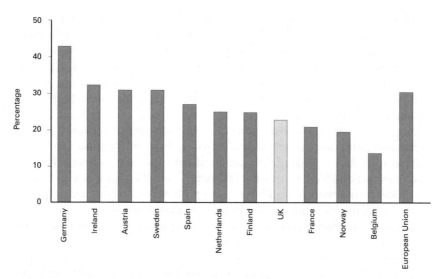

Figure 14.3 Share of manufacturing turnover from new/improved products, 1994–1996. Source: Eurostat (Community Innovation Survey) (reported in Department of Trade and Industry, 2001, p. 58).

14.4.4 *Product specification and quality*

The link between low skills and low product specification was introduced in Chapter 13. Del Bono and Mayhew (2001) argue that, if the UK is in a low-skills equilibrium, there should be evidence that its products are of a lower specification than those of its main competitors. The authors point to the case-study evidence, mainly from the NIESR comparisons of UK and German companies (Del Bono and Mayhew, 2001, pp. 9–13). The idea of the case studies was to match production units in terms of the type and quality of their output, with a view to exploring productivity differences. However, the problems the NIESR researchers experienced in finding matching establishments suggest that UK and German firms often operate in different quality ranges (segments) of the market. Mason and Wagner (2002, p. 88), for example, argue that:

> The German components industry also benefits from the greater involvement of German automotive industry in production of 'luxury' grades of car which contributes to a relatively high average value added per unit of output in many German supplier plants. In addition some German suppliers specialise in manufacturing high value added components and sub-assemblies which are simply not made any more in Britain.

Del Bono and Mayhew (2001, pp. 9–10) argue that 'the majority of these studies show Britain at a substantial disadvantage in producing goods and services of quality comparable to that observed in other European countries'.

Hooley *et al.* (1988) carried out a survey of a large sample of companies operating in the UK. Their findings are reassuring in that as many UK companies as foreign companies viewed their competitive advantage as arising from non-price factors. The results reported by Doyle *et al.* (1992), however, are less positive. Their survey of ninety US, Japanese and British companies competing in the UK market suggested that, while around 20 per cent of British companies viewed their products as being relatively cheap and 'down-market', none of the US or Japanese companies considered this a valid description of their activities. British companies perceived their competitive advantages to lie in low prices, traditional brand names and 'being British'. The results indicated that British firms are over-represented in low-value-added market segments; US companies tended to be in the high-technology niches; and, while Japanese firms covered all areas (including mass markets), they were increasingly entering high-value-added areas.

Del Bono and Mayhew (2001, pp. 17–33) consider what light import and export prices (and volumes) throws on international quality differentials. Taken at face value, the evidence suggests that the UK's comparative advantage is probably in the low-value-added activities, particularly in the early period (i.e. the 1970s). Oulton (1996) argues that while, on average, the quality of UK exports was about the same as those of Germany, Germany exhibited significantly higher volumes. In other words, Germany is less 'capacity constrained' because of its more highly skilled workers, which enables it to export higher volumes of high-quality goods. A number of such studies also include measures of R&D, patents and so on in import and export equations, as proxies for the changes in quality. Fagerberg's (1988) results suggested that non-price competitiveness is the principal factor influencing differences in international competitiveness and growth. Greenhalgh (1990) and Greenhalgh *et al.* (1994) demonstrated a role for some measure of 'innovation', such as patenting activity, on trade volumes and the balance of trade, although their impact on export prices could be positive or negative. Anderton (1996) reported that increases in UK patenting relative to other countries decreased import volumes, although the effect on export volumes was less clear cut. These results should be seen against the evidence presented in this chapter that the UK's R&D and patenting activity is not only low but has declined relative to those of many of its main competitors.

Thus, on balance, Del Bono and Mayhew (2001) conclude that 'in contrast to the Government's vision of a high skills/high value added economy, British producers tend to pursue a low specification – low skills strategy'.

14.4.5 *Evidence of trajectories*

This section explores data on trajectories in education, R&D and patenting. On balance, participation rates in higher education in the UK have been rising and, at least until recently, the government had a notional target of 50 per cent of young people entering higher education. However, one major consequence of the growing numbers of students has been falling unit funding (see Figure 14.4) – although the government is well aware of the current funding crisis in higher education and the implications for graduate quality if no action is taken.

The UK's track record in R&D was poor relative to its major international competitors during the second half of the twentieth century. The R&D/GDP ratio for the UK was about the same in the 1990s as it was in the 1960s. The trend of this ratio relative to the USA and Japan was markedly downwards (see Figure 14.5 for a comparison with Japan). Case-study evidence confirms this result:

> Not only is the scale of automotive R&D much larger in Germany than Britain but the gap appears to be growing as even some British-owned companies have recently started to cut back on R&D employment in Britain and expand it in Germany (or neighbouring countries). (Mason and Wagner, 2002, p. 93)

Worrying trends in UK patenting activity *vis-à-vis* the country's main industrial competitors have also been widely noted (Greenhalgh *et al.*, 2000; Patel and Pavitt, 1995). In a study of the activities of UK companies

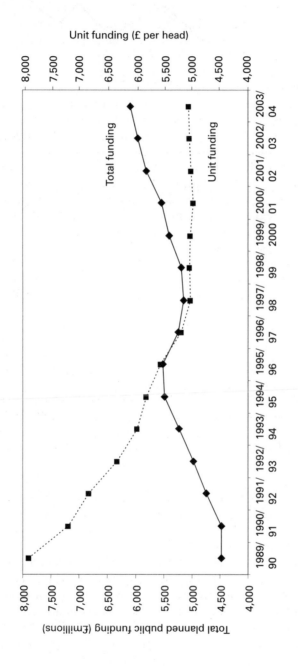

Figure 14.4 Comparison of total public funding of higher education (£million, 2001/2002 prices) and unit funding (£, 2001/2002 prices), 1989–2003. Source: Government white paper, *The Future of Higher Education*, Cm 5735 (2003).

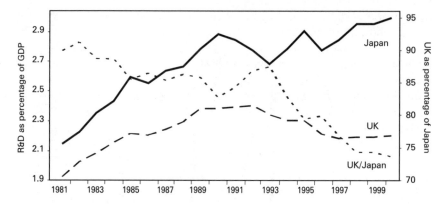

Figure 14.5 R&D expenditure per unit of GDP, UK and Japan, and the ratio of the two (UK/Japan, %), 1981–2000. Source: http://international.tamu.edu/eucenter/Teich%20Presentation.pdf.

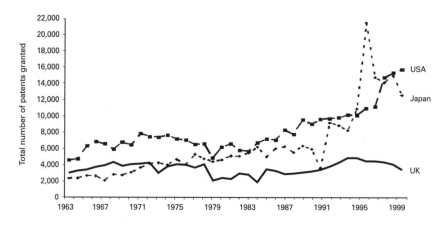

Figure 14.6 Number of patent grants in the UK, USA and Japan, 1963–1999. Source: Constructed from World Intellectual Property Organization historical data (see www.wipo.int/ipstats/en/).

in the 1980s and 1990s, Greenhalgh *et al.* (2000) concluded that 'a major fall ... in the rate of patenting in Britain appears not to be explained solely by a shift to applications directly via Europe. The fall in IP protection affects areas of historical importance to high technology production in the UK.' Figure 14.6 shows the total numbers of patents granted protection in each country (irrespective of the country of origin of the patent applications and the route sought for protection[4]). The important thing to note from Figure 14.6 is the static nature of the total UK activity, which rises by only about 12 per cent over the period as a whole. This small growth in activity should be compared with an approximately 3.5-fold increase in the USA and a 5.5-fold increase in Japan.[5] A further worrying trend is that, against the background of the largely static UK total patenting activity, the proportion of those patents granted to UK resident individuals and companies fell from about 35 per cent of the total at the beginning of the period down to about 10 per cent by the end. The USA shows a similar downward trend in the proportion from domestic sources (80 per cent to around 55 per cent), although against a background of a significant overall rise in patenting activity. The major growth in the total of Japanese patents in Figure 14.6, however, is associated with a growth in domestic activity from about 65 per cent to 85 per cent – Japan is one of the few economies to show such a trend in domestic activity.

14.5   Implications for government policy

14.5.1 *Background*

The evidence outlined above does not paint a very favourable picture of either the UK's position or of the key trends, such as in R&D and patenting – in most respects, the UK is punching below its weight. Where to begin, what to do and what consequences might flow from policy interventions are complicated questions – the fact that the system is complex and is, in part at least, adaptive, endogenously designed and evolutionary in nature makes policy design difficult and risky. Yet doing nothing is not an option.

The early literature focusing on changes to the NIS perhaps concentrated too much on the supply side of the system, while the current discussion focuses more on the interaction of supply and demand at each point in time within the system as a whole. This balance of policies on both the supply and demand sides is crucially important in the transitional phase as the government attempts to move the economy from a low-skills/low-innovation trajectory to a high-skills/high-innovation one. Increasing the skill levels is a waste of resources if the demand for skills (the wages paid and company profits) do not also rise; likewise, there is no use in stimulating the demand for higher-specification products if a lack of skills does not allow UK companies to produce them. It is essential for the changing supplies and demands of higher skills to be only marginally out of line, but on a rising trajectory, if the transition is to be smooth and successful.

It has been demonstrated that the effect on the growth of the economy of improvements to skills alone is severely limited unless these additional skills generate a more dynamic environment in which new technological and market niches evolve at a higher rate. While higher-quality labour is likely to raise both labour productivity and TFP, a limit is set by the higher incomes required by the more skilled labour and the need to maintain the rate of return on capital. Even if the improvements in labour quality give rise to new high-value-added niches, it seems likely that – insofar as skills predate the development of such niches – some form of government intervention may be required to match the nature and timing of the availability of the two.

A report by Branscomb and Auerswald (2003, p. 2), in outlining evidence of some of the underlying relationships known to be necessary for a successful NIS, suggests what is probably the current view of the way forward:

> Scholars have produced a solid body of knowledge about innovation systems; economic behaviour in the face of technological risk, uncertainty and incomplete information; and social capital, regional agglomeration and industry clustering. We now know that the early development of a novel technology depends on academic science, which generates the ideas that drive the innovation process; on the magnitude and geographical localization of knowledge spillovers; and on the social returns from investments in R&D, including those made by the federal government.

Again, while this brings together a wide range of the issues, if anything the emphasis tends to remain rather on the supply side; the discussion in section 14.5.8 attempts to redress this bias.

14.5.2 *Organization of government*

The days of the 'mission-oriented'[6] approach to large-scale, heavily subsidized R&D programmes (as in aerospace, telecommunications, etc.) – particularly linked to the development of 'national champions' – appear to be over (Scherer and Harhoff, 2000, p. 562; Walker, 1993, p. 185). However, there are grounds for government to step back from its ever-increasing demand for (and narrow interpretation of) 'value for money' – accepting only projects that will meet strict performance criteria, within budget. The government has to accept that, while strict accounting of research inputs and outputs is essential to good decision making, some proportion of the research projects it supports should be inherently risky and should not all be expected to break even or make a profit – it may be acceptable for a minority to do so, as long as the returns on this minority are sufficiently large. Scherer and Harhoff (2000, p. 562) argue as follows:

> Legislators and senior government leaders are likely to view government technology programs in which half the supported projects fail to yield appreciable returns and only one in 10 succeeds handsomely as a rather poor track record when in fact, by the standards of private sector markets it is quite normal. Those who are responsible for the allocation of financial resources to support the advance of technology should adjust their expectations accordingly.

In addition, the items that enter the government's calculation should be broader than the profits generated. Clearly, the government does not want to support unprofitable activities *per se*, but it should bear in mind the 'options' value of maintaining a capability in a particular area of science or technology. In addition, if the commercialized outcome is to create 1,000 jobs for a ten-year period, where the counterfactual would have been 1,000 individuals drawing benefits, then the social returns to the investment may be high even if the new company earns only normal profits.

Successive governments and, in particular, government departments need to build a capacity for corporate memory. This appears to be largely absent at the moment and is typified by the high rates of turnover of civil servants (albeit often between departments). Just as firms are expected to be learning organizations, so should the government as well – where are the 'learning silos' in government departments? Walker (1993, p. 187) makes exactly this point: 'In no other advanced country has the government department responsible for industrial policy so frequently changed its name, its internal organisation, or its Minister (six times in the 1980s alone, against twice in the Treasury)'. This has led to a lack of continuity of policy: 'Looking back over the past 30 years, one is struck, when comparisons are made with other countries, by the instability – and the lack of true cooperation – that have marked the state's relationship with the industrial sector in Britain' (Walker, 1993, p. 187). In addition, the results reported in the present book, particularly in the context of systems problems and failures, suggest the need for effective coordinated joint action by a number of government departments (notably the Department of Trade and Industry, the Department for Education and Skills, the Department for Work and Pensions, and the Treasury). While the present government appears to be making a concerted attempt to coordinate parts of the system, this still seems to be at an early stage and it is not at all clear how effective it is.

14.5.3 *Government support for the science and technology base*

The evidence suggests that public funding for higher education and R&D is too low in the UK. While a number of private sector companies working in areas close to the science base have become more involved with basic research, Arrow's (1962) arguments with regard to the inability of firms to appropriate the returns to basic research still apply. Again, such research, by its very nature, is highly risky and there should be no presumption by government that every project should be successful.

It might be argued that in areas where government-funded research is more applied, the risks should be lower and evidence should exist of similar rates of return to those sought by private investors. However, the Office of Technology Assessment (1986, p. 3) in the USA argues that, while the evidence suggests high private returns and even higher social returns to private sector R&D, 'Economists ... have not been able to show comparable returns, and at times been unable to show any returns, on Federal R&D expenditures, except for some applied research programmes in agriculture, aeronautics, and energy designed to improve industrial productivity'. This should not be too surprising, for at least two keys reasons. First, if there is a high private rate of return earned, then the government should leave research to the private sector – though it should take measures to encourage increased private investment where the social rate of return exceeds the private rate of return (see below). Second, in some of the areas where the government is directly involved in R&D, the outputs are difficult to quantify in economic terms. In practice, nearly two-thirds of the US Federal budget for applied R&D was reported to go into public goods whose value is not measured in economic terms (Office of Technology Assessment, 1986, p. 4) and, hence, it would be surprising to see any evidence of high economic rates of return.

The general view is that knowledge generated by publicly funded basic research has a large positive payoff when it or the resulting technologies and skills are disseminated within firms (Metcalfe *et al.*, 2003, p. 61). The OECD reports that a 1 per cent growth in publicly funded R&D leads to a 0.17 per cent increase in TFP in the long run (Griliches, 1995). Another study found at least a 30 per cent return to public R&D in pharmaceuticals (Guellec and van Pottelsberghe, 2001). One study concluded that public R&D is a complement to private R&D (Cockburn and Henderson, 2001). However, the UK government's funding is biased towards defence, where the spillovers to the private sector may be lower (Walker, 1993, pp. 177–178).

Popper and Wagner (2002, p. 36) argue that the portfolio of public research in the USA should:

(i)   have an element of stability, with sufficient levels of public funding for fundamental science and engineering;
(ii)   be based on a more informed process for deciding priorities and a balance across fields.[7]

Governments support private R&D in a wide variety of ways, including the provision of highly qualified researchers via the university system, spillovers from government-funded R&D units and tax breaks for R&D. The findings of Guellec and van Pottelsberghe (2001) are important here:

(i)   direct government funding of R&D performed by firms (either grants or procurement) has a positive effect on business R&D ($1 given to firms results in $1.7 of research);
(ii)   tax incentives have a positive (though rather short-lived) effect on business R&D;

(iii) stability is important – firms do not invest in additional R&D unless they are certain of the continuity of government support;

(iv) direct government funding and R&D tax incentives are substitutes – raising one reduces the effect of the other on business R&D;

(v) the effect of government funding on private R&D increases up to a point (i.e. where government funding represents about 13 per cent of business R&D) and then decreases;

(vi) defence research performed in public laboratories and universities crowds out private R&D, while civilian public research is neutral for business R&D.

14.5.4 *Legal and regulatory framework*

The IP framework is largely set under various international conventions (the European Patent Convention and the Patent Convention Treaty, etc.) and through the GATT/World Trade Organization rounds. The evidence suggests that countries with stronger IP frameworks, such as patent protection, have higher investments in R&D (Varakelis, 2001, p. 1067). Most commentators view the UK as having a favourable IP framework in the context of its NIS, but it is not without its problems. First, the current system was developed for and has evolved around established areas of technology. As a consequence, it is far from ideal in terms of balancing the encouragement of investment in new areas of science and technology with consumer welfare (in, for example, the areas of genetic discoveries, computer software and business methods). It seems important that the UK forms a well founded view about how these areas should be protected.[8] Second, the IP framework in the UK is not well suited to the needs of small companies. There are strong grounds for the UK to consider some policy, perhaps the introduction of 'petty patents' for minor inventions, for example, as a stimulus to incremental invention – an area where the present study suggests that the UK may be particularly weak. Small enterprises are put off patenting (and perhaps, thereby, from invention) by the potential threat of litigation by large and powerful companies. While it is possible, in principle, to insure against this threat, the costs for individual inventors and SMEs are simply too large. The government might investigate whether anything could be done to overcome these problems.

The government also needs to review the way in which regulations and standards are set, in light of the extent to which these encourage rather than stifle high-quality production and innovation. An example is the impact of strict controls in work on genetics (human cloning, genetically modified crops, etc.), which may have important effects on the UK science and technology base *vis-à-vis* countries in which the rules are more relaxed. Popper and Wagner (2002, pp. 46–49) see the need to review the process of setting standards in the context of improving the US NIS. They note, for example:

> Failure to agree on domestic standards for cellular telephony led to an alleged reversal of a usual source of US advantage. This lapse has been pointed to as a principal reason why non-US firms were able to capture both technological and market leads over their potential US competitors.

This may not imply more direct intervention by government in setting standards, but it calls for government's more proactive role as 'a convenor and provider of auspices for fostering and providing discussion of standards' (Popper and Wagner, 2002, p. 48).

It is essential that the accounting profession agrees some standard for the accounting of intangible assets. The time is ripe for such a change: significant advances in understanding of the measurement of intangibles have occurred in recent years; intangibles have become extremely important particularly in the knowledge-based economy that governments encourage. While there is a need for caution (with a view to avoiding stock market bubbles and crashes of the type seen in the high-technology sector), companies cannot effectively manage their core activities and the stock market cannot make rational investment decisions if the discretionary investments and the values of intangible assets are not known. While it might be assumed that investors build up a rational expectation of the various amounts, all the work on disclosure (e.g. on the effects of disclosure of R&D) suggest that, in the absence of such information, the market significantly underestimates the extent of R&D activity and MV.

14.5.5 *Government policies on education and training*

The general view seems to be that the supply of graduates and the contribution to the science base of UK universities is high and a relative area of strength. The earlier discussion to some degree supports this view, but there is little to suggest that the position is anything other than that which the fourth or fifth largest economy in the world should occupy. However, there is substantial evidence of a real problem with intermediate skills in the UK, in addition to the issues surrounding the relatively low levels of literacy and numeracy. Evidence has been provided about how low skill levels can deflect firms from incremental innovations that might lead to greater efficiency, longevity of products and maintenance of pay levels, rather than firms resorting to deskilling (see Chapters 9 and 13). In addition, it has been demonstrated that there are large externalities that arise from operating from a high skills base, with much lower costs of maintaining that base (incremental training) when all firms are highly skilled, rather than a minority of firms.

The evidence about management skills is not conclusive, but there is a clear need for UK managers to be of at least as high a quality as those of international competitors. There are strong grounds for arguing that management plays such a pivotal role that it is essential that management skills are assessed and validated. The government, perhaps through employer or professional bodies, needs to consider the introduction of guidelines for management training and qualifications. As a crude rule of thumb, it might be argued that corporate managers should be as qualified as those who take up professional occupations and that managers and proprietors should be as qualified as those in semi-professional occupations. Chapter 6 also provided evidence of the importance of social competences and skills among entrepreneurs – the evidence suggested that new start-ups were more likely to survive if such skills were present. It is not clear, given the enormous turnover of new businesses in the UK, that the vast majority of these entrepreneurs have the necessary skills.

A lack of quality of management is reflected in the shutting down of various options as being too risky. Higher-quality management is more likely to handle the risks of – and therefore take – a quality-increasing route than lower-quality management and, for this reason, management quality is central to the choice of product market strategy and goals. Booz Allen Hamilton Inc. undertook thirty-nine detailed interviews with managers of US companies regarding the trends influencing the R&D environment. A common result was the increasing pressures for R&D to deliver measurable results and demonstrable financial benefits (Branscomb and Auerswald, 2003, annex 1). The present book has argued, however, that companies (and governments) should not restrict their funding to projects that guarantee profits – they must recognize the risky nature of R&D and related activities. As part of this, the companies must assess their investments in R&D using new forms of decision rules and put management and other competences, as well as organizational systems, in place to help manage risk.

The earlier discussion suggested that the lack of focus on skills in the UK is not surprising. The skills are, broadly speaking, adequate for the outputs currently produced, but these goods and services are not of sufficiently high specification or quality *vis-à-vis* the UK's main international competitors, such as Germany, the USA and Japan. If there were a requirement for an upward movement in the specification of the products and services produced by UK companies, this would give rise to a wide range of skill problems and reported skill deficiencies. Hence, 'latent skills deficiencies' are present that would emerge as actual deficiencies if there was a concerted move 'up-market' (or to efficiency-increasing rather than cost-reducing strategies).

14.5.6 *Government coordination function*

It is perfectly possible for some parts of the NIS to be functioning well even though the whole is not. One of the reasons for this is a lack of coordination between different parts, possibly through a lack of particular skills (entrepreneurial skills) or inadequacies in particular institutions (e.g. a mechanism for funding high-risk ventures). There remains a general feeling – even if the concept appears outdated – that the UK is relatively good at inventing and relatively poor at innovating. Nelson and Rosenberg (1993, p. 12) provide an example: 'Great Britain provided a remarkable degree of intellectual leadership in the field of molecular biology, but most of the commercial exploitation of this research, so far, has been in the United States'.[9] Walker (1993, p. 180) argues that, in the UK, 'The connection between the physical sciences and engineering seems especially weak. One feature of Britain is that it is comparatively poorly endowed with "bridging" institutions, such as the Fraunhofer Gesellschaft in Germany.' Branscomb and Auerswald (2003) emphasize the importance of funding in the \$0.2–2.0 million range of high-risk ventures in the US economy. They believe that there may well be a market failure in this area caused by the lack of specialist knowledge and skills among venture capital sources. They argue:

> every high-technology innovation, by its nature, calls for specialized technical knowledge; and every radical innovation that expects to create a market that does not yet exist, can only be evaluated by someone with experience in new market creation in that segment of the business world. (Branscomb and Auerswald, 2003, p. 4)

14.5.7 *Clusters, networks and agglomerations*

The potential importance of buyer–supplier chains as sources of information and of stimulus for innovation was discussed in Chapter 11. Some commentators argue that 'close and mutually sustaining producer–user relations tend to be the exception rather than the rule in Britain' (Walker, 1993, p. 181). The problem may again be the result of the very market-oriented system that operates in the UK. Walker (1993, p. 181) suggests that 'The British tradition is for the consumer to have complete freedom of choice, and to have no special responsibility toward, or common cause with, indigenous suppliers'. The same is true throughout the supply chain and is likely to be exacerbated by the cost-oriented product market strategies of UK producers (e.g. when they buy inputs for their production process). Even companies such as Marks and Spencer, which was known for its preference for domestic suppliers, have been forced to modify this strategy.

On balance, the evidence of the present book has been that clusters are likely to be important to firm performance. The concept of clusters and agglomerations has arisen both in terms of the stimulus to technology and in terms of skills eco-systems (Finegold, 1999), suggesting that microcosms of the NIS may develop at local levels. This appears to be the view of other policy-oriented studies (Branscomb and Auerswald, 2003). However, it is clear that clusters are not a panacea – they cannot 'compensate for poor awareness of market conditions, failure to adapt to technological shifts, or better management of the process of innovation' (Metcalfe *et al.*, 2003, annex 1). In addition, it is one thing to observe the conditions prevailing that have led to a successful cluster and quite another to attempt to re-create these in some other context through government or regional policy (Schmitz and Nadvi, 1999). Metcalfe *et al.* (2003) argue that it is likely that government policy will be:

(i)   to act as a signpost to firms, institutions and networks;
(ii)   to provide information about who is active in what field;
(iii)   to promote the strengths of UK science and business abroad in order to be included in international networks;
(iv)   to act as a catalyst in areas of strategic interest.

However, the empirical results on clusters, linked to spillovers and externalities, suggest that this is such an important area that government might be forced into a broader and more active role.

Finally, in the case of one-off programmes, a number of countries appear to be focusing on programmes to alter the product market strategy of companies, linked to the introduction of technological change and the use of HPWPs. Ashton *et al.* (2003, pp. 16–21) report the example of Finland. Here the associated programme provides funding for three types of project:

(i)   basic analysis to identify the development needs;
(ii)   operationalization designed to improve productivity and the quality of working life;
(iii)   development of vertical or horizontal networks to support and test the potential of the changes for job creation in the economy.

The aim is not only to help individual companies and diffuse the benefits to other companies, but to build up an expertise among academics, managers and government – in other words, a national institutional capacity. Ashton *et al.* (2003, p. 19) argue that there is early evidence of positive effects on:

(i)   productivity and quality;
(ii)   management and leadership;
(iii)   equality;
(iv)   opportunities for improving individual competences;
(v)   cooperation and social relations.

14.5.8 *Government policies for the demand side*

The other element of the story lies in the sophistication of product demand. Porter and Ketels (2003, p. 26) argue that sophisticated consumers 'educate companies' and 'pressure them to produce superior goods and services'. They report that 'The UK ranks high on overall buyer sophistication'. This may well be the case among higher-income consumers, but it is much less clearly the case among lower-income groups (where potential sophistication may be high but cannot be exercised). It should be noted that the UK and the USA exhibit greater inequality in income distributions than most other industrialized countries. The implication appears to be that, while a small proportion of individuals may be able to exercise the highest levels of sophistication in buying, this may not be the case for the majority. A larger proportion of low-income groups may put pressure on companies to seek greater efficiency, and so lower costs and prices, with existing, ageing product lines. While the larger UK companies are generally competing in world markets and are not tied to the demands made by UK consumers alone, it is believed that such companies often appear to be operating in relatively older, lower-technology areas (Hogarth and Wilson, 2003). In addition, if the evidence of low product specifications in the UK is correct, this influences the level of sophistication in the buyer–supplier chains. The sophistication of product demand is not independent of the skills base and income levels (or distribution). If the economy becomes locked into a low-skills trajectory, it is inevitable that the sophistication of demand will follow the same pattern (even if latent sophistication is strong).

There is evidence that the government does not make full use of its purchasing activities to influence the extent of innovation and the demand for skills. In the case of the USA, for example, the Department of Defense and other government agencies that procure R&D services are required to ensure that a minimum of 5 per cent of total R&D expenditures go to small businesses. The issue of procurement is much more general, however, concerning all aspects of the government's purchasing activity (from both public and private sectors). Porter and Ketels (2003, p. 27) report that 'the UK ranks low on the sophistication of government procurement'. While it is a moot point as to whether changes in procurement policy alone might reverse a low-skills trajectory, it could at least play a more positive role.

Ashton *et al.* (2003, pp. 5–11) discuss changes in the shape of what they term the 'national institutional framework', either through the introduction of a German-style 'dual system', combining more formal off-the-job and more practical on-the-job training, or through the introduction of a French-style training tax or levy. While these can be viewed as changes to the supply side, the authors argue that the increased supply and the need to participate to take advantage of the system alter employers' demand-side behaviour. The impact of the well established German system on skill levels has been discussed at various stages throughout the present book, and evidence is emerging of the positive impact of the French system (OECD, 1999b). At various stages, the UK has experimented with aspects of both systems and, while there were specific reasons for their failure, there would probably be some reluctance to relive these lessons. In addition, their level of bureaucracy and their inherent inflexibility do not appear to match well with the UK's market-based approach.[10] The long-term credibility of any radically new system would require all the main political parties to agree to this approach as the long-term strategy for raising skill levels.

The example of the policy approach of Singapore is much more complex; that approach is designed to produce a system of complementary and cumulative effects on employers' demand for skills (Ashton *et al.*, 2003, pp. 21–30). The aim of the system is not only to raise the demand for skills, but to raise them to a level comparable with world best practice. The cumulative nature of the system is aimed at 'capturing' companies, in the sense that, once they adopt one part of the system, they are more likely to adopt other programmes. Again, the earlier chapters have provided considerable support for this cumulative type of approach and, in addition, it can be viewed as an extension of the clustering, network and agglomeration discussion in section 14.5.7.

The second group of measures operating on demand relate to one-off programmes that are intended to target employer and organization behaviour (Ashton *et al.*, 2003, pp. 11–21). The idea is that 'These operate to improve the product market performance, as well as through HPWPs that drive up the demand for skills' (p. 14). The first of these is the adoption of national and sectoral benchmarking systems, such as that developed by the American Society of Training and Development (ASTD) and the work of the US industry associations (Ashton *et al.*, 2003). This appears a much more detailed and sophisticated system than anything on offer in the UK at the time of writing. It is available online at all times[11] and enables companies to generate a free benchmarking report, based on the results of a completed questionnaire. From the perspective of the discussion throughout the present book, it provides feedback on various measures of intellectual capital within the company. Ashton *et al.* (2003, p. 13) note that:

> The system provides information on such items as intellectual capital measures and has tracked the spend on training within organisations, expenditure by type of courses, the changes in training methods and the emergence of the new technologies, new training technologies and their use and the process of training evaluation within companies.

While there are clearly limitations to this approach, in terms of both the coverage of the benchmarking and its voluntary nature, it appears to be a useful device for the assessment and dissemination of information about best practice – it may also aid the development of new accounting standards for intangible assets.

14.6   Conclusions

Some parts of the story are becoming clear, such as the role of risk and the importance of various forms of complementarities and synergies, virtuous and vicious circles. One fundamental point is that there is no reason, *per se*, why firms should set goals consistent with the best interests of society. The enterprise will choose a down-market, cost-reducing strategy if this route is more profitable than the alternative of an up-market, quality-improving strategy. The present chapter has argued that the choice made in practice is the result of a wide variety of influences, both internal (competences, skills, flexibility, etc.) and external to the firm (i.e. the incentive and institutional systems within which the firm operates – which for simplicity, with some provisos, the discussion termed the NIS). While the internal issues were dealt with in the earlier chapters, the present chapter has focused mainly on these external issues.

The empirical evidence in the present chapter does not paint the UK's position in a particularly favourable light. There are few, if any, areas of education, skills, science, technology and so on where the economy appears to be punching at or above its weight. While the discussion considered it difficult to think of the UK as currently trapped in a low-skills equilibrium, at least across the economy as a whole, it certainly has features consistent with this and, in addition, exhibits a number of unfavourable trends. The evidence suggests that there is a need for changes in a variety of government policies and interventions on both the demand and supply sides, which would change the balance from lower to higher product quality and skill demands. This is a difficult balancing act, requiring the level and mix of skills demanded to be broadly balanced with those supplied, preferably, from society's point of view, while the levels of both are rising. Thus, policies to shift public and private sector procurement towards higher-specification and higher-quality goods are needed, but balanced against improving skills and competences that enable these goods and services to be delivered by UK firms (rather than via imports).

Notes

1   The levels relate to the national vocational qualification classification, with higher numbers referring to higher levels of qualifications. Details can be found at www.dfes.gov.uk/nvq/what.shtml.
2   Some care needs to be exercised because of the bias caused by the use of the English language.
3   The website www1.oecd.org/publications/e-book/92-2001-04-1-2987/Annex_tables_ excel/At5.1.1_e.xls provides full details.
4   That is, the domestic patent office, the European Patent Office or the Patent Convention Treaty.
5   The 'blip' in the Japanese data in the mid-1990s was caused by problems associated with the introduction of an electronic application system.

6 The mission- versus the diffusion-oriented policy approaches can be traced to Ergas (1987). For an empirical application to the German economy, see Cantner and Pyka (2001).

7 The Foresight Programme in the UK, which has adopted a number of features of Japan's Science and Technology Agency/Ministry of International Trade and Industry R&D forecasting programme, appears to be a mechanism for this to happen. The Programme helps to capture academics, industrialists, policy makers, and so on in a constructive dialogue – along the lines of the Finnish experiment outlined in section 14.5.7.

8 There is some evidence that the World Intellectual Property Organization is being somewhat more proactive in developing new IP frameworks as the new areas of science and technology begin to emerge, with a view to international negotiations to establish an early date for their implementation.

9 Many other examples are provided by Metcalfe *et al.* (2003).

10 The overemphasis (from a societal viewpoint) of cost reduction among UK companies suggests that a training levy would be widely perceived as yet another financial burden (though the same is true, if less obvious, of the other measures discussed) and would meet stiff opposition. Note, however, that the current Singapore system actually taxes low-skills, low-wage employers to help pay for the system of training – providing a disincentive to move down-market or occupy a low-specification niche.

11 Details can be found at www.astd.org/astd.

References

Aaker, D.A. and J.G. Myers (1982). *Advertising Management*. Englewood Cliffs, NJ: Prentice Hall.

Abernathy, W.J. and K. Wayne (1974). 'Limits of the Learning Curve'. *Harvard Business Review*. September/October. pp. 109–119.

Acs, Z.J. and D.B. Audretsch (1990). *Innovation and Small Firms*. Cambridge, MA: MIT Press.

Acs, Z.J. and D.B. Audretsch (1993). 'Analysing Innovation Output Counts: The US Experience'. In A. Kleinknecht and D. Bain (eds). *New Concepts in Innovation Output Measurement*. Basingstoke: St Martin's Press. pp. 10–41.

Acs, Z.J. and D.A. Gerlowski (1996). *Managerial Economics and Organisation*. London: Prentice Hall.

Adler, P.S. (1988). 'Managing Flexible Automation'. *California Management Review*. Vol. 30. No. 3. pp. 34–56.

Aggarwal, R.K. and A.A. Samwick (1999). 'The Other Side of the Trade-Off: The Impact of Risk on Executive Compensation'. *Journal of Political Economy*. Vol. 107. No. 1. p. 65.

Agrawal, A., G. Harhalakis, I. Minis and R. Nagi (1996). 'Just-In-Time Production of Large Assemblies'. *IIE Transactions on Scheduling and Logistics*. Vol. 28. pp. 653–667.

Akella, S.R. and S.I. Greenbaum (1988). 'Savings and Loan Ownership Structure and Expense Preference'. *Journal of Banking and Finance*. Vol. 12. pp. 419–437.

Albert, M., D. Avery, F. Narin and P. McAllister (1991). 'Direct Validation of Citation Counts as Indicators of Industrially Important Patents'. *Research Policy*. Vol. 20. pp. 251–259.

Alchian, A. (1950). 'Uncertainty, Evolution and Economic Theory'. *Journal of Political Economy*. Vol. 58. pp. 211–221.

Alder, P. and K. Clark (1987). *Behind the Learning Curve: A Sketch of the Learning Process*. Working Paper. Boston, MA: Harvard Business School.

Aldrich, H. (1987). 'The Impact of Social Networks on Business Founding and Profit: A Longitudinal Study'. Paper presented at the Babson Entrepreneurial Conference, Malibu, CA.

Allen, J.M. and K. Norris (1970). 'Project Estimates and Outcomes in Electricity Generation Research'. *Journal of Management Studies*. Vol. 7. No. 3. pp. 271–287.

Altman, E.I. (1968). 'Financial Ratios, Discriminant Analysis and the Prediction of Corporate Bankruptcy'. *Journal of Finance*. Vol. 23. September. pp. 589–609.

Altman, E.I. (1983). *Corporate Financial Distress: A Complete Guide to Predicting, Avoiding and Dealing with Bankruptcy*. New York: John Wiley.

Altman, E.I., R. Avery, R. Essenbeis and J. Sinkey (1981). *Application of Classification Techniques in Business, Banking and Finance*. Greenwich, CT: JAI Press.

Amsden, A.H. (1989). *Asia's Next Giant: South Korea and Late Industrialisation*. Oxford: Oxford University Press.

Andersen, R.C., T.W. Bates, J.M. Bizjak and M.L. Lemmon (2000). 'Corporate Governance and Firm Diversification'. *Financial Management*. Vol. 29. No. 1. p. 5.

Anderton, B. (1996). *UK Trade Performance and the Role of Product Quality, Innovation and Hysteresis: Some Preliminary Results*. Discussion Paper No. 102. London: NIESR.

Andrews, R.L. and G.R. Franke (1991). 'The Determinants of Consumption: A Meta-analysis'. *Journal of Public Policy and Marketing*. Vol. 10. No. 1. pp. 81–100.

Anwar, M.F. and R. Nagi (1998). 'Integrated Scheduling of Material Handling and Manufacturing Activities for Just-In-Time Production of Complex Assemblies'. *International Journal of Production Research*. Vol. 36. No. 3. pp. 653–681.

Aoki, M. and R. Dore (1994). *The Japanese Firm: The Sources of Competitive Strength*. Oxford: Oxford University Press.

Argyris, C. (1973). *On Organizations of the Future*. Beverly Hills, CA: Sage.

Argyris, C. (1983). 'Action Science and Intervention'. *Journal of Applied Behavioural Science*. Vol. 19. pp. 115–140.

Arora, A., A. Fosfuri and A. Gambardella (2001). 'Specialised Spillovers, International Spillovers and Investment: Evidence from the Chemical Industry'. *Journal of Development Economics*. Vol. 65. pp. 31–54.

Arrow, K. (1962). 'Economic Welfare and the Allocation of Resources for Invention'. In R.R. Nelson (ed.). *The Rate and Direction of Inventive Activity*. Princeton, NJ: Princeton University Press. pp. 609–625.

Arthur, J.B. (1994). 'Effects of Human Resource Systems on Manufacturing Performance and Turnover'. *Academy of Management Journal*. Vol. 37. pp. 670–687.

Ashton, D., J. Sung and A. Raddon (2003). *Raising Employer Demand for Skills: Lessons from Abroad*. London: DTI.

Ashworth, J. (1997). 'A Waste of Time? Private Rates of Return to Higher Education in the 1990s'. *Higher Education Quarterly*. Vol. 51. No. 2. pp. 164–188.

Assmus, G., J.U. Farley and D. Lehmann (1984). 'How Advertising Affects Sales: Meta Analysis of Econometric Results'. *Journal of Marketing Research*. Vol. 21. pp. 65–74.

Attewell, P. (1995). 'Technology Diffusion and Organisational Learning: The Case of Business Computing'. In M.D. Cohen and L.S. Sproul (eds). *Organisational Learning*. Thousand Oaks, CA: Sage. pp. 203–229.

Avlonitis, G J. and B.G.S. James (1982). 'Some Dangerous Axioms of Product Elimination Decision Making'. *European Journal of Marketing*. Vol. 16. January. pp. 36–48.

Bahk, B-H. and M. Gort (1993). 'Decomposing Learning by Doing in New Plants'. *Journal of Political Economy*. Vol. 101. No. 4. pp. 561–583.

Bain, S.G. and P. Elias (1985). 'Trade Union Membership in Great Britain: An Individual-Level Analysis'. *British Journal of Industrial Relations*. Vol. 23. pp. 71–92.

Baird, A. and R. St-Amand (1995). 'Trust Within the Organization'. Public Service Commission Monograph. Ottawa. Canada. See www.psc-cfp.gc.ca/publications/monogra/mono1_e.htm#biblio. Last accessed 18 March 2005.

Baker, G.P., M.C. Jensen and K.J. Murphy (1988). 'Compensation and Incentives: Practice Versus Theory'. *Journal of Finance*. Vol. 18. pp. 593–616.

Baker, N.R. and J.R. Freeland (1975). 'Recent Advances in R&D Benefit Measurement and Selection Methods'. *Management Science*. Vol. 21. No. 10. pp. 1164–1175.

Balachandra, R. and J.H. Friar (1997). 'Factors for Success in R&D Projects and New

Product Innovation: A Contextual Framework'. *IEEE Transactions on Engineering Management*. Vol. 44. No. 3. pp. 276–288.

Baloff, N. (1966). 'The Learning Curve – Some Controversial Issues'. *Journal of Industrial Economics*. Vol. 78. No. 3. pp. 275–282.

Banerjee, A. and J.E. Owers (1992). 'Wealth Reduction in White Knight Bids'. *Financial Management*. Vol. 21. No. 3. p. 48–57.

Barbi, V. (2000). *Interlocking Directorship Networks: What Is Relevant for the Evolution and Change of the Networks*. Discussion Paper. Department of Economics, University of Siena.

Barkema, H.G. and L.R. Gomez-Mejia (1998). 'Managerial Compensation and Firm Performance: A General Research Framework'. *Academy of Management Journal*. Vol. 41. No. 2. p. 135–146.

Barnhart, S.W. and S. Rosenstein (1998). 'Board Composition, Managerial Ownership and Firm Performance: An Empirical Analysis'. *Financial Review*. Vol. 33. No. 4. pp. 1–36.

Baron, R.A. and C.D. Brush (1999). 'The Role of Social Skills in Entrepreneurs' Success: Evidence from Videotapes of Entrepreneurs' Presentations'. See www.babson.edu/entrep/fer/papers99/I/I_A/I_A.html. Last accessed 18 March 2005.

Baron, R.A. and G.D. Markman (1999a). 'The Role of Entrepreneurs' Behavior in Their Financial Success: Evidence for the Benefits of Effective Social Skills'. See www.babson.edu/entrep/fer/. Last accessed 18 March 2005.

Baron, R.A. and G.D. Markman (1999b). 'The Role of Personal Appearance Entrepreneurs' Financial Success: Effects and Mediating Mechanisms.' See www.babson.edu/entrep/fer/. Last accessed 18 March 2005.

Barry, R., D.L. Bosworth and R.A. Wilson (1997). *Engineers in Top Management*. Research Report. Institute for Employment Research, University of Warwick.

Bassi, L.J. and M.E. Van Buren (1999). 'Valuing Investments in Intellectual Capital'. *International Journal of Technology Management*. Vol. 18. Nos 5–8. pp. 414–432.

Bates, T. (1990). 'Entrepreneur Human Capital Inputs and Small Business Longevity'. *Review of Economics and Statistics*. Vol. 62. No. 4. pp. 551–559.

Baumol, W. (1982). 'Contestable Markets: An Uprising in the Theory of Industrial Structure'. *American Economic Review*. Vol. 72. pp. 1–15.

Baumol, W. (1993). 'Formal Entrepreneurship Theory in Economics: Existence and Bounds'. *Journal of Business Venturing*. Vol. 8. pp. 197–210.

Baysinger, B. and R.E. Hoskisson (1990). 'The Composition of Boards of Directors and Strategic Control: Effects on Corporate Strategy'. *Academy of Management Review*. Vol. 15. No. 1. pp. 72–87.

Beard, C. and C. Easingwood (1992). 'Sources of Competitive Advantage in the Marketing of Technology-Intensive Products and Processes'. *European Journal of Marketing*. Vol. 26. No. 12. pp. 5–18.

Beatty, R.P. and E.J. Zajac (1994). 'Managerial Incentives, Monitoring and Risk Bearing: A Study of Executive Compensation, Ownership and Board Structure in Initial Public Offerings'. *Administrative Science Quarterly*. Vol. 39. No. 2. p. 313.

Beaver, W. (1966). 'Financial Ratios as Predictors of failures'. *Empirical Research in Accounting, Selected Studies*. Supplement to *Journal of Accounting Research*. Vol. 4. January. pp. 71–111.

Bebchuk, L., J. Coates and G. Subramanian (2002). *The Powerful Anti-takeover Force of Staggered Boards: Theory, Evidence and Policy*. Discussion Paper No. 353. John M. Olin Center for Law, Economics, and Business. Harvard University. May.

Becker, G.S. (1964). *Human Capital*. New York: Columbia University Press for NBER.

Bell, R.M. (1972). *Changing Technology and Manpower Requirements in the Engineering Industry*. Brighton: Sussex University Press with the Engineering Industry Training Board.

Belliveau, M.A., C.A. O'Reilly and J.B. Wade (1996). 'Social Capital at the Top: Effects of Social Similarity and Status on CEO Compensation'. *Academy of Management Journal*. Vol. 39. pp. 1568–1593.

Bendixen, M.T. (1993). 'Advertising Effects and Effectiveness'. *European Journal of Marketing*. Vol. 27. No. 10. pp. 19–32.

Benito, A. (2001). *Oscillate Wildly: Asymmetries and Persistence in Company-Level Profitability*. Working Paper No. 128. London: Bank of England.

Ben-Zion, U. (1984). 'The R&D and Investment Decision and Its Relationship to the Firm's Market Value: Some Preliminary Results'. In Z. Griliches (ed.). *R&D, Patents, and Productivity*. Chicago: University of Chicago Press. pp. 299–312.

Berle, A. and G. Means (1932). *The Modern Corporation and Private Property*. New York: Macmillan.

Berndt, E.R. (1991). *The Practice of Econometrics: Classic and Contemporary*. Reading, MA: Addison Wesley.

Bhide, A. (1993). 'The Hidden Costs of Stock Market Liquidity'. *Journal of Financial Economics*. Vol. 34. pp. 31–51.

Biemans, W.G. and H.J. Setz (1995). 'Managing New Product Announcements in the Dutch Telecommunications Industry'. In M. Bruce and W.G. Biemans (eds). *Product Development: Meeting the Challenge of the Design–Marketing Interface*. Chichester: John Wiley.

Bird, B.J. (1989). *Entrepreneurial Behavior*. Glenview, IL: Scott Foresman.

Bishop, J.A. and J.H. Yoo (1985). '"Health Scare" Excise Taxes and Advertising Ban in the Cigarette Demand and Supply'. *Southern Economic Journal*. Vol. 52. No. 4. pp. 402–411.

Blackwell, D. (1956). 'An Analogue of the Minmax Theorem for Vector Payoffs'. *Pacific Journal of Mathematics*. Vol. 6. pp. 1–8.

Blasko, V. J. and C.H. Patti (1984). 'The Advertising Budgeting Practices of Industrial Marketers'. *Journal of Marketing*. Vol. 48. No. 4. pp. 104–110.

Blundell, R., R. Griffith and J. Van Reenan (1999). 'Market Share, Market Value and Innovation in a Panel of British Manufacturing Firms'. *Review of Economic Studies*. Vol. 66. July. pp. 529–554.

Booz Allen Hamilton Inc. (1982). *New Product Management for the 1980s*. New York: Booz Allen Hamilton Inc.

Boston Consulting Group (1973). 'The Experience Curve Reviewed, II: History'. *Perspectives*. No. 125. pp. 1–2. See www.bcg.com/publications/files/experiencecurvell. pdf. Last accessed 18 March 2005.

Bosworth, D.L. (1973). 'Changes in the Quality of Inventive Output and Patent Based Measures of Technological Change'. *Bulletin of Economic Research*. Vol. 25. No. 2. pp. 95–103.

Bosworth, D.L. (1976). 'Price and Quality Changes in Metal Working Machine Tools'. *Applied Economics*. Vol. 8. pp. 283–288.

Bosworth, D.L. (1983). 'Recent Developments in the Economics of Technological Change Literature'. *Economics*. Vol. 19. Part 3. No. 83. pp. 104–107.

Bosworth, D.L. (1986). *Intellectual Property Rights*. Royal Statistical Society and Economic and Social Research Council. Reviews of UK Statistical Sources. Vol. 19. Oxford: Pergamon Press.

Bosworth, D.L. (1996). 'Determinants of the Use of Advanced Technologies'. *International Journal of the Economics of Business*. Vol. 3. No. 3. 269–293.

Bosworth, D.L. (1999). *Empirical Evidence of Management Skills in the UK*. Skills Task Force Research Paper No. 18. Nottingham: Department for Education and Employment.

Bosworth, D.L. (2001). *Goals and Strategies: Empirical Evidence from the Employers' Skill Survey*. Report to the Council for Excellence in Management and Leadership. Manchester: UMIST.

Bosworth, D.L. and N.S. Gharneh (1996). 'Dynamic Activities and Firm Performance'. In K.H. Oppenlander and G. Poser (eds). *Business Cycle Survey: Forecasting Issues and Methodological Aspects*. Selected Papers from the 22nd Ciret Conference. Singapore. Aldershot: Avebury. pp. 231–250.

Bosworth, D.L. and C. Jacobs (1989). 'Management Attitudes, Behaviour and Abilities as Barriers to Growth'. In J. Barber, J.S. Metcalf and M. Porteous (eds). *Barriers to Growth in Small Firms*. London: Routledge. pp. 20–38.

Bosworth, D.L. and G. Jobome (2001). *Management Skills and Enterprise Performance: A Review of the Literature*. Report for the Council for Excellence in Management and Leadership. Manchester School of Management, University of Manchester Institute of Science and Technology.

Bosworth, D.L. and H. Mahdian (1999). 'Returns to Intellectual Property in the Pharmaceuticals Sector'. *Economie Appliquée*. Vol. 52. No. 2. pp. 69–93.

Bosworth, D.L. and P.A. Stoneman (1994). *An Efficiency study for the Water Industry*. A report by National Economic Research Associates for OFWAT. London: NERA.

Bosworth, D.L. and R. Wilson (2004). *Sectoral Management Priorities*. Report to the Social Skills Development Agency. Coventry: Institute for Employment Research, Warwick University.

Bosworth, D.L., R. Wilson and P. Taylor (1992). *Technological Change: The Role of Scientists and Engineers*. Aldershot: Avebury Press.

Bosworth, D.L., P. Dawkins and T. Stromback (1996a). *Economics of the Labour Market*. Harlow: Addison Wesley Longman.

Bosworth, D.L., P.A. Stoneman and U. Sinha (1996b). *Technology Transfer, Information Flows and Collaboration: An Analysis of the Community Innovation Survey*. Report to the European Innovation Monitoring System, DG XIII of the European Commission.

Bosworth, D., P. Dawkins, M.N. Harris and S. Kells (1997). *Diversification and the Performance of Australian Enterprises*. Working Paper No. 28/97. Melbourne: Institute for Applied Economic and Social Research, Melbourne University.

Bosworth, D., P. Dawkins, M.N. Harris and S. Kells (1999a). 'Business Focus and Profitability'. In P. Dawkins, M.S. Harris and S. King (eds). *How Big Business Performs: Private Performance and Public Policy*. St Leonards: Allen and Unwin. pp. 68–79.

Bosworth, D.L., A. Wharton and C. Greenhalgh (1999b). 'Intangible Assets and the Market Valuation of UK Companies: Evidence From Fixed Effects Models. Oxford Intellectual Property Research Centre'. *Electronic Journal of Intellectual Property Rights*. Working and Seminar Paper Series. WP 12/99. November.

Bosworth, D.L., R. Davies and R. Wilson (2001). *The Extent, Causes and Implications of Skill Deficiencies*. Research Report to the Department for Education and Employment. Institute for Employment Research, University of Warwick.

Bosworth, D.L., S. Massini and M. Nakayama (2002). 'The Role of Innovation and Quality Change in Japanese Economic Growth'. In J.S. Metcalf and U. Cantner (eds). *Proceedings of the Schumpeter Conference*, Manchester, 2002, pp. 291–318. Reprinted in *Journal of Evolutionary Economics*. Selected papers from the Schumpeter Conference, Manchester, 2000, pp. 135–162.

Bosworth, D.L., D. Filiou and M. Longland (2003). *Measuring the 'Quality' of Patents*. Report to the UK Patent Office. Manchester School of Management and St Peter's College, Oxford.

Bosworth, D., D. Filiou and M. Longland (2005a). 'New Measures for Company Benchmarking and Decision Making'. In D. Bosworth and E. Webster (eds). *The Management of Intellectual Property*. Cheltenham: Edward Elgar. (Forthcoming.)

Bosworth, D.L., S. Massini and M. Nakayama (2005b). 'Quality Change, Productivity Improvement and the Rate of Growth of the Japanese Economy'. *Japan and the World Economy*. Vol. 17. No. 1. pp. 1–23.

Boudreau, J.W. and P.M. Ramstad (1997). 'Measuring Intellectual Capital: Learning from Financial History'. *Human Resource Management*. Vol. 36. No. 3. pp. 343–356.

Boulding, K.E. (1978). *Eco-dynamics: A New Theory of Social Evolution*. Beverley Hills, CA: Sage.

Braglia, M. and A. Petroni (1999). 'The Shortcomings and Benefits Associated with the Implementation of MRP Packages: A Survey of Research'. *Logistics Information Management*. Vol. 12. No. 6. pp. 428–438.

Branscomb, L.M. and P.E. Auerswald (eds) (2000). *Taking Technical Risks: How Innovators Manage Risk in High-Tech Innovations*. Cambridge, MA: MIT Press. (References made in the present book are taken from the authors' manuscript, made available on the web.)

Branscomb, L.M. and P.E. Auerswald (2003). *Between Invention and Innovation: An Analysis of Funding for Early-Stage Technology Development*. Gaithersburg, MD: National Institute of Standards and Technology. See www.atp.nist.gov/eao/gcr02-841/gcr02-841.pdf. Last accessed 18 March 2005.

Branscomb, L.M., K.P. Morse, M.J. Roberts and D. Boville (2000). *Managing Technical Risk: Understanding Private Sector Decision Making on Early Stage Technology-Based Projects*. NIST GCR 00-787. Washington, DC: Department of Commerce.

Bresnahan, T., S. Stern and M. Trajtenberg (1996). *Market Segmentation and the Sources of Rents from Innovation: Personal Computers in the 1980s*. Working Paper No. 5726. Cambridge, MA: National Bureau for Economic Research.

Bresnahan, T., E. Brynjolfsson and L.M. Hitt (1999). *Information Technology, Work Place Organization and the Demand for Skilled Labor: Firm-Level Evidence*. NBER Working Paper No. 7136. Cambridge, MA: National Bureau for Economic Research.

Brewer, P.C., G. Chandra and C.A. Hock (1999). 'Economic Value Added (EVA): Its Uses and Limitations'. *SAM Advanced Management Journal*. Vol. 64. No. 2. pp. 4–11.

Broadbent, M. and J. Cullen (1993). *Managing Financial Resources*. Oxford: Butterworth-Heinemann.

Brooks, J. (1971). *Business Adventures*. Harmondsworth: Pelican.

Brown, J.S. and P. Duguid (1995). 'Organizational Learning and Communities of Practice: Towards a Unified View of Working, Learning and Innovation'. In M.D. Cohen and L.S. Sproul (eds). *Organizational Learning*. Thousand Oaks, CA: Sage. pp. 58–82.

Brusoni, S., P. Crisculolo and A. Geuna (2003). 'The Knowledge Base of the World's Largest Pharmaceutical Groups: What Do Patent Citations to Non-patent Literature Reveal?' Paper given at the ASEAT Conference, April 2003. University of Manchester.

Brutinni, A. (1975). 'Advertising and the Industrial Revolution'. *Monte Dei Paschi De Siena. Economic Notes*. Vol. 4. Nos 2–3. May–December. pp. 90–116.

Bryant, K., L. Lombardo, M. Healy, L. Bopage and S. Hartshorn (1996). *Australian Business Innovation: A Strategic Analysis*. Canberra: Department of Industry, Science and Technology.

Brynjolfsson, E. and L.M. Hitt (1993). 'Is Information Systems Spending Productive? New Evidence and New Results'. In *Proceedings of the 14th International Conference on Information Systems, Orlando, FL*. pp. 47–64.

Brynjolfsson., E. and L.M. Hitt (1995). 'Information Technology as a Factor of Production: The Role of Differences Among Firms'. *Economics of Innovation and New Technology*. Vol. 3. No. 4. pp. 183–200.

Brynjolfsson, E. and S. Yang (1999). *The Intangible Costs and Benefits of Computer Investments: Evidence from Financial Markets*. Working Paper. Sloan School of Management, Massachusetts Institute of Technology.

Brynjolfsson, E., L.M. Hitt and S. Yang (2000). *Intangible Assets: How the Interaction of Computers and Organizational Structure Affects Stock Market Valuations.* Working Paper. Sloan School of Management, Massachusetts Institute of Technology.

Burns, T. and G.M. Stalker (1961). *The Management of Innovation.* London: Tavistock.

Business Week (1992a). 'R&D Scoreboard'. 3 June.

Business Week (1992b). 'Global Innovation: Who's in the Lead'. 3 August.

Buzacott, J.A. (2000). 'The Impact of Worker Differences on Production Systems'. *11th International Working Seminar on Production Economics.* Innsbruck, Austria. Vol. 3. pp. 71–80.

Bygrave, W.D. & Timmons, J. (1997). 'Venture Capital: Reflections and Projections'. In D.L. Sexton and R. W. Smilor (eds). *Entrepreneurship 2000.* Chicago, IL: Upstart Publishing. pp. 29–46.

Cable, J. (1972). 'Market Structure, Advertising Policy and Inter-market Differences in Advertising Intensity'. In K. Cowling (ed.). *Market Structure and Corporate Behaviour.* London: Gray-Mills. pp. 107–124.

Cadbury, A. (1992). *Report of the Committee on the Financial Aspects of Corporate Governance.* London: Gee Publishing.

Calantone, R.J. and R.G. Cooper (1979). 'A Discriminant Model for Identifying Scenarios of Industrial New Product Failure'. *Journal of the Academy of Marketing Science.* Vol 7. No 3. pp. 163–183.

Campbell, R.S. and L.O. Levine (1983). 'Patent Analysis: Tracking Technology Trends'. *Battelle Today.* April. pp. 3–6.

Cantner, U. and A. Pyka (2001). 'Classifying Technology Policy from an Evolutionary Perspective'. *Research Policy.* Vol. 30. No. 5. pp. 759–775.

Capps, B.T. and M.D. Hattery (2000). 'Performance Measurement: Time for an Overhaul?' *Bank Accounting and Finance.* Vol. 13. No. 3. pp. 25–30.

Carley, K. (1995). 'Organizational Learning and Personnel Turnover'. In M. Cohen and L. Sproull (eds). *Organizational Learning.* Thousand Oaks, CA: Sage. pp. 230–266.

Carpenter, M.P. and F. Narin (1983). 'Validation Study: Patent Citations as Indicators of Science and Foreign Dependence'. *World Patent Information.* Vol. 5. pp. 180–185.

Carpenter, M.P., F. Narin and P. Woolf (1981). 'Citation Ratio to Technologically Important Patents'. *World Patent Information.* Vol. 3. pp. 160–163.

Casson, M.C. (1982). *The Entrepreneur: An Economic Theory.* Oxford: Robertson.

Castigionasi, J. and C. Ornaghi (2003). *An Empirical Assessment of the Determinants of Total Factor Productivity Growth.* Working Paper. Universidad Carlos III, Madrid.

Caves, R.E., M.D. Whinston and M.A. Hurwitz (1991). 'Patent Expiration, Entry, and Competition in the US Pharmaceutical Industry'. *Brookings Papers on Economic Activity: Microeconomics.* pp. 1–48.

Cawkell, A.F. (1977). 'Science Perceived Through the Science Citation Index'. *Endeavour* (New Series). Vol. 1. pp. 57–62.

Chamberlin, E.H. (1933). *The Theory of Monopolistic Competition.* Cambridge, MA: Harvard University Press.

Champy, J. (1995). *Reengineering Management: The Mandate for New Leadership.* New York: Harper Business.

Chan, S.H., J.D. Martin and J.W. Kesinger (1990). 'Corporate Research and Development Expenditures and Share Value'. *Journal of Financial Economics.* Vol. 26. pp. 255–276.

Chaney, P.K., T.M. Devinney and R.S. Winter (1991). 'The Impact of New Product Introductions on the Market Value of Firms'. *Journal of Business.* Vol. 64. No. 4. pp. 573–610.

Chatterjee, S. and B. Wernerfelt (1991). 'The Link Between Resources and Type of

Diversification: Theory and Evidence'. *Strategic Management Journal*. Vol. 12. pp. 33–48.

Chaudhuri, A. and M.B. Holbrook (2001). 'The Chain of Effects from Brand Trust and Brand Affect to Brand Performance: The Role of Brand Loyalty'. *Journal of Marketing*. Vol. 65. No. 2. pp. 81–93.

Chell, E., J. Haworth and S. Brearly (1991). *The Entrepreneurial Personality: Concepts, Cases and Categories*. London: Routledge.

Chesnais, F. (1992). 'Foreign Direct Investment and the Operations of Multinational Enterprises'. In B.-A. Lundvall (ed.). *National Systems of Innovation*. London: Pinter. pp. 264–295.

Chesnais, F. (1995). 'National Systems of Innovation, Foreign Direct Investment and the Operations of Multinational Enterprises'. In B.A. Lundvall (ed.). *National Systems of Innovation: Towards a Theory of Innovation and Interactive Learning*. London: Pinter.

Chi, T. and P. Nystrom (1998). 'An Economic Analysis of Matrix Structure, Using Multinational Corporations as an Illustration'. *Managerial and Decision Economics*. Vol. 19. pp. 141–156.

Child, J. (1972a). 'Organization Structure and Strategies of Control: A Replication of the Aston Study'. *Administrative Science Quarterly*. Vol. 17. pp. 163–177.

Child, J. (1972b). 'Organizational Structure, Environment and Performance: The Role of Strategic Choice'. *Sociology*. Vol. 6. pp. 1–22.

Child, J. (1973). 'Predicting and Understanding Organization Structure'. *Administrative Science Quarterly*. Vol. 18. pp. 168–185.

Cho, M.H. (1998). 'Ownership Structure, Investment and Corporate Value: An Empirical Analysis'. *Journal of Financial Economics*. Vol. 47. pp. 103–121.

Ciccotello, C.S. and C.T. Grant (1999). 'Corporate Governance and Shareholder Patience'. *Business Horizons*. Vol. 42. No. 6. p. 29.

Clancey, K. and R. Shulman (1994). *Marketing Myths That Are Killing Businesses: The Cure for Death-Wish Marketing*. New York: McGraw Hill.

Clutterbuck, D. and M. Devine (1985). 'Why Start-Ups Start'. *Management Today*. July–December.

Coase, R. (1937). 'The Nature of the Firm'. *Economica*. Vol. 4. pp. 386–405. Reprinted in L. Puttman and R.S. Randall (1996). *The Economic Nature of the Firm*. Cambridge: Cambridge University Press. Ch. 7.

Coats, P.K. and L.F. Fant (1993). 'Recognizing Financial Distress Patterns Using a Neural Network Tool'. *Financial Management*. Vol. 22. pp. 142–155.

Coch, L. and J. French (1948). 'Overcoming Resistance to Change'. Reprinted as L. Coch and J.R.P French, Jr. (1996). 'Overcoming Resistance to Change'. In H. Proshki and B. Seidenberg (eds). *Basic Studies in Social Psychology*. New York: Holt, Rinehart and Winston.

Cockburn, I. and Z. Griliches (1988). 'Industry Effects and Appropriability Measures in the Stock Market's Valuation of R&D Investment'. *American Economic Review: Papers and Proceedings*. Vol. 78. No. 2. pp. 419–423.

Cockburn, I. and R. Henderson (2001). 'Publicly Funded Science and the Productivity of the Pharmaceutical Industry'. In *NBER Innovation Policy and Economy*. Harvard, MA: MIT Press. pp. 1–34.

Cohen, K.J. and R.M. Cyert (1965). *Theory of the Firm*. Englewood Cliffs, NJ: Prentice Hall.

Cohen, M. and P. Bacdayan (1996). 'Organizational Routines Are Stored as Procedural Memory'. In M. Cohen and L. Sproull (eds). *Organizational Learning*. Thousand Oaks, CA: Sage. pp. 403–429.

Cohen, M. and L. Sproull (1996). 'Introduction'. In M. Cohen and L. Sproull (eds). *Organizational Learning*. Thousand Oaks, CA: Sage. pp. ix–xv.

Colley, R.H. (1961). *Defining Advertising Goals for Measured Advertising Results*. New York: Association of National Advertisers.

Comanor, W.S. and F.M. Scherer (1969). 'Patent Statistics as a Measure of Technical Change'. *Journal of Political Economy*. Vol. 77. No. 4. pp. 392–398.

Comanor, W.S. and T.A. Wilson (1974). *Advertising and Market Power*. Cambridge, MA: Harvard University Press.

Comment, R. and G.A. Jarrell (1995). 'Corporate Focus and Stock Returns'. *Journal of Financial Economics*. Vol. 37. pp. 67–87.

Committee on Corporate Governance (1998). *The Combined Code, London Stock Exchange Limited*. London: Gee Publishing.

Connolly, R.A. and M. Hirschey (1984). 'RD, Market Structure and Profits: A Value-Based Approach'. *Review of Economics and Statistics*. Vol. 66. No. 4. November. pp. 682–691.

Connolly, R.A. and M. Hirschey (1990). 'Firm Size and R&D Effectiveness'. *Economic Letters*. Vol. 37. pp. 277–281.

Conway, R.W. and A. Schultz (1959). 'The Manufacturing Progress Function'. *Journal of Industrial Engineering*. Vol. 10. January–February. pp. 39–53.

Conyon, M. and C. Mallin (1997). 'A Review of Compliance with Cadbury'. *Journal of General Management*. Vol. 2. No. 3. pp. 24–37.

Conyon, M. and S.I. Peck (1998). 'Board Control, Remuneration Committees and Top Management Compensation'. *Academy of Management Journal*. Vol. 41. No. 2. pp. 146–157.

Cooper, R.G. (1979). 'The Dimensions of Industrial New Product Success and Failure'. *Journal of Marketing*. Vol. 43. Summer. pp. 93–103.

Cooper, R.G. (1980). *Project New Prod: What Makes a New Product a Winner?* Montreal: Centre Quebecois d'Innovation Industrielle.

Cooper, R.G. and E.J. Kleinschmidt (1988). 'New Products: What Separates Winners From Losers?' *Journal of Product Innovation Management*. Vol. 4. No. 4. pp. 169–184.

Cooper, R.G. and E.J. Kleinschmidt (1990). *New Products: The Key Factors in Success*. Chicago, IL: American Marketing Association.

Copeland, T.E. and J.F. Weston (1992). *Financial Theory and Corporate Policy*. Reading, MA: Addison Wesley.

Corbett, G. (1997). 'The Benefits of Valuing Brands'. In R. Perrier (ed.). *Brand Valuation*. London: Premier Books. pp. 11–18.

Coriat, B. and O. Weinstein (2002). 'Organisations, Firms and Institutions in the Generation of Innovation'. *Research Policy*. Vol. 31. pp. 273–290.

Cotterill, R.W. and L.E. Haller (1997). *An Econometric Analysis of the Demand for RTE Cereal: Product Market Definition and Unilateral Market Power Effects*. Food Marketing Policy Center Research Report No. 35. Department of Agricultural and Resource Economics, University of Connecticut.

Covin, J.G. (1991). 'Entrepreneurial *versus* Conservative Firms: A Comparison of Strategies and Performance'. *Journal of Management Studies*. Vol. 28. No. 5. pp. 439–462.

Cowen, T. and D. Parker (1997). *Markets in the Firm: A Market Process Approach to Management*. Hobart Paper No. 134. London: Institute for Economic Affairs.

Cowling, K. and J. Cubbin (1972). 'Hedonic Price Indexes for United Kingdom Cars'. *Economic Journal*. Vol. 82. pp. 963–978.

Cowling, K. and D. Mueller (1978). 'The Social Costs of Monopoly Power'. *Economic Journal*. Vol. 88. pp. 727–748.

Cowling, K. and D. Mueller (1981). 'The Social Costs of Monopoly Power Revisited'. *Economic Journal*. Vol. 91. pp. 721–725.

Cowling, K., D. Metcalf and A.J. Rayner (1970). *Resource Structure of Agriculture: An Economic Analysis*. Oxford: Pergamon Press.

Craig, A. and S. Hart (1992). 'Where to Now in New Product Development Research?' *European Journal of Marketing*. Vol. 26. No. 11. pp. 2–49.

Crawford, C. (1991). *New Products Management* (3rd edn). Homewood, IL: Irwin.

Crocombe, G. (1991). *Upgrading New Zealand's Competitive Advantage*. Auckland: Oxford University Press.

Cubbin, J. and D. Leech (1983). 'The Effect of Shareholding Dispersion on the Degree of Control in British Companies: Theory and Measurement'. *Economic Journal*. Vol. 93. pp. 35–69.

Cudd, M. and R. Duggal (2000). 'Industry Distributional Characteristics of Financial Ratios: An Acquisition Theory Application'. *Financial Review*. Vol. 41. pp. 105–120.

Culkin, N., D. Smith and J. Fletcher (1999). 'Meeting the Information Needs of Marketing in the 21st Century'. *Marketing Intelligence and Planning*. Vol. 17. No. 1. pp. 6–12.

Cyert, R.M. and J.G. March (1963). *A Behavioural Theory of the Firm*. Englewood Cliffs, NJ: Prentice Hall.

Czinkota, M.R. and I.A. Ronkainen (1998). *International Marketing*. Fort Worth, TX: Dryden Press.

Daft, R.L., J. Sormunen and D. Parks (1988). 'Chief Executive Scanning, Environmental Characteristics, and Company Performance: An Empirical Study'. *Strategic Management Journal*. Vol. 9. pp. 123–139.

Dahya, J., J.J. McConnell and N.G. Travlos (2000). 'The Cadbury Committee, Corporate Performance and Top Management Turnover'. Manuscript. Purdue University.

Daily, C.M. and D.R. Dalton (1992). 'Financial Performance of Founder-Managed *versus* Professionally-Managed Small Corporations'. *Journal of Small Business Management*. Vol. 30. No. 2. p. 25.

Daily, C.M. and D.R. Dalton (1997). 'CEO and Board Chair Roles Held Jointly or Separately: Much Ado about Nothing?' *Academy of Management Executive*. Vol. 11. No. 3. p. 11.

Daily, C.M. and J.L. Johnson (1997). 'Sources of CEO Power and Firm Performance: A Longitudinal Assessment'. *Journal of Management*. Vol. 23. No. 2. p. 97.

Davidson, W.N., T. Pilger and A. Szakmary (1998). 'Golden Parachutes, Board and Committee Composition and Shareholder Wealth'. *Financial Review*. Vol. 33. No. 4. p. 17.

Davis, G.F. (1991). 'Agents without Principles? The Spread of the Poison Pill Through the Intercorporate Network'. *Administrative Science Quarterly*. Vol. 36. No. 4. p. 583.

Davis, G.F. and M.S. Mizruchi (1999). 'The Money Centre Cannot Hold: Commercial Banks in the US System of Corporate Governance'. *Administrative Science Quarterly*. Vol. 44. No. 2. pp. 215.

Deakin, E.B. (1972). 'A Discriminant Analysis of Predictors of Business Failure'. *Journal of Accounting Research*. March.

Debackere, K., A. Verbeek, M. Luwel and E. Zimmerman (2002). 'Measuring Progress and Evolution in Science and Technology – II: The Multiple Uses of Technometric Indicators'. *International Journal of Management Reviews*. Vol. 4. No. 3. pp. 213–231.

Del Bono, E. and K. Mayhew (2001). *The Specification and Quality of British Products*. SKOPE Working Paper Series. Department of Economics, University of Oxford.

Demsetz, H. (1983). 'The Structure of Ownership and the Theory of the Firm'. *Journal of Law and Economics*. Vol. 26. June. pp. 375–393.

Demsetz, H. (1997). 'The Firm in Economic Theory: A Quiet Revolution'. *American Economic Review*. Vol. 87. pp. 426–429.

Demsetz, H. and K. Lehn (1985). 'The Structure of Corporate Ownership: Causes and Consequences'. *Journal of Political Economy*. Vol. 93. pp. 1155–1177.

Department of Industry, Science and Technology (1996). *Australian Business Indicators: A Strategic Vision*. Canberra: Department of Industry, Science and Technology.

Department of Trade and Industry (2000). *Our Competitive Future: UK Competitiveness Indicators, 1999*. London: HMSO.

Department of Trade and Industry (2001). *UK Productivity Competitiveness Indicators*. London: Department of Trade and Industry.

Department of Trade and Industry (2003). *Competing in the Global Economy: The Innovation Challenge*. London: Department of Trade and Industry.

Department of Trade and Industry (2004). *The 2004 R&D Scoreboard*. London: Department of Trade and Industry.

Devine, P.J., N. Lee, R.M. Jones and W.J. Tyson (1985). *An Introduction to Industrial Economics* (4th edn). London: George, Allen and Unwin.

Dhalla, N.K. and S. Yuspeh (1976). 'Forget the Product Life Cycle Concept'. *Harvard Business Review*. January–February. pp. 102–110.

Dibb, S., L. Simpkin, W.M. Pride and O.C. Ferrel (2001). *Marketing Concepts and Strategies* (4th edn). Boston, MA: Houghton Mifflin.

Dixit, A.K. and R.S. Pindyck (1994). *Investment Under Uncertainty*. Princeton, MD: Princeton University Press.

Dixon, M.D. (undated). *The Patents Information Services of Derwent Publications Limited*. London: Derwent Publications.

Dodd, J. and S. Chen (1997). 'Economic Value Added'. *Arkansas Business and Economic Review*. Vol. 30. No. 4. pp. 1–8.

Dolan, R.J. and H. Simon (1996). *Power Pricing: How Managing Price Transforms the Bottom Line*. New York: Free Press.

Dollinger, M.J. (1984). 'Environmental Boundary Spanning and Information Processing Effects on Organisational Performance'. *Academy of Management Journal*. Vol. 27. pp. 351–368.

Donaldson, L. (1996). 'The Normal Science of Structural Contingency Theory'. In S.R. Clegg and C. Hardy (eds). *Studying Organization: Theory and Method*. London: Sage.

Donaldson, L. (1999). 'The Normal Science of Contingency Theory'. In S.R. Clegg and C. Hardy (eds). *Studying Organization: Theory and Method*. London: Sage.

Donaldson, L. (2001). *The Contingency Theory of Organizations*. Thousand Oaks, CA: Sage.

Dorfman, R. and P.O. Steiner (1954). 'Optimal Advertising and Optimal Quality'. *American Economic Review*. Vol. 44. pp. 826–836.

Doyle, P., J. Saunders and V. Wong (1992). 'Competition in Global Markets: A Case Study of American and Japanese Competition in the British Market'. *Journal of Business Studies*. Third quarter.

Drazin, R. and A.H. Van de Ven (1985). 'Alternative Forms of Fit in Contingency Theory'. *Administrative Science Quarterly*. Vol. 30. pp. 514–539.

D'Souza, J. and W.L. Megginson (1999). 'The Financial and Operating Performance of Privatised Firms During the 1990s'. *Journal of Finance. Papers and Proceedings*. Vol. 54. No. 4. pp. 1397–1438.

Duffy, M. (1996). 'Econometric Studies of Advertising Restrictions and Cigarette Demand: A Survey'. *International Journal of Advertising*. Vol. 15. No. 1. pp. 1–23.

Duffy, M. (1999). 'The Influence of Advertising on the Pattern of Food Consumption in the United Kingdom'. *International Journal of Advertising*. Vol. 18. No. 2. pp. 131–168.

Duffy, M. (2001). 'Advertising in Consumer Allocation Models: Choice of Functional Form'. *Applied Economics*. Vol. 33. No. 4. pp. 437–456.

Duffy, M. (2003a). 'On the Estimation of an Advertising-Augmented, Cointegrating Demand System'. *Economic Modelling*. Vol. 22. No. 1. pp. 181–206.

Duffy, M. (2003b). 'Advertising and Food, Drink, and Tobacco Consumption in the United Kingdom: A Dynamic Demand System'. *Agricultural Economics*. Vol. 28. pp. 51–70.

Dutta, P.K. (1999). *Strategies and Games: Theory and Practice*. Cambridge, MA: MIT Press.

Dutton, J. and R. Freedman (1985). 'External Environment and Internal Strategies: Calculating, Experimenting, and Imitating in Organizations'. In R. Lamb and P. Shrivastava (eds). *Advances in Strategic Management, Vol. 3*. Greenwich, CT: JAI Press.

Dutton, J. and A. Thomas (1984). 'Treating Progress Functions as Managerial Technology'. *Academy of Management Review*. Vol. 9. pp. 235–247.

Dwyer, L. and R. Mellor (1991). 'New Product Strategies of High Technology Firms'. *Asia Pacific International Forum*. No. 16. pp. 4–11.

Dyer, W.G. (1986). *Cultural Change in Family Firms*. San Francisco: Jossey-Bass.

Edquist, C. (2001). 'The Systems of Innovation Approach and Innovation Policy: An Account of the State of the Art'. Lead Paper, DRUID Conference, Aalborg. June.

Edwards, K.L. and R.J. Gordon (1984). *Characterisation of Innovations Introduced in the US Market Since 1992*. Glastonbury, CT: Futures Group.

Elias, P. (1992). 'Management Occupations'. In R.A. Wilson and R.M. Lindley (eds). *Review of the Economy and Employment, Occupational Case Studies*. Coventry: Institute for Employment Research, University of Warwick.

Engelsman, E.C. and A.F.J. Raan (1994). 'A Patent Based Cartography of Technology'. *Research Policy*. Vol. 23. pp. 1–26.

English, H.B. and A.C. English (1958). *A Comprehensive Dictionary of Psychological and Psychoanalytical Terms*. New York: Longman.

Epple, D., L. Argote and R. Devadas (1995). 'Organisational Learning Curves: A Method for Investigating Intra-plant Transfer of Knowledge Acquired Through Learning by Doing'. In M.D. Cohen and L.S. Sproul (eds). *Organizational Learning*. Thousand Oaks, CA: Sage. pp. 83–100.

Ergas, H. (1987). 'The Importance of Technology Policy'. In P. Dasgupta and P. Stoneman (eds). *Economic Policy and Technological Performance*. Cambridge: Cambridge University Press.

Ettorre, B. (1995). 'George Lorch Explains Economic Value Added'. *Management Review*. Vol. 84. No. 9. pp. 50–52.

European Commission (1994). *Innovation: The Community Innovation Survey. Status and Perspectives*. EUR 15378 EN. Directorate-General: Telecommunications, Information Market and Exploitation of Research. Luxembourg: Eurostat.

European Economics (2000). *Benefits of Trademarks and Infringement Damages Estimation*. London: European Economics. November. Draft.

Fagerberg, J. (1988). 'International Competitiveness'. *Economic Journal*. Vol. 98. No. 391. pp. 355–374.

Fama, E.F. (1980). 'Agency Problems and the Theory of the Firm'. *Journal of Political Economy*. Vol. 88. No. 2. pp. 288–307.

Fama, E.F. and M.C. Jensen (1983). 'Separation of Ownership and Control'. *Journal of Law and Economics*. Vol. 26. pp. 301–325.

Farmer, R.N. and B.M. Richman (1964). 'A Model for Research in Comparative Management'. *Californian Management Review*. Vol. 7. Winter. pp. 55–68.

Federico, P.J. (1958). *Renewal Fees and Other Patent Fees in Foreign Countries*. Study of the Subcommittee on Patents, Trade Marks and Copyrights of the Committee of the Judiciary US Senate, 85th Congress. Second Session Study No. 217. Washington, DC: Government Printing Office.

Feeny, S. and M. Rogers (2000). *R&D and Intellectual Property Scoreboard 2000*. Melbourne: Melbourne Institute.

Ferguson, J.M. (1974). *Advertising and Competition: Theory, Measurement, Fact.* Cambridge, MA: Ballinger.

Ferguson, P.R., G.J. Ferguson and R. Rothschild (1993). *Business Economics.* London: Macmillan.

Finegold, D. (1999). 'Creating Self-sustaining, High-Skill Ecosystems'. *Oxford Review of Economic Policy.* Vol. 15. No. 1.

Finegold, D. and G. Mason (1999). 'National Training Systems and Industrial Performance: US–European Matched Plant Comparisons'. *Research in Labour Economics.* Vol. 18. pp. 331–358.

Finegold, D. and Soskice, D. (1988). 'The Failure of Training in Britain: Analysis and Prescription'. *Oxford Review of Economic Policy.* Autumn. pp. 21–51.

Finkelstein, S. and R.A. D'Aveni (1994). 'CEO Duality as a Double-Edged Sword: How Board of Directors Balance Entrenchment Avoidance and Unity of Command'. *Academy of Management Journal.* Vol. 37. No. 5. pp. 1079–1108.

Finniston, M. (chair) (1980). *Engineering Our Future.* Cmnd. 7794. London: HMSO.

Flamholtz, E.G. (1986). *How to Make the Transition from an Entrepreneurship to a Professionally Managed Firm.* San Francisco: Jossey-Bass.

Fligstein, N. (1985). 'The Spread of the Multidivisional Form Among Large Firms, 1919–1979'. *American Sociological Review.* Vol. 50. pp. 377–391.

Fligstein, N. (1987). 'The Intraorganizational Power Struggle: Rise of Finance Personnel to Top Leadership in Large Corporations, 1919–1979'. *American Sociological Review.* Vol. 52. pp. 44–58.

Forbes, D.P. and F.J. Milliken (1999). 'Cognition and Corporate Governance: Understanding Boards of Directors as Strategic Decision-Making Groups'. *Academy of Management Review.* Vol. 24. No. 3. p. 489.

Foss, N.J. (1998). 'Real Options and the Theory of the Firm'. In R. Sanchez (ed). *Options Theory in Strategic Management.* London: Sage.

Foster, B.P. and T.J. Ward (1997). 'Financial Health or Insolvency? Watch Trends and Interactions in Your Cash Flows'. *Journal of the Academy of Accounting and Financial Studies.* Vol. 1. No. 1. pp. 33–37.

Franks, J. and C. Mayer (1997). 'Corporate Ownership and Control in the UK, Germany and France'. *Journal of Applied Corporate Finance.* Vol. 8. No. 1. pp. 30–45.

Fredriksen, Ø. and M. Klofsten (1999). 'CEO versus Board Typologies in Venture Capital–Entrepreneur Relationships'. See www.babson.edu/entrep/fer/papers99/XV/XV_A/XV_A.html. Last accessed 18 March 2005.

Freear, J. and W.E. Wetzel (1992). 'The Informal Venture Capital Market in the 1990's'. In D.L. Sexton and J.D. Kasarda (eds). *The State of the Art of Entrepreneurship.* Boston: PWS Kent. pp. 462–486.

Freeman, C. (1962). 'Research and Development: A Comparison Between British and American Industry'. *NIESR Economic Review.* Vol. 20. May.

Freeman, C. (1969). *Measurement of Output of Research and Experimental Development.* Statistical Reports and Studies. Paris: UNESCO.

Freeman, C. (2002). 'Continental, National and Sub-national Innovation Systems – Compementarity and Economic Growth'. *Research Policy.* Vol. 31. pp. 191–211.

Freeman, C. and L. Soete (1997). *The Economics of Industrial Innovation.* Cambridge, MA: MIT Press.

Freeman, R. (1971). *The Market for College Trained Manpower.* Cambridge: Cambridge University Press.

Freeman, R. (1975). 'Supply and Salary Adjustments to the Changing Science Manpower Market'. *American Economic Review.* Vol. 65. No. 1. pp. 27–39.

Freeman, R. (1976). 'A Cobweb Model of the Supply and Starting Salary of New Engineers'. *Industrial Labour Relations Review.* January.

Freeman, R. (1981). 'Response to Change in the U.S.' In R. M. Lindley (ed.). *Higher Education and the Labour Market*. Guildford: Society for Research into Higher Education.

Friedman, M. (1953). *Essays in Positive Economics*. Chicago, IL: University of Chicago Press.

Frydman, R., C.W. Gray, M. Hessel and A. Rapaczynski (1997). *Private Ownership and Corporate Performance: Evidence from Transition Economies*. Working Paper No. 26. London: EBRD.

Galbraith, J.K. (1967). *The New Industrial State*. Boston, MA: Houghton Mifflin.

Gartner, W.B. (1988). 'Who Is an Entrepreneur? Is the Wrong Question'. *American Journal of Small Business*. Vol. 12. No. 4. pp. 11–32.

Geletkanycz, M.A. and D.C. Hambrick (1997). 'The External Ties of Top Executives: Implications for Strategic Choice and Performance'. *Administrative Science Quarterly*. Vol. 42. No. 4. p. 654.

Getz, D. and J. Carlsen (2000). 'Characteristics and Goals of Family and Owner-Operated Businesses in the Rural Tourism and Hospitality Sectors'. *Tourism Management*. Vol. 21. No. 6. December. pp. 547–560.

Ghemawat, P. (1985). 'Building Strategy on the Experience Curve'. *Harvard Business Review*. March/April.

Ghosh, B.C., H.P. Schoch, D.B. Taylor, W.W. Kwan and T.S. Kim (1994). 'Top Performing Organisations of Australia, New Zealand and Singapore'. *Marketing Intelligence and Planning*. Vol. 12. No. 7. pp. 39–48.

Giacomino, D.E. and D.E. Mielke (1993). 'Cash Flows: Another Approach to Ratio Analysis'. *Journal of Accountancy*. Vol. 175. No. 3. pp. 55–58.

Gibb, J.R. (1978). *Trust: A New View of Personal and Organizational Development*. Los Angeles: Guild of Tutors Press.

Gibbons, M., R. Coombes, P. Saviotti and P.C. Stubbs (1981). *Innovation and Technological Change: A Case Study of the UK Tractor Industry, 1957–1977*. Discussion Paper. University of Manchester.

Gilfillan, S.C. (1964). *Invention and the Patent System*. Joint Economic Committee Congress of the United States. Washington, DC: Government Printing Office.

Gill, J. (1985). *Factors Affecting the Survival and Growth of the Smaller Company*. Aldershot: Gower.

Gill, R.T. (1974). *Economics: A Text with Included Readings*. London: Prentice Hall.

Goddard, J.A. and J.O.S. Wilson (1999). 'The Persistence of Profit: A New Empirical Interpretation'. *International Journal of Industrial Organization*. Vol. 17. No. 5. pp. 663–687.

Gomez-Mejia, L.R. (1994). 'Executive Compensation: A Reassessment and a Future Research Agenda'. In G.R. Ferris (ed.). *Research in Personnel and Human Resource Management*. Vol. 12. pp. 161–222. Greenwich, CT: JAI Press.

Gomez-Mejia, L.R., H. Tosi and T. Hinkin (1987). 'Managerial Control, Performance, and Executive Compensation'. *Academy of Management Journal*. Vol. 30. pp. 51–70.

Gomulka, S. (1990). *The Theory of Technological Change and Economic Growth*. London: Routledge.

Gort, M. and S-H. Lee (2003). *Managerial Efficiency, Organisational Capital and Productivity*. Discussion Paper. Center for Economic Studies, Bureau of the Census, Washington, DC.

Gort, M., H. Grabowski and R.M. McGuckin (1985). 'Organisation Capital and the Choice Between Specialisation and Diversification'. *Managerial and Decision Economics*. Vol. 6. March. pp. 2–10.

Grabowski, H.G. and D.C. Mueller (1978). 'Industrial Research and Development, Intangible Capital Stocks and Firm Profit Rates'. *Bell Journal of Economics*. Vol. 9. No. 2. pp. 328–343.

Grabowski, H.G. and J.M. Vernon (1992). 'Brand Loyalty, Entry and Price Competition in Pharmaceuticals after the 1984 Drug Act'. *Journal of Law and Economics*. Vol. 35. pp. 331–350.

Grabowski, H.G. and J.M. Vernon (1996). 'Longer Patents for Increased Generic Competition in the US'. *Pharmaco-Economics*. Vol. 10. pp. 110–123.

Granstrand, O. (1999). *The Economics and Management of Intellectual Property*. Cheltenham: Edward Elgar.

Grantham, L.M. (1997). 'The Validity of the Product Life Cycle in the High-Tech Industry'. *Marketing Intelligence and Planning*. Vol. 15. No. 1. pp. 4–10.

Greenbury, R. (1995). *Directors' Remuneration: Report of a Study Group Chaired by Sir Richard Greenbury*. London: Gee Publishing.

Greene, P.G. and T. Brown (1997). 'Resource Needs and the Dynamic Capitalism Typology'. *Journal of Business Venturing*. Vol. 12. No. 3. pp. 161–174.

Greenhalgh, C. (1990). 'Innovation and Trade Performance in the UK'. *Economic Journal*. Vol. 100. No. 400. pp. 105–118.

Greenhalgh, C. and M. Longland (2004). *Intellectual Property Scoreboards for the UK in 2000*. Working Paper. Oxford Intellectual Property Research Centre, St Peter's College, Oxford.

Greenhalgh, C., P. Taylor and R. Wilson (1994). 'Innovation and Export Volumes and Prices: A Disaggregated Study'. *Oxford Economic Papers*. Vol. 46. pp. 102–135.

Greenhalgh, C., M. Longland and D. Bosworth (2000). *Protecting Intellectual Property: British, European and American Patents and Trade Marks of Selected UK Companies, 1986–95*. Discussion Paper. Oxford Intellectual Property Research Centre, St Peter's College. Oxford.

Griliches, Z. (1958). 'Research Cost and Social Returns: Hybrid Corn and Related Innovations'. *Journal of Political Economy*. Vol. 66. pp. 419–431.

Griliches, Z. (1981). 'Market Value, R&D, and Patents'. *Economic Letters*. Vol. 7. pp. 183–187.

Griliches, Z. (1990). 'Patent Statistics as Economic Indicators: A Survey'. *Journal of Economic Literature*. Vol. 28. December. pp. 1661–1707.

Griliches, Z. (1992). 'The Search for R&D Spillovers'. *Scandinavian Journal of Economics*. Vol. 94. pp. 29–47.

Griliches, Z. (1995). 'R&D and Productivity: Econometric Results and Measurement Issues'. In P.A. Stoneman (ed.). *Handbook of the Economics of Innovation and Technological Change*. Oxford: Blackwell. pp. 52–89.

Griliches, Z. and H. Regev (1995). 'Firm Productivity in Israeli Industry'. *Journal of Econometrics*. Vol. 65. pp. 175–203.

Grossman, G.M. and O. Hart (1986). 'The Costs and Benefits of Ownership: A Theory of Vertical Integration'. *Journal of Political Economy*. Vol. 94. pp. 691–719.

Grossman, G.M. and C. Shapiro (1984). 'Informative Advertising with Differentiated Products'. *Review of Economic Studies*. Vol. 51. No. 1. pp. 63–81.

Guellec, D. and B. van Pottelsberghe de la Potterie (2001). *R&D and Productivity Growth: Panel Data Analysis of 16 OECD Countries*. Paris: OECD.

Hair, J.F, R.E. Anderson, R.L. Tatham and W.C. Black (1995). *Multivariate Analysis with Readings*. Englewood Cliffs, NJ: Prentice Hall.

Hall, B. (1993a). 'The Stock Market's Valuation of R&D Investment During the 1980s'. *American Economic Review: Papers and Proceedings*. Vol. 83. No. 2. pp. 259–264.

Hall, B. (1993b). *The Value of Intangible Corporate Assets: An Empirical Study of the Components of Tobin's Q*. Working Paper No. 93-207. Hoover Institute, Stanford University. University of California at Berkeley and NBER.

Hall, B.H. (2000). 'Innovation and Market Value'. In R. Barrell, G. Mason and M. O'Mahony (eds). *Productivity, Innovation and Economic Performance*. Cambridge: Cambridge University Press. pp. 177–198.

Hall, B.H., A.B. Jaffe and M. Trajtenberg (1998). *Patent Citations: A First Look*. NBER Working Paper No. 7741. Cambridge, MA: National Bureau for Economic Research.

Hamermesh, D. (1988). 'Plant Closures and the Value of the Firm'. *Review of Economics and Statistics*. Vol. 70. pp. 580–586.

Hampel, R. (1998). *Committee on Corporate Governance: Final Report*. London: Gee Publishing.

Han, K.C. and D.Y. Suk (1998). 'The Effect of Ownership Structure on Firm Performance: Additional Evidence'. *Review of Financial Economics*. Vol. 7. No. 2. p. 143.

Harhoff, D., F. Narin, F.M. Scherer and K. Vopel (1997a). *Citation Frequency and the Value of Patented Innovation*. Discussion Paper FS IV 97–26. Forschungsschwerpunkt Marktprozeß und Unternehmensentwicklung.

Harhoff, D., F.M. Scherer and K. Vopel (1997b). *Exploring the Tail of Patented Invention Value Distributions*. Discussion Paper No. FS IV 97–27. Forschungsschwerpunkt Marktprozeß und Unternehmensentwicklung.

Harrigan, J. (undated). *Cross-Country Comparisons of Industry Total Factor Productivity: Theory and Evidence*. Research Paper No. 9734. New York: Federal Reserve Bank.

Hart, H. (1957). 'Acceleration in Social Change'. In J.F. Cuber (ed.). *Technology and Social Change*. New York: Appleton-Century-Crofts. pp. 27–55.

Hart, H.C. (1949). 'Re Citation System for Patent Office'. *Journal of the Patent Office Society*. Vol. 31. p. 714.

Hart, O. (1995). 'Corporate Governance: Some Theory and Implications'. *Economic Journal*. Vol. 105. pp. 678–689.

Hart, O. (1996). *Firms, Contracts and Financial Structure*. Oxford: Oxford University Press.

Hart, S. (1989). 'Product Deletion and the Effects of Strategy'. *European Journal of Marketing*. Vol. 23. No. 10. pp. 6–17.

Hartley, K. (1965). 'The Learning Curve and its Application to the Aircraft Industry'. *Journal of Industrial Economics*. Vol. 13. March. pp. 122–128.

Hartmann, G.C. and M.B. Myers (2000). 'Technical Risk, Product Specifications and Market Risk'. In L.M. Branscomb and P.E. Auerswald (eds). *Taking Technical Risks: How Innovators Manage Risk in High-Tech Innovations*. Cambridge, MA: MIT Press. pp. 29–39. References made in the present book are taken from the authors' manuscript, made available on the web.

Hay, D.A. and D.J. Morris (1979). *Industrial Economics: Theory and Evidence*. Oxford: Oxford University Press.

Heidensohn, K. and N. Robinson (1974). *Business Behaviour: An Economic Approach*. Oxford: Philip Alan.

Helfert, E.A. (1994). *Techniques of Financial Analysis: A Practical Guide to Managing and Measuring Business Performance* (8th edn). Chicago, IL: Irwin Professional.

Helpman, E. (1998). 'Introduction'. In E. Helpman (ed.). *General Purpose Technology and Economic Growth*. Cambridge, MA: MIT Press. pp. 1–14.

Henderson, R.M. (1995). 'Technological Change and the Management of Architectural Knowledge'. In M.D. Cohe and L.S. Sproul (eds). *Organizational Learning*. Thousand Oaks, CA: Sage. pp. 359–375.

Henebry, K.L. (1996). 'Do Cash Flow Variables Improve the Predictive Accuracy of a Cox Proportional Hazards Model for Bank Failure?' *Quarterly Review of Economics and Finance*. Vol. 36. No. 3. pp. 395–409.

Herbert, R.F. and A.N. Link (1982). *The Entrepreneur*. New York: Praeger.

Hermalin, B.E. and M.S. Weisbach (1991). 'The Effects of Board Composition and Direct Incentives on Firm Performance'. *Financial Management*. Vol. 20. No. 4. p. 101.

Hiam, A. (1992). *Closing the Quality Gap: Lessons from America's Leading Companies*. Englewood Cliffs, NJ: Prentice Hall.

Hicks, D., T. Ishizuka, P. Keen and S. Sweet (1994). 'Japanese Corporations, Scientific Research and Globalization'. *Research Policy*. Vol. 23. No. 4. July. pp. 375–384.

Hirsch, W. (1952). 'Manufacturing Progress Functions'. *Review of Economics and Statistics*. Vol. 34. No. 2. pp. 134–155.

Hirsch, W. (1956). 'Firm Progress Ratio'. *Econometrica*. Vol. 24. No. 2. pp. 136–143.

Hirschey, M. (1982). 'Intangible Capital Aspects of Advertising and R&D Expenditures'. *Journal of Industrial Economics*. Vol. 30. No. 4. pp. 375–389.

Hobday, M. (2000). 'The Project-Based Organisation: An Ideal Form for Managing Complex Products and Systems'. *Research Policy*. Vol. 29. pp. 871–893.

Hodgson, G.M. (1998). 'Evolutionary and Competence-Based Theories of the Firm'. *Journal of Economic Studies*. Vol. 25. No. 1. pp. 25–56.

Hogarth, T. and R. Wilson (eds) (2003). *Tackling the Low Skills Equilibrium: A Review of Issues and Some New Evidence*. Research Report to the DTI. Institute for Employment Research, University of Warwick.

Hollander, S. (1965). *The Sources of Increased Efficiency: A Study of Du Pont Rayon Plants*. Cambridge, MA: MIT Press.

Holstrom, B. and J. Rogers (1998). 'The Boundaries of the Firm'. *Journal of Economic Perspectives*. Vol. 12. No. 4. pp. 73–94.

Hooley, G.J. and J.E. Lynch (1985). 'Marketing Lessons from the UK's High Flying Companies'. *Journal of Marketing Management*. Vol. 1. No. 1. pp. 65–74.

Hooley, G., J. Lynch, R. Brooksbank and J. Shepherd (1988). 'Strategic Market Environments'. *Journal of Marketing Management*. Vol. 4. No. 2. pp. 131–147.

Horne, J.V., K. Davis, R. Nicol and K. Wright (1990). *Financial Management and Policy in Australia*. New York: Prentice Hall.

Horsley Keogh Associates (1990). *Horsley Keogh Venture Study*. San Francisco. Reported in Scherer (1996).

Hoskisson, R.E. and M.A. Hitt (1990). 'Antecedents and Performance Outcomes of Diversification: A Review and Critique of Theoretical Perspectives'. *Journal of Management*. Vol. 16. No. 2. pp. 461–509.

Hoskisson, R.E., R.A. Johnson and D.D. Moesel (1994). 'Corporate Divestiture Intensity in Restructuring Firms: Effects of Governance, Strategy and Performance'. *Academy of Management Journal*. Vol. 37. No. 5. p. 1207.

Hu, A.G.Z. and A.B. Jaffe (2001). *Patent Citations and International Knowledge Flow: The Cases of Korea and Taiwan*. NBER Working Paper No. 8528. Cambridge, MA: National Bureau for Economic Research.

Huber, G.P. (1995). 'Organizational Learning: The Contributing Processes'. In M.D. Cohen and L.S. Sproul (eds). *Organizational Learning*. Thousand Oaks, CA: Sage. pp. 124–162.

Hudson, J. (2000). 'Generic Take-Up in the Pharmaceutical Market Following Patent Expiry: A Multi-country Study'. *International Review of Law and Economics*. Vol. 20. pp. 205–221.

Huffman, S.P. and D.J. Ward (1996). 'The Prediction of Default for High Yield Bond Issues'. *Review of Financial Economics*. Vol. 5. No. 1. pp. 75–89.

Huffman, W.E. and R.E. Evenson (1993). *Science for Agriculture*. Iowa City: Iowa State University Press.

Hurley, S.F. and S. Kadipasaoglu (1998). 'Wandering Bottlenecks: Speculating on the True Causes'. *Production and Inventory Management Journal*. Vol. 39. No. 4. pp. 1–4.

Hurwitz, M.A. and R.E. Caves (1988). 'Persuasion or Information? Promotion and the Shares of Brand Name and Generic Pharmaceuticals'. *Journal of Law and Economics*. Vol. 31. pp. 299–320.

Huselid, M.A. (1995). 'The Impact of Human Resource Management Practices on Turnover, Productivity, and Corporate Financial Performance'. *Academy of Management Journal.* Vol. 38. No. 3. pp. 635–672.

Hyams, M. and C. Oppenheim (1983). *Technological Forecasting Based Upon the Statistical Analysis of Patent Databases.* Infodial Paper. London: Derwent Publications.

IMD (2004). *IMD World Competitiveness Yearbook.* Geneva: World Competitiveness Centre, International Institute for Management Development.

Ingham, H. and S. Thompson (1995). 'Mutuality, Performance and Executive Compensation'. *Oxford Bulletin of Economics and Statistics.* Vol. 57. No. 3. pp. 295–308.

Jacobsson, S. and J. Philipson (1993). 'Indicators of Technological Activities – Comparing Educational, Patent and R&D Statistics in the Case of Sweden'. Paper presented at Säro Conference on Technical and Industrial Development, School of Technology Management, Chalmers University, Gothenberg.

Jaffe, A. (1986). 'Technological Opportunity and Spillovers of R&D: Evidence from Firms' Patents, Profits and Market Value'. *American Economic Review.* Vol. 76. No. 5. pp. 984–1001.

Jaffe, A.B. and M. Trajtenberg (1996). *Flows of Knowledge from Universities and Federal Labs: Modelling the Flow of Patent Citations over Time and across Institutional and Geographic Boundaries.* NBER Working Paper No. 5712. Cambridge, MA: National Bureau for Economic Research.

Jaffe, A.B., B. Hall and M. Trajtenberg (2000). *Market Value and Patent Citations: A First Look.* NBER Working Paper No. 7411. Cambridge, MA: National Bureau for Economic Research.

Jarrell, G.A., K. Lehn and W. Marr (1985). *Institutional Ownership, Tender Offers and Long-Term Investments.* Washington, DC: Office of the Chief Economist, Securities and Exchange Commission.

Jensen, C.M. (1986). 'Agency Costs of Free Cash Flow, Corporate Finance, and Takeovers'. *American Economic Review.* Vol. 76. May. pp. 323–329.

Jensen, M.C. (1988). 'Takeovers: Their Causes and Consequences'. *Journal of Economic Perspectives.* Vol. 2. pp. 21–48.

Jensen, M.C. and W.H. Meckling (1976). 'Theory of the Firm: Managerial Behaviour, Agency Costs and Ownership Structure'. *Journal of Financial Economics.* Vol. 3. pp. 305–360.

Jensen, M.C. and K.J. Murphy (1990). 'CEO Incentives – It's Not How Much You Pay, But How'. *Harvard Business Review.* May–June. pp. 138–153.

Johansen, L. (1972). *Production Functions: Micro and Macro, Short Run and Long Run Aspects.* Amsterdam: North Holland.

John, T.A. (1993). 'Accounting Measures of Corporate Liquidity, Leverage and Costs of Financial Distress'. *Financial Management.* Vol. 22. No. 3. pp. 91–100.

Johne, F.A. (1994). 'New Style Product Development: The Essential Ingredients'. In J. Saunders (ed.). *ESRC Studies into British Marketing.* London: Prentice Hall.

Johnson, A. and S. Jacobsson (2000). 'The Emergence of a Growth Industry: A Comparative Analysis of the German, Dutch and Swedish Wind Turbine Industries'. Paper presented at the Schumpeter Conference, Manchester.

Johnson, J.L., C.M. Daily and A.E. Ellstrand (1996). 'Boards of Directors: A Review and Research Agenda'. *Journal of Management.* Vol. 22. No. 3. p. 409.

Johnson, L.D. and B. Pazderka (1993). 'Firm Value and Investment in R&D'. *Management and Decision Economics.* Vol. 14. pp. 15–24.

Jones, C.C. (1998). *Introduction to Economic Growth.* New York: Norton.

Jorgenson, D.W. and B.M. Fraumeni (1992). 'Investment in Education and US Economic Growth'. *Scandinavian Journal of Economics.* Vol. 94. Supplement. pp. 51–70.

Jorgenson, D.W. and Z. Griliches (1967). 'The Explanation of Productivity Change'. *Review of Economic Studies*. Vol. 34. No. 99. pp. 249–280.

Jorgenson, D.W. and K.J. Stiroh (1995). 'Computers and Growth'. *Journal of Innovation and New Technology*. Vol. 3. Nos 3–4. pp. 295–316.

Jorgenson, D.W. and K.J. Stiroh (1998). *The Role of Computer Investment and Consumption in US Growth*. Mimeo. Harvard University.

Judge, W.Q. and C.P. Zeithaml (1992). 'Institutional and Strategic Choice Perspectives on Board Involvement in the Strategic Decision Process'. *Academy of Management Journal*. Vol. 35. No. 4. p. 766.

Kaplan, D. and L. Glass (1995). *Understanding Nonlinear Dynamics*. New York: Springer-Verlag.

Kaplan, R.S. and D.P. Norton (1992). 'The Balanced Scorecard – Measures That Drive Performance'. *Harvard Business Review*. January–February. pp. 71–79.

Kauffman, S., J. Lobo and W.G. Macready (2000). 'Optimal Search on a Technology Landscape'. *Journal of Economic Behavior and Organization*. Vol. 43. pp. 141–166.

Kay, J. (1991). 'The Economics of Mutuality'. *Annals of Public and Cooperative Economics*. Vol. 62. No. 3. pp. 309–318.

Kay, J. (1995). *Foundations of Corporate Success*. Oxford: Oxford University Press.

Kay, J. and A. Silberston (1995). 'Corporate Governance'. *National Institute Economic Review*. August. pp. 84–97.

Keat, P.G. and P.K.Y. Young (2000). *Managerial Economics: Economics Tools for Today's Decision Makers*. Upper Saddle River, NJ: Prentice Hall.

Keats, B.W. (1990). 'Diversification and Business Economic Performance Revisited: Issues of Measurement and Causality'. *Journal of Management*. Vol.16. No. 1. pp. 61–72.

Kellogg, D. and J.M. Charnes (2000). 'Real Options Valuation Methods for a Bio-technology Company'. *Financial Analysts Journal*. Vo. 56. No. 3. May/June. pp. 76–84.

Kesner, I.F. and R.B. Johnson. (1990). 'An Investigation of the Relationship Between Board Composition and Shareholder Suits'. *Strategic Management Journal*. Vol. 11. pp. 327–336.

Kettinger, W., V. Grover, S. Guha and A. Segars (1994). 'Strategic Information Systems Revisited: A Study in Sustainability and Performance'. *MIS Quarterly*. Vol. 18. pp. 31–55.

Kirzner, I.M. (1997). *How Markets Work: Disequilibrium, Entrepreneurship and Discovery*. IEA Hobart Paper No. 133. London: Institute for Economic Affairs.

Klaas, P. (2003). *Towards a Concept of Dynamic Fit in Contingency Theory*. Discussion Paper. Odense: University of Southern Denmark.

Kleinknecht, A. (1991). *Towards Literature Based Innovation Indicators*. Amsterdam: SEO.

Kleinknecht, A. (1993). 'Why Do We Need New Innovation Output Indicators? An Introduction'. In A. Kleinknecht (ed.). *New Concepts in Innovation Output Measurement*. London: St Martin's Press. pp. 1–9.

Kleinknecht, A. and J.O.N. Reijnen (1993). 'Towards Literature-Based Innovation Output Indicators'. *Structural Change and Economic Dynamics*. Vol. 4. No. 1. pp. 199–207.

Kleinschmidt, E.J. and R.G. Cooper (1995). 'The Relative Importance of New Product Success Determinants – Perception *versus* Reality'. *R&D Management*. Vol. 25. No. 3. July. pp. 281–299.

Kling, J. (1995). 'High Performance Work Systems and Firm Performance'. *Monthly Labour Review*. May. pp. 29–36.

Klofsten, M., M. Jonsson and J. Simon (1999). 'Supporting the Precommercialisation Stages of Technology-Based Firms: The Effects of Small Scale Venture Capitalism'. *Venture Capital*. Vol. 1. No. 1. pp. 83–93.

Knight, F. (1921). *Risk, Uncertainty and Profit*. New York: Houghton Mifflin.

Koshal, R.K. and S. Pejovich (1992). 'A Note on the Separation of Ownership From Control'. *Management International Review*. Vol. 32. Special Issue. pp. 103–104.

Kourteli, L. (2000). 'Scanning the Business Environment: Some Conceptual Issues'. *Benchmarking: An International Journal*. Vol. 7. No. 5. pp. 406–413.

Kroszner, R.S. and P.E. Strahan (1996). 'Regulatory Incentives and the Thrift Crisis: Dividends, Mutual-to-Stock Conversions and Financial Distress'. *Journal of Finance*. Vol. 51. No. 4. pp. 1285–1319.

Kroszner, R.S. and P.E. Strahan (1998). *What Drives Deregulation? Economics and Politics of the Relaxation of Bank Branching Restrictions*. Working Paper. Graduate School of Business Research Department. University of Chicago. Chicago. September.

Kusewitt, J.B. (1985). 'An Exploratory Study of Strategic Acquisition Factors Relating to Performance'. *Strategic Management Journal*. Vol. 6. April–June. pp. 151–169.

Lambin, J.J. (1976). *Advertising, Competition and Market Conduct in Oligopoly Over Time*. Amsterdam: North Holland.

Lamont, B.T. and C.A. Anderson (1985). 'Mode of Corporate Diversification and Economic Performance'. *Academy of Management Journal*. Vol. 28. December. pp. 926–934.

Lancaster, K. (1966). 'A New Approach to Consumer Theory'. *Journal of Political Economy*. Vol. 74. pp. 132–157.

Landström, H. (1990). 'Co-operation Between Venture Capital Companies and Small Firms'. *Journal of Entrepreneurship and Regional Development*. Vol. 2. No. 4. pp. 345–362.

Lant, T.K. and S.J. Mezias (1995). 'An Organizational Model of Convergence and Learning'. In M.D. Cohen and L.S. Sproul (eds) (1995). *Organizational Learning*. Thousand Oaks, CA: Sage. pp. 267–301.

Laursen, K. and N.J. Foss (2000). 'New HRM Practices, Complementarities, and the Impact on Innovation Performance'. Paper presented at the Econometrics of Trademarks and Patents Conference, Alicante, Spain.

Lawrence, P. and Lorsch, J. (1967). *Organization and Environment*. Cambridge, MA: Harvard University Press.

Layard R., S. McIntosh and A. Vignoles (2001). *Britain's Record on Skills*. Working Paper. Performance and Innovation Unit, London School of Economics.

Learning and Skills Council (2003). *Skills in England, Vol. 1*. Coventry: Learning and Skills Council.

Leibenstein, H. (1966). 'Allocative Efficiency vs. X-Efficiency'. *American Economic Review*. Vol. 56. No. 3. pp. 392–415.

Lev, B. and T. Sougiannis (1996). 'The Capitalisation, Amorisation and Value-Relevance of R&D'. *Journal of Accounting and Economics*. Vol. 21. pp. 107–138.

Levin R. and P. Reiss (1984). 'Test of a Schumpeterian Model of R&D and Market Structure'. In Z. Griliches (ed.). *R&D, Patents and Productivity*. Chicago: University of Chicago Press. pp. 175–208.

Levitt, B. and J.G. March (1988). 'Organisational Learning'. *Annual Review of Sociology*. Vol. 14. pp. 319–340.

Levy, H. (1991). 'Possible Explanations of No-Synergy Mergers and Small-Firm Effect by the Generalised Capital Asset Pricing Model'. *Review of Quantitative Finance and Accounting*. Vol. 1. pp. 101–127.

Levy, H. and M. Sarnat (1970). 'Diversification, Portfolio Analysis and the Uneasy Case for Conglomerate Mergers'. *Journal of Finance*. September. pp. 795–802.

Lichtenberg, F.R. (1995). 'The Output Contributions of Computer Equipment and Personnel: A Firm-Level Analysis'. *Economics of Innovation and New Technology*. Vol. 3. pp. 201–217.

Lieberman, M. (1984). 'The Learning Curve and Pricing in the Chemical Processing Industries'. *Rand Journal of Economics*. Vol. 15. No. 2. pp. 213–228.

Light, D.A. (1998). 'Performance Measurement'. *Harvard Business Review*. November–December. p. 17.

Likert, R. (1932). *A Technique for the Measurement of Attitudes*. New York: McGraw-Hill.

Likert, R. (1967). *The Human Organization: Its Management and Value*. New York: McGraw-Hill.

Lilien, G.L., A.J. Silk, J.M. Choffray and M. Rao (1976). 'Industrial Advertising Effects and Budgeting Practices'. *Journal of Marketing*. Vol. 40. No. 1. pp. 16–24.

Lloyd, W.P., J.H. Hand and N.K. Modani (1987). 'The Effect of the Degree of Ownership Control on Firm Diversification, Market Value and Merger Activity'. *Journal of Business Research*. Vol. 15. pp. 303–312.

Loomes, G. (1991). 'Experimental Methods in Economics'. In D. Greenaway, M. Bleaney and I.M.T. Stewart (eds). *Companion to Contemporary Economic Thought*. London: Routledge. pp. 593–613.

Lundberg, E. (1961). *Produktivitet och Rantabilitet*. Stockholm: P.A. Norstedt and Soner.

Lundvall, B.-A., B. Johnson, E.S. Andersen and B. Dalum (2002). 'National Systems of Production, Innovation and Competence Building'. *Research Policy*. Vol. 31. pp. 213–231.

Lynch, L. and S. Black (1995). *Beyond the Incidence of Training: Evidence from a National Employer's Survey*. NBER Working Paper Series No. 5232. Cambridge, MA: National Bureau for Economic Research.

Maclean, M. (1999). 'Corporate Governance in France and the UK: Long-Term Perspectives on Contemporary Institutional Arrangements'. *Business History*. Vol. 41. No. 1. pp. 88–116.

Main, B.G.M. and J. Johnson (1993). 'Remuneration Committees and Corporate Governance'. *Accounting and Business Research*. Vol. 23. pp. 351–362.

Mairesse, J. and P. Mohnen (1995). *Research and Development and Productivity – A Survey of the Econometric Literature*. Paris: Insee.

Mairesse, J. and M. Sassenou (1991). 'R&D and Productivity: A Survey of Econometric Studies at the Firm Level'. *Science, Technology and Industry Review: OECD*. Vol. 7. pp. 265–269.

Majumdar, S. (1998). 'The Impact of Human Capital Quality on the Boundaries of the Firm in the US Telecommunications Industry'. *Industrial and Corporate Change*. Vol. 7. No. 4. pp. 663–677.

Malerba, F. (1992). 'Learning by Firms and Incremental Technical Change'. *Economic Journal*. Vol. 102. No. 413. July. pp. 845–859.

Malerba, F. (2002). 'Sectoral Systems of Innovation and Production'. *Research Policy*. Vol. 31. pp. 247–264.

Malhotra, N.K. (1999). *Marketing Research: An Applied Orientation*. Englewood Cliffs, NJ: Prentice Hall.

March, J.G. (1981). 'Footnotes to Organisational Change'. *Administrative Science Quarterly*. Vol. 26. pp. 563–577.

March, J.G. (1995). 'Exploration and Exploitation in Organisational Learning'. In M.D. Cohen and L.S. Sproul (eds) (1995). *Organizational Learning*. Thousand Oaks, CA: Sage. pp. 101–133.

March, J.G., L.S. Sproul and M. Tamuz (1995). 'Learning from Samples of One or Fewer'. In M.D. Cohen and L.S. Sproul (eds). *Organizational Learning*. Thousand Oaks, CA: Sage. pp. 1–19.

Marris, R. (1964). *The Economic Theory of Managerial Capitalism*. London: Macmillan.

Marsh, P. (2001). 'New Millenniums Winners and Losers'. *Financial Times*. 29 October. p. 12.

Marshall, A. (1890). *Principles of Economics*. London: Macmillan.

Marshall, A.W. and W.H. Meckling (1959). *Predictability of Costs, Time and Success of Development*. RAND Corporation Working Paper No. P-1821. Santa Monica, CA: RAND Corporation.

Martin, P. (1996). 'Branded by Success'. *Financial Times*. 12 December. p. 18.

Mason, G. and K. Wagner (2002). *Skills, Performance and New Technologies in the British and German Automotive Components Industries*. Discussion Paper. London: National Institute of Economic and Social Research.

Mason, R.H. and M.B. Goudzwaard (1976). 'Performance of Conglomerate Firms: A Portfolio Approach'. *Journal of Finance*. Vol. 31. March. pp. 39–48.

Matheson, J.E. and M.M. Menke (1994). 'Using Decision Quality Principles to Balance Your R&D'. *Research–Technology Management*. Vol. 37. No. 3. pp. 38–43.

Matthews, R.C.O. and F.H. Hahn (1966). 'The Theory of Economics Growth: A Survey'. In *Surveys of Economic Theory: Growth and Development*. Vol. 11. Royal Economic Society. London: Macmillan. pp. 1–124.

McAfee, R.P., H.M. Mialon and M.A. Williams (2003). *What Is a Barrier to Entry?* Working Paper. Department of Economics, University of Texas, Austin.

McConnell, J.J. and H. Servaes (1990). 'Additional Evidence on Equity Ownership and Corporate Value'. *Journal of Financial Economics*. Vol. 22. pp. 595–612.

McGregor, D. (1967). *The Professional Manager*. New York: McGraw-Hill.

McGuinness, T. and K. Cowling (1975). 'Advertising and the Aggregate Demand for Cigarettes'. *European Economic Review*. Vol. 6. pp. 311–328.

McKenna, V. (1990). 'The Theory of Search in Labour Markets'. In D. Sapsford and Z. Tzannatos (eds). *Current Issues in Labour Economics*. London: Macmillan. pp. 33–62.

McKnight, P.J. and C. Tomkins (1999). 'Top Executive Pay in the United Kingdom: A Corporate Governance Dilemma'. *International Journal of the Economics of Business*. Vol. 6. No. 2. pp. 223–243.

McMeekin, A., S. Randles and A. Warde (2003). 'Professions, Firms and the Evolution of Knowledge: The Case of Market Research'. Paper presented to the ASEAT Conference Knowledge and Economic and Social Change, 7–9 April.

Megna, P. and M. Klock (1993). 'The Impact of Intangible Capital on Tobin's q in the Semiconductor Industry'. *AEA Papers and Proceedings*. Vol. 83. No. 2. May. pp. 265–269.

Melicher, R.W. and D.F. Rush (1974). 'Evidence on the Acquisition-Related Performance of Conglomerate Firms'. *Journal of Finance*. Vol. 29. March. pp. 141–149.

Mendelsson, H. and R.R. Pillai (1999). 'Information Age Organisations, Dynamics and Performance'. *Journal of Economic Behaviour and Organisation*. Vol. 38. pp. 253–281.

Mensch, G. (1978). '1984: A New Push for Basic Innovation'. *Research Policy*. Vol. 7. No. 2. pp. 108–122.

Mercer, D. (1993). 'A Two-Decade Test of Product Life Cycle Theory'. *British Journal of Management*. Vol. 4. No. 4. December. pp. 269–274.

Metcalfe, J.S. (1995). 'The Economic Foundations of Technology Policy: Equilibrium and Evolutionary Perspectives'. In P.A. Stoneman (ed.). *Handbook of the Economics of Innovation and Technological Change*. Oxford: Blackwell. pp. 409–512.

Metcalfe, J.S., *et al.* (2003). *Report of the DTI Innovations Review (Academic)*. Panel. 8th Draft. London: DTI.

Meyer, J.W. and B. Rowan (1977). 'Institutionalized Organizations: Formal Structure as Myth and Ceremony'. *American Journal of Sociology*. Vol. 83. No. 2. pp. 340–363.

Meyer, M. (2000). 'Does Science Push Technology? Patents Citing Scientific Literature'. *Research Policy*. Vol. 29. pp. 409–434.

Meyer, M., P. Milgrom and J. Roberts (1992). 'Organisational Prospects, Influence Costs and Ownership Changes'. *Journal of Economic and Management Strategy*. Vol. 1. pp. 9–35.

Michel, A. and I. Shaked (1984). 'Does Business Diversification Affect Performance?' *Financial Management*. Vol. 13. Winter. pp. 18–25.

Miles, D. (1993). 'Testing for Short-Termism in the UK Stock Market'. *Economic Journal*. Vol. 103. pp. 1379–1393.

Miles, D. (1995). 'Testing for Short-Termism in the UK Stock Market: A Reply'. *Economic Journal*. Vol. 105. pp. 1224–1227.

Milgrom, P. and J. Roberts (1990). 'The Economics of Modern Manufacturing Technology, Strategy and Organization'. *American Economic Review*. Vol. 80. No. 3. pp. 511–528.

Milgrom, P. and J. Roberts (1995). 'Complementarities and Fit: Strategy, Structure, and Organizational Change in Manufacturing'. *Journal of Accounting and Economics*. Vol. 19. pp. 179–208.

Miller, D. and P.H. Friesen (1982). 'Strategy Making and Environment: The Third Link'. *Strategic Management Journal*. Vol. 4. pp. 221–235.

Mills, J.R. and J.H. Yamamura (1998). 'The Power of Cash Flow Ratios'. *Journal of Accountancy*. Vol. 186. No. 4. pp. 53–59.

Minford, P. (1983). *Unemployment: Causes and Cures.* London: Martin Robertson.

Minguzzi, A. and R. Passaro (2001). 'The Network of Relationships Between the Economic Environment and the Entrepreneurial Culture in Small Firms'. *Journal of Business Venturing*. Vol. 16. No. 2. March. pp. 181–207.

Mintzberg, H., B. Ahlstrand and J. Lampel (1998). *Strategy Safari: A Guided Tour Through the Wilds of Strategic Management.* London: Prentice Hall.

Mitchell, L.A. (1993). 'An Examination of Methods of Setting Advertising Budgets: Practice and Literature'. *European Journal of Marketing*. Vol. 27. No. 5. pp. 5–21.

Moerland, P.W. (2000). 'Changing Models of Corporate Governance in OECD Countries'. In E.F. Rosenbaum, F. Bonker and H. Wagener (eds). *Privatisation, Corporate Governance and the Emergence of Markets*. Basingstoke: Macmillan. pp. 69–82.

Mohan, L. and W. Holstein (1994). 'Marketing Decision Support Systems in Transition'. In R. Blattberg, R. Glazer and J. Little (eds). *The Marketing Information Revolution*. Boston, MA: Harvard Business Press. pp. 230–252.

Montet, C. (1991). 'Game Theory and Strategic Behaviour'. In D. Greenaway, M. Bleaney and I.M.T. Stewart (eds). *Companion to Contemporary Economic Thought*. London: Routledge. pp. 343–365.

Morck, R., A. Shleifer and R.W. Vishny, (1988). 'Management, Ownership and Market Valuation: An Empirical Analysis'. *Journal of Financial Economics*. Vol. 20. pp. 293–315.

Moser, C. (1999). *Improving Literacy and Numeracy for Adults: A Fresh Start*. Report by the Working Group Chaired by Sir Claus Moser. London: Department for Education and Employment.

Mossman, C.E., G.G. Bell, L.M. Swartz and H. Turtle (1998). 'An Empirical Comparison of Bankruptcy Models'. *Financial Review*. Vol. 33. No. 2. pp. 35–54.

Mueller, D.C. (1967). 'The Firm Decision Process: An Econometric Investigation'. *Quarterly Journal of Economics*. Vol. 81. pp. 58–87.

Mueller, D.C. (1992). 'The Persistence of Profits'. In D.B. Papadimitriou and P. Sarbanes (eds). *Profits, Deficits and Instability*. London: Macmillan. pp. 82–102.

Mueller, E. and A. Spitz (2002). 'Do Owners Make Good Managers?' *Centrepiece: The Magazine of Economic Performance*. Vol. 7. No. 2. pp. 25–27.

Murphy, K.J. (1985). 'Corporate Performance and Managerial Remuneration: An Empirical Analysis'. *Journal of Accounting and Economics*. Vol. 7. pp. 11–41.

Murray, V.A. (1996). *Innovation and Firm Performance*. MSc Dissertation. Manchester School of Management, University of Manchester Institute of Science and Technology.

Myers, S.C. and C.D. Howe (1997). *A Life-Cycle Financial Model of Pharmaceutical R&D*. Program on the Pharmaceutical Industry, Massachusetts Institute of Technology. Quoted in Kellogg and Charnes (2000).

Nahapiet, J. and Ghoshal, S. (1998). 'Social Capital, Intellectual Capital, and the Organizational Advantage'. *Academy of Management Review*. Vol. 23. No. 2. pp. 242–266.

Narin, F. and E. Noma (1987). 'Patents as Indicators of Corporate Technological Strength'. *Research Policy*. Vol. 16. pp. 143–155.

Narin, F. and D. Olivastro (1988a). 'Technology Indicators Based Upon Patents and Patent Citations'. In A.F.J. Raan (ed.). *Handbook of Quantitative Studies of Science and Technology*. Amsterdam: Elsevier. pp. 465–507.

Narin, F. and D. Olivastro (1988b). 'Patent Citation Analysis: New Validation Studies and Linkage Statistics'. In A.F.J. van Raan, A.J. Nederhoff and H.F. Moed (eds). *Science Indicators: Their Use in Science Policy and Their Role in Science Studies*. Leiden: DSWO Press. pp. 465–507.

Narin, F., K.S. Hamilton and D. Olivastro (1997). 'The Increasing Linkage between US Technology and Public Science'. *Research Policy*. Vol. 26. No. 3. pp. 317–330.

Nelson, R. (1990). *What Is Public and What Is Private About Technology?* Working Paper. Columbia University, New York.

Nelson, R. (1991). 'Why Do Firms Differ, and How Does It Matter?' *Strategic Management Journal*. Vol. 12. pp. 61–74.

Nelson, R. and K. Nelson (2002). 'Technology, Institutions, and Innovation Systems'. *Research Policy*. Vol. 31. pp. 265–272.

Nelson, R. and N. Rosenberg (1993). 'Technical Innovation and National Systems'. In R. Nelson (ed.). *National Innovation Systems: A Comparative International Analysis*. Oxford: Oxford University Press. pp. 3–21.

Nelson, R. and S. Winter (1982). *An Evolutionary Theory of Economic Change*. Cambridge, MA: Harvard University Press.

Norburn, D., B.K. Boyd, M. Fox and M. Muth (2000). 'International Corporate Governance Reform'. *European Business Journal*. Vol. 12. No. 3. pp. 113–116.

OECD (1970). *The Measurement of Scientific and Technical Activities: Proposed Standard Practice for Surveys of Research and Experimental Development. The 'Frascati Manual'*. Directorate for Scientific Affairs. DAS/SPR/70.40. Paris: OECD.

OECD (1998). *Human Capital Investment – An International Comparison*. Paris: OECD.

OECD (1999a). *OECD Principles of Corporate Governance*. Ad Hoc Task Force on Corporate Governance. Paris: OECD.

OECD (1999b). *Managing Innovation Systems*. Paris: OECD.

OECD (2002). *Science, Technology and Industry Scoreboard, 2001 – Towards a Knowledge Based Economy*. Paris: OECD.

OECD (undated). *The Measurement of Scientific and Technological Activities. Oslo Manual*. Eurostat. European Commission. www.oecd.org/dataoecd/35/61/2367580.pdf.

Office for National Statistics (1994). *Census of Production* (CD-Rom). London: HMSO.

Office of Technology Assessment (1986). *Research Funding as an Investment: Can We Measure the Returns?* Washington, DC: Office of Technology Assessment.

O'Mahony, M. (1999). *Britain's Relative Productivity Performance, 1950–1996: An*

International Perspective. London: National Institute of Economic and Social Research.

Ordover, J.A. and R.D. Willig (1985). 'Antitrust for High-Technology Industries: Assessing Research Joint Ventures and Mergers'. *Journal of Law and Economics*. Vol. 28. May. pp. 311–333.

Oulton, N. (1996). 'Workforce Skills and Export Competitiveness'. In A. Booth and D. Snower (eds). *Acquiring Skills*. Cambridge: Cambridge University Press. pp. 201–230.

Oulton, N. and M. O'Mahony (1994). *Productivity and Growth: A Study of British Industry 1954–1986.* Cambridge: Cambridge University Press.

Pakes, A. (1986). 'Patents as Options: Some Estimates of the Value of Holding European Patent Stocks'. *Econometrica*. Vol. 54. pp. 755–784.

Pandya, A.M. and N.V. Rao (1998). 'Diversification and Firm Performance: An Empirical Evaluation'. *Journal of Financial and Strategic Decisions*. Vol. 11. No. 2. pp. 67–81.

Pantalone, C.C. and M.B. Platt (1993). 'Impact of Acquisitions on Thrift Performance'. *Financial Review*. Vol. 28. No. 4. pp. 493–522.

Patel, P. (2000). 'Technological Indicators of Performance'. In J. Tidd (ed.). *From Knowledge Management to Strategic Competence*. London: Imperial College Press.

Patel, P. and K. Pavitt (1995). 'Patterns of Technological Activity: Their Measurement and Interpretation'. In P. Stoneman (ed.). *Handbook of the Economics of Innovation and Technological Change*. Oxford: Basil Blackwell. pp. 14–51.

Pavlik, E.L. and A. Belkaoui (1991). *Determinants of Executive Compensation: Corporate Ownership, Performance, Size, and Diversification*. New York: Quorum Books.

Pearce, J.A. and S.A. Zahra. (1991). 'The Relative Power of CEOs and Boards of Directors: Associations with Corporate Performance'. *Strategic Management Journal*. Vol. 12. pp. 135–153.

Peckham, J.O. (1976). 'Advertising Established Brands'. *Nielsen Researcher*. No. 3. pp. 1–12.

Pedersen, T. and S. Thomsen (1999). 'Economic and Systemic Explanations of Ownership Concentration Among Europe's Largest Companies'. *International Journal of the Economics of Business*. Vol. 6. No. 3. p. 367.

Penrose, E. (1959). *The Theory of the Growth of the Firm*. Oxford: Basil Blackwell.

Percy, J. P. (1995). 'The Cadbury Report and Corporate Governance in the UK'. *CPA Journal*. Vol. 65. No. 5. p. 24.

Perrow, C. (1967). 'A Framework for the Comparative Analysis of Organizations'. *American Sociological Review*. Vol. 32. No. 3. pp. 194–208.

Pfeffer, J. (1994). *Competitive Advantage Through People*. Boston, MA: Harvard Business School Press.

Phelan, P. and S.E. Lewin (2000). 'Arriving at a Strategic Theory of the Firm'. *International Journal of Management Reviews*. Vol. 2. No. 4. pp. 305–324.

Pickering, J.F. (1974). *Industrial Structure and Market Conduct*. London: Martin Robertson.

Piercy, N.F. (1987). 'The Marketing Budgeting Process: Marketing Management Implications'. *Journal of Marketing*. Vol. 51. pp. 45–59.

PIMS (1998). *Evidence of the Contribution of Branded Consumer Goods to Businesses and to Economic Growth*. Research Report. London: Profit Impact of Market Strategy.

Pindyck, R.S. (1991). 'Irreversibility, Uncertainty, and Investment'. *Journal of Economic Literature*. Vol. 29. pp. 1110–1148.

Plossl, G. (1994). *Orlicky's Material Requirements Planning*. New York: McGraw Hill.

Polli, R. and V. Cook (1969). 'Validity of the Product Life Cycle'. *Journal of Business*. Vol. 42. No. 4. pp. 385–400.

Popper, S.W. and C.S. Wagner (2002). *New Foundations for Growth: The US Innovation System Today and Tomorrow.* MR-1388.0-OSTP. Santa Monica, CA: RAND Corporation.

Porter, M. (1985). *Competitive Advantage: Creating and Maintaining Superior Performance.* New York: Free Press.

Porter, M. (1990). *The Competitive Advantage of Nations.* New York: Free Press.

Porter, M.E. and C.H.M. Ketels (2003). *UK Competitiveness: Moving to the Next Stage.* DTI Economics Paper No. 3. London: HMSO.

Pozen, R. (1994). 'Institutional Investors: The Reluctant Activists'. *Harvard Business Review.* Vol. 72. No. 1. pp. 140–149.

Prahalad, C.K. (1983). 'Developing Strategic Capability: An Agenda for Top Management'. *Human Resource Management.* Vol. 22. pp. 237–254.

Prencipe, A. (2000). 'Breadth and Depth of Technological Capabilities in Complex Product Systems: The Case of the Aircraft Engine Control System'. *Research Policy.* Vol. 29. pp. 895–911.

Prencipe, A. (2004). *Change, Co-ordination and Capabilities.* SPRU Electronic Working Paper Series. Paper No. 120. Brighton: SPRU, University of Sussex.

Prescott, E. (1998). 'Needed: A Theory of Total Factor Productivity'. *International Economic Review.* Vol. 39. pp. 525–552.

Prescott, E.C. and M. Visscher (1980). 'Organisational Capital'. *Journal of Political Economy.* Vol. 88. June. pp. 446–461.

Price, D.J. de S. (1969). 'The Structures of Publication in Science and Technology'. In W. Gruber and G. Marquis (eds). *Factors in the Transfer of Technology.* MIT Press. Reprinted as 'Science and Technology: Distinctions and Interrelationships'. In B. Barnes (ed.) (1972). *Sociology of Science.* Harmondsworth: Penguin. pp. 166–180.

Prowse, S. (1994). *Corporate Governance in an International Perspective: A Survey of Corporate Control Mechanisms Among Large Firms in the United States, the United Kingdom, Japan and Germany.* BIS Economic Papers No. 41. Basle: Bank for International Settlements.

Quince, T. and H. Whittaker (2002). *High Tech Business in the UK: Performance and Niche Markets.* Working Paper No. 234. ESRC Centre for Business Research. Cambridge: Cambridge University Press.

Quintin, E. and J.J. Stevens (2003). *Growing Old Together: Firm Survival and Employee Turnover.* Working Paper. Federal Reserve Bank, Dallas.

Radner, R. (1992). 'Hierarch: The Economics of Managing'. *Journal of Economic Literature.* Vol. 30. pp. 1382–1415.

Rajbhandari, S.P. (1999). 'Changing Roles of Organisational Leaders in Modern Organisational Management'. *Administration and Management Review.* Vol. 1. No. 11. January. pp. 10–24.

Rappa, M., K. Debackere and R. Garud (1992). 'Technological Progress and the Duration of Contribution Spans'. *Technological Forecasting and Social Change.* Vol. 42. pp. 133–145.

Rediker, K.J. and A. Seth (1995). 'Boards of Directors and Substitution Effects of Alternative Governance Mechanisms'. *Strategic Management Journal.* Vol. 16. pp. 85–99.

Reich, R.B. (1991). *The Work of Nations: Preparing Ourselves for 21st Century Capitalism.* New York: Knopf.

Reid, G.C. (*circa* 2000). *The Development and Survival of New Small Businesses: Empirical Evidence for Scotland, 1994–97.* Centre for Research into Industry, Enterprise, Finance and the Firm, St Andrews University.

Reid, S.R. (1968). *Mergers, Managers and the Economy.* New York: McGraw Hill.

Richardson, G. (1964). 'The Limits to a Firm's Rate of Growth'. *Oxford Economic Papers.* Vol. 16. No. 5. March. pp. 9–23.

Rickne, A. (2000). *New Technology-Based Firms and Industrial Dynamics: Evidence from the Technological Systems of Biomaterials in Sweden, Ohio and Massachusetts.* Working Paper. Department of Industrial Dynamics, Chalmers University of Technology, Gothenberg.

Ries, A. and L. Ries (2002). *22 Immutable Laws of Branding: How to Build a Product or Service into a World-Class Brand.* New York: Harper Collins.

Rigby, D.L. (1991). 'The Existence, Significance and Persistence of Profit Rate Differentials'. *Economic Geography.* Vol. 67. pp. 210–222.

Rigg, M., P. Elias, M. White and S. Johnson (1990). *An Overview of the Demand for Graduates.* London: HMSO.

Ritchie, J., J. Eversley and A. Gibb (1982). 'Aspirations and Motivations of Would-Be Entrepreneurs'. In T. Webb, T. Quince and D. Watkins (eds). *Small Business Research.* Aldershot: Gower.

Robinson, C. (1997). Foreword. In I.M. Kirzner. *How Markets Work: Disequilibrium, Entrepreneurship and Discovery.* IEA Hobart Paper No. 133. London: Institute for Economic Affairs.

Rosenberg, N. (1991). 'Critical Issues in Science Policy Research'. *Science and Public Policy.* Vol. 18. No. 6. December. pp. 335–346.

Roth, A.E. (1988). 'Laboratory Experimentation in Economics: A Methodological Overview'. *Economic Journal.* Vol. 98. pp. 974–1031.

Rothwell, R. (1972). *Factors for Success in Industrial Innovation. Project SAPHO: A Comparative Study of Success and Failure in Industrial Innovation.* Science Policy Research Unit, University of Sussex.

Rothwell, R. (1992). 'Successful Industrial Innovation: Critical Factors for the 1990s'. *R&D Management.* Vol. 22. No. 3. pp. 221–239.

Rothwell, R. (1994). 'Industrial Innovation: Success, Strategy, Trends'. In M. Dodgeson and R. Rothwell (eds). *Handbook of Industrial Innovation.* Cheltenham: Edward Elgar. pp. 33–53.

Rubenson, G.C. and A.K. Gupta (1990). 'The Founder's Disease: A Critical Re-examination'. In *Babson Entrepreneurship Research Conference Proceedings, Wellesley, MA.* Babson College. pp. 167–183. See www.babson.edu/entrep/fer/front-90.html. Last accessed 18 March 2005.

Rumelt, R.P. (1986). *Strategy, Structure, and Economic Performance.* Boston, MA: Harvard Business School Press.

Runkel, K. and C.E. Brymer (1997). 'The Nature of Brands'. In R. Perrier (ed.). *Brand Valuation.* London: Premier Books.

Rutherford, D. (1992). *Dictionary of Economics.* London: Routledge.

Ruthven, P. (1994). *Leadership and Success in Corporate Australia.* IBIS Business Paper. Melbourne: IBIS.

Sampson, D. (2000). *Managerial Principles and Profitability.* In P. Dawkins, M. Harris and S. King (eds). *How Big Business Performs.* St Leonards: Allen and Unwin.

Sanders, B., J. Rossman and L.J. Harris (1958). 'The Economic Impact of Patents'. *Patent, Trademark and Copyright Journal.* Vol. 2. pp. 340–363.

Sanders, W. and M.A. Carpenter (1998). 'Internationalisation and Firm Governance'. *Academy of Management Journal.* Vol. 41. No. 2. pp. 158–178.

Satchell, S.E. and D.C. Damant (1995). 'Testing for Short Termism in the UK Stock Market: A Comment'. *Economic Journal.* Vol. 105. September. pp. 1218–1223.

Savery, L., T. Mazzarol and P. Dawkins (1994). *How Others See Us Competitively.* Perth: Institute for International Competitiveness, Curtin University.

Sawyer, M. (1981). *The Economics of Industries and Firms.* London: Croom Helm.

Scase, R. and R. Goffee (1980). *The Real World of the Small Business Owner.* London: Croom Helm.

Schankerman, M. and A. Pakes (1986). 'Estimates of the Value of Patent Rights in

European Countries During the Post-1950 Period'. *Economic Journal*. Vol. 96. No. 384. pp. 1052–1077.

Schein, E.H. (1968). 'Organisational Socialisation and the Profession of Management'. *Industrial Management Review*. Vol. 9. pp. 1–15.

Schein, E.H. (1985). *Organizational Culture and Leadership*. San Francisco: Jossey-Bass.

Schelling, T.C. (1960). *The Strategy of Conflict*. Cambridge, MA: Harvard University Press.

Schelling, T.C. (1966). *Arms and Influence*. New Haven, CT: Yale University Press.

Scherer, F.M. (1965). 'Firm Size, Market Structure, Opportunity, and the Output of Patented Inventions'. *American Economic Review*. Vol. 55. pp. 1097–1123.

Scherer, F.M. (1971). *Industrial Market Structure and Economic Performance*. Chicago, IL: Rand McNally.

Scherer, F.M. (1996). *The Size Distribution of Profits from Innovation*. Working Paper, Harvard University. ('Patents: What We Know; What Must We Learn?' Keynote Address. AEA The Econometrics of Innovation (Patents). Conference. Strasbourg.)

Scherer, F.M. and D. Harhoff (2000). 'Technology Policy for a World of Skew-Distributed Outcomes'. *Research Policy*. Vol. 29. pp. 559–566.

Schmitz, H. and K. Nadvi (1999). 'Clustering and Industrialisation: Introduction'. *World Development*. Vol. 27. No. 9. pp 1503–1514.

Schmookler, J. (1954). 'The Level of Inventive Activity'. *Review of Economics and Statistics*. Vol. 36. pp. 183–190.

Schmookler, J. (1966). *Invention and Economic Growth*. Cambridge, MA: Harvard University Press.

Schumpeter, J. (1947). *Capitalism, Socialism and Democracy*. London: Allen and Unwin. Reprinted as 'The Dynamics of Competition and Monopoly'. In A. Hunter (ed.) (1969). *Monopoly and Competition*. Harmondsworth: Penguin.

Scott, J.T. (1993). *Purposive Diversification and Economic Performance*. Cambridge: Cambridge University Press.

Seidel, A. (1949). 'Citation System for Patent Office'. *Journal of the Patent Office Society*. Vol. 31. p. 554.

Shafritz, J.M. and J.S. Ott (eds) (1992). *Xenophon, 'Socrates Discovers Generic Management'* (3rd edn). Classics of Organizational Theory. Belmont: Wadsworth.

Shane, S. and Cable, D. (1998). *Social Capital and the Financing of New Ventures*. Discussion Paper. Massachusetts Institute of Technology.

Shapiro, D.M. and L.N. Switzer (1993). 'The Stock Market Response to Changing Drug Patent Legislation: The Case of Compulsory Licensing in Canada'. *Managerial and Decision Economics*. Vol. 14. pp. 247–259.

Sharif, A.M. (2002). 'Benchmarking Performance Management Systems'. *Benchmarking*. Vol. 9. No. 1. pp. 62–85.

Shaver, K.G. and L.R. Scott (1991). 'Person, Process, Choice: The Psychology of New Venture Creation'. *Entrepreneurship Theory and Practice*. Vol. 16. No. 2. pp. 23–45.

Shaw, R.W. and S.A. Shaw (1977). 'Patent Expiry and Competition in Polyester Fibres'. *Scottish Journal of Political Economy*. Vol. 24. No. 2. pp. 117–132.

Shelling, T. (1960). *The Strategy of Conflict*. Cambridge, MA: Harvard University Press.

Shen, T.Y. (1970). 'Economics of Scale. Penrose-Effect, Growth of Plants and Their Size Distribution'. *Journal of Political Economy*. Vol. 78. No. 4. July. pp. 702–716.

Sheshinski, E. (1967). 'Tests of the "Learning by Doing" Hypothesis'. *Review of Economics and Statistics*. Vol. 49. November. pp. 568–578.

Shleifer, A. and R. Vishny (1989). 'Managerial Entrenchment: The Case of Manager-

Specific Investments'. *Journal of Financial Economics*. Vol. 25. November. pp. 123–139.

Shleifer, A. and R.W. Vishny (1997). 'A Survey of Corporate Governance'. *Journal of Finance*. Vol. 52. No. 2. pp. 737–783.

Short, H. (1999). 'Corporate Governance: Cadbury, Greenbury and Hampel – A Review'. *Journal of Financial Regulation and Compliance*. Vol. 7. No. 1. pp. 57–67.

Simmonds, P.G. (1990). 'The Combined Diversification Breadth and Mode Dimensions and the Performance of Large Diversified Firms'. *Strategic Management Journal*. Vol. 11. September. pp. 399–410.

Simon, H.A. (1959). 'Theories of Decision Making in Economics and Behavioural Science'. *American Economic Review*. Vol. 49. No. 3. pp. 253–283.

Simon, H.A. (1995). 'Bounded Rationality and Organisational Learning'. In M.D. Cohen and L.S. Sproul (eds). *Organizational Learning*. Thousand Oaks, CA: Sage. pp. 175–187.

Skills in England (2003). *Skills in England, Vol. 1*. Coventry: Learning and Skills Council.

Smith, A. (1776). *An Inquiry into the Nature and Causes of the Wealth of Nations*. London: Dent & Sons (1904).

Smith, K. (1996). 'The Systems Challenge to Innovation Policy'. In W. Polt and B.Weber (eds). *Industrie and Glueck. Paradigmenwechsel in der Industrie- und Technologiepolitik*. Vienna.

Smith, K.V. and J.F. Weston (1977). 'Further Evaluation of Conglomerate Performance'. *Journal of Business Research*. Vol. 5. March. pp. 5–14.

Smith, N.R. (1967). *The Entrepreneur and His Firm: The Relationship Between the Type of Man and Type of Company*. East Lansing, MI: Michigan University Press.

Solo, R. (1966). 'The Capacity to Assimilate an Advanced Technology'. *American Economic Review, Papers and Proceedings*. May. pp. 91–97. Reprinted in N. Rosenberg (1971). *The Economics of Technological Change*. Harmondsworth: Penguin. pp. 480–488.

Solow, R.M. (1956). 'A Contribution to the Theory of Economic Growth'. *Quarterly Journal of Economics*. Vol. 70. February. pp. 65–94.

Solow, R.M. (1991). 'Growth Theory'. In D. Greenaway, M. Bleaney and I.M.T. Stewart (eds). *Companion to Contemporary Economic Thought*. London: Routledge. pp. 393–415.

Song, J. (1993). *Investment Under Uncertain Property Rights*. Discussion Paper No. 93/4. Edinburgh: Heriot-Watt University.

Spence, M. (1981). 'The Learning Curve and Competition'. *Bell Journal of Economics*. Vol. 12. No. 1. Spring. pp. 49–70.

Stanworth, J. and J. Curran (1986). 'Growth and the Small Firm'. In J. Curran, J. Stanworth and D. Watkins (eds). *The Survival of the Small Firm, Vol. 2*. Aldershot: Gower.

Starr, J. and I. MacMillan (1990). 'Resource Cooptation via Social Contracting: Resource Acquisition Strategies for New Ventures'. *Strategic Management Journal*. Vol. 11. pp. 79–92.

Stevens, G.A. and J. Burley (1997). '3,000 Raw Ideas Equals 1 Commercial Success!' *Research and Technology Management*. Vol. 40. No. 3. pp. 16–27.

Stewart, M. (1983). 'Relative Earnings and Individual Union Membership in the UK'. *Economica*. Vol. 50. pp. 111–125.

Stinchcombe, A.L. (1990). *Information and Organisations*. Berkeley, CA: University of California Press.

Stoneman, P. and D. Bosworth (1994). *Feasibility Study for the Development of an Innovation Scoreboard*. Final Report to the DTI. London: Stoy Hayward Consulting.

Stoneman, P. and M. Karshenas (1993). 'Rank, Stock and Order Effects in the Diffusion of New Process Technologies: An Empirical Model of Adoption Duration'. *RAND Journal of Economics*. Vol. 24. No. 4. Winter. pp. 503–528.

Stoneman, P. and O. Toivanen (2001). 'The Impact of Revised Recommended Accounting Practices on R&D Reporting by UK Firms'. *International Journal of the Economics of Business*. Vol. 8. No. 1. pp. 123–136.

Stoneman, P., D. Bosworth and A. Gibbons (1992). *Investment, Productivity and Competitiveness in UK Manufacturing Industry*. Research Report. IER. Coventry: University of Warwick.

Stoneman, P., D. Bosworth and J. Roe (1994). *Water and Sewerage Industries: General Efficiency and the Potential for Improvement*. Report to OFWAT. February. Published (1998). London: OFWAT.

Storey, D. (1986). 'New Firm Formation, Employment Change and the Small Firm: The Case of Cleveland County'. In J. Curren, *et al.* (eds). *The Survival of the Small Firm, Vol. 2*. Aldershot: Gower Press. pp. 8–40.

Strickland, A.D. and L.W. Weiss (1976). 'Advertising, Concentration, and Price–Cost Margins'. *Journal of Political Economy*. Vol. 84. pp. 1109–1122.

Sundaramurthy, C.R., P. Rechner and W. Wang (1996). 'Governance Antecedents of Board Entrenchment: The Case of Classified Board Provisions'. *Journal of Management*. Vol. 22. No. 5. pp. 783–799.

Svennilson, I. (1963). *Economic Growth and Technical Progress – An Essay in Sequence Analysis*. OECD Conference on the Residual Factor and Economic Growth, 20–22 May. Paris: OECD.

Taylor, R. (1996). 'UK: Top Directors Report Increases of 14.5 *Per Cent*'. *Financial Times*. 29 April.

Teece, D. and G. Pisano (1994). 'The Dynamic Capabilities of Firms: An Introduction'. *Industrial and Corporate Change*. Vol. 3. pp. 547–556.

Teixeira, A. (2002). *On the Link Between Human Capital and Firm Performance*. Working Paper No. 121. Faculdade de Economia, Universidade do Porto, Porto.

Tellis, G.J. (1988). 'The Price Sensitivity of Competitive Demand: A Meta-analysis of Sales Response Models'. *Journal of Marketing Research*. Vol. 15. No. 3. pp. 331–341.

Thaler, R. (1988). 'Anomalies: The Ultimate Game'. *Journal of Economic Perspectives*. Vol. 2. pp. 195–206.

Tidd, J. and C. Driver (2000). 'Technological and Market Competencies and Financial Performance'. In J. Tidd (ed.). *From Knowledge Management to Strategic Competence*. London: Imperial College Press. pp. 94–125.

Tidd, J. and M.J. Trewhella (1997). 'Organizational and Technological Antecedents for Knowledge Acquisition and Learning'. *R&D Management*. Vol. 27. No. 4. pp. 359–375.

Tidd, J., C. Driver and P. Saunders (1995). 'Linking Technological, Market and Financial Indicators of Innovation'. *Economics of Innovation and New Technology*. Vol. 4. pp. 155–172.

Tijssen, R.J.W. (2002). 'Science Dependence of Technologies: Evidence from Inventions and Their Inventors'. *Research Policy*. Vol. 31. pp. 509–526.

Timmerman, A. (1994). 'Can Agents Learn to Form Rational Expectations? Some Results on Convergence and Stability of Learning in the UK Stock Market'. *Economic Journal*. Vol. 104. July. pp. 777–797.

Tirole, J. (1990). *The Theory of Industrial Organisation*. Cambridge, MA: MIT Press.

Tobin, J. (1969). 'A General Equilibrium Approach to Monetary Theory'. *Journal of Money, Credit and Banking*. Vol. 1. No. 1. pp. 15–29.

Tolbert, P.S. and L.G. Zucker (1999). 'The Institutionalisation of Institutional Theory'. In S.R. Clegg and C. Hardy (eds). *Studying Organization: Theory and Method*. London: Sage. pp. 169–184.

Tomer, J.F. (1981). 'Organisational Change, Organisational Capital and Economic Growth'. *Eastern Economic Journal*. Vol. 7. January. pp. 1–14.

Townsend, J., F. Henwood, G. Thomas, K. Pavitt and S. Wyatt (1981). *Science and Technology Indicators for the UK: Innovations in Britain Since 1945*. Brighton: Science Policy Research Unit, University of Sussex.

Trajtenberg, M. (1990). 'A Penny for your Quotes: Patent Citations and the Value of Innovations'. *RAND Journal of Economics*. Vol. 21. No. 1. pp. 172–187.

Tushman, M.L. and R. Katz (1980). 'External Communication and Project Performance: An Investigation into the Role of Gatekeepers'. *Management Science*. Vol. 26. pp. 1071–1085.

Unland, M. and B.H. Kleiner (1996). 'New Developments in Organising Around Core Competences'. *Work Study*. Vol. 45. No. 2. pp. 5–9.

van der Eerden, C. and F.H. Saelens (1991). 'The Use of Science and Technology Indicators in Strategic Planning'. *Long Range Planning*. Vol. 24. June. pp. 18–25.

van Horne, J.C. (1998). *Financial Management and Policy* (11th edn). Englewood Cliffs, NJ: Prentice Hall International.

van Witteloostuijn, A. (1990). *Rationality, Competition and Evolution: Entry Deterrence in Dynamic Barrier Market Theory*. Dissertation No. 90-1. University of Limberg, Maastricht.

Varakelis, N.C. (2001). 'The Impact of Patent Protection, Economy Openness and National Culture on R&D Investment: A Cross-country Empirical Investigation'. *Research Policy*. Vol. 30. pp. 1059–1068.

Venkatraman, N. (1991). 'IT Induced Business Re-configuration'. In M.S. Scott (ed.). *The Corporation of the 1990s: IT and Organisational Transformation*. New York: Oxford University Press. pp. 122–158.

Venture Economics (1988). *Venture Capital Performance*. Boston, MA. Quoted in Scherer (1996).

Vernon, J.M. and R. Nourse (1973). 'Profit Rates and Market Structure of Advertising Intensive Firms'. *Journal of Industrial Economics*. Vol. 22. No. 1. pp. 1–20.

Virany, B., M.L. Tushman and E. Romanelli (1995). 'Executive Succession and Organisational Outcomes in Turbulent Environments: An Organisational Learning Approach'. In M.D. Cohen and L.S. Sproul (eds). *Organizational Learning*. Thousand Oaks, CA: Sage. pp. 302–329.

Volpin, P.F. (2002). *Governance with Poor Investor Protection: Evidence from Top Executive Turnover in Italy*. CEPR Discussion Paper No. DP3229. London: CEPR.

Walker, W. (1993). 'National Innovation Systems: Britain'. In R.R. Nelson (ed.). *National Innovation Systems: A Comparative Analysis*. Oxford: Oxford University Press. pp. 158–191.

Ward, J. and J. Peppard (2002). *Strategic Planning for Information Systems*. Chichester: Wiley.

Waring, G. (1996). 'Industry Differences in the Persistence of Firm-Specific Returns'. *American Economic Review*. Vol. 86. December. pp. 1253–1265.

Watkins, D. and J. Watkins (1986). 'The Female Entrepreneur in Britain: Some Results of a Pilot Study with Special Emphasis on Educational Needs'. In M. Scott, A. Gibb, J. Lewis and T. Faulkner (eds). *Small Firms Growth and Development*. Aldershot: Gower.

Weber, R. (1989). 'Games with Incomplete Information'. In J. Eatwell, M. Milgate and P. Newman (eds). *Game Theory*. New York: Norton. pp. 149–155.

Weick, K.E. (1995). 'The Non-traditional Quality of Organizational Learning'. In M.D. Cohen and L.S. Sproul (eds). *Organizational Learning*. Thousand Oaks, CA: Sage. pp. 163–174.

Weingartner, M.H. (1966). 'Capital Budgeting of Interrelated Projects: Survey Synthesis'. *Management Science*. Vol. 12. No. 7. pp. 485–516.

Weitzman, M.L., W. Newey and M. Rabin (1981). 'Sequential R&D Strategy for Synfuels'. *Bell Journal of Economics*. Vol. 12. No. 2. pp. 574–590.

Wennekers, S., R. Thurik and F. Buts (1999). *Entrepreneurship, Economic Growth and What Links them Together*. EIM: Zoetermeer.

Westphal, J. and E.J. Zajac (1995). 'Who Shall Govern? CEO/Board Power, Demographic Similarity and New Director Selection'. *Administrative Science Quarterly*. Vol. 40. pp. 60–83.

Whisler, T.L. (1988). 'The Role of the Board in the Threshold Firm'. *Family Business Review*. Vol. 1. pp. 309–321.

White, R.K. and R. Lippitt (1960). *Autocracy and Democracy: An Experimental Inquiry*. New York: Harper.

Whittington, R., M. Mayer and F. Curto (1999a). 'Chandlerism in Post-war Europe: Strategic and Structural Change in France, Germany and the United Kingdom, 1950–1993'. *Industrial and Corporate Change*. Vol. 8. No. 4. pp. 519–551.

Whittington, R., A. Pettigrew, S. Peck, E. Fenton and M. Conyon (1999b). 'Change and Complementarites in the New Competitive Landscape: A European Panel Study, 1992–1996'. *Organisational Science*. Vol. 10. No. 4. pp. 583–600.

Wild, K. and M. Scicluna (1997). 'Accounting for Brands: The Practitioner's Perspective'. In R. Perrier (ed.). *Brand Valuation*. London: Premier Books. pp. 87–98.

Wildsmith, J.R. (1973). *Managerial Theories of the Firm*. London: Martin Robertson.

Willard, G.E., D.A. Krueger and H.R. Feeser (1992). 'In Order to Grow, Must the Founder Go: A Comparison of Performance between Founder and Non-founder Managed High Growth Manufacturing Firms'. *Journal of Business Venturing*. Vol. 7. pp. 181–194.

Williamson, O.E. (1963). 'Managerial Discretion and Business Behaviour'. *American Economic Review*. Vol. 53. December. pp. 1032–1057.

Williamson, O.E. (1967a). *The Economics of Discretionary Behaviour*. Chicago, IL: Markham Press.

Williamson, O.E. (1967b). 'Hierarchical Control and Optimal Firm Size'. *Journal of Political Economy*. Vol. 75. pp. 123–138.

Williamson, O.E. (1975). *Markets and Hierarchies*. New York: Free Press.

Williamson, O.E. (1985). *The Economic Institutions of Capitalism: Firms, Markets and History*. Cambridge: Cambridge University Press.

Williamson, O.E. (1986). *Economic Organization: Firms, Markets and Policy Control*. New York: New York University Press.

Williamson, O.E. (1988). 'Corporate Finance and Corporate Governance'. *Journal of Finance*. Vol. 43. No. 3. pp. 567–591.

Williamson, O.E. and N. Bhargava (1972). 'Assessing and Classifying the International Structure and Control Apparatus of the Modern Corporation'. In K. Cowling (ed.). *Market Structure and Corporate Behavior: Theory and Empirical Analysis of the Firm*. London: Gray-Mills. pp. 125–148.

Wills, G. (1972). *Technological Forecasting*. Harmondsworth: Penguin.

Wilson, R.A. (1986). 'Changing Pay Relativities for the Highly Qualified'. In *Review of the Economy and Employment, 1985/6, Vol. 2*. Coventry: Institute for Employment Research. Chapter 2. pp. 30–48.

Winter, S.G. (1964). 'Economic Natural Selection and the Theory of the Firm'. *Yale Economic Essays*. Vol. 4. pp. 225–272.

Wood, W. (1992). 'Who Is Running British Business?' *Industrial Management and Data Systems*. Vol. 92. No. 6. pp. 13–16.

Woodward, J. (1958). *Management and Technology*. London: HMSO.

Woodward, J. (1965). *Industrial Organization: Theory and Practice*. Oxford: Oxford University Press.

Wright, P.M., G.C. McMahon and A. McWilliams (1994). 'Human Resources and Sustained Competitive Advantage: A Resource-Based Perspective'. *International Journal of Human Resources Management*. Vol. 5. pp. 301–326.

Wright, T. (1936). 'Factors Affecting the Cost of Airplanes'. *Journal of the Aeronautical Society*. Vol. 3. pp. 122–128.

Youndt, M.A., S.A. Snell and D.P. Lepak (1996). 'Human Resource Management, Manufacturing Strategy, and Firm Performance'. *Academy of Management Journal*. Vol. 39. pp. 836–866.

Zahra, S. and G. George (2002). 'Absorptive Capacity: A Review, Reconceptualisation, and Extension'. *Academy of Management Review*. Vol. 27. No. 4. pp. 185–203.

Zantout, Z.Z. and G.P. Tsetsekos (1994). 'The Wealth Effects of Announcements of R&D Expenditure Increases'. *Journal of Financial Research*. Vol. 17. No. 2. pp. 205–216.

Zeckhouser, R.J. and J. Pound (1990). 'Are Large Shareholders Effective Monitors? An Investigation of Share Ownership and Corporate Performance'. In G.R. Hubbard (ed.). *Asymmetric Information, Corporate Finance and Investment*. Chicago, IL: University of Chicago Press.

Zhou, Y. (2004). *Derivatives Usage, Disclosure and Risk Management of UK Non-financial Firms*. PhD Thesis. University of Manchester School of Science and Technology.

Name index

Subject index

absorptive capacity 219–220, 299, 316–318, 327n, 376
advertising 11
  brand development 238–265, 243–244, 246–251, 251–263, 359–361
  competition and rivalry 186, 187, 239, 242–243, 246–251, 254–256, 353
  counterfeiting 257–258
  decision 11, 240–245, 245–248
  definition 239–240
  determinants of 11
  discretionary 4, 11, 38, 62, 63, 67, 208, 238, 239, 243–244, 247, 248, 251–263, 265n, 331, 332
  elasticity of demand 56, 239, 240, 241–242, 246–248, 251, 264n
  high-performance work practices (HPWPs) 13
  impact on demand and performance 11, 76, 186–190, 239, 243, 245–251, 251–264, 356
  intangible assets 184, 189, 240, 258
  intensity 48, 189, 242, 248
  market information 76–77, 98
  market promotion 238–240, 253–254, 256–257, 260, 263, 355
  monopoly power 11, 239
  new product launch 11, 252–253, 352
  optimal 239, 240–245
  pool 242–243
  product life-cycle 352–359, 365n
  R&D 11, 13, 184, 239, 258–260, 352, 353, 356
  risk 239, 252–253
  strategy 114, 116, 125, 242–243, 257–258
  sunk costs 203, 252

  trademarks 260
  welfare 11, 239, 245–246

brands 187
  advertising and brand elasticities 247, 249–251, 251–257
  brand development 238–265
  company structure 275
  conjoint analysis of brand value 80–81
  definition 240, 264
  hedonic analysis of brand value 95–97
  infringement 257–258
  life expectancy and long-lived brands 256, 353, 357–359
  performance 258–263, 264n
  platforms 356–357, 357–359
  price 246
  R&D 201
  trademarks 257

clusters
  high-performance work practices (HPWPs) 222, 228
  market segments 356–357
  spatial 372, 386, 392–393, 395
  technology 90, 372, 386, 392–393, 395
conjoint analysis 72, 78, 80–82, 95, 97
corporate governance 9, 41, 42, 125, 153, 155, 157–179, 366
  codes and best practice 9, 158, 161–163, 164–166, 171–173, 177, 178
  management and ownership 166–169, 169–173, 331
  strategy 174–175, 177
  transaction costs 17, 22, 24, 25, 27, 160–161

443